The Rameau Compendium

The Boydell Composer Compendium Series

The aim of the Composer Compendium series is to provide up-to-date reference works on major composers and their music that can both provide instant information and act as a gateway to further reading. The authors are all leading authorities on the composers in question who have been given the remit not only to assemble and present already existing data but also, where appropriate, to make personal interpretations, to introduce new facts and arguments and to shed light on the many discourses surrounding the chosen musicians from their lifetime up to the present day.

The core of each volume is a dictionary section with entries for people, institutions and places connected with the composer; musical, analytical and historical terminology of particular relevance to them; significant events in the reception history of their music; the genres in which they composed; individual compositions or groups of compositions – in short, anyone and anything judged to be pertinent. Entries in the dictionary section are carefully cross-referenced to each other and also to a very comprehensive bibliography section at the end of the volume. Between the dictionary and the bibliography there is a work list based on the latest information, and the volume is prefaced by a concise biography of the composer. Numerous music examples and illustrations are included. By means of this simple formula, the series aims to provide handbooks of wide and durable interest responding to the needs of scholars, performers and music-lovers alike.

Michael Talbot
Series editor

Proposals are welcomed and should be sent in the first instance to the publisher at the address below. All submissions will receive prompt and informed consideration.

Boydell & Brewer, PO Box 9, Woodbridge, Suffolk, IP12 3DF
email: editorial@boydell.co.uk

Previous volumes in this series:

The Vivaldi Compendium, Michael Talbot, 2011
Also available in paperback

The Rameau Compendium

Graham Sadler

THE BOYDELL PRESS

First published 2014
The Boydell Press, Woodbridge
Paperback edition 2017

ISBN 978 1 84383 905 7 hardback
ISBN 978 1 78327 192 4 paperback

The Boydell Press is an imprint of Boydell & Brewer Ltd
PO Box 9, Woodbridge, Suffolk IP12 3DF, UK
and of Boydell & Brewer Inc.
668 Mt Hope Avenue, Rochester, NY 14620–2731, USA
website: www.boydellandbrewer.com

A CIP catalogue record for this book is available
from the British Library

The publisher has no responsibility for the continued existence or accuracy
of URLs for external or third-party internet websites referred to in this book,
and does not guarantee that any content on such websites is,
or will remain, accurate or appropriate

This publication is printed on acid-free paper

Fakenham Prepress Solutions, Fakenham, Norfolk NR21 8NN

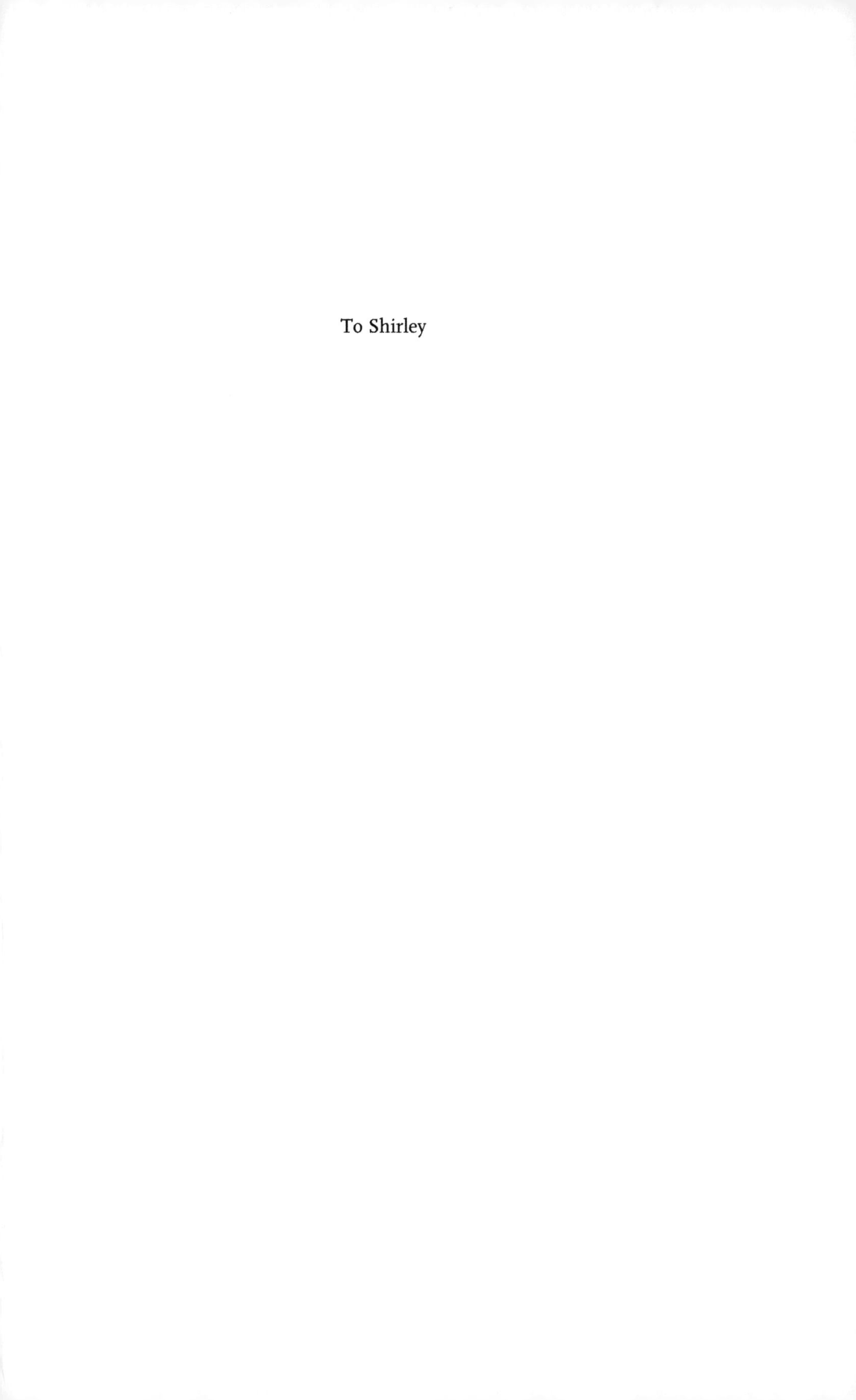

To Shirley

Contents

Illustrations

Introduction

More by accident than design, the publication of this Compendium coincides with the 250th anniversary of Jean-Philippe Rameau's death in 1764. For all that such commemorations have their uses in focusing a spotlight on the individual concerned, there is nevertheless no need to justify the present project on those grounds alone. Interest in Rameau has increased enormously during the past fifty years. His operas are no longer regarded as peripheral by performers but are increasingly staged in the world's major opera houses and festivals. His keyboard and other chamber music has established itself in the mainstream of the French Baroque repertory, while the stature of his activity as a music theorist continues to grow as the extraordinary sophistication of his achievement in this sphere is more widely recognized. These welcome developments have gone hand in hand with a huge increase in the amount of scholarly research on Rameau and his period. Archival studies have added 'new' facts to his biography, lost works have come to light, and there is scarcely an aspect of his multifarious activity as composer, theorist, teacher or performer that has not benefited from closer scrutiny and reassessment. Even so, the sheer quantity and diversity of recent research can sometimes appear daunting. While a substantial proportion of such work has been published in English, much of it appears in French or other languages, and some material is not readily accessible. Hence the need for a reference work that not only provides up-to-date information on a broad range of topics relating to Rameau and his world but also draws attention to the most authoritative writings on the subject.

The lion's share of the compendium – well over four-fifths of its content – is devoted to the Dictionary section. Here I have aimed at maximum breadth and diversity, with a wide range of entries on persons, places, institutions, musical works, theoretical writings and many other matters connected with Rameau. The coverage extends to some possibly unexpected areas: even the most seasoned Ramellian may be surprised – but, I hope, intrigued – to find such keywords as 'Goethe', 'Fandango' or the 'Noblemen and Gentlemen's Catch Club'. Still, the focus of the book is unashamedly 'Rameau-centric'. Pleasing though it might have been to include entries on all the more important musicians and intellectuals active in France during the composer's lifetime, I have deliberately limited the choice to those with whom a specific link to Rameau can be demonstrated. The same is true of musical and dramatic genres, technical and critical terms, and so on. Special prominence is given to French terminology of the period. During the seventeenth and much of the eighteenth centuries, France maintained a performing tradition quite distinct from that of Italy and elsewhere – a tradition, moreover, for which the 'international' Italian musical terminology is often unsuited. I have therefore included in the Dictionary many French terms on generic distinctions, notational peculiarities, performance practice and the like, particularly those that have been widely adopted in modern writings on the composer and his era.

It goes without saying that the Dictionary is not designed to be read from A to Z. (Inquisitive minds may nevertheless be tempted to continue reading by some possibly unexpected juxtapositions: 'Divertissement' and 'Do do, l'enfant do', for instance, or '*Parodie*' and 'Paroles qui ont précédé le Te Deum'.) Rather, a system of asterisks provides cross-references from one entry to another. To avoid cluttering the text, asterisks are used in moderation. Given that each of Rameau operas, cantatas, motets and keyboard publications has its own Dictionary entry, as do all the component pieces with 'character' titles and all the theoretical writings other than minor pamphlets, I have not asterisked the titles of such items except when a cross-reference might shed particular light on the matter under discussion. In the case of keywords that comprise more than one word, the asterisk is normally placed after the final one, at least whenever the individual words are capitalized or in italic (e.g., Concert Spirituel*; *scènes d'action**); in other instances, placement after the first word sometimes seems preferable. An asterisk may, for the sake of convenience, appear after a plural word, even when the relevant keyword is singular.

Quotations from French texts are normally given in English translation only, although the original is also included in the case of passages of verse and, occasionally, where the wording is especially colourful or my translation somewhat free. In each case, the text of the original may be found in one or more of the items cited at the end of the entry. If the French derives from eighteenth-century sources, I have not normally modernized spelling or accentuation. The same is true of the titles of works by Rameau and others, except those that occur with variant spellings in multiple authoritative sources, where I have used my discretion.

With a few exceptions, Dictionary entries end with one or more cross-references to the Bibliography. These take the form of six-letter sigla, normally made up of the first three letters of the author's name followed by the first three of a prominent word in the title (e.g., *AntFre* for James R. Anthony, *French Baroque Music from Beaujoyeulx to Rameau*, or *BoyFam* for Marie-Thérèse Bouquet-Boyer, 'Rameau et l'esprit de famille'). Where the reference is to an item with two authors, the siglum comprises the first three letters of both names. Unavoidably, the same three initial letters sometimes refer to different authors (*Bou* for Bourde, Bouissou and Boucher etc.). In a few cases, I have introduced a variant (*Baz* for Bardez) to avoid items by one writer interrupting a sequence of items by another.

The keywords in the Dictionary and the sigla in the Bibliography are listed in alphabetical order following the word-by-word system. I make an apparent exception in the case of French titles that begin with a definite article (e.g., *Les Amants trahis* or *L'Ambigu de la folie*). Here, instead of relegating the article to the end of the keyword, I retain it at the start. Nevertheless, each of these titles appears in the alphabetical sequence dictated by its initial noun ('Amants', 'Ambigu' etc.) This exception does not, of course, apply to proper names that begin with a definite article ('La Borde', 'Le Maure' etc.).

The Dictionary is preceded by a brief biography. This is intended to provide an overview of the principal events in Rameau's life and to indicate the range of his activities and personal contacts. Asterisks are not used in this section, since the great majority of the names of persons, towns and institutions are the subject of individual Dictionary entries. For the same reason, the Biography does not footnote sources of reference, on the grounds that these can usually be located by way of the relevant keywords.

Numerous individuals and institutions have assisted me in the preparation of this volume. On the often murky questions relating to Rameau iconography,

I have much benefited from the advice of Florence Gétreau, of the Centre National de la Recherche Scientifique. Erik Kocevar was kind enough to share with me many archival discoveries on the Rameau family, all of which will eventually be reported in volume VI/6 of *Jean-Philippe Rameau: Opera Omnia* (OOR). Among the many scholars who allowed me to read their work prior to publication, I am indebted to Antonia Banducci, David Charlton, Marie Demeilliez, Don Fader, Thomas R. Green, John Hajdu Heyer, Peter Holman, Bertrand Porot, Michael Talbot, Thomas Vernet, Cynthia Verba, Kees Vlaardingerbroek, Beverly Wilcox and Valérie de Wispelaere. Patrick Florentin gave me unlimited access to his rich collection of books, scores and other material relating to Rameau, now housed in the Bibliothèque musicale François-Lang at the Abbaye de Royaumont. I have enjoyed the support of Sylvie Bouissou and her colleagues at the Institut de Recherche sur le Patrimoine Musical en France, in particular Nathalie Berton, Cécile Davy-Rigaux, Pascal Denécheau and Denis Herlin. Among those who have supplied factual or other material, I am especially grateful to Jane Clark, Alan Curtis, Mary Cyr, Laurence Decobert, Marie Demeilliez, Pascal Denécheau, Charles Dill, Jean Duron, Florence Gétreau, Tula Giannini, John Hajdu Heyer, Rebecca Harris-Warrick, Bénédicte Hertz, Douglas Hollick, Thomas Leconte, Simon McGuire, Lois Rosow, Lionel Sawkins, Saraswathi Shukla and Jonathan Williams. Thanks are due to the institutions named in the list of illustrations for permission to reproduce the items detailed there. I also wish to thank Michael Middeke, my commissioning editor at Boydell, and his assistant editor Megan Milan for their invaluable advice and encouragement. Above all, I owe a huge debt of gratitude to the series editor, Michael Talbot, who has been a tower of strength and support at every stage of the project.

Graham Sadler
September 2013

For this paperback edition, I have taken the opportunity to correct a few factual errors and to add details of recent publications to the bibliography. These include a collection of essays originating in the Paris Rameau conference of 2014, a special Rameau issue of *Early Music*, and Sylvie Bouissou's 1000-page biography of the composer. The sigla assigned to these items have been added, where appropriate, to the entries in the Dictionary.

Graham Sadler
February 2017

Biography

With tongue firmly in cheek, Sir William Walton once advised all sensitive young composers to die by the age of thirty-seven (*New York Times*, 4 June 1939); in so doing, they would escape the 'critical damnation' of failing to live up to their early promise. Happily, Rameau was not around to heed this advice. By that age he had composed little more than one slender volume of keyboard pieces and a handful of motets and cantatas; nor had he published a word of the forty or so theoretical writings that between them were to transform the way in which the scientific basis of music is understood, and established him as the founder of modern harmonic theory. In short, the composer would never have come to be regarded as one of the most important figures in French – and, indeed, European – musical history.

Rameau was, in fact, the classic late developer. After dropping out from school, he spent most of his first forty years in the relative obscurity of the French provinces. The first of his theoretical works was not published until he was thirty-nine. As for his operatic career, one early biographer claimed that the composer left it 'until the ordinary mortal begins to decay' before making his debut at the Paris Opéra – a slight exaggeration, given that Rameau was only fifty when *Hippolyte et Aricie* was premiered in 1733. It is nonetheless salutary to recall that by that date, his younger contemporaries Bach and Handel had composed most of the works for which they are best remembered. By contrast, some nine-tenths of Rameau's output belongs to his last three decades, between 1733 and his death in 1764 at the age of almost eighty-one. Thus, while the foundation of his musical idiom belongs to the Baroque period, much of the surface detail became increasingly influenced by *galant* or *rococo* developments.

Rameau was evidently secretive about his early life. To his early biographer Michel-Paul-Gui de Chabanon, the whole of the first forty years were absolutely unknown: the composer 'never talked about them to his friends, not even to Madame Rameau his wife'. Thanks to archival and other research, the picture is less blank, if still patchy. Born in Dijon, Jean-Philippe was baptized on 25 September 1683, the son of Jean Rameau and Claude de Martinecourt. He is known to have been the eighth of twelve children and the eldest surviving son. His birthplace in the cour Saint-Vincent on the rue Saint-Michel still exists (now 5–7 rue Vaillant). Despite their modest means, the family maintained influential connections; the composer's godparents, for example, were both from noble families connected with the Burgundian *parlement*. His father, a local organist, was apparently the first professional musician in a family that came to include several notable keyboard players: Jean-Philippe himself, his younger brother Claude-Bernard and sister Marie-Claude (Catherine), Claude's son Jean-François – the eccentric 'neveu de Rameau' of Diderot's novel – and Jean-François's half-brother Lazare.

Rameau *père* apparently took responsibility for his children's early musical education: according to Hugues Maret, 'he taught them music even before they had learnt to read'. Eventually, at about the age of twelve, Jean-Philippe was sent to the Collège des Godrans. He did not, however, distinguish himself there and left in his mid-teens without completing the course – a decision possibly influenced by the death of his mother in July 1697. At this school Rameau doubtless made his first acquaintance with music theatre, which was an important element in the curriculum of such Jesuit colleges. In Dijon he may also have attended touring opera productions. Two recently discovered legal documents of 1699 indicate that Rameau was already active as a musician in the city by the age of sixteen, probably as deputy to his father, who held several organist posts concurrently.

Dijon at that time enjoyed a lively cultural life, and among its luminaries were several men who had visited Italy and acquired an interest in Italian music. This might explain the young Rameau's decision, in his late teens, to travel to Italy – a highly unusual venture for a French musician of his generation. Although the visit was evidently short and he is said to have travelled no further than Milan, it helped to establish a lifelong interest in Italian music. Maret claimed that on his return to France Rameau joined a touring theatrical troupe that gave performances in Provence and Languedoc. It emerges, however, that the Rameau in question was the dancing-master Pierre Rameau (no relation, as far as we know).

On 14 January 1702 Jean-Philippe was appointed temporary *maître de musique* at the metropolitan church of Notre-Dame des Doms in Avignon. By 1 May, however, he had taken up a post as organist at Clermont Cathedral, his duties including not only playing but also some 'learned instruction' and organ tuning. The contract, signed on 30 June, was for six years, though in the event he served no more than four. This is the earliest indication of Rameau's unfortunate tendency to resign from organist posts long before the agreed termination date.

By 1706, but more likely towards the end of 1705, Rameau had moved to Paris. He initially lodged opposite the Franciscan monastery, where his idol Louis Marchand was organist. When Rameau's *Premier livre de pièces de clavecin* was published in 1706, he had already succeeded Marchand as organist at the Collège Louis-le-Grand and was also organist at the monastery known as the Pères de la Mercy. On 12 September he won a competition for the post of organist at Sainte-Marie-Madeleine-en-la-Cité, but when the judges learnt that he was unwilling to relinquish his other two posts, they appointed the runner-up. Rameau had also by now established a relationship with the publishing firm of Ballard, which printed his bawdy drinking song 'Lucas, pour se gausser de nous' in 1707 and later, it seems, commissioned his *Traité de l'harmonie*.

Rameau must have returned to Dijon towards the end of 1708 to succeed his father as organist at Notre-Dame, since a contract dated 27 March 1709 stated that he had already been in post for about three months. This contract, in which he agreed to share the post with the organ-builder's son, stipulated a period of six years. Typically, however, Rameau left the post after only three years: a document of 1 September 1712 names him as 'organiste à Lyon'. By May or June 1713 he had been appointed organist at the Jacobins monastery in Lyon, and in July of that year he was described as 'maistre organiste et musicien de cette ville' when the city authorities paid him for organizing and composing music for a concert to celebrate the Treaty of Utrecht. This is the earliest indication that he had moved beyond the composition of keyboard music. Indeed, several of his 'concert' motets, among them *Deus noster refugium* and *Quam dilecta*, evidently date from his years in Lyon. On 13 December 1714, the day of his father's death, Rameau drew his salary and travelled to Dijon for the funeral and to make the necessary legal arrangements; he remained there for the wedding of his brother Claude-Bernard on 10 January 1715, though by March of that year he had returned to Lyon.

On 1 April 1715 Rameau signed a second contract as organist at Clermont Cathedral. His premature departure a decade earlier seems not to have alienated the cathedral chapter, since this time the contract specified a period of twenty-nine years. His duties once again specified 'learned instruction'; indeed, to judge from the so-called 'Clermont notes', his teaching activities were now extensive and included a substantial course in continuo realization (*accompagnement*) and music theory. Most of Rameau's *cantates françoises* evidently date from this second period at Clermont; it was there, too, that the greater part of his *Traité de l'harmonie* must have been written. Rameau was still at Clermont in May 1722, when he was paid for taking part in three Rogation Day processions. He finally left for Paris shortly afterwards, once again well before his contract expired. (This time it had no fewer than twenty-one years to run.)

Rameau had probably arrived in Paris by June 1722, and was to live there, with occasional excursions, for the rest of his life. The immediate reason for his move was the need to supervise the production of the *Traité de l'harmonie* which, he states, had been typeset in Paris while he was still at Clermont. Indeed, the printing of this work had evidently begun some three years earlier. Nevertheless, numerous errors remained, and before the treatise was published Rameau included a lengthy supplement of corrections, plus a revised or possibly new preface and other changes. The *Traité* was eventually issued soon after his arrival in the capital; an enthusiastic review by the Jesuit mathematician Louis-Bertrand Castel was published in the October–November 1722 issue of the *Journal de Trévoux*.

The appearance of Rameau's monumental 450-page *Traité*, followed by the *Nouveau systême de musique théorique* in 1726, earned him a formidable reputation in France. Thanks to Castel's review, Rameau's writings also attracted increasing attention abroad, though not without meeting some resistance: Johann Mattheson proved particularly hostile to certain aspects of Rameau's theories. Shortly after the appearance of the *Nouveau systême*, Rameau sent a copy to the Royal Society in London – the first of numerous attempts to secure approval for his work from foreign academies and scholars.

Incongruous though it may seem in view of his newfound eminence as a theorist, Rameau's first compositions in Paris consisted of incidental music to a farcical *opéra comique*, *L'Endriague*, given at the Théâtre de la Foire in 1723. The invitation to provide music for this work came from its author, Alexis Piron, a fellow Dijonnais and probably one of the few people in Paris Rameau would already have known. In his three subsequent collaborations with Piron at the Fair theatres, he contributed less music. Yet in spite of the lack of prestige attached to the Théâtre de la Foire, the composer made useful contacts, among them Louis Fuzelier, future librettist of *Les Indes galantes*.

On 10 September 1725 Rameau attended a performance at the Théâtre-Italien by two American Indians from Louisiana. He was soon to characterize their dancing in the harpsichord piece 'Les Sauvages'. This was one of the works Rameau referred to in his oft-quoted letter of 1727 to the dramatist Houdar de La Motte, the text of which shows that he was already planning his operatic debut. During the mid- and late 1720s, more of his music appeared in print. A second keyboard collection, the *Pièces de clavessin*, was issued in 1724, followed by the *Nouvelles suites de pièces de clavecin* and the *Cantates françoises à voix seule*, both undated but evidently published in 1729 or 1730, a year or two later than has long been assumed. One of the cantatas, *Le Berger fidèle*, had by then been performed at Anne Danican Philidor's Concert Français in 1728.

On 25 February 1726, now aged forty-two, Rameau married the 19-year-old Marie-Louise Mangot, an accomplished musician. She bore him four children, of whom three survived infancy: Claude-François, Marie-Louise and Marie-Alexandrine. By all accounts, their family life was happy. Mme Rameau's father, Jacques Mangot, was a musician in the king's service, as was her brother Jacques-Simon Mangot, who later made Rameau's music known at the court of Parma and acted as intermediary in correspondence between Rameau and padre Martini.

In spite of his growing reputation as a theorist, composer and teacher of harmony, *accompagnement* and singing, Rameau was unable to secure an organist's appointment for many years after reaching Paris. The title-pages of his music printed in the 1720s, unlike those of previous publications, give no current post; that of the *Nouveau système* describes him as 'formerly organist of Clermont Cathedral'. In 1727 he competed for the post of organist at the church of Saint-Paul but lost out to Louis Daquin. By 1732, however, Rameau had become organist at Sainte-Croix de la Bretonnerie and, by 1736, at the Jesuit Collège Louis-le-Grand once again. He still held the former appointment in 1738 but not the latter.

Although Rameau did not make his operatic debut until he was fifty, it is clear from passages in the *Traité*, from his letter to La Motte in 1727 and from later remarks, that it had long been his ambition to write for the Paris Opéra (the Académie Royale de Musique). The final impetus, it was widely claimed, was provided by Michel Pignolet de Montéclair's powerful biblical opera *Jephté*, premiered in February 1732. The impact of Rameau's first opera, *Hippolyte et Aricie* (1733), was immense. Initial reactions ranged from excitement and admiration to bewilderment and disgust. This work gave rise to a long-running dispute between the conservative Lullistes, as the anti-Rameau faction was known, and the composer's supporters, the Ramistes (or Ramoneurs). The Lullistes, who formed a powerful cabal, were variously motivated by a distaste for the quantity, complexity and allegedly Italianate character of Rameau's music, and by the fear that the new style would annihilate the traditional repertory, above all the works of their revered Lully. There was an element of professional jealousy on the part of certain composers and librettists, among them André Campra and Pierre-Charles Roy, and Rameau also had to contend with the ill-will of some of the Opéra performers. The dispute continued to rage around Rameau's second opera two years later: according to an anonymous contributor to the *Observations sur les écrits modernes* in 1735, the music was 'a perpetual witchery [...] I am racked, flayed, dislocated by this devilish sonata of *Les Indes galantes*'. With the production of *Dardanus* in 1739, the Lulliste-Ramiste dispute took on a frenzied character: Rameau was the target of numerous satirical engravings and poems; one of the latter led to an unseemly brawl between the composer and its perpetrator, Pierre-Charles Roy. Although the Lulliste-Ramiste dispute abated during the following decade as the public came to terms with the composer's powerful and sophisticated idiom, echoes could still be heard in the early 1750s. Yet despite the controversy, Rameau's first five operas were in no way failures. *Castor et Pollux* and *Dardanus*, the least successful at their first appearance, had honourable runs of twenty-one and twenty-six performances respectively. The two *opéras-ballets* proved even more popular: *Les Indes galantes* was performed sixty-four times between 1735 and 1737, *Les Fêtes d'Hébé* seventy-one times in 1739 and 1740.

Rameau was initially taken aback by the ferocity of the Lulliste-Ramiste dispute; Chabanon quotes him as saying: 'I thought my style would succeed; I have no other; I will compose nothing more'. Yet the composer soon began to revel in his newly launched operatic career: according to Castel, he even considered abandoning his work on music theory, since at that stage he felt he could pursue this no further. The composer's first visits to court began in December 1733; between then and 1740, all his operas to date were performed at the Concerts de la Reine, the singers sometimes including his wife.

Almost immediately after the première of *Hippolyte et Aricie*, Rameau began the first of three collaborations with Voltaire. The libretto and much of the music of the ill-fated *Samson* had been written and rehearsed by October 1734. This opera ran into censorship problems, however, and was subsequently abandoned. At the time of this first collaboration with Voltaire, Rameau was beginning his last with Piron – not this time at the Théâtre de la Foire but on the exalted stage of the Comédie-Française. *Les Courses de Tempé*, one of the few pastoral plays staged there, was given a single performance, in August 1734.

At the time of his operatic debut, Rameau enjoyed the patronage of the prince de Carignan, a powerful figure at the Académie Royale de Musique. The composer is known to have benefited from the prince's lavish hospitality at the Hôtel de Soissons on several occasions; moreover, he may have been introduced to freemasonry there, since the Carignan residence hosted a number of masonic gatherings in the 1730s. Rameau's association with the prince lasted until at least November 1735. By the following August, however, he had transferred his allegiance to the tax-farmer Le Riche de La Pouplinière, one of the wealthiest men in France and an influential patron of the arts. It seems likely that Rameau was invited into this household, as music director, by his devoted pupil Thérèse Deshayes, La Pouplinière's mistress and future wife. He became an influential figure there: Jean-Jacques Rousseau ruefully noted that 'Rameau made it rain and shine, as they say, in that house'. There, too, he received firm backing during the Lulliste-Ramiste dispute and associated with a wide circle of artists and literary figures. The latter included numerous future librettists, though he would already have met many of these if, as later claimed, he was a member of the convivial literary dining club known as the Caveau.

Rameau's only major theoretical work of the period 1733–49 was *Génération harmonique* (1737), dedicated to the members of the Académie Royale des Sciences. Once again, Rameau sent a copy to the Royal Society in London but evidently received no response. By the time this treatise appeared, his circle of friends and acquaintances in the world of science and mathematics had widened considerably and included Dortous de Mairan and the abbé Étienne-Simon de Gamaches. Moreover, he is now known to have been a founder member of a discussion group established in the previous decade by the mathematician Moreau de Maupertuis. During the 1730s Rameau was embroiled in a number of polemical exchanges, initially with a 'second musician' (possibly

Montéclair) on the subject of *accompagnement* and the *basse fondamentale*; then with his former friend Castel, whose reviews of his writings had become increasingly critical; and finally with Louis Bollioud-Mermet, a mathematician and astronomer in Lyon, who took issue with his views on temperament. In each case Rameau defended his cause with characteristic verve.

From December 1737, notices in the *Mercure de France* and elsewhere announced that Rameau had established a School of Composition, where up to twelve pupils would meet each week for three two-hour classes. Teaching materials for the course survive in the manuscript 'L'Art de la basse fondamentale', while his pupils include a number of composers, among them Claude Balbastre and Pietro Gianotti.

The period from 1740 to 1744 was uncharacteristically slack by the standards of Rameau's mature years. He produced no theoretical writings, while his musical output was limited to the publication of the *Pièces de clavecin en concerts* (1741) and the revision for their first revivals of *Hippolyte et Aricie* (in 1742), *Les Indes galantes* (1743) and *Dardanus* (1744). There is reason to suspect a quarrel with the Opéra management, which may well explain his lack of enthusiasm for a libretto of *Pandore* that Voltaire offered him in 1740 and likewise for an anonymous libretto intriguingly entitled *Orphée aux enfers*. At all events, the composer's productivity revived sharply soon after Louis-Armand Thuret was replaced by François Berger as Opéra director in May 1744. A year earlier, Rameau had apparently been persuaded to participate as conductor at Jean Monnet's newly revitalized Opéra-Comique.

The immediate stimulus to Rameau's renewed creative activity was a series of commissions, three of them from the court, which resulted in the production of four substantial dramatic works in 1745. For the festivities surrounding the Dauphin's wedding he composed *La Princesse de Navarre* (his second collaboration with Voltaire) and *Platée*; for the celebration of the victory of Fontenoy he wrote *Le Temple de la Gloire* (again with Voltaire) and *Les Fêtes de Polymnie*. This last work initiated a long collaboration with Louis de Cahusac, resulting in at least seven operas.

On 4 May, shortly after the Dauphin's wedding, Rameau received a royal pension of 2000 *livres* and the title *compositeur de la musique de la chambre du roi* – an exceptional honour, since this title was normally conferred only on an existing member of the royal musical establishment. Thus was officially inaugurated a closer association with the court: from 1745 onwards, more than half of Rameau's stage works were intended for court premieres. One of these, *Les Surprises de l'Amour* (1748), was written as a vehicle for the marquise de Pompadour's theatrical talents in her Théâtre des Petits Cabinets. There is evidence that, at the time of his first royal pension, Rameau had not been financially well-off. After *Le Temple de la Gloire* Voltaire generously donated his own fee to Rameau, whose 'fortune is so inferior to his talents'. (On the other hand, Rameau was already said to have worked with librettists only if they surrendered their fees to him.) In 1750 the king, Louis XV, accorded the composer a further pension of 1500 livres, payable from the Opéra's revenues, although this pension was not actually honoured until 1757.

The five years 1745–49 were among Rameau's most productive: no fewer than ten new works were performed at the Opéra and/or at court. By 1749 his works dominated the stage to such an extent that the comte d'Argenson, who had oversight of the Académie Royale de Musique, felt compelled to limit the number of Rameau's operas staged there to one (some reports suggest two) per year, to avoid discouraging other composers. Rameau was furious: according to Charles Collé, he withdrew a *tragédie en musique* that he and his librettist Cahusac had already submitted for performance. Indeed, evidence suggests that his relationship with the management of the Académie Royale de Musique was again not good, and on several occasions he was to express his resentment at the small amount he was paid in relation to the huge sums his works had earned for the Académie.

Despite such frustrations, Rameau had reached the height of his popularity around 1750. The Lulliste-Ramiste dispute was effectively over, and he had the support of a wider cross-section of the French public than ever before. His position at court was secure, he enjoyed the esteem of most of the intellectuals, including many who were later to side against him, and his works were widely performed in the provinces. The extent to which he had won over the audiences and performers at the Opéra can be judged by a report in the *Mercure de France* for May 1751:

> At Wednesday's performance [of *Pigmalion*] M. Rameau, who had only just recovered from a long and dangerous illness, appeared at the Opéra in one of the rear boxes. His presence aroused a murmur that began in the stalls and spread rapidly throughout the whole audience. Then suddenly there broke out a general applause and – something that had never been seen before – the assembled orchestra added their rapturous cheers to those of the *parterre*. [Rameau] shared with the public the pleasure of an excellent performance. That night it seemed that all the actors were striving to excel themselves.

Such spontaneous demonstrations of respect and affection were to become more common during the 1750s. Even so, audiences remained slow to respond to new works: it was frequently noted that his operas achieved real success only when they were revived.

Rameau's operatic activities in the mid- and later 1740s had left little time for theoretical work, but in 1750 he broke an 13-year silence in this field with the publication of *Démonstration du principe de l'harmonie*. (This long silence supports Castel's claim that in the mid-1730s Rameau felt he could develop his theoretical work no further.) For this treatise he had the 35-year-old Denis Diderot as collaborator, hence the clarity and elegance of what is generally considered one of his most mature theoretical works. The *Démonstration* was approved by members of the Académie Royale des Sciences, including Jean le Rond d'Alembert. Rameau sent copies to the Royal Society (once again without result) and to the Swiss mathematician Jean II Benouilli.

In 1745 two events took place that were to sow the seeds of Jean-Jacques Rousseau's undying hatred of Rameau. Having completed *Les Muses galantes*, an *opéra-ballet* modelled on Rameau's *Les Indes galantes*, Rousseau solicited Rameau's opinion of it. In his *Erreurs sur la musique de l'Encyclopédie* (pp. 41–42) Rameau recalls this encounter:

> Some ten or twelve years ago, a certain person ['un Particulier'] had a ballet of his, which was later offered to the Opéra and rejected, performed at M. [de La Pouplinière's]. I was struck by finding in it very beautiful instrumental airs in a

purely Italian style, and at the same time all that is worst in the French style in the vocal and instrumental parts, including *ariettes* with the dullest vocal line supported by the loveliest Italian accompaniments. This contrast surprised me, and I asked the composer a few questions, which he answered so badly that I saw clearly what I had already guessed, that he had written only the French music and had pillaged the Italian.

Rousseau was later to admit that he had had some help from François André Danican Philidor in composing this piece (hence, no doubt, the stylistic discrepancies). Later that year, he had a similarly humiliating experience when asked to recycle the divertissements of Rameau's *La Princesse de Navarre* for further performance at court under the title *Les Fêtes de Ramire*. Rousseau's efforts were so harshly criticized that the work was sent back to Rameau. At all events, Rousseau gained no credit from the episode. From then on, he seldom missed an opportunity to speak in scathing or hostile terms of the compositions, and to a lesser extent the theories, of his former idol.

When Rameau's irrepressible nephew Jean-François was sent to prison in 1748 for insulting the Opéra directors, the composer was asked by the authorities 'how long he deemed it fitting that [the nephew] should stay there'. Rameau evidently suggested that Jean-François be deported to the colonies, but this was evidently beyond the secretary of state's powers; the miscreant was released three weeks later.

During his final thirteen years Rameau's operatic activity declined sharply. Apart from two major works (*Les Paladins* and *Les Boréades*), his composition was limited to small-scale pastorales and *actes de ballet* and to the revision of earlier works for revivals, notably *Castor et Pollux* and *Zoroastre*. From 1749 until 1757 Rameau remained on bad terms with the Opéra management. Of his new works from 1752 onwards, only *Les Paladins* was given there; the rest were performed solely at court. *Les Boréades*, possibly begun as early as 1747, is now known to have been prepared for performance not at the Opéra but at the royal residence of Choisy in June 1763; it had been rehearsed two months earlier in Paris and Versailles, but subsequently abandoned and never performed in the eighteenth century. Until his last year, Rameau nevertheless continued to take an active part in new productions and in revivals, giving his views on the distribution of roles and regularly attending rehearsals both in Paris and at court.

No doubt advancing age, and the ill health to which the composer and others increasingly alluded, contributed to the reduction in the quantity, if not necessarily the quality, of Rameau's compositions. But this slackening coincided with a remarkable resurgence of activity in his theoretical work: from 1752 he produced some twenty-three writings. Many are short pamphlets, but more weighty works include the *Observations sur notre instinct pour la musique* (in part a reply to Rousseau's notorious *Lettre sur la musique françoise*), the *Code de musique pratique* and his recently discovered final treatise *Vérités également ignorées et interessantes tirées du sein de la nature*, formerly known only in fragmentary form. In 1752 his pupil d'Alembert performed the invaluable service of publishing the *Éléments de musique théorique et pratique suivant les principes de Mr Rameau*, in which the master's theories are expounded with exceptional clarity and elegance, though not without a certain amount of oversimplification and distortion. A letter of about 1750 from the 33-year-old Alembert to the 67-year-old Rameau reveals that the two were at this stage on very cordial terms. In 1757 d'Alembert's book was translated into German by Rameau's lifelong admirer F.W. Marpurg.

Rameau's contacts with foreign scholars increased markedly in this period as he sought wider recognition. Beginning in 1750, he entered successively into correspondence with Gabriel Cramer (Geneva), Johann II Bernoulli (Basle), Christian Wolff (Halle), Leonhard Euler (Berlin), Giovanni Poleni (Padua), J.B. Beccari, padre Martini and F.M. Zanotti (Bologna). He even sent a treatise on canon, now lost, to the Noblemen and Gentlemen's Catch Club in London. Although he had also communicated with many French scientists and scholars over the years, the list now widened to include the aesthetician Charles Batteux, the architect Charles-Étienne Briseux and the scholar François Arnaud, all of whom were to prove influential.

At the start of the 1750s Rameau still had the support of most of the intellectuals (with the obvious exception of Rousseau), and was championed both as a composer and theorist by Diderot, d'Alembert and Melchior von Grimm. During the Querelle des Bouffons, however, Grimm and others found it expedient, partly for extra-musical reasons, to side against the principal living exponent of French music. Rameau was soon to break with Diderot and d'Alembert as well, in a polemic concerning the music articles in the *Encyclopédie*. Rameau had declined the invitation to write these, and they were eventually entrusted to Rousseau (who later complained that Diderot had allowed him only three weeks and that this had impaired their quality). Rameau, however, was never shown them before publication: possibly Rousseau had seen to that. His pride doubtless hurt, he initially kept silent, despite repeated provocation by Rousseau, about what he perceived to be the failings in the music articles. But with the publication of the fourth volume of the *Encyclopédie* in 1754, Rameau could no longer hold back. In *Erreurs sur la musique dans l'Encyclopédie* (1755) and subsequent pamphlets, he launched a fierce attack on Rousseau. By the time Diderot and d'Alembert had been fully drawn into the conflict, when they defended Rousseau in the preface to the sixth volume of the *Encyclopédie* (1756), Rameau had alienated all the principal *philosophes*. Yet even without this increasingly vituperative quarrel, these men could never have allied themselves with the latest developments in Rameau's thinking, in particular when this took on a mystical, metaphysical or even theological tone.

The break with the *philosophes* must have been desperately disappointing to Rameau, since it had long been his ambition to be accepted as a thinker. 'Can it not be clearly seen', he wrote to Diderot and Alembert in 1757, 'that in honouring me with the titles "artiste célèbre" and "musicien" you wish to rob me of the one [i.e., "philosophe"] which I alone among musicians deserve, since I was the first to have made music a science by the discovery of its natural principle?' He must have been equally disappointed never to have been elected to the Académie Royale des Sciences. True, the Académie had shown a high regard for his work and had endorsed his *Démonstration du principe de l'harmonie* in 1750. But otherwise the nearest he came to such an honour was in 1752 when, along with several other distinguished Burgundians, he became an associate member of a distinguished Dijon literary society. When this ceased to exist in 1761, he was elected to its victorious rival, the Académie des Sciences, Arts et Belles-Lettres de Dijon.

After nearly two decades, Rameau's association with La Pouplinière came to an end in 1753. Although the financier had separated from his wife, Thérèse Deshayes, five years earlier, the composer and Mme Rameau stayed on, spending each summer at La Pouplinière's country home and even living for a time in an apartment in his Paris residence. But in 1753 La Pouplinière's new mistress established herself there and soon made life unbearable for a number of residents, including Rameau and his wife. At the same time, the financier seemed keen to replace his venerable 70-year-old music director with a more fashionable musician. Maret claimed that the final rift came when La Pouplinière installed another composer in his house. If so, that composer cannot (as has been conjectured) have been Johann Stamitz: although he was eventually to succeed Rameau in the financier's household, Stamitz arrived in Paris only in 1754.

In his last years, Rameau made feverish attempts to finish his theoretical work, now more important to him than composition. Indeed, he had come to regret the time spent on the latter, which had deflected him from his principal goal. A rare glimpse of the aged Rameau is provided by a letter of November 1763 to the businessman Casaubon, in which his disquiet that time was running out is all too apparent. Very few personal letters of this sort have survived. According to his son Claude-François, who as a youth had often served as messenger boy and amanuensis, Rameau burned most of his papers and other effects.

By now Rameau was comparatively rich, having amassed a considerable fortune from his royal pensions, pupils' fees, payments from the Opéra and, until 1753, his patron La Pouplinière. There was also revenue from the sale of books, scores and pamphlets. Numerous details survive of his investments, many of them taken out in favour of his children and other relatives. When François Rebel and François Francœur took over as joint directors at the Opéra in 1757, they belatedly honoured the royal pension of 1500 *livres*, granted in 1750 and payable from the theatre's revenues. Three years earlier, Rameau helped his son Claude-François buy the coveted title of *valet de chambre* in the king's service, providing 17,500 of the necessary 21,500 *livres*. On several other occasions he gave financial help to members of his family circle, among them his sister Marie-Claude (Catherine) and brother-in-law Jacques-Simon Mangot.

Rameau died at his home in the rue des Bons-Enfants on 12 September 1764, three weeks after contracting a violent fever. He was buried the next day in his parish church of Saint-Eustache. Five months earlier, he had received Letters of Nobility from Louis XV; among the papers found after his death is proof that the necessary registry fees were paid. The posthumous inventory of his estate, valued at 199,426 *livres*, itemizes the composer's mainly threadbare wardrobe and a single dilapidated harpsichord, but reveals that a writing desk in his wife's room contained coins worth 40,584 *livres*. Indeed, less than four months after the composer died, Mme Rameau was able to provide a grand 'society' wedding for her 20-year-old daughter Marie-Alexandrine, who Rameau, according to Collé, had sworn would never marry in his lifetime.

Three memorial services were held in Paris, two of them organized by the Académie Royale de Musique and one by François André Danican Philidor. Similar commemorations took place in various provincial towns, among them Marseilles, Orléans and Avignon. On 25 August 1765 Hugues Maret, secretary of the Dijon academy of which Rameau had been a member, delivered a carefully researched *Éloge historique*; published the following year, this is one of the most valuable sources of information on the composer's life. Numerous epitaphs appeared in the press and elsewhere; curiously, most of these chose to emphasize Rameau's achievements as a theorist rather than a composer, though some are couched in terms that could apply to both: 'To write Rameau's epitaph | Everyone exercises his genius. | One line suffices: | In this tomb lies the God of Harmony'.

Descriptions of Rameau's physique agree on his height and build: 'though much taller than Voltaire, he was just as gaunt and emaciated' (Grimm); 'he was lean and scraggy, with more the air of a ghost than a man' (Chabanon); 'like a long organ pipe with the blower absent' (Piron). Collé and Grimm give extremely unflattering and doubtless jaundiced accounts of his personality. 'Rameau was by nature harsh and unsociable; any feeling of humanity was foreign to him; [...] his dominant passion was avarice' (Grimm); 'he was a difficult person and very disagreeable to live with; [...] he was, furthermore, the most uncivil, the most unmannerly and the most unsociable man of his day' (Collé). All these accounts are by those who had axes to grind or who knew Rameau only as an old and by now eccentric man; the picture they paint is thus almost certainly distorted or incomplete. Sadly, there are few accounts from his earlier years to provide balance, though snippets of evidence from the 1730s and 1740s hint at a far more sociable individual with a taste for conviviality, as do the playful texts of his drinking songs and canons.

Rameau's musician friends included Balbastre, Chabanon and Duport. Jean-Baptiste Gautier-Dagoty drew attention to his generosity of spirit towards gifted composers: 'Far from feeling overshadowed by the success of others, he hastened to applaud the talents of his contemporaries'. Rameau's modesty and shyness were noted by his friend Chabanon:

> He loved fame, no doubt, since he had gained so much of it [...], but I am convinced that he was little concerned about his own; indeed it sometimes embarrassed him. At the Opéra he was seen to hide away, to shun the attention of the public who applauded him. This was not to display a false modesty: he was incapable of such a thing, and all artifice was foreign to him. [...] He liked to affirm the talents of others as much as his own, and if he sometimes showed too much pride in his discoveries about music, it was less because these brought him honour than because he sensed how useful they were.

Although the charge of avarice cannot be dismissed, against this must be set his many acts of generosity to family members.

As a keyboard player Rameau excelled in continuo realization (*accompagnement*). Although he never acquired an organist post of any great prestige after he settled in Paris in 1722, his playing at Sainte-Croix-de-la-Bretonnerie attracted many music lovers, while Marmontel described him playing 'pieces of astonishing vitality' on the organ at La Pouplinière's country mansion. Maret's assessment, though second-hand, derives from those who were well acquainted with Rameau's playing: 'Less brilliant in execution, perhaps, than Marchand's but more learned, his touch yielded nothing in delicacy to that of Clérambault'. Maret had nevertheless been told, possibly by Balbastre, that Claude-Bernard Rameau was a better player than his older brother.

By the time of his death Rameau's cantatas, motets and harpsichord music had long fallen out of fashion, though some of the keyboard works remained on sale in the 1760s. A number of his dramatic works were revived at the Opéra in the years immediately after his death, but few survived in the repertoire beyond 1770 and fewer still beyond the middle of that decade, when the operas of Gluck, Piccinni and Sacchini were taking Paris by storm. Those of his works that did survive were, like the rest of the 'ancien répertoire', subjected to the now-customary revisions and disfigurements. Some opera lovers, albeit a tiny minority, deplored what they saw as this corruption of taste; Rameau's tireless advocate Jacques-Joseph-Marie Decroix, reminiscing many years later, even saw it as a contributory cause of the French Revolution.

Rameau's theoretical works suffered a similar – if less catastrophic – decline. In the years after the composer's death, interest in the speculative side of his writings waned sharply; the *coup de grâce* as far as the bulk of his work was concerned came in 1801, when the Paris Conservatoire decided to reject his harmonic system in favour of a utilitarian system by Charles-Simon Catel (1773–1830). Yet a number of Rameau's most important discoveries and insights had subtly infiltrated the thinking even of those who were generally opposed to his work. Key principles such as the inversion of chords, the primacy of triads and seventh chords, and the *basse fondamentale* were widely accepted, as were the system of harmonic generation and the recognition of the subdominant as one of the three pillars on which the tonal system is founded. If certain aspects of Rameau's theoretical writings have been now shown to be questionable or plain wrong, the core of his work has been accepted into the very fabric of our thinking about harmony and still forms the basis of traditional approaches to the teaching of the subject.

The rehabilitation of the music took longer. If Rameau the composer was remembered at all amid the revolutionary fervour at the end of the eighteenth century, it was as a representative of the hated and discredited Ancien Régime. In the early decades of the following century, the music of the entire Lully-Rameau period was regarded in France with shame or derision. Seen in this light, Hector Berlioz's appreciative comments on passages from *Castor et Pollux* in the *Revue et Gazette musicale* (1842) run wholly counter to the prevailing view. The beginnings of a Rameau revival later in the century were hampered by the lack of adequate editions of the music; even so, excerpts from his works appeared increasingly if sporadically in concert programmes, while the centenary of his death was celebrated in his native Dijon in 1864 with some magnificence. Yet not until the upsurge of French nationalism in the wake of the Franco-Prussian War of 1870–71 did the revival gain real momentum, especially after the establishment by Camille Saint-Saëns of the magnificent, if flawed, *Œuvres complètes* (1894–95). The turn of the century witnessed more frequent and larger-scale performances mounted at the Schola Cantorum and elsewhere, awakening the enthusiasm of Claude Debussy among others. Meanwhile, serious archival studies by Michel Brenet, Henri Quittard, Lionel de La Laurencie and other scholars provided a sound basis for subsequent biographies.

One major impediment to the performance of Rameau's music at that time was the lack of a performance tradition that could do justice to his ornamentation, rhythms and orchestration, while the problem of performing his operas

at modern pitch, about a tone higher than intended, created extreme diffi-
culties. Not until the end of the twentieth century, with the establishment of a
historically informed performance tradition, has a viable alternative emerged.
Admittedly, no one would claim that musicologists have unearthed more than
a fraction of the relevant historical evidence (or ever will). Performers, for
their part, tend to be quite selective about which bits of this evidence they are
prepared to be informed by, and instrument makers are sometimes pressured
into taking liberties in the interests of reliability and convenience. Still, the
balance sheet is nowadays more positive than negative. The fact that Rameau
operas now appear frequently at major festivals and opera houses is eloquent
testimony to the work of countless scholars, instrument makers and performers
who, in recent decades, have tried to recreate the unique sound-world for which
these works were intended.

Dictionary

Abaris Rameau's last opera is sometimes referred to as *Abaris, ou Les Boréades*, a modern conflation of the titles by which the work was originally known. The two surviving full scores bear the title *Les Boréades**, as do all but nine of the forty-nine vocal and instrumental part-books, and this is the form of the title found in all contemporary archival documents. The remaining nine part-books are entitled *Abaris*, the name of the male protagonist. The original set of performing parts eventually entered the Decroix collection, which explains why Decroix* himself refers to the work, in *L'Ami des arts* (1776), as *Abaris*. He is nevertheless the only eighteenth-century writer to do so. *BouBor, BouHer, BouPas, DecAmi, DecRam, KinRam, TérAba.*

L'Absence In his carefully researched *Éloge historique de Mr Rameau*, Hugues Maret* mentions that Rameau had written a cantata with this title in Clermont*, presumably during his second period there (1715–22). Maret evidently got his information from Michel Pélissier de Féligonde (1729–67), secretary of the Académie de Clermont. No source of this work has been located, however. *MarÉlo, SchFam, TunCan.*

Académie des Sciences, Arts et Belles-Lettres de Dijon Founded in 1725, this scientific and literary society was granted letters patent in 1740. It later became associated with a literary group formed in 1752 by Richard de Ruffey (1706–94), who in that year invited several distinguished non-resident Burgundians – Rameau among them – to become associate members of his group. The grateful composer sent a copy of two recently published articles, 'Réflexions sur la manière de former la voix' and 'Extrait d'une réponse de Mr Rameau à M. Euler sur l'identité des octaves', which were reviewed by members of the group. When Ruffey's society was wound up in 1761, Rameau was invited to join the newly invigorated Académie de Dijon by its president, Charles de Brosses*. At about that time, the academy acquired a copy of Caffieri's* bust of Rameau. After the composer's death, the society's permanent secretary Hugues Maret* was commissioned to prepare an *Éloge historique de Mr Rameau*, a superbly documented obituary that was read at a meeting in August 1765 and later published. *GirAut, LauGen, MarÉlo, RamCtw.*

Académie Royale de Musique The institution colloquially known as the Opéra took its official title of Académie Royale de Musique in 1672, when Louis XIV granted Lully* letters patent to take over Pierre Perrin's 'Académies d'Opéra', founded three years earlier. Almost throughout the Lully-Rameau period the company occupied the Palais-Royal* theatre. Despite its royal status, the Académie received no formal state subsidy; nevertheless the terms of its royal *privilège* ensured a monopoly over the public representation of opera throughout France. This was jealously guarded by successive directors, who supplemented the income from ticket and other sales by licensing provincial opera-houses and demanding royalties from spoken theatres for the right to include a strictly limited amount of music. For much of the Opéra's history, the *privilège* was owned by impresarios, who tried to run the establishment as a going concern while remaining ultimately answerable to the current secretary of state. The director at the time of Rameau's operatic debut in 1733 was Louis Thuret*. When he resigned in 1744, the *privilège* passed to François Berger*, who held it until his death in 1747. Berger's period as director and that of his successor Tréfontaine* proved financially disastrous, to the extent that Louis XV decided in 1749 to give control of the Opéra to the city of Paris. The institution was administered by a succession of official *inspecteurs* until 1757, when Rebel* and Francœur were jointly accorded the *privilège*. They were succeeded in 1767, three years after Rameau's death, by Berton* and Trial. *CamAca, ChaRou, DurAca, GorOpé, RosDes, SerOpé, WooSad.*

Académie Royale des Sciences   Music traditionally played a part in discussions at the French Royal Academy of Sciences, founded in 1666. For Rameau, the goal of having his theoretical writings officially approved by this scientific institution, second in prestige only to the Royal Society* in London, was of vital importance. His first known contact was in 1737, when he asked permission to dedicate *Génération harmonique* to the academy's members. A short but positive appraisal of the manuscript, by Ferchault de Réaumur (1683–1757), Dortous de Mairan* and the abbé de Gamaches*, was summarized in an extract from the academy's registers, which Rameau proudly included at the end of the published work. His fulsome letter of dedication* calls for the academicians' support in his future efforts to discover the secrets of the science of music. He must nevertheless have been disappointed that their report fell short of an official approbation. Rameau's second attempt to gain this recognition began on 19 November 1749, when he read a 'Mémoire où l'on expose les fondemens du système de musique théorique et pratique', written with the assistance of Diderot*. This 'Mémoire', which was to form the basis of the *Démonstration du principe de l'harmonie* (1750), marks the beginning of Rameau's association with d'Alembert*. The brilliant young mathematician drafted a glowing report signalling the academy's view that harmony, previously guided by 'arbitrary laws or blind experience', had become a science to which the principles of mathematics could be more usefully applied. The published *Démonstration* notes the academicians' approval and includes their report as a 39-page supplement. Rameau's final appearance at the Académie took place on 4 April 1759, when he read his essay 'Réflexions sur le principe sonore'. By now, in the course of a rancorous dispute with the editors of the *Encyclopédie*, Rameau had broken with most of the leading *philosophes*, including d'Alembert, whom the academicians asked to examine the 'Réflexions'. No report was ever forthcoming. A revised version of this work was published as *Nouvelles réflexions sur le principe sonore*, included as a supplement to the *Code de musique pratique* (1760). *ChrTho, CohAca, RamCtw.*

Acante et Céphise, ou La sympathie   This three-act *pastorale héroïque** was first performed at the Académie Royale de Musique* on 19 November 1751 during celebrations to mark the birth of the duc de Bourgogne. (The suggestion by Robert Fajon that it had also been presented before the court at Choisy the previous day seems far-fetched, given the logistics of transporting the sets, costumes, instruments and cast ten miles from Choisy and setting them up in a single day.) Marmontel's* libretto is inspired by *la féerie** of Middle-Eastern myth; it centres on a talisman given to the eponymous lovers by their guardian fairy Zirphile, which imparts the telepathic power (the 'sympathie'

of the subtitle) to experience each other's feelings even when separated. This
communication by talisman, together with Zirphile's initiatory voyage and
the lovers' ordeals, suggest that the opera, like several of Rameau's others,
articulates newly fashionable themes connected with freemasonry* – in this
case, the place of women within the order. It was widely believed that women
could not be trusted with the masonic secret and were hence excluded from
most lodges. The present libretto may be seen as part of a reaction against
this exclusion; thus when Acante and Céphise are tortured in an attempt to
worm the telepathic secret out of them, it is Céphise who repeatedly proves
the more steadfast and prevents her lover from disclosing it. (Marmontel was
later jailed for not 'outing' a freemason – an example, perhaps, of life imitating
art.) In a surprise denouement, Zirphile predicts the birth of a Bourbon prince.
That apart, the plot has no connection with the royal birth, and it is probable
that this feature was a late addition if, as seems likely, the opera was press-
ganged at the last minute (the commission dates from no earlier than June
1751) into celebrating the royal event. The same may well be true of the opera's
programme overture, its three sections entitled 'The nation's good wishes',
'Fireworks' (involving cannon* shots) and 'Fanfare' (imitating the cries of 'Vive
le roi'). This work includes the earliest surviving parts for clarinets* in French
opera. The spelling 'Achante' encountered in some modern sources derives
from a misprint in the proofs of the engraved score, eventually corrected by
Rameau. *BouHer, ChaRou, FajAch, GirRam, MasOpé.*

Accent   The *accent* is one of the ornaments most frequently encountered in the
performing parts used by the singers who created Rameau's operas. In these
sources it is notated by a caret (∧) placed over the staff, above or to the right
of the note to which it applies. This indicates a vocal inflection in which the
singer briefly and delicately sounds the diatonic note above, usually towards
the end of the main note. The *accent*, associated exclusively with expressions
of strong emotion, is consistently found on exclamations and other highly-
charged syllables ('Ah!', '*hé*-las!', '*trem*-ble', 'cru-*el*-le'). The emotional impact
was intensified by a crescendo to the upper note, followed by a diminuendo.
See also **Ornaments added in rehearsal**. *CyrEss, GreSou, McGSpa, NeuOrn, NeuPer,
SawNou, WilAna .*

Accompagnement   When Castel*, in his review of the *Traité de l'harmonie*, wrote
that Rameau 'excelled in the art of accompaniment', he meant that the composer
was particularly skilled at realizing the continuo bass. This aspect of performance was one that Rameau discussed many times in his theoretical writings,
since he considered 'accompaniment' to be the surest way of becoming properly
sensitive to harmony. It was through his experience of teaching accompaniment
that he first conceived the principle of the *basse fondamentale**, as is revealed
by the so-called 'Clermont notes'* prepared in the later 1710s. In Rameau's
view, the fundamental bass presented a more effective alternative to the *règle
de l'octave** which was then the standard aid to continuo realization. An even
simpler system, first discussed during his polemic with a 'second musician'
(possibly Montéclair*) between 1729 and 1731, was more fully explained in his
*Dissertation sur les différentes métodes d'accompagnement pour le clavecin** (1732),
and involved both a drastic reduction in the number of symbols and a new
approach to the connecting of chords. *ChrRèg, ChrTho, CohCor, RamCtw, RouDic.*

Accompanied keyboard music   Though better described as chamber music with obbligato keyboard, the genre nowadays known as accompanied keyboard music came to prominence during the mid-eighteenth century. The new genre, which co-existed with rather than replaced the continuo-accompanied sonata, evolved as a consequence of the growing prestige of the harpsichord as a solo instrument. Indeed, it brought about a role-reversal, in that the formerly subservient keyboard came to the fore, while the melody instrument(s) took on a largely accompanying role. Rameau's principal contribution to the genre is the *Pièces de clavecin en concerts** of 1741. In his preface to the score, the composer acknowledges that it had been the success of Mondonville's* *Pièces de clavecin en sonates* (undated but now believed to have been published in or about 1738) that prompted him to adopt a similar design in his own volume. Further examples of the genre may be found in two of Rameau's earlier publications. The preface to the *Pièces de clavessin** of 1724 indicates that 'several pieces' in the collection could be played in other keys: the Musette en rondeau in E major, for example, could be transposed to C major 'in order to be played with the viol'. The E minor *rigaudon* could be played in D minor, probably for the same purpose. In the preface to the published score of *Les Indes galantes*, condensed into 'Quatre grands concerts'* (c.1736), Rameau indicates that although the instrumental movements had been adapted as *pièces de clavecin*, this should not prevent their being played with other instruments doubling the written-out harpsichord part. *BouHer, CyrVio, GusFul, FulAcc, HerMor, KidSon, RpeKey, SadInd.*

Achille et Déïdamie   One of the more unusual manifestations of the Lulliste-Ramiste* dispute occurs in this *tragédie en musique** by Danchet and Campra*, premiered in 1735. The prologue is set at the foot of Mount Parnassus in front of a monument to the Goddess of Harmony and Muse of Poetry. The monument is surmounted by statues of Lully* and Quinault* crowned with laurels. Melpomene, Muse of Tragedy, praises the talents of these revered founders of French opera. Addressing the Graces, she assures them that all art languishes without their attributes, adding that whereas Learning ('le Savoir') may surprise, it cannot touch the heart without their help. Such comments, in the context of the Lulliste-Ramiste dispute, would have been interpreted as a veiled criticism of Rameau: his operatic style was regarded by his detractors as lacking in grace and excessively learned ('savant'), hence incapable of moving the emotions. Thus Danchet and Campra, in associating themselves with such sentiments, were siding openly with the Lulliste faction. Given that Campra was currently the *inspecteur* at the Académie Royale de Musique*, this must have complicated his relationship with Rameau. *BarCam, HarPro, MasLul.*

Acte de ballet   One of the many sub-species of French opera, the *acte de ballet* is a self-contained work equivalent in length and character to a single entrée* of an *opéra-ballet**. It was a form of opera that Rameau apparently enjoyed writing: his output includes eight works of this sort, including such fine examples as *Pigmalion* and *La Guirlande*. Most were designed to be performed independently alongside other works, not necessarily his own. Several of those that have survived as *actes de ballet* – *La Naissance d'Osiris*, *Mirthis* and probably *Anacréon* – were originally intended as part of a projected *opéra-ballet* entitled *Les Beaux Jours de l'Amour**. *AntFre, GreSou, HarBal, MasOpé.*

Actéon   *See* **Diane et Actéon.**

À demi jeu   In his autograph and published scores Rameau preferred to use French rather than Italian terminology for dynamic* marks. The literal meaning of *à demi jeu* (often abbreviated as *à demi*) is 'at half-play' or 'at half-strength', hence the term approximates to *mezzo-forte*. Although Jean-Jacques Rousseau* also equated it with *sotto voce*, Rameau appears not to have used *à demi* in this sense. Unlike *doux**, which could indicate the temporary halt to woodwind doubling of the outer string parts, *à demi jeu* did not imply a reduction in the number of players. *GreSou, MasOpé, RouDic.*

Adoucissez   To indicate diminuendos or crescendos* Rameau sometimes used an early form of the 'hairpin' signs, but more often employed such words and phrases as *adoucissez* ('get softer') and *en adoucissant* ('getting softer'). In *Les Boréades* the final chord of the overture, sustained for three bars, is marked 'adoucir toujours en mourant' ('get steadily softer in dying away'), while the start of the entr'acte* between Acts III and IV bears the indication above the *violon* part: 'adoucissez insensiblement pour être touj[ours] doux avec les flutes' ('get imperceptibly softer in order to continue softly with the flutes'). *GreSou, MasOpé.*

'L'Agaçante'   The title of this movement, from the *Pièces de clavecin en concerts* (1741), must be interpreted figuratively rather than literally. Whereas in modern French 'acaçant(e)' means 'irritating' or 'annoying', the primary meaning of the verb *agacer* in Rameau's day was 'to set the teeth on edge', which hardly seems appropriate to this playful movement. However, the word could also be used to mean 'to provoke or excite by words, actions or glances', as in the phrase 'c'est une coquette qui agace tout le monde' (*Dictionnaire de l'Académie Française*, 1762). The *Dictionnaire de Trévoux* (1771) applies the word to 'the thousand little things a woman says or does to attract someone who does not displease her'. It was presumably such meanings that Rameau had in mind. This piece is one of five that the composer arranged for solo harpsichord. He was later to include re-workings of the movement in *La Princesse de Navarre* (1745) and *Zoroastre* (1749). Comparison of these different versions provides useful clues to the interpretation of ornaments and to the practice (or avoidance) of *notes inégales**. *DicAut, HerMor, RpeKey, SadBor, SadZo1, SadZo2.*

Agréments   Rameau's contemporaries would have understood an *agrément*, in the musical sense, to be anything that made a melody more pleasing. More narrowly, the word was applied to the grace notes and ornament symbols used in vocal and instrumental music. In his *Premier livre de pièces de clavecin* (1706) and *Pièces de clavessin* (1724) Rameau provides explanations of how the symbols in each volume should be interpreted (the 1724 table is shown overleaf); in other publications he makes clear that these explanations apply to all his harpsichord music, including the arrangements from *Les Indes galantes* published as 'Quatre grands concerts'*. The keyboard *agréments* differ from the ornament symbols in his cantatas and operas, where Rameau restricts himself, as was standard practice, to grace-notes and the + sign (usually indicating a trill), together with the occasional *accent** and the ⌣ sign. This last, when it occurs in ascending movement, normally indicates a *pincé**. *See also* **Ornaments added in rehearsal**   *CyrEss, CyrSin, McGSpa, NeuOrn, RpeKey, SadInd, SawNou, WilAna.*

Table of ornaments in Rameau's *Pièces de clavessin* of 1724 (Paris, Bibliothèque Nationale de France, Département de la Musique, Vm⁷. 1873). Reproduced by permission.

'Ah ! loin de rire, pleurons'   *See* **Modulating canon.**

Air   In the Lully-Rameau period, this multifaceted term encompassed a wide range of forms and genres. It was not restricted to vocal music: the terms *air de ballet*, *air de danse* and *air de violon* denoted instrumental pieces, the first two being dance movements in staged entertainments. Vocal airs were often classified by their subject matter, as in Ballard's* monthly collections *airs sérieux et à boire*, to which Rameau contributed a modulating* canon and a duo. In the operatic repertory an air was often categorised according to its language (*air italien**), character (*air gracieux, air tendre*) or dramatic context (*air de dialogue, air de divertissement**, air de monologue**, air des scènes*). In the operas of Rameau and his contemporaries, a passage marked 'air' could be as short as six bars and scarcely distinguishable from the surrounding recitative, though most were rather longer and more developed in their form and melodic character. Apart from *airs de divertissement* and *airs de monologue*, however, few had the dimensions or the degree of musical elaboration of a typical aria in a contemporary Italian opera. *See also* **Ariette; Maxim air; Simile air.** *AntFre, GirRam, MasOpé, VerRec.*

Air de monologue   The rational Gallic mind found it difficult to accept the Italian custom of punctuating recitative dialogues with extended arias; the idea of one character waiting around while another voiced his emotions at length seemed faintly absurd. For that reason, musical expansion within the *scènes d'action** of French opera was from the outset limited mainly to *petits airs**. No such objection could be levelled at the soliloquy, however, and the *air de monologue* thus established itself as a staple and welcome component of opera from the time of Lully* onwards. *Monologues* usually though not invariably occur at the start of an act, where they help prepare the emotional tone of the ensuing scene. By the mid-eighteenth century the majority were cast in *da capo* form. That apart, Rameau's *monologues* have little in common with the Italian *da capo* aria. The vocal line, often akin to a heightened recitative and modelled on the rhythms of impassioned speech, includes few if any textual repetitions and no technical display. Despite such apparent restrictions, these *monologues* include many of the composer's profoundest expressions of human sentiments, as in the abject grief of Télaïre's 'Tristes apprêts' (*Castor et Pollux*, I, 3) or the misery of Abaris's 'Lieux désolés' (*Les Boréades*, IV, 2). In these and other *monologues*, the orchestra plays a vital role in projecting the emotional character, no more so than in 'Lieux funestes' in the 1744 *Dardanus* (IV, 1), with its powerful bassoon obbligato; one contemporary considered that, even without the words, this music eloquently conveyed the sorrow and rigours of Dardanus's cruel imprisonment. *AntFre, GirRam, GirTra, MasOpé, NauDra.*

Air italien   Despite his youthful trip to Milan*, Rameau is known to have set only one Italian text, the aria 'Fra le pupille' in the entrée* 'Les Fleurs' from *Les Indes galantes* (1735). In incorporating an *air italien* into this opera, he and his librettist Fuzelier* harked back to a practice that had been fashionable at the turn of the seventeenth and eighteenth centuries, but had long waned with the emergence of the *ariette**, the French equivalent of the extended *da capo* aria. 'Fra le pupille' seems to have sparked a revival of interest in the *air italien*, several of which may be found in the immediate successors of *Les Indes galantes*, notably Rebel* and Francœur's *Scanderberg* (1735) and Mlle Duval's *Les Génies* (1736). Rameau's aria, like most French *airs italiens* of the period, adopts the outward form and some stylistic elements of the *aria di bravura*, though its technical demands on the singer are limited by comparison with an equivalent aria by Vivaldi* or Handel*. *AntFre, CyrEss, CyrSin, GirRam, MasOpé.*

Airs sérieux et à boire   See **Ballard, Jean-Baptiste Christophe**

Alberti, Domenico   When the *Messe des morts* by Jean Gilles* was adapted for use at memorial* services marking the death of Rameau, two of its movements were replaced by *contrafacta** based on Rameau's own music. A further adaptation was the insertion of a 'Pie Jesu', recently identified by John Hammond as a reworking of the aria 'Caro sposo' by Domenico Alberti (c.1710–46). Although Alberti's text is taken from Apostolo Zeno's libretto *Cajo Fabricio*, this setting appears to be an independent concert aria. Music by Alberti had entered the Concert Spirituel* repertory as early as 1749, and a number of unidentified arias were performed there in 1763 and 1764; given that one surviving source of 'Caro sposo' derives from the Concert Spirituel library, this aria may well have been among them. Had Rameau particularly admired it there or at the house of his former patron La Pouplinière*, where the piece may also have been performed? Or did the organizers of the memorial service include it merely because it had proved popular at the Concert Spirituel? Whatever the case, the sentiments expressed by this aria, in which a widow grieves for her husband, seem apt as a basis for this 'Pie Jesu', though a modern eyebrow might be raised, in such a context, at the degree of vocal virtuosity on display. *CucPou, HamMem.*

Alembert, Jean Le Rond d'   Co-editor of the *Encyclopédie* and one of the pre-eminent mathematicians of the Enlightenment, d'Alembert (1717–83) first came into contact with Rameau's music theory in 1749, when he was appointed by the Académie Royale des Sciences* to examine a manuscript 'Mémoire' that Rameau had submitted for the Académie's approval; the 'Mémoire', written with help from Diderot*, was to become the basis of the *Démonstration du principe de l'harmonie*, published the following year. The deductive nature of Rameau's methodology struck a chord with d'Alembert, as is clear from his glowing report, and he became an enthusiastic advocate for Rameau's ideas. It was at about this time that d'Alembert began lessons in music theory from Rameau and embarked on the task of turning the clumsy expression of his mentor's writings into well-structured and readable prose – a task that resulted in the *Élémens de musique théorique et pratique suivant les principes de M.ʳ Rameau** (1752). This publication drew a touchingly grateful response from the composer. The following year, d'Alembert singled Rameau out for special praise in the 'Discours préliminaire' to the *Encyclopédie*; as editor of the music articles, he also ensured that Jean-Jacques Rousseau's* contributions on music theory were not disrespectful towards Rameau. But when the composer, inflamed by the tone of some of Rousseau's subsequent publications, attacked the author in *Erreurs sur la musique dans l'Encyclopédie*, d'Alembert felt obliged to defend his contributor. The resulting exchange of open letters, increasingly acrimonious in tone, led to an irrevocable breach between Rameau, d'Alembert and his fellow editor Diderot. *BerPri, CanPhi, ChoPré, ChrTho, CohAca, DalElé, IshDal, IshQue, KafEnc, KinRam, OliEnc, RamCtw, VerMus.*

Algieri, Pietro   The Venetian painter and stage designer Pietro Algieri (dates of birth and death unknown) was from 1735 an assistant to Servandoni* at the Académie Royale de Musique*. In 1748 he succeeded Boucher* there as *premier décorateur*. One of his first tasks was to design an unprecedented amount of new scenery for Rameau's *Zoroastre* (1749), the first production mounted after the city of Paris took control of the Académie; invoices by Algieri and his assistant Pajot provide a wealth of information about the designs, colours, construction materials and stage effects. Jérôme de La Gorce has plausibly suggested Algieri as designer of a number of cardboard *maquettes* (set models) prepared in the 1750s and 1760s for productions that include Rameau's *Dardanus, Les Surprises de l'Amour* and *Zaïs*. In many of these the design is symmetrical, though in others this symmetry is restricted to the side wings, the backdrops being painted in oblique perspective. *GorDec, GorSet, HowNeo, SadZo1.*

Allard, Marie   After appearing as a child dancer in her native Marseille and later in Paris at the Comédie-Française, Marie Allard (1742–1802) studied dancing with Gaetano Vestris*, by whom she had a child, the future star dancer Auguste Vestris (1760–1842). Marie's debut at the Académie Royale de Musique* in the 1761 revival of Rameau's *Zaïs* was an instant success, and she was soon hailed as the natural successor to Mlle Camargo* in the genre of *danse haute*. According to Noverre*, she was an excellent *pantomime* who always tastefully choreographed her own entrées* without the aid of the official ballet master*. By the time she retired in 1781, she had appeared in well over forty-five operas and ballets, including the Mozart-Noverre ballet-pantomime *Les Petits Riens* (1778). *BouHer, CamAca, NovLet, SadZaï.*

Les Amants trahis   Scored for two singers, obbligato *basse de viole* and continuo, this is one of the relatively few *cantates françoises** to require more than one voice. As is often the case in such works, it lacks the element of narrative, a defining feature of the solo cantata. Rather, the text consists entirely of a dialogue between the jilted lovers Damon and Tircis, the one insouciant, the other despairing. Although notated in the treble clef, the part of Damon is primarily intended for a *haute-contre*. Given that one of the two surviving manuscript sources is dated 1721, the work was probably composed during Rameau's second period at Clermont*. The virtuoso *basse de viole* part includes perilous leaps and multiple stoppings of up to six notes. From the fact that many of these chords make use of few if any open strings, Mary Cyr has suggested that parts of the score have been transposed up a semitone from D to E♭, perhaps at the request of a singer. *CyrCan, CyrChr, CyrEss, CyrPer, DorCan, MonBou, SadCou, TunCan.*

L'Ambigu de la folie   Having begun his dramatic career in Paris at the Théâtre de la Foire*, Rameau was evidently tempted back at the height of his fame to take part in a gala production in 1743. The impresario Jean Monnet* had just taken over the direction of what was by now known as the Opéra-Comique* and was eager to raise its artistic standards. Among his first productions was *L'Ambigu de la folie, ou Le ballet des dindons*, a highly acclaimed *parodie** by Charles-Simon Favart (1710–92) of Rameau's *opéra-ballet** *Les Indes galantes*. The performers included three young dancers – Louise-Madeleine Lany*, Mlle Puvigné* and Jean-George Noverre* – who distinguished themselves in a *pas de trois* from the entrée 'Les Fleurs' in Rameau's *opéra-ballet*. To supervise these child prodigies, Monnet engaged three renowned dancers, Marie Sallé*, Louis Dupré* and Jean-Barthélemy Lany*. Sets and costumes were designed by the distinguished painter François Boucher*. Given such a star line-up, Monnet's claim that the orchestra was directed by 'M.ʳ Rameau' cannot be dismissed. Some commentators have suggested that the Rameau in question was the composer's brother Claude-Bernard* or his nephew Jean-François*, yet neither was in Paris in 1743. Besides, any reference to 'M.ʳ Rameau' at this date automatically indicated

Jean-Philippe, all others being qualified as *frère, neveu, fils* etc. If, as is generally believed, the composer had quarrelled with the Opéra management in the early 1740s, he may have relished the chance to direct his own music in the newly-refurbished Opéra-Comique, where the account books show that artists could be engaged for periods as short as two weeks. *MelPar, PorNov, PorPre, SadPir.*

Amelot manuscript   One of the main sources of information on the Paris Opéra during the Lully-Rameau period, this manuscript was commissioned by the secretary of state Antoine-Jean Amelot de Chaillou (1732–95), hence the shorthand label by which the *Mémoires pour servir à l'histoire de l'Académie royale de musique vulgairement l'Opéra depuis son établissement en l'année 1669 jusques et y compris l'année 1758* are often known. As well as relating in substantial detail the administrative, financial and artistic history of the Paris Opéra in the Lully-Rameau period, it provides invaluable biographical information about the Académie's singers, players and other employees. The original is now in the Bibliothèque Royale, Brussels; a copy is preserved in the Bibliothèque Nationale de France (Bibliothèque-Musée de l'Opéra), Paris. *ChaPol, CyrCho, CyrSin, GreSou, SerOpé.*

Amiot, Joseph-Marie   In 1754 the Jesuit missionary Amiot (1718–93) sent to Paris a manuscript report of his experiences in China. His comments on Chinese music were later used by Rameau (*Nouvelles réflexions sur le principe sonore*, 1760) as the basis of a hypothesis that Chinese and Greek music evolved from the same source. Amiot's *Mémoire sur la musique des chinois* (1776) took Rameau to task, however, for introducing errors into his account of the Chinese system. In his *Mémoires concernant les chinois* (1779) the Jesuit reveals that he had played Rameau's harpsichord pieces 'Les Sauvages' and 'Les Cyclopes' to the Chinese, together with music by Michel Blavet, but his listeners could make nothing of these examples of Western music. *See also* **Orgue de barbarie**. *ChrTho, LabEss, SavAme.*

Anacréon   This is one of two independent one-act pieces by Rameau with the same title. (The other is discussed as 'Anacréon' below). It was first performed on 24 October 1754 as part of the celebration of the birth of the duc de Berry (the future ill-starred Louis XVI) during the French court's annual *voyage* to Fontainebleau. Cahusac's* libretto is unusual in several respects. First, it features a historical personage, the ancient Greek lyric poet Anacreon, rather than a character from myth or legend. Second, it makes no use of *le merveilleux** (the supernatural), which suggests that it was conceived for a theatre with no stage machinery; indeed, there is reason to believe that the work was originally composed for Madame de Pompadour's Théâtre des Petits Cabinets*, the role of Chloë presumably being intended for the marquise herself to sing. The work may even have been designed as the final entrée* of *Les Beaux Jours de l'Amour**, an abandoned *opéra-ballet**. The sources of *Anacréon* classify it as a *ballet héroïque**, although in its surviving state it more logically belongs to the genre of *acte de ballet**. *See also* **Fragments**. *BouHer, GirRam, GreSou, MasOpé, RicFon, SawNou, SawPig, WilAna.*

'**Anacréon**'   Not to be confused with the Rameau-Cahusac *Anacréon** of 1754, this is a setting of a libretto by Pierre-Joseph Bernard*, composed as an additional entrée* for *Les Surprises de l'Amour* (1748) when that work was revived in 1757. Like Cahusac*, Bernard features the ancient Greek poet

Anacreon, who debates with the Maenads the question of whether love and wine are compatible. Bernard, whose life had been largely given over to practical experiment in both domains, answers the question in the affirmative. The music includes a *sommeil** that alludes to several passages in Vivaldi's *Le quattro stagioni*. *See also* **Modulating canons.** *BouHer, BouSu2, EmmPyg.*

Andante Although Rameau preferred to use French indications of tempo and expression, his scores from the mid-1740s onwards occasionally include the Italian term *andante* (see illustration on p. 82). In France this was often taken to denote not only a moderate speed (as elsewhere in Europe) but also to warn against the use of *notes inégales**. That the latter function was usually Rameau's intention is revealed by various clues. In the production* score of the 1744 *Dardanus*, Isménor's recitative 'Quel transport me saisit!' (IV, 2) bears the engraved marking *andante*, to which Rameau later added 'doux et notes égales' (softly and with equal notes) alongside the violin staff. In the engraved score of *Platée*, the air 'C'est pour mon divertissement' (II, 3) is marked 'notes égales' at the start of the *ritournelle*, and 'croches égales' (equal quavers) at the singer's first entry, while the production score bears the autograph annotation 'andante' at the start of the movement. The use of the Italian time signature 2/4 in conjunction with *andante* likewise warns against *notes inégales*. There is, however, one exception to this interpretation of the term in Rameau's music: the *ariette** 'Non, non, une flame volage' in *La Naissance d'Osiris* is marked 'andante, et lourée' and is dominated by a lilting dotted figure in 6/8. Here *andante* appears to indicate the tempo only, since the term *louré** implies that the dot should be slightly lengthened. By Rameau's time, it seems unlikely that *andante* still carried the connotation that the bass notes should be detached, as indicated by Brossard at the start of the century. *BroDic, GreSou, HefRhy, MasOpé.*

Annonce Towards the end of a dramatic dialogue, at the point when the participants of a divertissement* are about to appear, it was the custom in French opera for the orchestra to interrupt the recitative with an *annonce* – often the opening phrase of one of the pieces in the divertissement. Where appropriate, this would feature instruments emblematic of the participants (hunting horns*, *musettes** etc.) and would sound as if played at a distance, to signal their approach. Occasionally the *annonce* has no connection with a divertissement, as in the entrance of the jailer Orcan at the start of the first scene of *Les Paladins*. *HarBal, MasOpé.*

Anthony, James R. With the publication in 1978 of his *French Baroque Music from Beaujoyeulx to Rameau*, Anthony (1922–2001) did much to turn a period largely neglected by Anglophone musicians into a thriving area of scholarship and performance. Although the end-point of this classic study is 1733 (the date of Rameau's first opera), the book provides an informative, richly illustrated and readable account of the institutions, milieux and genres within which Rameau worked; the revised, expanded edition (1997) includes a wide-ranging, 79-page bibliography. The focus of Anthony's other writings is the *préramiste** period, with particular emphasis on Lully* and *opéra-ballet**. *AntFre, AntOpé, HajLul.*

Antier, Marie A native of Lyons, the soprano Marie Antier (1687–1747) became a pupil of the legendary singer Marthe Le Rochois, creator of the title roles in Lully's* *Armide* and Charpentier's* *Médée*, among many others. On her first appearance at the Académie Royale de Musique*, in 1711, Mlle Antier was an immediate success with the public, and during the next three decades she took part in as many as five productions per year. Like her teacher, she was an outstanding actress, renowned for her dignified posture and *jeu de théâtre**, and she excelled in powerfully dramatic roles. By the time Rameau made his operatic debut, the beauty of her voice was beginning to fade; she nevertheless had the distinction of creating the major roles of Phèdre in *Hippolyte et Aricie*, Phani in *Les Indes galantes* and Phébé in *Castor et Pollux*. She retired in 1741. *BenMus, BouHer, PieCon, PouJél, RivFil, SadInv, TunCan, ValLyo.*

'Apothéose de Rameau'   In the Musée d'Art et d'Histoire at Toul is a fine oil painting by Jean-Jacques Le Barbier (1717–1826) entitled 'Apothéose de Rameau'. Commissioned by the prince de Conti for the music room at the Enclos du Temple in Paris, it forms a pair with a tribute to Lully* by the same artist, which likewise survives in the Toul collection. In an Arcadian setting, a female figure places a floral crown on a bust of Rameau, plainly modelled on the one by Caffieri*. Hanging from the plinth is a medallion representing Sophie Arnould*, renowned during the 1760s and 1770s for her interpretations of the great female roles in Rameau and other operas. The paintings date from some time between the completion of the bust (1760) and the prince's death (1776). *GétPor.*

Aquilon et Orithie   In a much-quoted letter to La Motte* of 1727, Rameau refers to this cantata as 'L'Enlèvement d'Orithie', stating that it was written 'a dozen years ago'. This would place its composition either at the end of his time in Lyon* or the start of his second period at Clermont*. One version of the cantata survives as a set of manuscript parts dated 1719. Rameau later revised the work extensively for inclusion in his *Cantates à voix seule**, published in 1729 or 1730. *Aquilon et Orithie* is scored for bass voice with violin obbligato. The direction 'violons' in the published score suggests that this version of the work was conceived with orchestral rather than chamber performance in mind. *BouHer, CyrCan, CyrChr, CyrEss, CyrPer, DorCan, MonBou, RaySav, SadCan, TunCan, ZasApp.*

Argenson, Antoine-René de Voyer, marquis de Paulmy d'   Although the marquis de Paulmy (1722–87) held a number of major diplomatic appointments, he is perhaps more widely remembered for his outstanding collection of books and *objets d'art*. As grand bailiff ('balli') of the Artillery, he lived at the Arsenal in Paris; there he assembled a library of some 100,000 volumes that now forms the basis of the Bibliothèque de l'Arsenal (Bibliothèque Nationale de France), still housed in the original building. Many of the marquis's books, which include scores and librettos of Rameau operas, bear prefatory annotations written or dictated by him. These are of some interest in revealing the tastes and opinions of a man of great refinement. *GasPau.*

Argenson, Marc-Pierre de Voyer de Paulmy, comte d'   In 1750 Rameau dedicated his *Démonstration du principe de l'harmonie* to the comte d'Argenson (1696–1764), secretary of state for war and a supporter of many prominent intellectuals, among them Diderot* and d'Alembert*, who dedicated to him the *Encyclopédie*. The count had recently taken over responsibility for the city of Paris, thus assuming overall charge of the Académie Royale de Musique*. Valérie de Wispelaere and Thomas Vernet have recently discovered a letter from Rameau of 12 April 1752, addressed to an unnamed recipient who can only be the comte d'Argenson, to whom the writer had also sent a manuscript version, now lost, of the forthcoming *Nouvelles réflexions de Mr Rameau sur sa 'Démonstration du principe de l'harmonie'*. This letter, in the hand of Rameau's son Claude-François*, begins by extolling the treatise's virtues in revealing a unifying principle that governed all the arts. Rameau claims that if the king knew of the exceptional quality of his work, he would recompense him, so as to encourage emulation by others. The composer then asks for a meeting to discuss his concerns about the Académie – the lack of sufficient singers to sustain the traditional repertory ('les anciens Opéra') and the need to avoid a situation in which the directors are forced to mount only lightweight works because of the imminent departure of star singers (he was thinking of Marie Fel* and Pierre Jéliote*). While no reply from d'Argenson has survived, Rameau's request for proper financial reward seems to have been noted: a substantial payment of 2,400 *livres* to the composer in 1753 'for his past services' has recently been identified by David Charlton. *ChaPol, RamCwt, SerOpé, WisVer.*

Argenson, René-Louis de Voyer de Paulmy, marquis d'   Elder brother of the comte d'Argenson and father of the marquis de Paulmy d'Argenson (see above), the marquis d'Argenson (1694–1757) held the post of French foreign secretary from 1744 until 1747 and also pursued a literary career. His manuscript journal and memoirs, though primarily concerned with political matters, reveal something of his conservative tastes in music and ballet. They were first published together in 1859 as *Journal et mémoires du marquis d'Argenson*. His manuscript 'Notices sur les Œuvres de théâtre' provide numerous lively if opinionated comments on plays and operas from the Lully-Rameau period. *ArgMém, ArgNot.*

Ariette   Paradoxically, the French used this diminutive of 'air' for what, in the opera of Rameau's day, was their equivalent of the extended Italian *da capo* aria. Unlike in other types of French aria, the text of the *ariette* was regarded as subservient to the music, thus justifying a degree of musical expansion and vocal display. In Rameau's early operas, the degree of virtuosity in such *ariettes* as 'Rossignols amoureux' (*Hippolyte et Aricie*) and 'Brillez, astres nouveaux' (*Castor et Pollux*) is modest by comparison with the typical Italian bravura aria of the time, being limited mainly to brief vocalises on standard words or syllables. In the later Rameau operas, however, many of the *ariettes* call for considerable virtuosity, as in 'Un horizon serein' (*Les Boréades*) or, more spectacularly, 'Aux langueurs d'Apollon' (*Platée*), with its delicious send-up of an Italian cadenza. Moreover, Rameau greatly augmented the number of *ariettes* in such works; from the late 1740s onwards, they are allotted increasingly to principal characters rather than minor ones, and sometimes occur in the *scènes d'action**. The formal design likewise became less standard, with elaborate multi-sectional structures replacing the traditional *da capo*. *AntFre, GirRam, MasOpé, VenCom.*

Ariosti, Attilio   In *Génération harmonique** Rameau draws attention to certain 'admirable scenes' in Italian opera in which the enharmonic* genre is used to good effect. He specifically mentions the accompanied recitative 'Spirate, o iniqui marmi' from the prison scene in *Il Coriolano* by Attilio Ariosto (1666–1729). When Ariosti's opera was first performed at the King's Theatre in London in 1723, this scene had been the smash hit; as such, it was doubtless in the repertory of the performers from the Royal Academy of Musick who gave concerts in Paris the following summer. This might explain the presence in the Bibliothèque Nationale de France of no fewer than three manuscript copies of this single scene, plus an exemplar of the published score of the opera. In Ariosti's recitative, the second section includes enharmonic progressions not unlike those in 'L'Enharmonique'* and 'La Triomphante'*, which Rameau mentions in the same section of *Génération harmonique*. Whether or not these similarities are coincidental, Ariosto's accompanied recitative seems to have influenced Rameau in other respects. If we assume that he studied the Ariosti piece while preparing his new treatise, published in 1737, it is revealing to note correspondences between this piece and Télaïre's monologue from *Castor et Pollux*, which also appeared that year. Not only are the chromatic progressions and melodic contours similar (see the examples below), but both accompaniments feature an off-beat, three-note bassoon figure set against slow-moving strings – a style of writing without precedent in French opera. (To make the comparison clear, the first example has been transposed up a major third, the note values of the second example halved, and ornaments omitted.) Moreover Ariosti's piece was surely in Rameau's mind when he composed the monologue 'Lieux funestes' in the 1744 version of *Dardanus*. This likewise takes place in a prison scene; it features an obbligato line for bassoons; and the opening *ritournelle** includes chromatic progressions remarkably similar to those in Ariosti's recitative. *BarEnh, BreJeu, GirRam, LinAri, LinPat.*

(a) Arosti, *Coriolano*, III, 5

(b) Rameau, *Castor et Pollux*, I, 3

Arnaud, François (abbé)   Arriving from his native Provence in 1752, the abbé Arnaud (1721–84) gained a considerable reputation with his first publication, the *Lettre sur la musique à M. le Comte de Caylus* (1754), in which he sets out a plan for a treatise on musical analysis, sadly never completed. From this it becomes clear that he and Rameau had already discussed the expressive power of rhythm. The composer was much taken with the young abbé's lively intellect and sought his help in drafting both the *Prospectus* (1757) and the *Code de musique pratique* (1760). Arnaud, who was considered one of the most eloquent writers of his generation, not only improved Rameau's notoriously contorted prose* style but also evidently contributed ideas of his own. Three personal letters from Rameau to Arnaud reveal the warmth of their friendship. It was to Arnaud that the composer confided that if he were thirty years younger he would go to Italy and take Pergolesi as his model. 'I would subject my harmony to that truth of declamation which must be the musician's only guide. But in one's sixties, one realizes that one must stay as one is. Experience tells us what needs to be done, but the spirit refuses to obey.' *See also* **Orgue de barbarie.** *ChrTho, GirRam, LabEss, MasLet, RamCtw, TieRam.*

Arnould, Magdaleine-Sophie   The soprano Sophie Arnould (1740–1802) made a name for herself at the age of only five, when she sang before members of the French royal family. Having studied singing with Marie Fel* and acting with the famous tragedienne Mlle Clairon (1723–1803), she made a huge impact at the Académie Royale de Musique* at her debut in 1757: the *Mercure de France**, enthusing about the beauty of her voice and the warmth of her acting, declared that she had already become 'the queen of this theatre'. Although her voice was not strong, she made up for this by her stage presence, drawing tears from the audience in numerous tragic roles. She created the part of Argie in *Les Paladins* and would have played Alphise in *Les Boréades** had the planned premiere taken place. One of her greatest successes was as Télaïre in the 1764 revival of *Castor et Pollux.* She proved well suited to the Italianate music of Gluck, distinguishing herself in *Iphigénie en Aulide* (1774); by now, however, her voice was declining, and she was passed over for the title role of *Alceste.* She retired in 1778. *See also* **Balbastre's harpsichord.** *BouHer, BouBor, CamAca, CamSpe, ChaRou. PieCon, PouJél, RivFil, TroArn.*

Arpègement   In his table of keyboard ornaments of 1724, reproduced on p. 20, Rameau distinguishes two kinds of arpeggiation – the *arpègement simple* or simple spread chord, and the *arpègement figuré*, in which the arpeggio includes a non-harmony note (the leading-note in Rameau's table). Both are indicated by a diagonal stroke through the stem, the direction of the diagonal indicating the direction of the spread. The *arpègement figuré* also has a vertical wavy line after the chord. Like many French contemporaries, Rameau exemplifies only an on-beat start to the arpeggiation, though whether this indicates an invariable practice is far from certain. In his opera scores the diagonal line is sometimes used with the same meaning. More often, however, arpeggiated string chords are designated by the abbreviation 'harp.' (i.e., *arpégé*). *See also* **Articulation.** *CyrPer, NeuPer.*

'L'Art de la basse fondamentale'   Some time before c.1744, Rameau completed a manuscript entitled 'L'Art de la basse fondamentale', intended as a textbook for the School of Composition* he had established in 1737. This 310-page manuscript, probably in the hand of a pupil, mainly comprises a discussion of the *basse fondementale** in relation to consonant and dissonant chords and to the figured bass. This textbook is probably identical with the 'method of composition' mentioned in *Démonstration du principe de l'harmonie* (1750), which Rameau claims he had been forced to abandon some years earlier; he was nevertheless entrusting it to a person 'very capable of making both himself and the public profit from it'. That person, at least when Rameau wrote those words, may have been d'Alembert*: the manuscript is preserved in the d'Alembert archive of the Institut de France, and the great mathematician later expressed the hope of publishing 'a complete method of composition' if ever he found the necessary three or four years for this task. But work on the *Encyclopédie* clearly took precedence and the project was put aside. Almost two decades later, Rameau's former pupil Pietro Gianotti* published *Le Guide du compositeur* (1759), a tutor-book that has been shown to be based entirely on the content of Rameau's manuscript, albeit abridged, reorganized and expressed in more lucid prose. Importantly, Gianotti includes the music examples lacking in the manuscript. Given that this book appeared while Rameau was still alive, we must assume that the composer was happy for his protégé to make good use of material that he himself was no longer in a position to exploit. *ChrBas, ChrTho, KneRou, MarVie, RamCtw, RouArt.*

Articulation   Rameau used a fairly restricted range of articulation signs. Much the most frequent of these is the slur, normally indicated with great care in his own manuscripts and engraved scores, though less so in scribal copies; indeed, several autograph annotations in production* scores reveal Rameau's concerns about the accuracy of the slurs in the players' part-books. Sometimes he or his scribes would write a combined slur and tie, a double curve where a slur over two or more notes is elongated as a tie to the note that follows. One distinctive use of the slur is to indicate slurred* tremolo, a kind of intensity vibrato. Other articulation markings occur far less often in Rameau's music. Among those symbols in the keyboard music that relate to articulation rather than to ornamentation are the *suspension**, the *son coupé** and the *arpègement** or arpeggiation. The latter two are indicated respectively by a vertical* stroke and a diagonal line through the stem, symbols that occur not only in the harpsichord publications but also in opera scores. Further verbal indications of articulation in the operas include *pincé* (pizzicato*) and *détaché*. Rameau's only other articulation symbol is the superscript* dot – not necessarily used to signify staccato. *See also* **Nourrir**; **Underlay slurs.**   *BouPri, GreSou, HefRhy, McGSpa, MasOpé, SaiInt.*

Augmented mediant chord   In the fourth volume of *A General History of Music* (1789), Charles Burney* drew attention to one of his pet hates in French music – the 'chord of the superfluous fifth, which makes all nature shudder except our Gallic neighbours'. Burney cites a passage in Rameau's 1754 *Castor et Pollux* where, in his view, this chord is 'continued so long that it distorts the countenance of every other hearer, like *hiera picra* ['holy bitter', a pungent medicament]'. The offending chord, nowadays described as an augmented mediant chord, occurs at the asterisk in the example opposite; it consists of an augmented triad on the third degree of the minor scale – in this case E♭, G (supplied by the continuo) and B♮ – usually, as here, with a superimposed seventh (D) and ninth (F). Burney was right to associate this expressive dissonance with France: its use can be traced back to Louis Couperin in the 1660s, while Charpentier* and some of his successors were to make it a speciality. But the chord was also adopted by many foreign composers influenced by French music, prominent among them J.S. Bach. *BurHis, GirRam, MasOpé, MooAug.*

Rameau, *Castor et Pollux* (1754 version), III, 1

Autreau, Jacques   The poet, painter and playwright Jacques Autreau (1657–1745) is best remembered in opera circles as the librettist of *Platée*. He first made his name in the theatre in 1718 with a smash-hit comedy *Le Port à l'anglois*, the first French play given at the newly re-established Théâtre-Italien*. As a friend of La Pouplinière*, Autreau is presumed to have met Rameau when the latter joined the financier's circle in the mid-1730s, and it was evidently soon afterwards that the *Platée* project was conceived; indeed, according to the marquis d'Argenson*, La Pouplinière himself had a major hand in writing the libretto. However, Rameau's falling-out with Thuret* and the Opéra management in or around 1740 caused the project to be shelved. By the time it was revived for a projected production at the Paris Opéra in 1745, the octogenarian Autreau had entered the Hôpital des Incurables, and Rameau had bought the rights to the libretto. At the last minute *Platée* was pressed into service for the Dauphin's wedding celebrations at Versailles, at which point Le Valois d'Orville* made some minor textual revisions. *ArgNot, BarPla, BouHer, ChaRou, GirRam, GreSou, MasOpé, VlaTed.*

'Avec du vin, endormons-nous'   *See* **Modulating canon.**

Aved, Jacques André Joseph   A well-known oil painting said to be of Rameau shows a musician dressed in a scarlet jacket and plucking a violin. This portrait, currently displayed in the Musée des Beaux-Arts, Dijon, was for much of the twentieth century widely if not unanimously accepted as the work of Jacques Aved (1702 66), a respected French portraitist trained in Amsterdam. Serious doubts remain, however, concerning both the attribution to Aved and the identity of the sitter. The portrait, which is neither signed nor dated, bears no title. The earliest mention of its existence, in 1805, names Rameau as the subject but identifies the artist as Chardin*. It was not until the early twentieth century that Pierre Dorbec and, later, Georges Wildenstein argued the case for Aved. Other art historians, most recently Florence Gétreau, have been reluctant to accept this attribution. Regarding the subject matter, the only wholly reliable depictions of Rameau's likeness date from the 1760s, when the composer was an old man, and are thus of limited help in the authentication process. A modicum of support comes from Maret's* carefully researched *Éloge historique de M.ʳ Rameau*, which states that 'it was with a violin in hand that he composed his music'. Moreover, the posthumous* inventory of Rameau's estate lists a scarlet jacket, though unlike the one in this portrait, it was embroidered with gold thread and had gold buttons. It nevertheless seems strange, in view of Rameau's renown as both composer and theorist, that the portrait was never exhibited at the Salon de Peinture during his lifetime or issued as an engraving.

Given such uncertainly, the most that can be claimed is that the painting is 'possibly by Aved' and is 'said to represent Rameau'. An anonymous eighteenth-century copy formerly in the André Meyer collection was auctioned at Sotheby's in 2012. A further copy, by Jean-Baptiste Félix France (b. 1844) 'after Chardin', now hangs in the Musée de la Musique, Paris. The portrait was also reproduced as a lithograph by Eugène Nesle (1822–71). *GétPor, MarÉlo.*

Avignon   On 14 January 1702 Rameau was appointed *maître de musique* at the metropolitan church of Notre-Dame des Doms in Avignon. This was the only one of his many ecclesiastical appointments in which he was director of music and thus in charge of the singers, rather than only an organist. It was evidently a temporary appointment, since the post had already been accepted by Jean Gilles*, who, in the event, never took it up. Rameau's stay in the city was brief: in May of that year he moved to Clermont* as cathedral organist. Still, the memory of his association with Avignon remained alive: on 20 October 1764, soon after news of his death reached the city, an elaborate Requiem Mass was organized at Notre-Dame des Doms, when the music included Gilles's *Messe des morts* and a *De profundis* attributed to Pergolesi. According to one of the priests, this Mass was offered by the city's musicians as a mark of their affection for a composer who had once directed the music at this church. *BouRam, BreJeu, HajGil, HamMem, QuiJeu, RodAvi, TiéRam, ZasApp.*

Avison, Charles   The chamber music of the Northumbrian composer Avison (1709–70) provides a rare example of Rameau's influence in England as a composer rather than as a theorist. Soon after the publication of Walsh's* edition of Rameau *Pièces de clavecin en concerts* (as *Five Concertos for the Harpsichord*) in 1750, Avison had these works performed at the Newcastle Musical Society, of which he was director. He subsequently composed three sets of *Six Sonatas* for harpsichord with accompaniment of two violins and cello, as op. 5 (1756), op. 7 (1760) and op. 8 (1764); these are among the earliest examples of accompanied* keyboard music in England and take their inspiration (if not their style) from the example of Rameau, whose 'spirited Science' Avison praises in the Advertisement to his *Six Sonatas*, Op. 8. *FulAcc, HerMor, KidEme.*

Balbastre, Claude-Bénigne   Having been taught in his native Dijon* by his father and possibly by Claude Bernard Rameau*, Balbastre (1727–99) settled in Paris in 1750 and enrolled in Jean-Philippe Rameau's School of Composition*. Among his keyboard works are numerous arrangements of overtures and airs from the operas of Rameau and others. His performance of the *Pigmalion* overture on the organ at La Pouplinière's* country house at Passy was praised by Rameau, and the younger man made something of a speciality of playing such pieces at the Concert Spirituel*, to great acclaim. In January 1763, the 79-year-old Rameau, his wife and daughter Marie-Alexandrine were among the witnesses to the marriage of Balbastre and Marie Geneviève Hotteterre. When Hugues Maret* was collecting material for the *Éloge historique de M.ʳ Rameau*, Balbastre provided him with much biographical detail, including a few insights into Rameau's approach to composition. His admiration for his former teacher is evident in the superb decoration of one of his harpsichords, commissioned soon after Rameau's death (see next entry). *BreJeu, GiaHot, GirRam, MarÉlo, PieCon, QuiJeu.*

Balbastre's harpsichord   A significant number of depictions of Rameau appear on decorated* harpsichord lids. When Burney* visited Balbastre* in 1770, he was shown the Frenchman's 'fine Rucker [*sic*] harpsichord which he has had painted inside and out with as much delicacy as the finest coach or even snuff-box I ever saw at Paris'. On the inside of the lid was 'the story of Rameau's most famous opera, Castor and Pollux; earth, hell, and elysium are there represented; in elysium, sitting on a bank [...] is that celebrated composer himself; the portrait is very like, for I saw Rameau in 1764'. In 1983 Laurence Libin revealed that this decoration now forms part of a grand piano by Erard and Zeitter made in 1874. On the nameboard is the music of a 'Pastorale par M.ʳ Balbastre le 6 Aoust [August] 1767', thus providing a date for the refurbishment of the instrument Burney was to see three years later. The depiction of scenes from *Castor et Pollux** relates to the 1764 revival at the Paris Opéra. Rameau, having belatedly been awarded Letters of Nobility*, is wearing the blue sash and star of the Ordre de Saint-Michel; he is sitting on a bank, crowned with a wreath. Given the evident care with which the composer is portrayed, this decoration may also preserve the likenesses of those who took the principal roles at that revival. Castor and Pollux, played respectively by Pillot* and Gélin*, are shown in a fraternal embrace, while their beloved Télaïre (Sophie Arnould*) sits to one side. On the leaf of the lid, Phébé (Mlle Chevalier*) is shown at the mouth of Hades, her costume strikingly reminiscent of a Boquet* design for this revival. Florence Gétreau proposes Pierre-Antoine Baudouin* as the artist, not only on stylistic grounds but also because he designed these specific scenes for the 1764 production. The current location of this extraordinary instrument, formerly in the private collection of Barbara Piasecka Johnson and sold at Sotheby's on 8 June 2005, is unknown. *LibPor, GétPor.*

Ballard, Jean-Baptiste Christophe   In 1715, on the death of his father Christophe, Jean-Baptiste Christophe Ballard (1663/65–c.1750) inherited the publishing house of Ballard, which had enjoyed a virtual monopoly on music printing in France since the sixteenth century. Among other projects, he continued publication of the *Recueils d'airs sérieux et à boire*, issued monthly between 1695 and 1724. Rameau contributed two pieces to this important series – the *air à boire* 'Lucas, pour se gausser de nous'* (February 1707) and the modulating* canon 'Avec du vin, endormons nous' (November 1719). In the December 1719 issue of the *Recueils*, Ballard states that he had already begun printing Rameau's *Traité de l'harmonie* and that this publication, which he claims to have commissioned, would be ready in six months' time. In the event, the treatise did not appear until 1722 after a troublesome production process. Rameau was evidently not deterred, since he entrusted Ballard with the publication of his next treatise, the *Nouveau système de musique théorique* (1726). *See also* **Dissertation sur les différentes métodes [sic] d'accompagnement.** *BouHer, DevLes, GosTre, GouRec, RamCtw, ZasApp.*

Ballet   To the modern mind, ballet does not usually include singing. In its early development, and particularly in the seventeenth-century *ballet de cour*, however, vocal music formed an essential component of this art-form. Such was the French national obsession with dance that when an indigenous style of opera emerged, ballet was from the outset an indispensable ingredient: it played a significant role in the *tragédie en musique** established by Lully* in the 1670s and assumed even greater importance in the lighter genres that developed later. Yet genres like *opéra-ballet** and *ballet héroïque**, despite the use of the word 'ballet' in their labels, are essentially operas in which dance happens to be a major ingredient. By Rameau's day, certain works were classified in scores and librettos simply as 'ballet', as in the case of *Les Fêtes d'Hébé* and *La Guirlande*. The former, however, is more logically classed as an *opéra-ballet** and the latter as an *acte de ballet**. AntFre, BouHer, HarBal, HarTou, MasOpé.

Ballet figuré In his treatise *La Danse ancienne et moderne* (1754) Louis de Cahusac* coined this term for one or more dances in which a group of dancers perform some mimed action related to the main plot. Cahusac's own librettos are particularly rich in *ballets figurés*, for which he often provided detailed stage directions. Although such *danses d'action* (to use Cahusac's alternative term) had featured in several of Lully's* operas, this kind of mime subsequently fell out of fashion until the 1730s: the renewal of interest may be seen in the nine-movement 'Ballet des Fleurs' in *Les Indes galantes*, a fine example of the *ballet figuré* even though this term did not yet exist. At its best, this sort of *pantomime** could contribute significantly to the plot development: in *Zoroastre* (IV, 5), for example, the demons enact a ceremony during which a statue of Zoroastre bursts into flame, which is taken as a good omen and motivates the ensuing action; in *Naïs* (I, 7) Neptune's courtship of the heroine takes place during an extended representation of an athletics competition; while in *Les Boréades* (II, 6) the *ballet figuré* in which the nymph Orithie is abducted by the North Wind prefigures the fate of the heroine Alphise. *See also* **Sallé, Marie.** BouLiv, CahDan, FaiSty, HarBal, HarTou, LawGes, MasOpé, McCEng, McCSal, NovLet.

Ballet héroïque Coined by Fuzelier* in his libretto for Collin de Blamont's *Les Fêtes grecques et romaines* (1723), this term defined a sub-species of *opéra-ballet** in which each entrée* features one or more heroes from ancient history (as opposed to mythology), the adjective 'heroic' thus being used – initially, at least – in a more restricted sense than in the genre label *pastorale héroïque**. Fuzelier points out that, unlike the Italians, French librettists had never drawn material from history. In later operas, however, Fuzelier's term was used with little consistency, as is illustrated by the half-dozen works by Rameau to which it was applied. Only two, *Les Fêtes de Polymnie* and *Anacréon*, include known historical characters, and neither work conforms to Fuzelier's model, in that such characters appear in only one entrée of the former ('L'Histoire'), while the latter comprises a single act rather than a succession of entrées. *Les Indes galantes*, though adopting the *opéra-ballet* configuration, features characters from modern life or, in the case of the prologue, from mythology. As for *Les Fêtes de l'Hymen et l'Amour*, its prologue and three entrées include only mythological characters. Meanwhile *Zaïs*, categorized as a *ballet héroïque* in all primary sources, and *Naïs*, which is so labelled in several, have continuous plots developed across three or four acts. In these and many other operas, there is little to justify the adjective 'héroïque' other than the fact that the cast includes one or more mythological heroes or gods. In sum, the term *ballet héroïque* is virtually meaningless as a genre label as far as Rameau's operas are concerned, and all the above works are nowadays usually assigned to more appropriate, if sometimes anachronistic, generic categories. BouHer, MasBal, MasOpé.

Ballet masters The Académie Royale de Musique* employed a *maître de ballet* whose duties were to choreograph the dance music, direct the ballet rehearsals

and ensure good order among the members of the dance troupe. At the time of
Rameau's debut at the Académie in 1733, the *maître de ballet* was Michel Blondy*,
who held this post until his death in 1739; he must therefore have been responsible for the choreography of the composer's first five operas. Antoine Bandieri
de Laval* (1698–1767) took over as *maître de ballet* from then until 1748, when
he was succeeded by Jean-Bathélemy Lany*, who was assisted by Gaëtan
Vestris*, his deputy since 1761. The Académie's regulations of 1714 stipulated
that the dancers' roles be allocated not by the *maître de ballet* but by the *inspecteur*
in consultation with the composer. It was nevertheless the ballet master who
decided which dancers would participate in which pieces. He or his assistant,
the *maître de salle*, was required to be present at all rehearsals and performances
to ensure that the choreography was appropriately executed. Whenever possible,
the *maître de ballet* was also expected to attend the thrice-weekly dance classes
directed by the *maître de salle*. Contemporary librettos sometimes name the
'compositeur des ballets', who was normally but not always the *maître de ballet*:
in 1748, for example, the ballet music of *Zaïs* was choreographed by François
Antoine Malter*. *See also* **Dehesse, Jean-Baptiste**. *BouHer, BouLiv, DurAca, SerOpé.*

Ballet-pantomime   *See* **Pantomime**.

Ballot de Sovot   Counsellor-at-law in the French *parlement* and an amateur
writer, Ballot de Sovot or Sauvot (d.1761, forenames unknown) was a resident
at La Pouplinière's* country house at Passy, where Rameau also spent each
summer. In 1748 he adapted an entrée* from La Motte's* *Le Triomphe des Arts*
as the libretto for *Pigmalion*; he was also responsible for some minor revisions
to the text of the 1749 *Platée* and, he claimed, to the 1754 *Castor et Pollux*. In
1753, during the Querelle des Bouffons*, he was wounded in a duel with the
castrato Caffarelli, who had made disparaging remarks about French music.
His brother, Sylvain Ballot, was Rameau's solicitor. *BarPla, BouHer, CucPou,
GreSou, GirRam, LegPla, MalPla, MasOpé.*

Barbarine, Mlle   *See* **Campanini, Barbara**.

Baroque   Rameau has the dubious distinction of being the first composer
whose music was labelled 'baroque', a wholly derogatory epithet at that time.
The term occurs in a satirical letter published during the Lulliste-Ramiste*
dispute and provoked by the 1733 premiere of *Hippolyte et Aricie* ('Lettre de M***
à Mlle *** sur l'origine de la musique', *Mercure de France**, May 1734). The
anonymous author lampoons a 'ballet' (i.e., opera) by a certain composer who,
though unnamed, can only be Rameau. The music of this work is characterized
as unnatural, noisy, restless, overcharged with dissonance and lacking in melody,
grace or expression – all negative qualities consistent with the word *baroque* as
then understood. The term recurs in the sense of bizarre or outlandish in a
poem by a prominent Lulliste, Jean-Baptiste Rousseau*, which circulated widely
in 1739 around the time of the *Dardanus* premiere. Aimed at Rameau and his
imitators, it begins: 'Distillateurs d'accords baroques | Dont tant d'idiots sont
férus, | Chez les Thraces et les Iroquois | Portez vos opéras bourrus' (You who
distil the bizarre harmonies | With which so many fools are smitten, | Take your
boorish operas | To the Thracians and Iroquois). The word *baroque* retained this
pejorative meaning for at least a century before it was eventually adopted in its
present sense to denote a historical period. *DacDar, MasLul, PalBar.*

Basses In his autograph manuscripts and in most of the engraved opera scores, Rameau scrupulously differentiates between the groups of instruments intended to play the bass line in a given movement or section. In particular, he distinguishes the continuo instruments of the *petit chœur** (often indicated with the abbreviation 'B.C.') from the *basses du grand chœur** (normally labelled 'Basses' or 'B.ses'). These two groups had quite separate roles and, for much of a given work, did not combine. As well as using the above terms, Rameau frequently clarifies the transition from one group to another with two short diagonal lines (//). The only exceptions to this labelling system occur in the scores of his earliest operas, where 'B.C.' often appears in contexts where later scores would use the label 'Basses'. There is, however, no reason to believe that this discrepancy reflects a change of performance practice. Rather, it indicates a rationalization of the labelling itself, as the distribution of continuo figures (invariably associated only with the *petit chœur*) confirms. *CyrBas, GreSou, SadKey.*

Basse de viole During his second period at Clermont* (1715–22), Rameau evidently enjoyed the services of a highly skilled *basse de viole* player, as several of his early cantatas performed there, notably *Les Amants trahis, Aquilon et Orithie* and *L'Impatience*, include virtuoso parts for a seven-string bass viol. These include rapid passage-work, perilous leaps and, in the case of *Les Amants trahis*, numerous multiple-stopped chords. By the time Rameau turned to opera in the 1730s, the *basse de viole* was falling rapidly out of fashion and had largely been eliminated from the Paris Opéra orchestra; even so, *Les Indes galantes* is one of several works from that decade requiring bass notes a third below the cello range. At court, the bass viol player Jean-Baptiste Forqueray (1699–1782) took part in *La Princesse de Navarre* (1745), while the orchestra of Madame de Pompadour's Théâtre des Petits Cabinets* included two 'violes'. Rameau was also to include one of the most demanding bass viol parts ever written in his *Pièces de clavecin en concerts* of 1741. *See also* '**La Forqueray**'. *CyrCan, CyrEss, CyrPer, CyrVio, SadOrc.*

Basse de violon The bass member of the violin family in seventeenth-century French orchestras was the *basse de violon*, an instrument perceptibly larger than the cello and tuned a whole tone lower ($Bb'–F–c–g$). It remained in use in the early eighteenth century and evidently formed part of the orchestra for which Rameau wrote his early motet *Deus noster refugium**, which repeatedly exploits its lowest open string in the more turbulent passages. By the 1730s, when Rameau made his debut at the Académie Royale de Musique*, the *basse de violon* had been largely superseded by the cello (*violoncelle*). Confusingly, however, the older term – often abbreviated to *basse(s)* – continued to be used in scores, performing parts and archival documents as a synonym for *violoncelle* until the mid-century and beyond. *CyrBas, MasOpé, GorOrc, SadOrc, SpiZas.*

Basse fondamentale Rameau was not the first to show that all inversions of triads are related to a single root, but he was the first to extend this concept to all chords, including sevenths. He distinguished two basses for each chord: the actual notated bass, and the root or 'fundamental bass'. In any chord sequence, a separate bass line could be notated below the actual bass (see the illustration opposite) to show the movement of the root progression. With the aid of this *basse fondamentale*, Rameau developed the concept that the actual or implied dissonance in every chord other than that of the tonic is the generative force

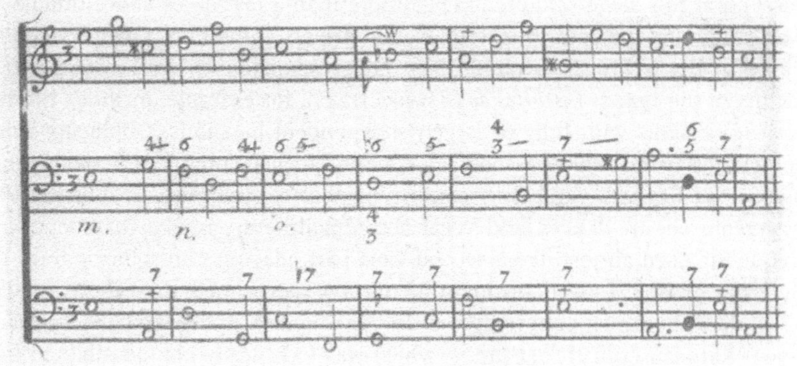

Rameau, *Code de musique pratique*, 1760 (Paris, Bibliothèque Nationale de France, Rés. V. 1616), supplement of music examples, plate 22. Reproduced by permission.

of harmonic movement, this being perceptible in its simplest form as the resolution of a dominant seventh onto a tonic triad. He conceived of all music as a series of interlocking cadences comprising dissonance and resolution, in which most of the points of repose are evaded. Rameau managed to explain for the first time the roles of consonance and dissonance in defining a given key and in creating the sense of direction in standard chord progressions. In practical terms, too, the *basse fondamentale* provided a welcome relief from the mass of rules and exceptions found in contemporary figured bass manuals. Although not published until 1722, Rameau's concept of the *basse fondamentale* had already formed in his own mind during his years in Lyon* (1712–15) or even earlier. Moreover, the so-called 'Clermont notes'* reveal that he was using it as a teaching aid during the period 1715–22. *ChrBas, ChrTho, DucVal, LesRam, LesThe, RamCtw.*

Basse-taille This term originally denoted a characteristic French voice-type* mid-way between *taille** and *basse* – the approximate equivalent of baritone. In the repertory of the *motet** *à grand chœur*, where the choruses are often in five parts, the next-to-lowest was allotted to *basse-taille*. The chorus of the Académie Royale de Musique*, by contrast, was disposed in four parts, the lowest being referred to indiscriminately as *basse* or *basse-taille*. During Rameau's operatic career the range of this part increased from *G–e* (sounding approximately a whole tone lower than modern concert pitch) to *F–f*. The term *basse-taille* was also used for solo roles with the slightly higher range of *G–f♯*. In Rameau's day this male voice-type was second in importance only to the *haute-contre**, and was thought particularly suited to the portrayal of gods, kings, fathers, magicians and unhappy lovers. *CyrCho, MasOpé.*

Bassoon In view of Rameau's resourceful treatment of the bassoon, it seems strange that his name seldom appears in the specialist literature. In his operas of the 1730s, he followed tradition in using the instrument mainly to double the bass and to take part in the classic *trio des hautbois* episodes, with only the occasional obbligato passage; even so, there was no real precedent in France for the expressive intensity of the obbligato for unison bassoons in Télaïre's 'Tristes apprêts' (*Castor et Pollux*, I, 4). While Rameau's obbligato writing for bassoon at this stage seldom ascends more than a few notes above middle *c'*, we already find the occasional high *a'*, and players at the Paris Opéra evidently jibbed at his technical demands. The huge expansion in the bassoon's role begins in the 1740s; *Les Fêtes de l'Hymen* (1747), for example, includes twenty-one movements with fully or largely independent bassoons. Obbligatos now sometimes feature two bassoon lines, often labelled 'premiers bassons' and 'deuxièmes bassons', and thus confirming that a minimum of four players was required. In dances and vocal accompaniments, unison bassoons are frequently used almost like a second viola part, playing non-soloistic lines in the tenor register. Indeed, the instruments now spend much time above middle *c'*, while *a'* becomes commonplace. In *Les Paladins* (1760) and *Les Boréades* (1763) Rameau even risked the *b'♭* which was technically just possible on the four-keyed instrument. *See also* **Air de monologue**; **Ariosti, Attilio**; *Nourrir les* **sons**. *CucPou, GorOrc, MasOpé, SadInv, SadOrc, SpiZas.*

Batteries   The application of this term in a musical context during Rameau's lifetime ranged from string tremolandos to rapid drum beats and arpeggiations. In the preface to his *Pièces de clavessin* of 1724 the composer distinguishes three species of keyboard *batterie*: virtuoso figurations involving the rotation of the hand over the thumb; brisk alternations where 'the hands between them make the consecutive movement of two drumsticks'; and hand-crossing of the kind where 'the left hand passes over the right to play alternately the bass and the treble.' For Rameau, this last was a feature in which 'the eye shares the pleasure that the ear receives'; indeed, it was one he claims to have invented, or at least to have been the first to demonstrate in print. He directs the reader to 'Les Cyclopes' in this volume for examples of all three kinds of *batterie*. J.S. Bach appears to have borrowed some of these techniques, as did Domenico Scarlatti*, who would doubtless have encountered them when he visited Paris in the mid-1720s. *SadSca, YeaAwk, WilAnx.*

Batteur de mesure   The tradition of using a 'time-beater' at the Académie Royale de Musique* dates from the time of Lully*. Iconographical evidence from the 1740s reveals that the *batteur de mesure* stood facing the stage with his back to the orchestral players, most of whom also faced the stage in a broad semicircle. He held a short but solid baton, which was sometimes used to beat time audibly on the music stand; the extent to which this practice was employed, however, was greatly exaggerated during the Querelle des Bouffons* by writers such as Grimm* and Jean-Jacques Rousseau*, in their attempts to undermine the French operatic tradition. Rather, the evidence suggests that the solo vocal music, at the very least, was co-ordinated by the baton visually rather than audibly; moreover, the *batteur de mesure* did not participate in the recitative. Even so, the fact that he faced the singers rather than the players suggests that his role as 'interpreter' in the modern sense was somewhat limited, though reforms in this respect were made in the mid-century and, in any case, the placement of the players allowed for easy visual communication with the on-stage performers. No doubt, too, details of interpretation were worked out during rehearsals*, for which the Académie made generous provision. A *règlement* of 1714 states that the *batteur* was responsible not only for keeping time in performances and rehearsals but also for maintaining orchestral discipline. It also reveals that composers could, if they wished, direct rehearsals* of their own operas; Rameau is known to have taken advantage of this opportunity, and there is reason to believe that he may occasionally have directed performances of his works at the Académie, as was also his right. At the start of his operatic career, the *batteur de mesure* was Jean-Féry Rebel (1666–1747), who was succeeded in 1739 by his son François. Although the younger Rebel* was officially replaced by André Chéron (1695–1766) in 1749, he continued to conduct first performances of new operas. During the 1750s Chéron was assisted by Pierre de La Garde and Antoine Dauvergne. In 1759 the post was awarded to Pierre-Montan Berton*, who remained *batteur de mesure* until after Rameau's death. The production* scores of the period are full of markings by successive *batteurs*. Rameau would often communicate his intentions to such men by means of annotations in these scores, as in *Les Paladins* (II, 6), where he asks the conductor to make sure that the singer follows the beat in the fast passages ('Faites suivre la mesure à Orcan dans les vites'). *See also* **Graffigny, Madame de**. *ChaMaî, ChaRou, GreSou, GorOrc, SadPat.*

Baudouin, Pierre-Antoine Son-in-law and pupil of Boucher*, Baudouin (1723–69) specialized in genre paintings and miniatures. His occasional work for the Académie Royale de Musique* included the scenery designs for the 1761 revival of *Castor et Pollux*. He is believed to be the artist who decorated Balbastre's* harpsichord with a portrait of Rameau surrounded by scenes from this opera. One of his risqué genre paintings, engraved by Voyez*, depicts a bust of Rameau and the score of *Castor*. *GétPor.*

Les Beaux Jours de l'Amour Rameau's *La Naissance d'Osiris* and *Mirthis**, which survive as isolated *actes de ballet**, were originally conceived as part of a projected *opéra-ballet** entitled *Les Beaux Jours de l'Amour*. In the autograph scores of both works Rameau wrote this collective title at the top of the first page but eventually crossed it out, presumably after the project had been abandoned. Internal evidence in the two autographs suggests that these works were composed alongside the Rameau-Cahusac *Anacréon*, which may have been intended as a further entrée* in this *opéra-ballet**. From these and other clues, Thomas Green has suggested that *Les Beaux Jours de l'Amour* was originally conceived for performance in Madame de Pompadour's Théâtre des Petits Cabinets*, perhaps as early as 1750. If so, the otherwise unattributed libretto of *Mirthis* is presumably by Cahusac*, author of the other two works. *BouHer, BouRam, GirRam, GreSou, MasOpé, RicFon, WilAna.*

Beffara, Louis-François A Parisian police commissioner from 1792 to 1816, Beffara (1751–1838) was renowned for his collection of some eighty documents relating to the Paris Opéra and other theatres. Although many of these were destroyed by fire during the days of the Commune in 1871, a number have survived, including the autograph manuscript of his 'Dictionnaire alphabétique des auteurs qui ont composé des opéras-ballets et autres pièces lyriques pour le théâtre de l'Académie Royale de Musique'. Compiled in 1783–84 and now conserved in the Bibliothèque Nationale de France (Bibliothèque-Musée de l'Opéra), Paris (Rés. 602–603), this carefully researched dictionary incorporates material derived from authoritative sources, including some which perished in the fire. *LajBib.*

Bérard, Jean Antoine As an opera singer, the *haute-contre** Bérard (1710–72) was initially slow to gain public approval: having entered and almost immediately left the Académie Royale de Musique* in 1733, he returned three years later and was tried out in solo roles, only to be 'totally booed and hissed' (as an Académie register of 1738 puts it) in Rameau's *Les Indes galantes*. In subsequent roles he was to 'astonish the entire audience, surpassing himself to an amazing degree'; yet he never progressed beyond minor roles and retired in 1745. Bérard is mainly remembered for his treatise *L'Art du chant* (1755), regarded by La Borde* as a summation of vocal practice during the Lully-Rameau era. Although the author was accused of plagiarizing *L'Art ou les principes philosophiques du chant* by Joseph Blanchet (1724–78), much of the most valuable material in his treatise derives from first-hand experience as a soloist at the Académie. He describes a far wider range of vocal ornaments than is found in any other comparable treatise and shows by means of lengthy music examples how these were applied in movements by Rameau and others. *CyrEss, CyrSin, JouBér, LabEss, McGSpa, SadInv.*

Le Berger fidèle   Performed at the Concert Français* on 22 November 1728 by the star singer Catherine-Nicole Le Maure*, *Le Berger fidèle* was described in the *Mercure de France** as a 'nouvelle cantate', and Rameau subsequently published it, along with *Aquilon et Orithie**, in his *Cantates à voix seule** published in 1729 or 1730. By the latter date this volume had been acquired for use at the Concerts de la Reine*. The cantata is scored for *dessus** (soprano) and two obbligato violin parts. To judge from the marking 'violons' on unison lines, it may originally have been intended for orchestral rather than chamber performance. In 1739 Rameau revised the second of the three airs for use in *Les Fêtes d'Hébé* (III, 3) as 'L'Objet qui règne dans mon âme'. *BouHer, CyrChr, CyrEss, DorCan, MonBou, SadAsp, TunCan, ZasApp.*

Berger, Jean-François   A former *receveur-général des finances* in the Dauphiné region, Berger (d.1747) was granted the *privilège* to direct the Académie Royale de Musique* in 1744, in succession to Thuret*. His period of management was, however, beset with problems – disputes with other theatres over breaches of legal agreements; complaints that expenditure on costumes and scenery had not risen sufficiently; loss of revenue, despite an indemnity of 45,000 *livres* when his performers were summoned for long periods to perform at court. Following the discovery, in 1746, that he had increased the Académie's already massive debts by 400,000 *livres*, he fell ill and died the following year, a broken man. Despite such apparent failure, Berger's brief administration saw the premieres at court or in Paris of five Rameau operas, including such major works as *Platée* and *Les Fêtes de l'Hymen et l'Amour*. Berger's *privilège* was eventually purchased by Tréfontaine*. *ChaPol, ChaRou, MalHip, SerOpé, WooSad.*

Bergiron du Fort-Michon   In 1713 Jean-Pierre Christin* and Nicolas-Antoine Bergiron de Briou, seigneur du Fort-Michon (1690–1768), founded the Académie des Beaux-Arts, a concert-giving society in Lyon*. Rameau doubtless encountered both men and the newly founded Académie during his years in this city between 1712 and 1715. Bergiron was not only the society's librarian but also assembled a large collection of manuscript scores, including ten of Rameau operas. The provenance of these manuscripts was for many years a puzzle, but Bénédicte Hertz has recently shown that they are all in Bergiron's own hand. After his death the collection was sold, and many of the manuscripts were acquired by Gaspard Cauvin*. A decade or so later, the ten Rameau volumes were bought by Decroix* and were eventually bequeathed to the Bibliothèque Nationale de France. Given that the manuscripts include choral and orchestral inner parts missing in many other sources, Bergiron evidently had access to authoritative sources – perhaps even by way of the composer himself, who remained in contact with the Académie. *BouHer, HerMot, WolŒu.*

Berlioz, Hector   In an age when the general attitude towards French music of the Lully-Rameau period was one of undisguised scorn, Berlioz expressed a rather more nuanced view in four articles on Rameau published in the *Revue et Gazette musicale* in 1842. On the one hand, he drew attention to what he saw as the 'tangle of errors and contradictions' in Rameau's music theory and to the 'unimaginable awkwardness and triviality' of the overture to *Castor et Pollux*. On the other (and unlike virtually all his French contemporaries), he could appreciate the colour, energy and harmonic richness of some of Rameau's choruses, while the A major gavotte in the *Castor* prologue struck him as 'gracious, tender and tinged with a gentle melancholy'. His highest praise was reserved for the monologue 'Tristes apprêts' in the same opera: 'Gluck himself has very few pages finer than Télaïre's celebrated air. [...] Everything serves to make this one of the most sublime conceptions of dramatic music'. Not for the best part of half a century would such positive comments on Rameau's music be expressed again in France. *EllEar, FauCas, GirRam, MapEar, MasOpé, PisPar.*

Bernard, Pierre-Joseph   After distinguishing himself in the army, the poet Bernard (1708–75) gained the protection of the comte de Coigny and Madame de Pompadour, who secured for him a substantial income and the leisure to indulge his epicurean tastes. Gentil-Bernard, as he was known, was a founder-member of the Caveau*, a convivial literary dining club formed in or around 1729, of which Rameau is said to have been a member. In 1736 Bernard was briefly involved in La Pouplinière's* circle, and it may well have been there that he and Rameau agreed to collaborate on *Castor et Pollux*. Bernard's poem for this opera has been described, with some justification, as the finest eighteenth-century French libretto (Masson). It reflects Voltaire's* reforming views in emphasizing a high-minded brotherly love rather than the conventional romantic entanglements. Bernard's subsequent librettos, *Les Surprises de l'Amour* (written for Madame de Pompadour's Théâtre des Petits Cabinets*) and the entrée 'Anacréon'* added to this work for the 1757 Paris production, are less innovative, though elegant and well constructed. It is just possible that the libretto of *Les Paladins** is also by Bernard. *CucPou, DilMon, MalCas, MasOpé, GirRam, GirTra, GreSou, VerDra.*

Bernouilli, Jean II   On 18 February 1750, as part of a campaign to gain international recognition for his theories, Rameau sent a copy of his newly published *Démonstration du principe de l'harmonie* to Bernouilli (1710–90), a member of the distinguished Swiss family of mathematicians and at that time professor of mathematics at the University of Basel. In another letter, dated 27 April, Rameau promised to send a second exemplar of the *Démonstration*, since the first, despatched via the French ambassador in Geneva, had still not arrived. In the second letter, Rameau admits the need for approximations ('des àpeuprès') in tempering intervals, which suggests that Bernouilli had raised some practical matters of this kind. His overall reactions to Rameau's work must nevertheless have been encouraging, for the composer wrote again, on 26 April 1752, enclosing a copy of his *Nouvelles réflexions sur la Démonstration du principe de l'harmonie*. Sadly, Bernouilli's side of the correspondence has not survived. *GirRam, JacNou, RamCtw.*

Berton, Pierre-Montan   After an itinerant early life, Pierre-Montan Berton (1727–80) won the post of *batteur de mesure** at the Académie Royale de Musique* in 1755. In this capacity he directed numerous operas by Rameau and others, and many production* scores include his characteristic red-crayon markings indicating such matters as tempo, articulation and the number of repeats of component sections. In 1767 he became co-director of the Académie with Jean-Claude Trial (1732–71), retiring eleven years later. The *Almanach des spectacles pour l'année 1781* published a posthumous list of his works, including details of the many operas in the 'ancien répertoire' he had refurbished ('raccommodé'). These include six by Rameau. Berton's revisions range from the substitution of individual movements or scenes to the wholesale re-orchestration of *Castor et Pollux* for revivals in the late 1760s and 1770s. *BouHer, CamAca, ChaRou, RosDes, SadZaï, WebWan.*

Binary form   Rameau's handling of binary form in his keyboard works shows a steady progression. In the *Premier livre de pièces de clavecin* of 1706 he still occasionally employs the traditional French technique of balancing simple, elegant phrases that are rhythmically similar but melodically independent, with a half-close in the tonic key before the first repeat. In the later collections, motivic organization becomes increasingly tighter, and the integration of the two sections by 'rhyming' terminations, structural symmetry and other means is far closer. None of the solo pieces, however, comes as near to sonata* form as 'La Pantomime'* in the *Pièces de clavecin en concerts*, with its brief but unmistakable modulatory development section and clear-cut recapitulation. The binary movements in Rameau's operas rarely include the traditional type in which the two parts of the structure have little if any thematic connection. While some of his binary pieces are essentially monothematic, an increasing number introduce sharp contrasts; this is especially true of the *pantomimes** and *ballets figurés** in which the mimed action demanded a variety of themes and moods. Many of Rameau's production* scores bear annotations clarifying the repeat structure (e.g., '2 commencements, une fin'), presumably agreed by composer, conductor and choreographer. *See also* **Reprise**. *MasOpé.*

Blondy, Michel   Taught by his uncle, the celebrated dancer and choreographer Pierre Beauchamps (1631–1705), Michel Blondy (c.1676–1739) entered the Académie Royale de Musique* in 1691 and soon established himself as the leading exponent of the *danse haute**, excelling in such character roles as furies and demons. In 1729 he succeeded Guillaume Louis Pécour (1653–1729) as ballet master* at the Académie, in which capacity he was responsible for the choreography for Rameau's first five operas. Among his pupils were Mlles Sallé* and Camargo*. *DurAca, ChrInt, SadDan.*

'La Boiteuse'   The title of this movement from the *Pièces de clavessin* of 1724 is derived from *boiteux* (lame), and the piece itself mischievously captures the rickety gait of someone with a limp – not necessarily female. A possible prototype for this movement is 'Le Gaillard-Boiteux' in François Couperin's* third book of *Pièces de clavecin* (1722), likewise in compound time and marked to be played 'dans le goût Burlesque'. Rameau's title was reused by Simon Luc Marchand in *Pièces de clavecin avec [...] violon, hautbois, violoncelle ou viole* (1747). *ClaCon, GirRam, GusFul, RpeKey.*

Bollioud-Mermet, Louis   By the age of 30, Louis Bollioud-Mermet (1709–94) had been elected to the Académie des Beaux-Arts and the Académie des Sciences et des Belles-Lettres in his native Lyon*, becoming permanent secretary of the combined academies from 1758. Although his main contributions to these societies were in the fields of mathematics and astronomy, he also took an interest in music theory. In 1740 he presented a paper on the tuning of instruments, in which he claimed that Rameau's advocacy of equal temperament* had 'determined nothing'. This event was reported in the *Mercure de France** in July 1740. The following May the *Mercure* published a letter from 'someone interested in Rameau's works' – i.e., Rameau himself – calling on the Lyon academy to publish the paper in full. When the academicians sent the text to the *Mercure*, the editor evidently forwarded a copy to Rameau, who immediately wrote to Jean-Pierre Christin*, the academy's secretary, insisting that the misleading and slanderous criticism of his ideas be corrected. As it happens, Bollioud's paper, which survives in the academy's archives, does not take issue with the theoretical basis of equal temperament but rather with its practicability. To some extent his criticism was justified, given the imprecision of Rameau's description of the tempering of fifths in *Génération harmonique*; even the author conceded that these were 'arbitrary'. While Rameau soon lost interest in this controversy, it continued to rage at the academy for several decades. Bollioud was later to launch an attack on all things modern in the music of his day; his book *De la corruption du goust dans la musique françoise* (Lyon, 1746) was one of the last sallies in the Lulliste-Ramiste* dispute. *BarTem, ChrTho, CleAct, CohEqu, HerMot, MasLul, ValAca, ValLyo.*

Boquet, Louis-René   Renowned throughout Europe as a costume designer, Louis-René Boquet (1717–1814) was associated with the Académie Royale de Musique* from about 1748, and collaborated on designs for the 1752 revival of *Les Fêtes de l'Hymen et de l'Amour* at Fontainebleau. He succeeded Martin as designer in c.1758. While details of Boquet's activities at the Académie are sketchy, more is known about his work for the Menus-Plaisirs* and the numerous court productions in which he participated. He also worked for Monnet* and Noverre* at the Opéra-Comique*, where he introduced innovations through the use of free-standing pieces of scenery to complement the traditional flats; it is possible that he adopted this innovatory approach in his subsequent work for the Académie. Although no stage designs by Boquet survive, sketches and watercolours of many of his delightful rococo costume designs have been preserved. Some five hundred of these were made for Noverre's ballets, while many others were intended for productions at the Académie. *GorDec, LesOpé, MasOpé, StaSer, TesBoq.*

Les Boréades   It was long accepted that this *tragédie en musique**, one of Rameau's finest works, was in rehearsal at the Paris Opéra, but then abandoned when the composer died in September 1764. However, Sylvie Bouissou* has revealed that the opera had already been rehearsed at Versailles and Paris in April 1763 by performers from the Musique du Roi and the Paris Opéra, for inclusion in the entertainments during the court's *voyage* to the palace of Choisy later that year. The work was nevertheless replaced in the schedule, the most plausible explanation being that the Opéra's Palais-Royal* theatre had burnt down during the rehearsal period; in the resulting upheaval, the challenge of preparing such a technically demanding new opera must have proved insuperable. Moreover, the fact that the libretto articulates ideas that may have been considered subversive – notably the freedom of thought embodied in the heroine's decision to abdicate the throne rather than submit to a loveless dynastic marriage – may also have influenced the decision to abandon the production. The libretto is plausibly attributed to Cahusac* in two independent eighteenth-century sources, thus the work's gestation must have begun considerably earlier, given that Cahusac died in 1759. Indeed, Thomas Green has shown that autograph fragments of the work survive in a source which may date from as early as 1747. *See also* **Abaris**. *BouHer, BouPas, BouRam, DilMon, GreSou, KinRam, PazBor, RicFon, TérAba, VerDra.*

Borée database Maintained by the Institut de Recherche en Musicologie (IRéMus), this database comprises almost 2000 bibliographical references to material relating to Rameau and his works, established by an ongoing and systematic examination of books, articles and other publications. It may be freely consulted online at www.iremus.cnrs.fr/base-de-données/boree.

Boucher, François Best known for his idealized rococo pastoral scenes and genre paintings, François Boucher (1703–70) was associated intermittently with the Académie Royale de Musique* over a thirty-year period from 1737, principally between 1742 and 1748 as its chief designer. He adopted a supervisory role there, limiting his actual painting mainly to decorative backdrops. For all his artistic talent, Boucher was untrained in the principles of architecture; accordingly, he usually opted for the less demanding symmetrical type of set design. From time to time, however, he produced sets with an oblique perspective, as in his acclaimed design for the entrée* 'La Danse' in the 1764 production of Rameau's *Les Fêtes d'Hébé*. Boucher was also involved in opera productions at court, including Madame de Pompadour's Théâtre des Petits Cabinets*, and at Monnet's* Opéra-Comique*. Sadly, our information on his designs is largely limited to contemporary descriptions in the press and elsewhere. *MasOpé, SadPir, StaSer.*

'La Boucon' The dedicatee of this 'air gracieux' from the *Pièces de clavecin en concerts* (1741) may possibly be Étienne Boucon (d.1735), a stockbroker well known as a music lover and patron of the arts. However, the Boucon in question is far more likely to be his eldest daughter, Anne-Jeanne (1708–80), an outstanding harpsichordist and, according to Marpurg*, a pupil* of Rameau. The piece has a gentle, melancholy elegance that may well characterize her playing. Two other harpsichord pieces, by Jean Barrière (*Sonates et pièces pour le clavecin*, c.1740) and Jacques Duphly* (first book of *Pièces de clavecin*, 1744) bear her name. In 1747 she married the composer Mondonville*. A fine portrait by Quentin de La Tour* shows her sitting in front of a harpsichord upon which is the score of 'Pièces de clavecin de Madame de Mondonville'. Sadly, these pieces have not survived. *BouHer, GirRam, GusFul, HerMor, MacMon, RpeKey.*

Bouffons   *See* **Querelle des Bouffons**.

Bouissou, Sylvie   Having graduated from the University of Paris IV in 1986 with a doctoral thesis on Rameau's *Les Boréades*, Sylvie Bouissou is a director of research at the Centre National de Recherche Scientifique, assigned until recently to the Institut de Recherche sur le Patrimoine Musical en France (now the Institut de Recherche en Musicologie), which she established in 1996. Since 1991, when she founded the Société Jean-Philippe Rameau*, she has been editor-in-chief of OOR*, the complete critical edition of Rameau's music. *BouBor, BouCri, BouHer, BouHi1, BouHi2, BouPas, BouPri, BouSu1, BouSu2.*

Bourbonnois, Mlle   Neither the forenames nor the dates of birth and death of this singer are known. A popular soprano at the Concert Spirituel* between 1728 and 1746, she entered the Académie Royale de Musique* in 1735, initially without salary, and later that year she created the role of Roxane in *Les Indes galantes*. Her style of singing was well suited to *ariettes** and similar decorative airs, as is borne out by her roles in Rameau operas, among them that of Amour (Cupid) which she created both in *Les Fêtes d'Hébé* and in *Dardanus*. She retired in 1747. *BouHer, PieCon, PouJél, SadInv, ValLyo.*

Brenet, Michel   Marie Bobillier (1858–1918), who wrote under this pseudonym, was a music historian of astonishingly wide interests that stretched from the fifteenth to the nineteenth century. Her study of Rameau's fifty-year 'youth', together with Quittard's* contemporaneous investigation of the same period, uncovered numerous archival documents, and corrected errors and misconceptions in earlier writings; it remains essential reading, as do her studies of concert life in France and Rameau's use of clarinets. *BreCla, BreCon, BreJeu, BreLib, BreNot.*

Brosses, Charles de   In 1739 and 1740, shortly before he became president of the Burgundian *parlement*, Brosses (1709–77) made a tour of Italy. The many letters he wrote during his visit, first published in 1799, include abundant information on the concerts and operas he attended there. (Some of these 'Italian' letters apparently survive in revised versions.) Naturally their chief value for the music historian relates to Italian music, but they often make revealing comparisons with the equivalent French musical and operatic tradition. Surprisingly, perhaps, the author notes hearing Rameau's harpsichord music played – 'and played well' – in Italy. Brosses's subsequent correspondence reveals him to be an operatic reformer, firmly pro-Italian during the Querelle des Bouffons* and in favour of establishing an Italian opera company in Paris. His views on Rameau are mixed. On the one hand, he finds the composer's harmonic idiom problematic and several of his operas inferior to Lully's*; on the other, he evidently tried to persuade Rameau to reset the librettos of Quinault* and La Motte*: such re-settings, he later wrote, could not equal Lully in their recitative but would be superior in every other respect. *See also* **Académie des Sciences, Arts et Belles-Lettres de Dijon**. *AgaLet, BézBro, BroBou, ChaRou, GirRam.*

Burney, Charles (Dr)   On a trip to Paris in 1770, the music historian Charles Burney (1726–1814) visited Balbastre's* house, where he was shown a magnificently decorated harpsichord adorned with a portrait of Rameau. Burney, who claims to have 'seen' the composer in 1764, pronounced this to be a good likeness. Like most British music-lovers of his day, he detested the French style of music and the way it was performed. Indeed, one reviewer of Burney's *The Present State of Music in France and Italy* (1771) took him to task for his 'bitterness and invective against the French'. Not surprisingly, the book caused an outcry in France, and the author was obliged to apologize to his many French friends for his hostile and disparaging remarks on their native music. Undeterred, he planned to translate this work into French and submit it for 'correction' to his friend Diderot*. Burney's treatment of Rameau in the fourth volume of *A General History of Music* (1789) is more balanced and includes a detailed assessment of *Castor et Pollux*, which he had seen in Paris. Yet although the English writer generally admired Rameau's instrumental music, he was sharply critical of certain harmonic procedures and the frequent changes of metre in the vocal music. Moreover, he saw little value in Rameau's theoretical writings, which he evidently had difficulty in understanding. *See also* **Augmented mediant chord**. *BurHis, GétPor, LibPor.*

Cadence   In his table of keyboard ornaments of 1724 (see p. 20) Rameau illustrates three kinds of *cadence*, or trill: the unprepared variety beginning on the upper auxiliary; the *cadence appuyée* (a 'supported' trill in which the upper note is emphasized before the oscillations begin) and the *double cadence**, which includes a two-note termination. In practice, simple *cadences* were sometimes performed as supported trills, as is suggested by the example below. The 'reprise' on the second staff is essentially a transposed reworking of the main theme on the first staff, though each of the *cadences appuyées* is replaced by a simple *cadence*; it is thus likely that, in this context, the performer was expected to interpret all these *cadences* as supported trills. The symbols in Rameau's 1724 ornament table apply only to the keyboard repertory: elsewhere, the composer indicates trills with a + and, where necessary, shows the preparation either in

(a) Rameau, 'L'Agaçante', *Pièces de clavecin en concerts*

(b) 'L'Agaçante', opening bars of *reprise*

(c) *Zoroastre*, 'Entrée des Indiens', II, 4 (transposed down a fifth) fully-measured notes (see the third staff below) or, more often, as grace-notes. By 1760 he had come to prefer the term *tremblement* for a trill, reserving 'cadence' for its modern meaning as a point of musical repose. In Rameau's day the variety of possible trills was much greater than is generally supposed: Jean Bérard's *L'Art du chant* (1755), for example, includes no fewer than seven types of *cadence*. Given that Bérard* sang in the premieres of Rameau operas between 1736 and 1745, his testimony is of special significance. *See also* **Coulé**; **Ornaments added in rehearsal** *BérArt, CyrEss, NeuOrn, NeuPer, SadInv, SawNou.*

Caffieri, Jean-Jacques After winning the Prix de Rome in 1748, Caffieri (1725–92) spent four years studying classical sculpture in Italy. As sculptor to Louis XV, he gained a reputation for his portrait-busts. Several versions of his bust of Rameau are known to have existed. A terracotta version, dated 1760 and once the property of the Académie des Sciences, Arts et Belles-Lettres de Dijon*, is now displayed at the city's Musée des Beaux-Arts (see illustration on the back cover). A plaster version was exhibited at the Paris Salon of 1761. Diderot*, who attended this exhibition and knew Rameau well, described the bust as striking: 'it is made cold, thin and dry, just like he is; and it captures very well his affected refinement and precious smile [sa finesse affectée et son souris précieux]'. Caffieri donated this version to the Bibliothèque de Sainte-Geneviève, Paris, where it still survives. A marble copy was exhibited at the 1771 Salon and stood in the foyer of the Académie Royale de Musique* but was destroyed in the fire of 1781. The posthumous inventory of Rameau's estate lists a plaster bust, which was presumably a further version. Caffieri's bust is depicted in several works of art, among them 'Apothéose de Rameau'*, 'Dialogue de Lulli, Rameau et Orphée'*, an engraving by Voyez* and the lid of a harpsichord formerly in the Cailleux* collection. *DawBus, GétPor, LauDoc.*

Cahusac, Louis de During a collaboration that lasted a dozen years or more, Cahusac (1706–59) provided Rameau with librettos for at least seven works. Those of *Les Fêtes de Polymnie* (1745), *Les Fêtes de l'Hymen et de l'Amour* (1747), *Zaïs* (1748), *Naïs* and *Zoroastre* (both 1749), *Anacréon* and *La Naissance d'Osiris* (both 1754) all bear his name, while the libretto of *Les Boréades* is attributed to him in two independent sources. There is also some reason to believe that he was author of the enigmatic *Mirthis* and *Zéphire*. In 1743 Cahusac was appointed secretary to the Comte de Clermont (1709–71), Grand Master of the French Grand Masonic Lodge, and he later worked for another prominent freemason, the comte de Saint-Florentin (1705–77). While no surviving document proves that Cahusac was a freemason (masonic records are badly incomplete for this period), his sympathies for the brotherhood are clear from the presence in his librettos of prominent symbols and themes associated with freemasonry*, notably in *Les Fêtes de l'Hymen et de l'Amour*, *Zaïs*, *Zoroastre* and *Les Boréades*. Cahusac was widely reviled in literary circles: Collé describes him as a mere 'word-flunkey [une espèce de valet de chambre parolier], whose servility of spirit bent him everything that Rameau willed'. Yet it is now generally conceded that he had undoubted strengths as a librettist, not least in his ingenious use of well-researched 'local colour', his skill at integrating the obligatory divertissement* into the plot, and his development of the *ballet figuré**. Cahusac was the author of the treatise *La Danse ancienne et moderne* (1754) and a number of articles on music and dance in Diderot* and d'Alembert's* *Encyclopédie*; between them, these writings constitute one of the earliest coherent theories of French lyric theatre. Cahusac was often criticized for his overuse of the supernatural – *le merveilleux**. From his writings it becomes clear that, for him, this was not a weakness but a source of strength: through the well-judged use of the supernatural, all the arts could more easily combine to astonish and bewitch the spectator, which in Cahusac's view was one of the prime functions of opera. *BetCah, BouBor, BouRam, CahDan, ChaRou, DilMon, GirRam, GreSou, KinPoé, KinRam, MasOpé, SadZaï, SadZo1, SouCah, SouFêt, VerDra, WilAna.*

'Cailleux' harpsichord lid   Among a number of decorated* harpsichord lids that feature Rameau's likeness is one formerly in the Cailleux collection but whose present location is unknown. The decoration features a bust of Rameau adorned with a floral crown, the bust itself clearly modelled on that of Caffieri* dating from 1760. Florence Gétreau identifies the painting as representing scenes from *Les Indes galantes*; it depicts the entry of two heroes, one dressed in a leopard skin, accompanied by an 'on-stage' orchestra including oboe, violins and continuo, while a troupe of dancers performs to a pipe and tabour. Given that *Les Indes galantes* was revived in 1761, 1765 and 1769, this harpsichord decoration was doubtless a posthumous tribute to the composer, like others of its kind. Gétreau attributes the decoration to the circle of the Saint-Aubin* brothers. *GétHer, GétPor.*

de Caix   In *Génération harmonique* Rameau names two *musiciens ordinaires de la musique du roi* whom he had consulted on matters of tuning: the violinist Jean-Pierre Guignon* and the viol player 'M. Dequai'. Although the latter has sometimes been identified as Louis de Caix d'Hervelois (c.1680–c.1755), that cannot be so, since this particular 'de Caix' was never a member of the *musique du roi*. Rameau's royal musician must have been either François-Joseph de Caix, *le père* (d. after 1751) or Barthélemy de Caix *le fils* (b. c.1716), both of whom were viol players in the king's service during the period when *Génération harmonique* was in preparation. Rameau's musician provided evidence that viol players normally slightly 'fortified' (i.e., widened) the perfect fourths between the outer strings, so that the major third between the two middle ones would not be too wide – evidence which the composer used to bolster his argument in favour of equal temperament*. *BenMus, BenVer, MacMus, RamCtw.*

Camargo, Marie-Anne Cupis de   Generally known in her day as Mlle Camargo or 'La Camargo', Marie-Anne Cupis (1710–70) was born in Brussels, where her Italian father was a dancing master. At the age of about 10 she was sent to Paris to study under the celebrated ballerina Françoise Prévost (1660–1741); her dance-style was also influenced by such star male dancers as Michel Blondy* and Louis Dupré*, from whom she learned the kind of virtuosic steps hitherto practised only by men – *cabrioles, entrechats coupés, jetés battus* and the like. Her debut at the Académie Royale de Musique* in 1726 caused a sensation, and she immediately established herself as the outstanding female practitioner of the *danse haute**. With the arrival a year later of Marie Sallé*, prime exponent of the *danse basse**, a rivalry developed, and the two dancers' respective styles provoked lively debate between conservative and progressive dance-lovers. Mlle Camargo's career was interrupted in 1734 by a serious on-stage accident, and she temporarily retired three years later on the orders of her lover, the comte de Clermont. As a consequence, the only Rameau opera she danced in during the 1730s was *Hippolyte et Aricie*, where she appeared as a *matelotte* (sailor girl) and a shepherdess. After her return to the Académie in 1741 she performed in the premieres of almost all of Rameau's new works and revivals, before retiring definitively in 1751. Mlle Camargo danced mainly in lively pieces, in which her nimbleness and gaiety were hugely admired. To give herself more freedom of movement, she shortened the skirts of her costumes to above the ankle and lowered the heels of her dance-shoes. She was widely credited with being the first to wear the *caleçon de securité* (male drawers), which eventually became obligatory for all acrobatic female dancers. *See also* '**La Cupis**'. BouHer, CahDan, CamAca, ChsInt, FaiSty, NovLet, SadDan, TesCor, VlaTed.

Campanini, Barbara   A native of Parma, Barbara Campanini (1721–99) came to Paris with her husband Antonio Rinaldi ('Fossani') at the age of 18, where she was known as Mlle Barbarine. She made her debut at the Académie Royale de Musique* during the first run of *Les Fêtes d'Hébé* (1739). Her athletic style of dancing, which included *entrechats à huit*, was an instant success with amateurs of the *danse haute**, though the marquis d'Argenson was one of those conservatives who hoped it would not catch on. To exploit this style, Rameau added several dances to the second entrée* of *Les Fêtes d'Hébe*, where she appeared as the Génie de la Victoire; she also distinguished herself as a *pantomime**, and the 'Airs italiens de la première pantomime' that she danced with her husband in this opera were later published separately by Mme Boivin. Later in 1739 she appeared in *Dardanus*. She was still in Paris in 1741, returning there briefly in 1743 after a tour of London and Vienna. ArgMém, BerPan, BouHer, ChaRou, DaiCor, DavHer, MasOpé, RolCos.

Campra, André   Towards the end of his long and distinguished career as an opera composer, Campra (1660–1744) became *inspecteur général* at the Académie Royale de Musique* in 1730 and thus presumably took part in the selection of Rameau's first opera, *Hippolyte et Aricie*. His famous remark to the prince de Conti ('My Lord, there is enough music in this work to make ten operas; this man will eclipse us all') suggests a mixture of admiration and anxiety. However, the prologue to his opera *Achille et Déidamie** (1735), produced during the Lulliste-Ramiste* dispute, adopted a pointedly Lulliste stance. Outside the theatre, the two composers are known to have collaborated at the Collège Louis-le-Grand*, where Campra was *maître de musique* during Rameau's tenure as organist in the 1730s. AntFre, BarCam, DemCam, GirRam, RosDes.

Canevas   Though sometimes used as a synonym for *parodie**, the term *canevas* refers to the framework (literally 'canvas') on which a poet was expected to base the words of the *parodie*. It usually took the form of a doggerel poem indicating the metre and the number of syllables in each line of the pre-existing music (Gautier de Montdorge's* *Réflexions d'un peintre sur l'opéra** includes a spoof example.) The discipline imposed by this procedure caused friction between Rameau and certain librettists, among them Voltaire* and Collé*. For Montdorge, the constraint of following a pre-ordained stress-pattern while limiting oneself to 'the list of words approved by the Opéra' ('les mots enregistrés au Théâtre lyrique') – i.e., those that were considered to 'sing' well – made it well-nigh impossible to produce passable verse; he ridiculed the process that resulted in such platitudes as 'les langueurs sans allarmes, | ces rigueurs et ces larmes, | ces fadeurs et ces charmes'. The objections voiced by Montdorge and others are often cited as evidence of Rameau's intransigence in dealing with librettists. But while the composer was certainly a demanding task-master, the fact remains that the creation of a successful *parodie* demanded a modicum of musical acumen, something which none of the above writers is known to have possessed. Rather, they seem to have been incapable of understanding Rameau's criticisms of their work. *BesVol, ColJou, GreSou, MasOpé, SchCan, SchRam.*

Cannon fire   One of the more unusual sound* effects featured in Rameau's operas occurs in *Acante et Céphise*. This opera, written to celebrate the birth of the duc de Bourgogne, begins with a programme overture whose second movement is entitled *Feu d'artifice* (Fireworks). To add a touch of realism, Rameau notates a part for cannon, its repeated shots being indicated in the score by the letter *C* above the bass staff. Presumably, some kind of mortar was employed, similar to those used at the Paris Opéra to represent lightning flashes. This virtuosic movement evidently made a huge impact in more than one sense. According to one eye-witness, 'the whole gamut of artillery fire is found in this new and unique piece. The boom of the cannons, the bursting of bombs, the speed of the rockets, the flashing sky [...], all this is painted in the most virile colours'. *FajAca, GirRam, MasOpé.*

Canon   Within Rameau's output the independent vocal canon may seem to occupy an insignificant place: of those that survive, only four are indisputably his. Yet the composer is known to have written a *Traité de la composition des canons en musique** 'with many examples', and he thought it worth sending a manuscript of this to the Noblemen and Gentlemen's Catch Club* in 1763. Surviving examples confirm an interest in the modulating* canon, two examples of which are printed in the *Traité de l'harmonie* (1722). One further canon, 'Mes chers amis, quittez vos rouges bords'*, attributed to Rameau by La Borde*, is a 'cadran harmonique' (harmonic sundial). These and all others attributed to him are infinite canons, in which the end of the melodic line leads back to the beginning. The texts are mostly playful or (as in 'Ah! loin de rire' and 'Mes chers amis') mock-serious. Until recently it was thought that Rameau had eschewed the scatological genre. However, evidence has emerged that the raunchy three-part canon 'L'Épouse [*or* La Femme] entre deux draps'* attributed to Couperin* may possibly be by Rameau. One eighteenth-century source attributes the famous *Frère Jacques* to Rameau. *BouHer, BouRam, ClaCon, GosTre, LabEss, MonBou, RobCat, SchFam.*

Cantate françoise   It has become customary to retain this 'period' spelling as a convenient shorthand for the French species of secular cantata that emerged in the early eighteenth century. Hundreds of such works appeared between c.1703 and 1730, the majority in published form. Surprisingly, perhaps, Rameau contributed only one volume to this flood of publications – the *Cantates françoises à voix seule**, issued in 1729 or 1730, which includes *Aquilon et Orithie** and *Le Berger fidèle**. Five others, all but one of them composed before he settled in Paris in 1722, survive in manuscript. In a letter of 1727 to La Motte*, Rameau explained his reluctance to publish these works: manuscript copies of his early cantatas had circulated so widely that 'I have not thought it worth having them engraved [...] unless I could add a few others, which I cannot for lack of words' – surely a somewhat disingenuous excuse. His *Cantates françoises* are nevertheless described as 'livre premier', which suggests that by then he intended to publish further works of this sort. That he did not do so is doubtless related to the sudden decline in popularity of the genre after 1730. *BouHer, CyrCan, CyrChr, DorCan, FadInv, MonBou, SadOrc, TunCan, ZasApp.*

Cantate pour le jour de la Saint-Louis Rediscovered by Mary Cyr in 1979, this work survives in a score in Rameau's hand. The calligraphic nature of the handwriting suggests that it served as the model for a presentation score (now lost) prepared for an unnamed dedicatee. As the text of the first recitative indicates, the work celebrates 'the name of a friend whom I adore'; Rameau nevertheless provided an alternative version of the final air for use 'when the cantata is not used on St Louis's Day' (25 August). Physical evidence assembled by Thomas Green narrows down the dating; the reverse side of one of the *collettes** bears a rejected passage from *Castor et Pollux*, completed in 1737, while the paper was manufactured before 1742. It is thus tempting to imagine that the cantata text was the one sent to Rameau by Voltaire* in 1735 for performance at the prince de Carignan's* residence. This hypothesis gains support from the fact that all three airs include an unlabelled obbligato part written, unusually, in the treble clef rather than the French* violin clef – an Italianate notational feature possibly requested by Guignon*, the prince's Italian violinist. The first air borrows from a sonata in F (TWV42) by Telemann*, who was in Paris in 1737 and 1738. *BesVol, BouHer, CyrEss, CyrNew, GreSou, MonBou.*

Cantates à voix seule Though described on the title page as 'livre premier', this was Rameau's only cantata publication. The composer may have planned a second volume in 1735, since he solicited suitable texts from Voltaire*, who provided him with at least one (possibly the *Cantate pour le jour de la Saint-Louis**). The present book comprises two works 'avec symphonie': *Le Berger fidèle* and *Aquilon et Orithie*. The volume is undated, and until recently the publication date was usually given as 'c.1728'. However, Mary Cyr has proposed the more plausible dating of 1729 or 1730: Johann Gottfried Walther's* 'Rameau' article in his *Musicalisches Lexicon* (1732) shows that the book had not appeared by the end of 1728 when Boivin published his 1729 catalogue, now lost; and the engraver signs herself Mlle Louise Roussel, hence the volume pre-dates her marriage in September 1730, after which time she signed herself Mme Leclair. *BouHer, CyrChr, CyrEss, DorCan, MonBou, TunCan, ZasApp.*

'Capitation des acteurs' It was the custom at the Académie Royale de Musique* to mount an annual series of performances for the benefit of the singers, dancers and other personnel. During the period of Rameau's operatic career, there were normally three such performances per year, scheduled towards the end of the winter season. As a form of redistributive taxation on the Académie's revenues, net profits were paid pro rata to Académie employees in proportion to their annual salary. Although the selection of works was decided by the director, the artists themselves exerted pressure on the management to choose operas that were popular with audiences. Thus the particular choices may be seen as a barometer of taste. As such, they confirm the fact that the public was slow to warm to Rameau's operas: during the 1730s and 1740s, only one entire work, *Les Indes galantes*, was selected for capitation performances, although individual entrées* of this and two other Rameau *opéras-ballets** were included in the 1740, 1744 and 1749 performances. It was not until 1755 that his *tragédies en musique** began to be chosen, even though *tragédies* by several other composers (Lully* especially) had long been staple fare on such occasions. *DenSer, SerOpé.*

Caricatures   Unlike the satirical* engravings that circulated during the Lulliste-Ramiste* dispute, several caricatures issued during the 1760s and 1770s made some attempt to capture Rameau's physical characteristics. The earliest is mentioned in Grimm's* obituary of the composer (1764): 'As he was constantly seen walking in public, M. de Carmontelle* drew him from memory a few years ago. This little engraving is wittily done and much resembles him'. Carmontelle's etching, entitled 'Rameau, Musicien', captures the stooped posture mentioned in an eye-witness description by Sébastien Mercier: 'since he was bent, [Rameau] always walked at the Palais-Royal [gardens] with his hands behind his back to keep his balance.' This caricature was copied directly or indirectly by other engravers, each of whom added embellishments. In 'La Caricature du Celebre Rameau' by a certain 'B.S.', the image appears in mirrored form (a sign that it was copied from Carmontelle's original), but now shows the composer in an avenue of trees. This image was in turn copied in an anonymous etching (see the illustration in the entry 'Rameau, Jean-Baptiste'* [*sic*]), which features an elegant woman seated on the left-hand side. A delightful etching by Charles-Philippe Campion de Tersan (1736–1819), dated 1765, shows Rameau and Voltaire* in animated conversation. The two figures are depicted as similar in height; in reality this was not so, as Mercier's* description of Rameau confirms: 'Much taller than M. de Voltaire, he was as gaunt and desiccated as him [aussi hâve et sec que lui]'. Once again, the figure of Rameau is copied directly (i.e., in mirror image) from Carmontelle, as is the engraving by Joseph Marie Vien (1716–1809) that forms the frontispiece of an anonymous and undated primer, *Le Petit Rameau*. One curiosity of these related engravings is that all except the last include a small chair; in the copies, this appears on the right- or left-hand side, according to whether the engraving is based directly on Carmontelle or derived from one of the copies. *See also* **Livre de caricatures.** *CerMcG, GétPor.*

Carignan, Victor-Amédée I, prince de   At around the time of his operatic debut, Rameau evidently enjoyed the patronage of the prince de Carignan (1690–1741). This colourful and dissolute figure, described by Barbier as 'a man who played all sorts of roles except prince', was probably the most powerful individual at the Académie Royale de Musique*, where he is described in administrative documents as 'inspector' or, more accurately, 'protector'. Evidence in the correspondence of Voltaire* shows that Rameau had already come under the prince's protection by December 1733, two months after the premiere of *Hippolyte et Aricie*. This association continued until at least November 1735, during which period Rameau was evidently a frequent visitor to the Hôtel de Soissons, the prince's Paris residence, and took part in celebratory events there. By August 1736, however, Rameau had transferred his allegiance to the tax-farmer La Pouplinère*, with whom he remained until 1753. Among the prince de Carignan's grand schemes was a plan, eventually abandoned, to build a new opera house in the grounds of the Hôtel de Soissons. It may have been there that Rameau first became associated with freemasonry*, since the prince allowed his residence to be used for masonic gatherings in the 1730s. *BarChr, BesVol, BouRam, BoyTur, CucPou, GrmCor, HenAri, LinPat, RosDes, SadPat.*

Carmontelle, Louis Carrogis, *known as* Carmontelle (1717–1806) is nowadays remembered for such diverse achievements as the invention of an early form of magic lantern and the creation of landscape gardens, notably the Parc Monceau in Paris. From 1758 he was in the service of the Orléans family at the Palais-Royal; here he came into frequent contact with members of the aristocracy and distinguished visitors, many of whom he depicted in pencil, gouache and water-colour. His portraits, of which some six thousand survive, were often executed within a few hours. In addition to his famous representation of the eight-year-old Mozart, Carmontelle portrayed a number of other musicians, including the opera singers Mlle Chevalier* and Sophie Arnould*. His portrait of Rameau, dated 1760, survives in the Musée Condé, Chantilly. It shows the composer seated in an armchair, poised to write on a sheaf of papers. At some distance is a Hemsch-style two-manual harpsichord, its lid closed. On the floor are various books, the top one opened to reveal its title, *Code de musique [pratique]**, belonging to a book which Rameau had published that same year. The water-colour captures the composer's bony physique. An etching of this portrait was made by Jean-Baptiste Delafosse (1721–55), while Carmontelle's depiction of the composer was copied to some degree in various other etchings and medallions. The artist also drew a caricature* of Rameau, stooped and walking with his hands behind his back, which spawned many imitations. Grimm* claimed that it was a good likeness. *ChlCar, GétPor, GrmCor.*

Casanova, Giacomo Girolamo In 1751 the famous Venetian adventurer Casanova (1725–1798) was invited to choose a French libretto to translate into Italian for performance during Carnival the following year at the royal theatre in Dresden. His brief was to select a work that lent itself to elaborate scene-changes and featured ballets related to the plot. In *Histoire de ma vie*, Casanova discusses his choice of the 1749 version of Cahusac's* libretto for *Zoroastre* and the difficulty of adapting the translation to Rameau's music. Casanova's choice of this particular opera is undoubtedly connected with his recent initiation into the order of freemasonry* at Lyon in 1750. The Dresden event was reported in the *Mercure de France** (May 1752), which states that the production had followed literally the plan of the original décor, choreography and stage machinery. Yet although the *Mercure* gives examples of 'tous les grands tableaux' of Rameau's music that had been included, only the ballet music and one of Rameau's choruses were actually used, the rest of the music being by Johann Adam (c.1705–79). Indeed, the libretto in the Sächsische Landesbibliothek – Staats- und Universitätsbibliothek Dresden states baldly: 'Texte de Casanova, musique d'Adam'. The score has not survived. *GauJug, SadZo1.*

Casaubon A rare glimpse of the octogenarian Rameau as he struggled to complete his life's work as a theorist is captured in his letter of November 1763 to a certain Casaubon, a syndic to the Compagnie des Indes. To judge from its content, Rameau had asked this wealthy businessman for some unspe-cified favour; he had, however, made the tactical error of requesting a simple yes-or-no reply, and Casaubon evidently took offence at Rameau's brusque tone. The composer begins his reply with profuse apologies for having seemed insulting, but claims that 'the time I take up to write concerning my domestic affairs is very precious to me since I steal it from Him whom I fear and who does not fail me, in order to bring to light new discoveries'. He claims that he was forced to communicate his thoughts in abbreviated form because of 'a lack of brainpower and eyesight, and because I cannot concentrate nowadays for more than two hours during the daytime'. This touching admission is all the more precious, given that very few of Rameau's personal letters of the sort have survived. Casaubon may be the dedicatee of 'La De Casaubon' in Duphly's* *Troisième livre de pièces de clavecin* (1756). *RamCtw.*

Castel, Louis-Bertand   Rameau's association with the Jesuit mathematician, physicist and journalist Castel (1688–1757) began soon after the publication of the *Traité de l'harmonie* in 1722. Enthralled by this treatise, Castel sought out Rameau through a mutual friend and soon began theory lessons with him. He later claimed to have introduced Rameau to the 'birdsongs noted in Kircher' (i.e., in *Musurgia universalis*, 1650), among them the hen and nightingale, and to have sketched out 'the outlines of pieces that imitate the truth of Nature'. While Rameau's birds in 'Le Rappel des oiseaux'*, 'La Poule'* and elsewhere do not sing the same songs as Kircher's, the composer was undoubtedly stimulated in the mid-1720s to produce a series of magnificent descriptive movements drawn not only from nature but also from the theatre. Castel's enthusiastic review of the *Traité* in the Jesuit *Journal de Trévoux** brought Rameau's work to the attention of a wide – indeed, a European – readership. Reviewing the *Nouveau système de musique théorique* six years later, Castel had become distinctly cooler. By the early 1730s his views had diverged sharply from Rameau's. This, he claimed, was why he refused the offer of all Rameau's research papers in 1733. (At that date the composer felt he had reached the limit of his 'speculation' and considered abandoning music theory in favour of his newly launched operatic career.) This was apparently their last meeting. Two years later, Castel's article 'Nouvelles expériences d'optique & d'acoustique' (*Journal de Trévoux*, 1735) contained the implication that Rameau had not sufficiently acknowledged his debt to certain earlier scholars. Rameau and Castel exchanged open letters, the tone of which is stiffly courteous. But when Castel wrote a grudging and equivocal review of *Génération harmonique* (1737), Rameau unleashed a riposte of such withering sarcasm that the *Journal de Trévoux*, which had hitherto published the entire polemic, evidently refused to print it; the review appeared instead in the independent *Le Pour et contre* (1738). Voltaire's* characteristically witty 'Lettre à Mr. Rameau' congratulating Orpheus Rameau on vanquishing Euclid Castel appeared later the same year. *BesVol, GirRam, RamCtw.*

Castor et Pollux   Rameau's third opera, a *tragédie en musique** on a libretto by Pierre-Joseph Bernard*, was premiered at the Académie Royale de Musique* on 24 October 1737. At first, the Opéra audience did not particularly warm to the work, comparing it unfavourably with Rameau's previous operas which, though initially controversial, had by then gained support among open-minded opera-goers. While *Castor* was by no means a failure, its first run of twenty-one performances was noticeably shorter than those of *Hippolyte et Aricie* (about forty) and *Les Indes galantes* (sixty-four). The coolness is partly explained by the unusual choice of subject – the brotherly love of the twins Castor and Pollux, the one mortal and the other immortal – rather than the romantic variety to which French opera normally gave a central place. Equally unusual is the fact that Castor does not appear on stage until Act IV. After an exceptionally long interval of eighteen years, *Castor* was revived in 1754 at the height of the Querelle des Bouffons*. The prologue was omitted and a new, expository first act inserted before the original Act I. To compensate for this, Acts III and IV were telescoped into one, and the libretto pruned by well over a quarter of its length. This time, it was ecstatically received and was widely regarded as a more effective counterblast to the Bouffons' supporters than any of the pro-French pamphlets. By the time it was revived again in 1764, equally triumphantly, *Castor* had come to be regarded as one of Rameau's crowning achievements. After the composer's death it remained in the Académie's repertoire until 1785, though increasingly disfigured by cuts, substitutions and re-orchestrations. *BouHer, BucSup, ChaRou, DilCre, DilMon, FauCas, GirRam, GirTra, HerCas, LibPor, MalCas, NoiHip, VerDra.*

Cauvin, Gaspard Alexis   Little is known about Cauvin, an eighteenth-century book collector whose library included numerous manuscripts of works by Rameau, Lalande* and Mondonville*. The ten Rameau volumes, eventually acquired by Decroix* in the 1770s or later, are of special value because they include inner parts missing from other sources. For many years the provenance of these so-called 'Cauvin' manuscripts was unknown, but Bénédicte Hertz has recently identified the scribe as Bergiron* du Fort-Michon, co-founder of the Académie des Beaux-Arts de Lyon. *BouDen, BouHer, DecRam, HerMot, WolŒu.*

Caveau   In or around 1729, a group of poets, playwrights and bons vivants founded a dining society in Paris which took its name from the basement ('caveau') in Landelle's tavern, where meetings took place. The monthly dinners lasted for up to ten hours, creating a convivial atmosphere that led to the creation of numerous satirical verses sung to popular melodies. The members of the original Société du Caveau, dissolved in 1739, included Piron*, Fuzelier*, Bernard*, La Bruère*, Collé* and Jéliote*. The earliest evidence that Rameau was a member appears in an account of the Caveau's early history published by Pierre Laujon in 1811. Laujon, who joined a re-incarnation of the society in 1762, frankly admits that his evidence was hearsay, so it must be treated with considerable caution. Anyone whose image of Rameau is of a curmudgeonly, unsociable individual will find the idea of his participating in such dissolute gatherings far-fetched. Still, there are glimpses in the composer's biography of a more genial, epicurean side to his personality; moreover Rameau's output includes a number of drinking songs. *LauDoc, LegVau, LevCav.*

Chabanon, Michel-Paul-Gui de   One of the first writers to produce an obituary of Rameau was Chabanon (1730–92): his *Éloge de Mr Rameau* was approved for publication on 28 October 1764, only about six weeks after the composer's death. Whether or not Chabanon was a composition pupil*, he was certainly a close friend during Rameau's final years; the *Éloge*, while not uncritical of certain aspects of the composer's music and theoretical work, is an eloquent testament to the writer's sincere admiration and affection. Chabanon paints a moving portrait of the old man, apparently lost in thought but actually shying away from compliments. He reports various confidences – that Rameau almost abandoned composition during the Lulliste-Ramiste* dispute, such was the outcry that greeted his first opera; and that in his last years he considered his musical imagination ('génie') to be worn out. The *Éloge* was Chabanon's first publication. He went on to make a name for himself as an influential writer on aesthetics, his *Observations sur la musique* (1779) being one of the earliest French writings to assert the autonomy of purely instrumental music. *CanPhi, ChaÉlo, GirRam, ReiCha, VenCom.*

Character piece The use of descriptive or evocative titles, though widespread in seventeenth-century French lute music, was less common in the contemporary harpsichord repertory. At the start of the following century it was still rare: Rameau included only a single example, 'Vénitiénne' [*sic*], in his *Premier livre de pièces de clavecin* of 1706. Not until 1713, with the appearance of the first book of *Pièces de clavecin* by François Couperin*, did the fashion for character titles really take off. The term 'pièce de caractère', while not in general use at that time, may be found in the fifth book of *Pièces de viole* (1725) by Marin Marais; two years later, Rameau was to draw attention to the way his harpsichord piece 'Les Sauvages' had 'characterized' the dancing of American Indians. It should not be assumed that the article *la* (as in 'La Rameau' or 'La Lapoplinière') indicates a female subject: rather it refers to 'la pièce...'. Exceptionally, the masculine article is used in such titles as 'Le Lardon'* and 'Le Vézinet'*. *ClaCon, FulPor, GirRam, GusFul.*

Chardin, Jean-Baptiste Siméon A much-reproduced portrait of a musician in a scarlet jacket, often said to represent Rameau, is nowadays generally attributed to Joseph Aved*. This attribution is no longer unanimously accepted, however, not least because the earliest surviving ascription names Chardin (1699–1779) as the artist. This attribution, dating from as late as 1805, is nevertheless problematic; indeed, it now seems unlikely that the identity of the artist will ever be resolved. As to whether the sitter is Rameau, this remains equally questionable. *GétPor.*

Charpentier, Marc-Antoine Of all Rameau's predecessors at the Paris Opéra, the composer with whom he bears the closest affinity is Charpentier (1643–1704). The parallels are striking: both men came late to writing full-scale music drama, making their debut at the Opéra at the age of fifty; both developed an intense harmonic idiom that proved unpalatable to conservative music lovers, who also attacked them for excessive stylistic borrowings from Italy; and both were labelled *savant* (learned, erudite), which for many opera-goers meant 'too clever by half'. Although Charpentier had died by the time Rameau arrived in Paris, his huge legacy of scores, including the operas *David et Jonathas* (1688) and *Médée* (1693), was available for study in the Bibliothèque du Roi. Moreover, soon after Rameau's arrival, the former work was revived at the Collège Louis-le-Grand*, on 10 February 1706. Assuming the young composer had already been appointed organist at the college, as seems likely, he would have taken part in this production, probably as continuo player. His first opera *Hippolyte et Aricie* may even include a reminiscence of Charpentier's powerful *tragédie*. Hippolyte's soliloquy, illustrated opposite, bears a remarkable resemblance to Saul's monologue 'Objet d'une implacable haine' in *David et Jonathas*. Over and above the textual similarity ('Ah! faut-il ... perdre...?' ['Ah! must I ... lose...?']), there is the resemblance between Saul's vocal line and that of Rameau's flutes and violins, which both begin with a syncopated falling fifth and rising fourth and have a similar descending contour. The resemblance is enhanced by the rhythmically unsettled counterpoint between voice and accompaniment. To make comparison easier, viola parts in both extracts have been omitted, as have Rameau's ornaments; the Charpentier extract is transposed up a tone and its note-values halved. *BreJeu, CesCha, KocOrg, QuiJeu, ZasApp.*

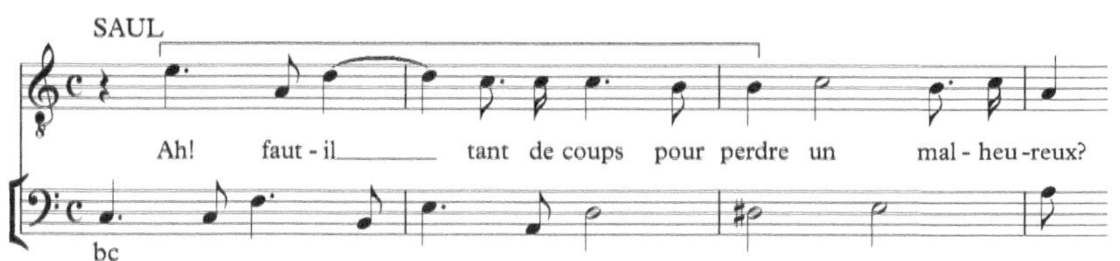

(a) Charpentier, *David et Jonathas*, III, 2

(b) Rameau, *Hippolyte et Aricie*, IV, 1

Chassé de Chinais, Claude-Louis-Dominique de   Born into a noble Breton family that suffered financial ruin in the 1720s, Claude Chassé (1699–1786) entered the Académie Royale de Musique* as a *basse-taille** in 1720 or 1721. He soon impressed with his strong stage presence, wide vocal range and impeccable diction, though his trills were sometimes criticized as goat-like. David Garrick* considered him 'ye best *actor* I have seen hitherto' in France, and the singer was similarly held up as a model in this respect by Jean-Jacques Rousseau*. In 1737 Chassé left the Académie in an attempt to regain his noble rank but returned in 1742 with equal success, which he maintained until his retirement in 1756. Among the numerous roles he created were many of the most powerful in Rameau's operas: Thésée in *Hippolyte et Aricie*; Huascar in *Les Indes galantes*; Pollux in *Castor et Pollux*; Abramane in *Zoroastre*. *BenMus, BouHer, CamAca, ChaRou, GarDia, MacMus, PouJél, RouDic, SadInv.*

Chevalier, Marie-Jeanne Fesch, *known as* Mlle   A pupil of the composer Royer*, Marie Chevalier (1722–89) made her debut at the Académie Royale de Musique* in 1740. The beauty of her voice and the nobility and refinement of her *jeu de théâtre** won her a considerable reputation. She excelled in representations of furies and sorceresses. Among the numerous roles she created were many in Rameau operas: Mnémosine and Stratonice in *Les Fêtes de Polymnie*; Érigone and Plautine in *Le Temple de la Gloire*; Orthésie in *Les Fêtes de l'Hymen et de l'Amour*; Érinice in *Zoroastre*; Uranie in the 1757 version of *Les Surprises de l'Amour*. She retired from the Opéra in 1766. *See also* **Balbastre's harpsichord.** *BouHer, CamAca, ChaRou, PieCon, PouJél, RivFil.*

Chorus   One aspect that distinguishes the French Baroque operatic tradition from many others of the day is its emphasis on the chorus. At the Académie Royale de Musique* virtually every act of every opera during the Lully-Rameau period provided extensive scope for choral singing. The Académie's chorus was a substantial body of singers. In Rameau's day its size grew from between thirty and thirty-four in the 1730s to at least forty during the 1750s and 1760s. Given that the Palais-Royal* theatre was fairly small, a professional chorus of such dimensions must have made quite an impact. The chorus normally comprised four voice parts; by now, the treble line (*dessus**) was sung exclusively by women, adult males taking the remaining parts (*haute-contre**, *taille** and *basse* or *basse-taille**). The balance always favoured the outer parts, as may be judged from the numbers on each line in *Les Indes galantes* in 1735–36 (respectively, 13, 6, 6 and 8) and *Zaïs* in 1748 (16, 7, 7, 10). The chorus was normally disposed in an arc around the edge of the performing area, with half of each voice-type on the *côté du roi* (King's side, stage left) and half on the *côté de la reine* (Queen's side, stage right). The male singers occupied the inner part of the arc, between the two groups of women. The chorus's deportment came in for growing criticism: however vivid the text and music of a given movement, the singers tended to stand motionless with their arms crossed, an aspect of performance practice unlikely to appeal to modern audiences. Various attempts were made to remedy this state of affairs, particularly by Cahusac*, but with limited success, at least in Rameau's lifetime. For opera performances at court, the chorus could sometimes be considerably larger, though disposed in similar proportions. When Rameau's motet *In convertendo** was performed at the Concert Spirituel* in 1751, the chorus included thirty-nine singers. *See also* **Petit chœur.** *CyrCho, CyrEss, CyrGes, MasOpé, RosPer, SadInv.*

Christin, Jean-Pierre   Widely remembered as the inventor of the Celsius thermometer, Christin (1683–1755) was also a co-founder of the Académie des Beaux-Arts de Lyon in 1714. In that capacity, he evidently got to know Rameau during the composer's time as organist in the city between 1712 and 1715. On 3 November 1741, in the course of a spat with Bollioud-Mermet* on the subject of keyboard temperament, Rameau wrote a stern letter to Christin, now the Académie's permanent secretary, insisting that the public be disabused of the 'false ideas' that a certain individual (i.e., Bollioud) was spreading about him in the Académie's name. The strength of Rameau's feelings may be judged by his frequent underlinings to emphasize individual words and phrases. Although the Académie never issued an apology or a correction, Christin may have dissuaded Bollioud-Mermet from publishing his paper. However, the claim that the surviving manuscript of Bollioud's text is a revised version, toned down at Christin's insistence, has been shown by Albert Cohen to be groundless. *BreJeu, CohEqu, GirRam, HerMot, RamCtw, ValLyo.*

Clarinet   The first French opera to include clarinets was Rameau's *Zoroastre* (1749), in which two supernumeraries, Schieffer and Raiffer, took part. The engraved score, our main source of this version of the work, gives no indication of where the clarinets played, perhaps because the engraving had reached too advanced a stage when the players were hired. Two years later, for *Acante et Céphise* (1751), the Académie Royale de Musique* hired Procksch and Flieger, clarinettists in the orchestra of Rameau's patron La Pouplinière*. This work includes a dozen movements in which these instruments have obbligato lines. The score specifies clarinets in C, A and D, frequently used in two parts. Oboe and clarinet never double each other, and in only two movements are these two families of instrument found together, despite the fact that clarinets are elsewhere used in combination with flutes, bassoons, horns and/or trumpets. Rameau evidently over-estimated the players' abilities, since the surviving materials reveal numerous cuts and simplifications. Thereafter, Rameau made no further use of clarinets except to suggest where they might play in his last opera, *Les Boréades*, since he had evidently heard that they might be available for the projected court performances at Choisy in 1763. The production* score includes eight autograph annotations relating to clarinets, six of them indicating passages where they could replace the oboes (or, in one case, violins). It is perhaps no coincidence that all three of these operas allude in one way or another to the rituals or tenets of freemasonry*, with which the clarinet was to be increasingly associated towards the end of the century. There is, however, no way of knowing whether this instrument had already acquired such associations in France during Rameau's lifetime. True, *Acante et Céphise* makes frequent use of the 'masonic' combination of clarinets and horns, but the fact that such writing often occurs in scenes featuring the evil genie Oroès and his followers surely argues against a masonic connection. Not until the 1770s did clarinettists become permanent members of the Académie Royale de Musique. By that time, it was common practice for clarinet parts to be added to revivals of existing operas, Rameau's among them. *See also* **Double clefs.** *AutCol, BreCla, BouBor, CotMaç, CucPou, FajAca, GorOrc, LauCla, SadOrc, SpiZas.*

Clermont Although the ancient city of Clermont was officially amalgamated with the neighbouring Montferrand in the seventeenth century, it was still generally known as Clermont en Auvergne rather than (as now) Clermont-Ferrand. Rameau's two periods as cathedral organist ran from 1 May 1702, for about three-and-a-half years, and from 1 April 1715, for seven. From 22 August 1721 until his departure the following year, Rameau seems to have shared his post with an organist named Marchand, a member of a local family of musicians. The anecdote that he gained early release from one of these periods of service by playing the organ in a disagreeable manner is possibly a case of mistaken identity: a well-documented incident of this nature, with his brother Claude-Bernard Rameau* as the miscreant, took place in Dijon* in 1736. A contemporary description of the organ at Clermont Cathedral reveals that it had fifteen stops on the *grand orgue*, ten on the *positif* and four each on the pedals and echo organ. Visitors to the cathedral in the 1860s were shown a large Louis XIV armchair that was proudly known as 'le fauteuil de Rameau'. Contracts of 1702 and 1715 stipulate that the composer was to play during the Offices and on solemn feast days, give 'learned instruction' to one chorister or other designated person and keep the reed pipes in tune. To judge from the 'Clermont notes'*, it was during his time in the city that Rameau began to consolidate his work on

Anon., view of Clermont Cathedral seen from the rue des Notaires, c.1820-30 (Paris, Bibliothèque Nationale de France, Est. Réserve VE-26 [Q]). Reproduced by permission.

music theory. Several of his *cantates françoises** evidently date from his second period there. *See also* **Basse de viole.** *BouRam, ChrTho GirRam, GosTre, MarAuv, MonBou, RamCtw, TiéRam, WelCle, ZasApp.*

'Clermont notes'   In *Génération harmonique**, Rameau mentions that he had acquired an interest in aspects of music theory by the age of 'seven or eight'. Not until his second period at Clermont*, however, do we find evidence of sustained work in this field. In 1958 René Suaudeau published extracts from several of the composer's autograph manuscripts, then located at Clermont-Ferrand, which included a course of theory exercises and a list of books that the composer had consulted in the episcopal library. These so-called 'Clermont notes' reveal that Rameau had already framed his concept of the *basse fondamentale** as a way of simplifying the rules of harmony and *accompagnement**. The papers were eventually acquired in the early nineteenth century by the Anglo-French composer George Onslow (1784–1853), a native of Clermont. Sometime after Suaudeau had examined them, they were dispersed among members of the Onslow family in Britain and South America. All attempts to trace them have so far failed. *ChrTho, GirRam, RamCtw, SuaCle, SuaInt, ZasApp.*

Cochin, Charles-Nicolas *le jeune*   The engraver and designer Charles-Nicolas Cochin* (1715–90) was known as 'le jeune' (the younger) or 'le fils' to distinguish him from his father, who was also called Charles-Nicolas and also an engraver. Among his works is a magnificent engraving of the final scene of Rameau's *La Princesse de Navarre*, as performed in the Grande Écurie, Versailles, in 1745. This shows the stage design in considerable detail, and reveals the presence of spectators on either side of the stage during the performance. The scene features a group of *figurants** executing a group dance. In front of the stage can be seen the large orchestra directed by the *batteur de mesure**. Cochin's design for the *Triomphe de Rameau**, though now lost, was used as the basis of a satirical* engraving by C.M. Fessard. *ChaMaî, GétPor, GétSat, LesOpé, MalPri.*

Code de musique pratique   Rameau's *Code de musique pratique, ou Méthodes pour apprendre la musique même à des aveugles* is the summation of his life's work as a teacher of composition, singing and *accompagnement**. The volume was completed by 1757, and a *Prospectus* advertising it for sale by subscription was published that year; but despite the date of 1760 on the title-page, the *Code* did not appear until 1761 because of a delay in producing the 'Nouvelles réflexions sur le principe sonore', added as an independent final section. The *Code* comprises seven 'methods' of radically different length: (1) the rudiments of music, capable of being taught 'even to the blind' (*aveugles*); (2) a brief essay on keyboard hand position, recapitulating ideas first stated in the *Pièces de clavessin* of 1724; (3) a method of voice production that develops material from his 'Réflexions sur la manière de former la voix' (*Mercure de France*, 1752); (4) a 55-page method of *accompagnement* in which, significantly, there is no mention of the reforms he had proposed in his *Dissertation sur les différentes métodes d'accompagnement* of 1732; (5) a composition method comprising nine chapters, which reworks material from his manuscript 'L'Art de la basse fondamentale'*; (6) a short discussion of accompanying without continuo figures; and (7) a 'méthode pour le prélude' (i.e., improvisation). All this solid practical and technical advice sits rather oddly alongside the supplementary 'Nouvelles réflexions sur le principe sonore', with its quasi-Rosicrucian arguments that the *corps sonore** was the key to all the arts and sciences. *See also* **Académie Royale des Sciences; Arnaud, abbé François.** *ChrTho, RamCtw, VerMus.*

***Colla parte* doubling**   When an instrumental line doubles a vocal one, *partitions réduites** in Rameau's day often saved space by combining the two lines onto a single staff. This sometimes had the effect of obscuring rhythmical differences that would be apparent in a full score. A case in point concerns phrase endings involving the so-called mute* '*e*' (*e muet*) which, despite its name, was normally pronounced in French poetry. Rameau's autograph and other authoritative full scores reveal that, in such doublings, the rhythm of the so-called feminine ending involving the mute '*e*' (e.g., 'don-*ne*', ♩♪₇) was usually adapted on the relevant instrumental staves either to ♩. or to ♩ ₇; in other words, it was not the norm for the instruments to articulate separately the note value given to the mute '*e*'. *See also* **Versification**.

Collé, Charles   A minor playwright and versifier, Collé (1709–83) achieved some limited success in the spoken theatre but is mainly remembered for his diary covering the period 1748 to 1772, published posthumously as *Journal historique, ou Mémoires littéraires* (Paris, 1807). Collé was a founder-member of the Caveau*, where he is presumed to have met Rameau; the two men also belonged to La Pouplinière's* circle. In 1752 Collé devised a 'prologue-ballet' entitled *Les Vendanges de la Folie*, in which elaborate *parodies** of movements from eight Rameau operas are interspersed with popular *vaudevilles**. The same year, he wrote a libretto for *Le Jaloux corrigé*, a pastiche 'opéra bouffon' that was performed at the Paris Opéra in 1753 alongside Jean-Jacques Rousseau's* *Le Devin du village*. Undeterred by the cool reception of his work, Collé began a collaboration with Rameau. Unfortunately, the premiere of *Daphnis et Églé**, scheduled for performance before the court at Fontainebleau on 30 October 1753, was cancelled at the last minute. Collé was humiliated by this debacle; whereas he had hitherto been a staunch admirer of Rameau, his subsequent references to the composer are wholly negative. This is not untypical of Collé's behaviour: beneath a veneer of bonhomie, the diarist reveals a bitter personality, quick to settle scores with opponents. It is in this light that his vitriolic, *ad hominem* 'obituary' of Rameau must be read. *See also* **Rameau, Marie-Alexandrine**. *ChaRou, ColJou, CucPou, GirRam, GreSou, MasOpé, RicFon.*

Collège des Godrans, Dijon   In a letter of 1744 to the abbé Mongeot*, Rameau states that he had attended the theatre since the age of twelve – i.e., from about 1695. Given that Dijon* did not have a municipal theatre until 1718, Rameau was probably referring to his experience as a pupil at the Collège des Godrans, the secondary school founded in 1581 with a legacy from a former president of the Burgundian *parlement*, Odinet Godrans. Like other Jesuit schools, the college included performances of tragedies and ballets in its curriculum. Although details of productions during Rameau's schooldays are sadly lacking, we may surmise from those at comparable Jesuit schools that they were elaborate and included stage machinery and scenic effects.

In view of his later achievements, it is surprising that the young Rameau did not distinguish himself at the college; according to a classmate, he would sing or write music during lessons. (On his own admission, he had begun considering aspects of music theory from the age of seven or eight.) Certain anecdotes suggest that Jean-Philippe's written French was defective at this time, and indeed his prose* style in the theoretical works and elsewhere is notable for its lack of clarity. The college buildings are now used as the municipal library. *See also* **Génération harmonique**. *BreJeu, GirAut, QuiJeu, ZasApp.*

Collège Louis-le-Grand   The title page of Rameau's *Premier livre de pièces de clavecin* (1706) indicates that the composer held two organist posts in Paris, one of them at the 'Jésuites de la Ruë S^t. Jacques'. This was the Collège Louis-le-Grand, the most prestigious school in France, where the Jesuits offered a secondary education to some three thousand boys. (Among the pupils at that date was Rameau's future collaborator Voltaire*.) Rameau may have acquired this post on the recommendation of his mentor Louis Marchand*, who been organist there from 1700 until at least 1703. The instrument, which had been rebuilt and enlarged in 1691, included eight stops on the *grand orgue*, six on the *positif*, a five-rank 'cornet' on the *récit*, and a single 8' flute on the pedals. According to the title page of the second edition of Rameau's *Premier livre*, published in 1708, the composer was still in his post at the Jesuits, though he had left by the end of that year. Some three decades later, after the start of his operatic career, he returned there as organist, being appointed by 1736; his return was short-lived, however, as he was no longer in post in 1738. *BarCam, BreJeu, BouHer, BouRam, DemCam, GirRam, KocOrg, QuiJeu, ZasApp.*

Collette   In Rameau's autograph manuscripts and production* scores, corrections or revisions are often written on pieces of paper pasted over the original passage. Such paste-overs, which vary in size from tiny rectangles to whole pages, are often nowadays referred to as *collettes*. Rameau's are usually made from discarded sheets of music paper of which he had used only one side. Most of the *collettes* have subsequently been 'lifted', allowing the rejected music on the reverse side to be examined. This has proved particularly revealing in matters of chronology, since it is often possible to establish the date of rejected material of the obverse side of the *collette*. *GreGen, GreSou, GreTra, GreZép.*

Comédie-ballet   In the 1660s, before the establishment of French opera, Molière and Lully* devised a genre of stage work in which a spoken play was interspersed with *intermèdes* (musical interludes) that were related in some way to the main plot. *Le Bourgeois gentilhomme* (Molière-Lully, 1670) and *Le Malade imaginaire* (Molière-Charpentier*, 1673) proved particularly durable examples of the genre. After the playwright's death, the *comédie-ballet* genre went into decline, though works of this sort continued to appear sporadically. The spoken plays are not invariably comedies in the accepted sense, as in the case of *La Princesse de Navarre* (1745), Rameau's sole essay in the genre. *See also* **Les Paladins**. *AntFre, GirRam, MasOpé.*

Comédie-Française   In 1680 Louis XIV signed a decree amalgamating several existing theatre troupes into one company with a monopoly over spoken theatre in the Paris region. In 1698 the Comédie-Française moved into a new theatre in the rue des Fossés-Saint-Germain on the left bank of the Seine, remaining there until 1770. Despite competition from the Théâtre-Italien* and the Théâtre de la Foire*, the troupe maintained its reputation as the bastion of the French classical tradition and the most prestigious theatre company in France. Rameau's only formal association with the Comédie-Française was in 1734 as composer of the divertissements* to *Les Courses de Tempé*, a *pastorale* by Piron*, though he is known to have attended performances of other works. *BouHer, ConPir, PirŒu, ProPir, SadPir.*

Comédie lyrique   In denoting an all-sung dramatic work with a continuous plot distributed over several acts, this eighteenth-century term proves useful for differentiating operas of this kind from *comédies-ballets**, which include spoken dialogue. Such a neat distinction was not, however, consistently practised in the mid-century: Rameau's two essays in the genre, for instance, are usually referred to in contemporary sources as 'ballet bouffon' (*Platée*) and 'comédie-ballet' (*Les Paladins*), respectively. *AntFre, BouHer, ChaRou, LajBib, GirRam, MasOpé.*

Compositeur de la chambre du roi   On 4 May 1745 Rameau was accorded a royal pension of 2,000 *livres* per year and the title of *compositeur de la chambre du roi*, in recognition of Louis XV's 'esteem and benevolence' towards a composer whose works had been 'universally applauded'. This was an honour normally granted only to an existing member of the king's musical establishment. In Rameau's case, however, it was effectively a reward for the two operas he had composed for the court, *La Princesse de Navarre* and *Platée*, both premiered there earlier that year. In the Letters* of Nobility granted to Rameau in 1764, and on his death certificate, this title is given as *compositeur du cabinet du roy*, the word 'cabinet' in this context indicating a post funded by the king's personal exchequer. *AntFre, BenMus, BenVer, LauDoc, MacMus, RidVol.*

Concert   Over and above its use in the conventional modern sense and in the titles of such organizations as the Concert Spirituel*, the French word *concert* was applied to a variety of multi-movement works designed for a heterogeneous chamber or orchestral ensemble. The word thus has no direct connection with *concerto* in its eighteenth-century sense, though the London publisher Walsh* was unaware of this when Rameau's *Pièces de clavecin en concerts* were issued under the title of *Five Concertos for the Harpsichord*. One characteristic of many of the compositions whose title includes the word 'concerts' is that they require instruments of different families; hence Rameau's *Pièces [...] en concerts* call for harpsichord, violin or flute, bass viol or second violin, while the anonymous arrangement of these pieces as *Six concerts de Mʳ Rameau* is scored for strings and bassoon. The extreme of diversity in this respect is reached in Rameau's own arrangement of movements from *Les Indes galantes* as 'Quatre grands concerts'*. These include not only the orchestral movements, arranged for harpsichord or 'other instruments', but also various solo vocal items and choruses. While the score includes vestiges of the work's orchestral scoring (including trumpets and drums), performers were free to arrange these *concerts* for any available combination of instruments. *AntFre, BouHer, BouRam, BreCon, FulAcc, HerMor, RpeKey.*

Concert Français   When the Concert Spirituel* was founded by André Danican Philidor* in 1725, the terms of its *privilège* excluded the programming of music with vernacular texts. In order to present works of this kind, Philidor established what became known as the Concert Français, in which French divertissements* and cantatas appeared alongside concertos, motets and Italian arias. The series ran from 1727 to 1733. Concerts – as many as six or more per month – took place throughout the year in the Salle des Suisses in the Tuileries Palace. Philidor managed to recruit some of the finest singers of the day, in particular Mlle Le Maure*, who at the age of twenty-three had temporarily 'retired' from the Académie Royale de Musique*: it was she who gave the first performance of Rameau's *Le Berger fidèle* in 1728. Concerto soloists included Leclair* and Guignon*. No records survive of the number of performers involved, but programmes often included works that required substantial orchestral forces. *BreCon, TunCan.*

Concert Spirituel   Founded in 1725, the Concert Spirituel was France's most important showcase for the performance of non-operatic music. Concerts took place in the Salle des Suisse at the Tuileries on religious festivals, when the Opéra was closed. Unlike the Concert Français*, this concert series was not allowed to present music with French words, hence its programmes included a preponderance of instrumental music and Latin motets. We can be sure that Rameau, a keen concert-goer, attended this series and thus kept abreast of developments in French and, increasingly, European musical styles. However, only one of his motets is known to have been given there: *In convertendo** was performed during Holy Week 1751, when the performers included a chorus of thirty-nine and an orchestra of thirty-four, of which twenty-six were string players. This motet was nevertheless received with little enthusiasm, and thereafter Rameau seems to have decided not to compete with Mondonville*, acknowledged as the undisputed master in this field. *See also* '**Paroles qui ont précédé le Te Deum**'.   *BreCon, FavMot, GreSou, HeaCon, PieCon, SpiZas.*

Concerts de la Reine   Soon after her arrival in France as Louis XV's bride in 1725, Queen Maria Leszczyńska asked Destouches* to establish a series of what came to be known as the 'Concerts de [or *chez*] la Reine'. These concerts, conducted by the current *surintendant* of the Musique du Roi, took place frequently – generally at least twice a week – either in the queen's apartments or elsewhere at Versailles, and sometimes at other royal residences. As such, the series constituted the most active musical institution at court. The staple fare comprised French cantatas alongside concert performances of operas in the current repertory of the Académie Royale de Musique*, the latter being performed over the course of several days. During the period 1725 to 1753, only eight of Rameau's operas ever appeared in the programmes, however; and whereas certain works by Lully, Destouches, Collin de Blamont and others were revived repeatedly during that time, most of the chosen Rameau operas were given no more than once – a reflection of the queen's conservative taste. Performers included star singers from the Opéra, as well as those from the *musique de la reine*, and players from the *musique du roi*. Rameau's wife, Marie-Louise Mangot*, took part occasionally as a singer. *BreCon, ChaRou, DraBla, RicFon, SadOrc, TunCan.*

Continuo group, *see **Petit chœur**.*

Contrafactum   Although the terms *contrafactum* and *parodie** both denote the practice of substituting one text of a musical setting for another, the former term is generally reserved for the substitution of sacred rather than secular words. Movements from Rameau's operas were occasionally adapted in this way, as in the 'Paroles qui ont precédé le Te Deum'* and Requiem*. The version of the *Messe des Morts* by Gilles* performed at memorial* services for Rameau included *contrafacta* derived from *Castor et Pollux* and from an aria by Domenico Alberti*. *BouHer, CucPou, HamMem.*

Contrebasse   Introduced as something of a curiosity around 1700, the *contrebasse* (double bass) had established a secure place in the orchestra of the Académie Royale de Musique* by the time Rameau made his debut there in 1733. Until 1765 the Académie officially employed only one double bass. (Evidence of a second player before that date is unreliable.) The player was a member of the *petit chœur**, taking part in airs and accompanied recitatives but doubling the cellos of the *grand chœur** in the overture and some other fully scored movements. Corrette, writing in 1773 about the instrument's early days in France, says that the preferred instrument had four strings tuned *E′–A′–D–G* and was often but not always fretted. Usually, the player in the Opéra orchestra read from a part labelled *basse continue* or *basse générale* shared by other members of the *petit chœur*. However, a few separate *contrebasse* parts have survived. In these, the instrument often plays a simplified version of the bass line, which it doubles variously at the unison and the sub-octave (see the examples below). More surprisingly, perhaps, the instrument is sometimes given the root of the chord while the cellos play the third, or it sustains the bass during more active lines for the cellos. This is an aspect of performance practice to which today's historically informed players have proved generally resistant. *CyrBas, CyrEss, GreDou, GorOrc, SpiZas.*

(a) Rameau, *Les Boréades*, 'Air un peu gai', II, 6

(b) *Zaïs*, Overture, revised version

(c) *Les Fêtes d'Hébé*, 'Bois chéri des amours', I, 1

Corps sonore   At the heart of Rameau's theoretical output was the *corps sonore*, a term for any vibrating string or other 'sonorous body' that generates overtones above its fundamental frequency. Although he had not yet adopted this term in his *Traité de l'harmonie* (1722), Rameau nevertheless used a monochord to show that all the chords that constitute standard harmony were generated from one fundamental sound (the *son fondamentale*). In later treatises he was to argue that the *corps sonore*, which he had now validated not only by mathematical but also by empirical means, was the unique principle of harmony, since it alone engendered all the elements and laws that governed musical practice. So convinced was he of this concept that, towards the end of his life, he began making increasingly exaggerated claims – that the *corps sonore* was the progenitor of all the arts and sciences based on proportions, and that it proved the essential unity of the world and even the existence of God. He may have derived such elements of pantheistic and Deist philosophy from the esotericism increasingly associated with freemasonry* from the mid-century onwards. Interestingly, several of Rameau's operas from the late 1740s onwards introduce representations of the *corps sonore* at moments of enlightenment or revelation: at such points the composer builds up sustained, widely-spaced chords comprising the notes of the harmonic series, to create an effect that Geoffrey Burgess aptly describes as Rameau's 'magic wand'. In the example below, at the point in *Zaïs* where Oromazès and the Spirits of the Elements prepare the denouement, the final bars present notes 1–6, 8, 12 and 16 of the harmonic series in their natural order, except that note 5 (oboe F♯) is transposed up an octave. *BerPyg, BurCor, ChrCor, ChrTho, LesRam, VerMus.*

Rameau, *Zaïs*, IV, 3

Coulé The descending appoggiatura was generally known in France as a *coulé* (spelt 'coulez' in Rameau's table of keyboard ornaments of 1724 reproduced on p. 20). Like the *port de voix**, this ornament is indicated by a curved bracket before the note and, as Rameau's realization shows, was played 'super-legato', the appoggiatura being released only after the resolution was sounded. In his table, the composer indicates only the on-beat resolution, though comparison of parallel passages reveals that a pre-beat interpretation is often required; this is illustrated in the music example in the *cadence** entry, where the explicit rhythmic notation of bar 5 is a guide to the realization of the *coulé* on the last beat of bar 20. This same example illustrates that outside the keyboard context the *coulé* was notated as a grace note (see the final bar of the third extract). *CyrSty, McGSpa, NeuOrn, NeuPer.*

'La Coulicam' The suggestion that the title of this movement from the *Pièces de clavecin en concerts* (1741) was intended as an anagram of *l'ami cocu*, 'the cuckolded friend', has long been discredited. 'Coulicam' is actually a phonetic spelling of Kouli Khan, the name of a Persian sufi-king who featured in the recently published *Histoire de Thamas Kouli-Kan, sophi de Perse* (1740–41) by Jean-Antoine Du Cerceau. It is unlikely that Rameau had read this book; rather, its topical subject was probably suggested by one of the 'persons of taste and skill' who named certain of the pieces in his collection, in which case Rameau spelled it as he heard it pronounced. On one exemplar of the 1752 edition, the title has been altered by hand to read 'La KouliKam', though when and by whom is not clear. Certainly the boisterous *batteries**, including ostentatious hand-crossings, may well have brought to mind the character of this belligerent monarch. *BouHer, BreJeu, GirRam, HerMor, RpeKey.*

Counterpoint of timbres   The term *contrepoint des timbres* was coined by Paul Marie Masson* to denote a kaleidoscopic style of orchestration particularly evident in Rameau's later operas, where different instrumental colours are superimposed and juxtaposed in ever-changing combinations. For instance, in the second section of the overture to *Zaïs*, which represents the disentangling of the four elements (Earth, Air, Fire and Water) from primordial Chaos, each element is characterized by its own thematic motifs and orchestral colours. *MasOpé, SadOrc.*

Couperin, François   Living and working in much the same areas of Paris, Rameau and his great contemporary François Couperin 'le grand' (1668–1733) must surely have crossed paths from time to time; yet there is nothing in their biographies to link them specifically. (François was certainly not the 'Coprin' who competed with Rameau for the post of organist at the church of Saint-Paul* in 1727.) As with Bach and Handel*, it is customary to couple their names together, but we should remember that Couperin was twenty-five years older than Rameau; moreover, the generation gap is exaggerated by the fact that the vast majority of Rameau's output was composed after Couperin's death and belongs to a genre (opera) that the older man never attempted. Even in the keyboard repertory, most of Rameau's harpsichord pieces were written after the bulk of Couperin's were published and they rarely betray much obvious influence. In the wake of Couperin's first book (1713), Rameau did, admittedly, adopt the new fashion for character* pieces, but he continued to show a lively interest in the traditional dance movements. A closer affinity between the two men is seen in their theoretical writings, which reveal a shared interest in *accompagnement** and a desire to inculcate good habits in young players. *See also* **Suite**. *AntFre, ClaCon, FulPor, GirRam, SadCou, TunCou.*

Couplet   In eighteenth-century French keyboard music, the intermediate sections of a rondeau movement were often referred to as *couplets*. Rameau, however, preferred the term *reprise**.

Les Courses de Tempé   One year after his debut at the Paris Opéra, Rameau undertook a final collaboration with Alexis Piron*. *Les Courses de Tempé*, a three-act *pastorale*, was staged at the Comédie-Française on 30 August 1734, to considerable acclaim. Rameau's music was limited to the concluding divertissement*, which comprised a shepherds' chorus, two vocal airs, a duet and *vaudeville**, plus two instrumental movements: a contest between the shepherdesses ('Lutte de bergères') and a 'Danse des bergères'. The marquis d'Argenson* described Rameau's divertissement as 'pretty and well performed'. All that survives of the music is the melodic line of the vocal items, first published in 1776. *ArgNot, ConPir, PirŒu, ProPir, SadPir.*

Crescendo and diminuendo   Rameau indicates gradual increases and decreases in volume by various means. His first opera, *Hippolyte et Aricie*

(1733), and a number of subsequent works make use of an early form of the 'hairpin':  Montéclair* claimed to have invented these symbols, which he recommended to 'M. de Planes' (Giovanni Antonio Piani), who then used them in his *Sonate a violino solo e violoncelle col cimbalo*, published in Paris in 1712. Often, however, Rameau preferred to indicate crescendos and diminuendos by such words or phrases as *enflez**, *en enflant le son*, *adoucissez** or *en adoucissant*. A representation of the rising dawn in *Zaïs* bears the rubric: 'chaque instrument entre ici un temps après l'autre, d'abord doux, puis en enflant insensiblement, jusqu'au plus fort' ('here each instrument enters one after the other, softly at first, then getting imperceptibly louder until they reach *fortissimo*'). Indications of this sort appear often enough in Rameau's output to belie a claim by Chabanon*, in 1772, that 'nuances from soft to loud, continually and gradually applied, are among the refinements of his art that Rameau made little use of'. *See also* **Dynamic marks** *GreSou, MasOpé.*

Croches blanches   This rather misleading term (literally 'white quavers') denotes the style of notation shown below, where crotchets, quavers and shorter values appear with void note-heads and with one or more flags or hooks. Though first developed in England and France during the fifteenth century, this notation fell into disuse in those countries and, by the seventeenth century, was primarily associated with Italy. Re-imported to France in the 1670s by Charpentier*, this notation was initially adopted there mainly by composers with strong Italian sympathies. There is no reason to believe that *croches blanches* had any tempo implications: they were associated almost exclusively with **3/2**, a metre that already indicated a slow tempo. Rameau used this void notation on only one occasion: in the cantata *Orphée*. *ThpCro, TunCou.*

'La Cupis'   Although the Cupis family included the legendary dancer Marie-Anne Cupis, known as Mlle Camargo*, the title of this movement from the *Pièces de clavecin en concerts* (1741) almost certainly refers to one of her brothers, the cellist François *le cadet* (1732–1808) or, more likely, the violinist and composer Jean-Baptiste Cupis *l'aîné* (1711–88). Given that Jean-Baptiste's wife gave birth to a son in the year Rameau's collection appeared, 'La Cupis' may even have been intended as a *berceuse* for Jean-Baptiste *le jeune*, a future cellist; certainly, its tender, rocking movement supports this hypothesis. Rameau included a sumptuous orchestral re-working of the piece, entitled 'Air tendre pour les Muses', as part of a *ballet figuré** in *Le Temple de la Gloire* (1745). *BeaDan, BouHer, GirRam, GusFul, HerMor, LetCam, RpeKey, SadBor, ValTed.*

Cuvillier, Louis-Antoine   The principal *taille** soloist at the Académie Royale de Musique* during the first half of Rameau's operatic career, Cuvillier (d.1752) made his debut there in 1725 and retired in 1750. An official inventory of 1738 describes him as a good actor and musician with a voice 'unique in its class'. For Rameau, Cuvillier created several distinctive roles, among them Arcas, Tisiphone and the 2$^\text{e}$ Parque (*Hippolyte et Aricie*), Adario (*Les Indes galantes*) and Momus (*Les Fêtes d'Hébé*). His son, identified in librettos and press reports as Cuvillier *fils*, sang as a *haute-contre** from 1738 to 1740 and as a *basse-taille* from 1749 to 1755; among his greatest successes was the creation of the role of Soothsayer in Jean-Jacques Rousseau's* *Le Devin du village* in 1752. *BouHer, CamAca, ChaRou, CyrCho, PieCon, SadInv.*

70 **'Les Cyclopes'** The technical *tour de force* in Rameau's *Pièces de clavessin* of 1724 is undoubtedly 'Les Cyclopes', an evocation of the one-eyed giants of classical mythology. The piece may well have been inspired by the Cyclops in Lully's* *Persée* (1682): this opera had recently been revived at the Paris Opéra, in November 1722, and was thus one of the first productions that Rameau, an avid opera-goer, would have seen when he settled in the city that year. In a prefatory essay to the 1724 book, the composer discusses various innovative *batteries**, directing the reader to 'Les Cyclopes' for examples of their use. Domenico Scarlatti* may well have encountered this piece during his visits to Paris in the 1720s: its main theme appears repeatedly in his G major sonata K547, and in half-a-dozen other sonatas he uses the Frenchman's newly-developed left-hand rotation technique. *GirRam, RpeKey, SadSca, YeaAwk.*

Dance songs and choruses The French sometimes apply the term 'danses chantées' to vocal airs or choruses that are based on the music of a ballet movement. Such pieces may be found in the majority of operatic divertissements*, where they are usually performed in alternation with the dance itself, their texts acting as a complement to, and an outgrowth of, the expressive character of the ballet. Many of these songs are straightforward *parodies**, in which words are adapted to the dance melody; in others, however, the thematic material of the dance becomes the starting point for an independent vocal movement. While most dance songs are for one or more solo singers, others may be allotted to the *petit chœur** or the full chorus, sometimes in alternation with soloists. Rameau was fond of reworking pieces from his harpsichord collections as dance songs in his operas – initially, during the Lulliste-Ramiste* dispute, as a way of increasing the popular appeal of these works. The sumptuous reworking of the musette from the 1724 *Pièces de clavessin* as the chorus 'Suivez les lois' (*Les Fêtes d'Hébé*, III, 8) illustrates the variety of vocal scorings employed in movements of this kind. The original rondeau refrain (R) and two *couplets** (C) are adapted thus: R (chorus) + R (duo and chorus) + C¹ (solo) + R (duo) + R (chorus) + C² (solo and duo) + R (duo) + R (chorus). *AntFre, BetCho, CyrHéb, GirRam, HarBal, MasOpé, SadBor.*

Dandrieu, Jean-François As a harpsichord composer, Dandrieu (c.1681–1738) was regarded as second in importance only to Couperin* and Rameau. His only known interaction with the latter, however, was in 1706, when he formed part of the jury that awarded Rameau the organist post at Sainte-Marie-Madeleine-en-la-Cité*. There are nevertheless numerous parallels between their respective keyboard outputs. Both men published their first collections in the first decade of the eighteenth century, then turned to other things before issuing two 'mature' collections at similar dates in the 1720s. In these later publications, moreover, both composers displayed an interest in extended pattern* variations, a genre which is seldom found in earlier eighteenth-century harpsichord music but which flourished in later decades as a result of their example. Both also chose similar character* titles: 'Les Tourbillons', 'L'Indifférente', 'La Timide', 'La Follette'*, 'L'Entretien des Muses' (cf. Dandrieu's 'Le Concert des Muses'). Both also took a close interest in pedagogy, as revealed by Dandrieu's detailed fingerings in his third book (1734) and in Rameau by the extensive preface to his second book (1724), where he discusses keyboard technique. *BouHer, FraDan, GusFul, SadHan.*

Danse basse The adjective 'basse' denotes the traditional style in which the dancer's feet glide along the ground, such dancing being associated with grace, elegance and modest expression. *CahDan, HilDan, MasOpé, NovLet.*

Danse d'action   *See **Ballet figuré***

Danse haute During the early eighteenth century, the traditional *danse basse** was increasingly threatened by the emergence of the *danse haute* – an athletic style of ballet characterized by leaps, pirouettes, entrechats and other virtuoso steps. For many traditionalists, the newer style was considered in bad taste, especially when executed by women; devotees of the *danse haute*, by contrast, saw it as a welcome invigoration of the French dance tradition. Matters came to a head in the late 1720s, when a dispute erupted between the rival partisans of Mlle Sallé* and Mlle Camargo*, prime exponents, respectively, of the old and new dance styles. This wrangle continued in parallel with the Lulliste-Ramiste* dispute and was to some extent interlinked with it, since Rameau's ballet music was seen as providing unprecedented opportunities for the *danse haute*. *CahDan, LanBel, MasOpé.*

Daphnis et Églé This one-act *pastorale héroïque** was scheduled for performance on 30 October 1753 during the court's annual *voyage* to Fontainebleau, as an after-piece to the spoken comedy *La Fausse antipathie* by Nivelle de La Chaussée (1692–1754). However, the opera appears to have been withdrawn from the schedule because of negative reactions to the previous day's dress rehearsal. The decision to cancel the production was taken largely in response to the generally poor performing standards which bedevilled the entertainments during the 1753 *voyage* and which are believed to have prompted Rebel* and Francœur's resignation as directors of the Académie Royale de Musique* the following month. Collé's* libretto was also criticized as lacking in dramatic interest, and Élie Fréron recounts that Rameau himself was 'given a good dressing down' ('celui-ci a eu la tête lavée') by the duc de Richelieu*, the official in charge of court entertainments. *Daphnis et Églé* remained unperformed in the eighteenth century, though the semi-public dress rehearsal on 29 October 1753 is sometimes regarded as the work's *de facto* premiere. Rameau's autograph score survives, as does the original set of parts copied for the Fontainebleau production. *BouHer, ChaRou, ColJou, GirRam, GreTra, GreSou, KocDap, MasOpé, RicFon.*

Daquin, Louis-Claude In a competition for the organist post at the church of Saint-Paul* in 1727, Rameau was beaten by Daquin (1694–1772), previously organist at the monastery known as the Petit Saint-Antoine. Daquin had been a child prodigy: at the age of six he played the harpsichord to Louis XIV; two years later he conducted his own *Beatus vir* at the Sainte-Chapelle. He was also regarded as the best improviser of his generation. Rameau harboured no resentment against Daquin after his defeat: during a conversation with Balbastre* in later life, he praised his former rival as the only composer to resist the current decline in taste: 'he has always preserved for the organ the majesty and the graces that befit it'. Daquin's son, the writer Pierre-Louis d'Aquin de Château-Lyon (1720–?96), championed Rameau during the Querelle des Bouffons*, devoting a whole chapter of his *Siècle littéraire de Louis XV, ou Lettres sur les hommes célèbres* (1754) to a eulogy of his music. *AquSiè, BreJeu, GirRam, GusFul, MarÉlo, QuiJeu, SgaDic.*

Dardanus The first performance of Rameau's fifth opera took place at the Académie Royale de Musique* on 19 November 1739. Appearing at the height of the long-running Lulliste-Ramiste* dispute, *Dardanus* sharply divided opinion. Even before the premiere, the rival views of those who had attended rehearsals* circulated in *nouvelles à la main** and in private correspondence, while the Ramoneurs* had to counter an attempted cabal on the part of the Lullistes. Despite a respectable first run of twenty-six performances, *Dardanus* was harshly criticized for various absurdities in the libretto and for the Act IV *sommeil** in which the principal melody reminded irreverent listeners of the nursery rhyme 'Do do, l'enfant do'*. The opera was said to be so full of music that for three hours the orchestral musicians scarcely had time to sneeze. Yet in purely musical terms this version of the opera is one of Rameau's most inspired creations, encompassing the widest emotional range of all his works. Unfortunately, the dramatic momentum generated by the plot is too often impeded by ill-motivated twists and turns. The response of Rameau and his librettist La Bruère* to such criticism was characteristically drastic. For the 1744 revival they undertook a thorough-going revision, and only the prologue and first two acts remained recognizably the same. The remaining three acts were largely rewritten, to the extent that they have an entirely new plot with fewer supernatural interventions. Rameau could describe this version, with little exaggeration, as a 'nouvelle tragédie' on the title page of the 1744 engraved score. Compared with the original, this version excited little comment, though the figure of twenty-two performances suggests only modest success. Revived again in 1760 with further, if less drastic changes, *Dardanus* proved to be a triumph: it was widely acclaimed as one of Rameau's finest achievements and remained in the Opéra repertory until 1771. La Bruère's libretto, adapted by Nicolas-François Guillard, was reset by Sacchini in 1784. *BouHer, BucSup, DacDar, DavHer, DilMon, GirRam, GirTra, GorSet, GreSou, LalDar, LegVoi, MalDar, PitDar, VerDra, WooSad.*

'La Dauphine' In 1777 Claude-François Rameau* sent Decroix* various items he had inherited from his father, including an autograph manuscript of this harpsichord piece. Although Claude-François listed 'La Dauphine' among the items to be returned, the autograph survives in the Decroix collection, along with two copies made by Decroix's scribe. One of the latter bears the annotation 'Pièce composée pour madame La Dauphine, mère de Louis XVI'. From this slender evidence, Charles Malherbe* concluded that the movement was improvised on the occasion of the marriage in 1747 of Louis (1729–65), Dauphin of France, to Maria-Josepha of Saxony (1731–67). While any such link with the royal wedding is pure conjecture, there is no reason to doubt that Rameau wrote the piece for this particular Dauphine, who was the dedicatee of keyboard publications by Jean-Baptiste Forqueray and Jean-Baptiste Cardonne (1730–after 1792), and was herself a skilled harpsichord player. That Rameau intended it as a gift is suggested by the nature of a further source – one that has given rise to some misunderstanding. In his 1958 edition of Rameau's keyboard music, Erwin Jacobi* included a facsimile of another autograph of 'La Dauphine', which was then located in the Bibliothèque Nationale de France, but has since disappeared. Although Jacobi initially accepted this source as genuine, he later considered it 'a skilfully prepared master-copy of the unique autograph which is in the Decroix collection'. Jacobi's opinion has been accepted by subsequent editors of Rameau's keyboard works. However, Thomas Green has shown that this manuscript is without doubt a second autograph, copied directly from the first. The calligraphic nature of the copy and the fact that it bears Rameau's own signature – the only one of his music manuscripts to do so – suggest that it was the actual copy presented to Her Royal Highness. Assuming it was written no earlier than 1747, 'La Dauphine' post-dates Rameau's four keyboard collections. *BouHer, CyrSty, GreSou, GusFul, JacPiè, MalPiè, SadLet, SchFam.*

Dauvergne, Antoine   *See* **Pupils**

'De la méchanique des doigts sur le clavessin'   This important essay, included in the preface to the first edition of Rameau's *Pièces de clavessin* (1724), is described on the title page as 'a method [...] by which are taught the means to achieve a perfect execution on this instrument'. It provides sound advice, applicable to organ as well as harpsichord, on such matters as posture, hand position, fingering, economy of movement, independence of the fingers and smoothness of execution. Rameau stresses the importance of practising with separate hands and of executing *tremblements* or *cadences** with 'light and brisk' movements. He also distinguishes between *roulements** and *batteries**. This essay was omitted from subsequent editions, as the composer was already working on 'a complete system of harpsichord finger technique'. Yet although he was to discuss certain aspects of keyboard technique in his *Dissertation sur les différentes métodes d'accompagnment pour le clavecin, ou l'orgue* (1732) and *Code de musique pratique* (1760), the promised 'complete system' never materialized. *RamCtw, RpeKey.*

Débité   It was generally agreed that recitative in Rameau's day was executed less rapidly than it had been in Lully's*. If the theorist De Rochement is to be believed, the women were more to blame for this than the men: writing in 1754, he maintained that 'most of our female singers do not declaim [*débitent*] at all: they merely sing'. Yet it is clear that Rameau himself wished to keep the recitative moving where appropriate. In his production* scores and in performing parts used by the singers themselves, the recitative is frequently marked 'débité'; this, as Jean-Jacques Rousseau explains, indicated that the singer should speed up the tempo ('presser le mouvement') in order to render the words in a speech-like manner. Rameau's scores also include the direction 'plus débité' and, in one case, 'scène débitée vivement sans agréments' ('scene delivered rapidly without ornaments', *Les Paladins*, II, 2). *CyrEss, CyrSin, GreSou, MasOpé, McGSpa, RouDic.*

Debussy, Claude Achille   In 1903 Debussy attended an open-air performance by the Schola Cantorum of *La Guirlande*, the first Rameau opera to be revived since the eighteenth century. This experience is said to have prompted Debussy's famous war cry: 'Vive Rameau, à bas Gluck', a characteristically forthright expression of his view that French taste had been corrupted by exposure to the Germanic musical tradition. In subsequent writings Debussy vaunted Rameau as a model of French musical purity. First-hand exposure to

La Guirlande and later to *Castor et Pollux* and *Hippolyte et Aricie* helped clarify his notion of what constituted Frenchness in music – clarity, elegance, simple and natural declamation, and especially the 'desire to please'. Pollux's air 'Nature, Amour' (*Castor*, II, 1), which he heard in 1903, struck him as so personal in character and so novel in construction that Rameau seemed almost a contemporary whom one could go up to and congratulate after the performance. Even so, Debussy's *Hommage à Rameau*, published two years later in the first set of *Images*, reveals no discernable influence of eighteenth-century music other than in being a sarabande. In 1908 Debussy edited *Les Fêtes de Polymnie* as part of the Rameau *Œuvres complètes**; he reportedly did not enjoy the editing experience, however, and farmed out some of the work to a young pianist, Francisco de Lacerda. *DubVan, EllEar, GirRam, MasOpé, SusDeb.*

Decorated harpsichord lids   The apotheosis of Rameau is depicted on a number of surviving harpsichord lids, all apparently painted during the 1760s. The instruments include Balbastre's* harpsichord, another by Donzelague* dating from 1716 but repainted after Rameau's death, and a third formerly in the Cailleux* collection. *GétHer, GétPor, LibPor.*

Decroix, Jacques-Joseph-Marie   Our knowledge of Rameau's music would be immeasurably poorer were it not for the 27-volume collection of his works assembled by Decroix (1746–1826), a native of Lille. In addition to holding high-ranking legal and financial appointments in this city, Decroix also followed a literary career as co-author of the tragedy *Almanzor* (1771) and co-editor of the Kehl edition of Voltaire's* works. Though only eighteen when Rameau died, he developed a burning enthusiasm for every aspect of the composer's musical output. By 1776 he had amassed sufficient materials to propose that the young Louis XVI, no less, should commission a complete Rameau edition. Although this proposal fell on deaf ears, Decroix went to considerable lengths to locate reliable source materials. A number of 'shopping lists' in his hand itemize specific movements or performing parts that he wished to locate. He gained access to authoritative sources and maintained a lengthy correspondence with the composer's son Claude-François*, who lent him a number of Rameau's scores and other materials, some of them autograph. Decroix's collection, which was donated to the Bibliothèque Nationale de France by his heirs in 1843, is of particular value in conserving inner choral and orchestral parts, often lacking in other sources. It also preserves variants and passages that had been rejected when a work was revised. Decroix himself had numerous Rameau scores copied, some in his own hand, but he also acquired reliable manuscripts, notably a set of ten full scores recently identified as being in the hand of Bergiron* du Fort-Michon. His book *L'Ami de arts* (1776), mainly devoted to a spirited defence of Voltaire and Rameau, is invaluable for its biographical details, as is his 'Rameau' entry in the *Biographie Michaud* (1824); the autograph manuscript of the latter discovered by Herbert Schneider includes many passages of interest omitted in the published version. *BouDen, BouHer, DecAmi, DecBio, HerMot, LebDec, LebFon, SadLet, SadZo1, SchFam, WolŒu.*

Dedications   Apart from a few years under the protection of the prince de Carignan*, Rameau seems to have shied away from aristocratic patronage*. His first theoretical work, *Traité de l'harmonie* (1722), proudly bears the dedication

'Au Public'. *Génération harmonique* (1737) and *Démonstration du principe de l'harmonie* (1750) are dedicated respectively to the Académie Royale des Sciences* and to the comte d'Argenson*, an honorary member of this academy and dedicatee of Diderot* and d'Alembert's* *Encyclopédie*. The published scores of the vast majority of his compositions include no dedication. One exception is *Les Fêtes d'Hébé* (1739), dedicated to 'S[on] A[ltesse] S[érénissime] Madame la Duchesse Douairière', probably Louise Françoise de Bourbon (1673–1743), widow of Louis III de Bourbon-Condé. Rameau thanks the duchess for 'the protection with which your Most Serene Highness has honoured my earliest works', though what this protection entailed is not revealed. *BouHer, RamCtw, SadPat, WisVer.*

Dehesse, Jean-Baptiste François An actor, dancer and one of the most inventive choreographers of his time, Dehesse (1705–79) was ballet master at the Théâtre-Italien* from 1738 until 1757. He was an influential advocate and exponent of *pantomime**, eschewing allegorical subjects in favour of believable narratives derived from everyday life. Between 1747 and 1751 he directed the ballets in works staged at Madame de Pompadour's Théâtre des Petits Cabinets*, among them those for Rameau's *Les Surprises de l'Amour*. *BouHer, ChaRou, LecDeh, WaeGes.*

Delafosse, Jean Charles Among rejected* portraits of Rameau is one engraved by Delafosse (1734–89) after Carmontelle* and bearing the inscription 'Rameau'. A later hand has added 'Lambert', and the sitter has indeed been identified as M. de Saint-Lambert, portrayed in a Carmontelle watercolour dated 1760 now in the Musée Condé at Chantilly. *ChlCar, GétPor.*

Delatour Although the title role of *Platée* is firmly associated with Pierre Jéliote*, who is famously portrayed in this *travesti* part by Charles-Antoine Coypel (1694–1752), this singer took part in only a single performance of the work: at the royal court in 1745. Once the opera had been transferred to the Académie Royale de Musique* in 1749, it was Delatour (d. after 1786) who took over the role, both in that production and in the 1754 revival. Throughout his career at the Académie, from 1740 until his retirement in 1756, Delatour had been overshadowed by Jéliote*, yet he seems to have found his niche in portraying this vain marsh nymph. (Indeed, Jéliote may have preferred not to appear before the Paris public in this unflattering guise.) *BarPla, BouHer.*

Démonstration du principe de l'harmonie On 19 November 1749 Rameau presented a lecture to the Académie Royale des Sciences* entitled 'Mémoire ou l'on expose les fondemens du système de musique théorique et pratique'. In the preparation of this, he had the assistance of Denis Diderot*, as a way of increasing his chances of gaining the academy's approbation. The 'Mémoire' survives in two different manuscripts, the first a fair copy of the lecture, the second a heavily revised version evidently incorporating technical material originally distributed as a hand-out. This later version was to become the basis of the *Démonstration du principe de l'harmonie*, published the following year. By then, the work had received the Académie's approval, thanks to an enthusiastic report by d'Alembert* and others. As a consequence of Diderot's assistance, the *Démonstration* is generally agreed to be the best-written of Rameau's theoretical works. It belongs to the sub-group of exclusively theoretical writings, its main aim being to demonstrate that the *corps sonore** represents the unique principle of music. Some of Rameau's material – including the use of the word 'démonstration' (proof), to which d'Alembert was later to take exception – appears to have been slipped in by the author after the text had received the Académie's approval. By now, Rameau had altered his view on the subdominant, which he explains as a product of musical experience rather than as a natural phenomenon. The treatise includes a renewed discussion of tuning systems, in which Rameau's preference for equal temperament* becomes clear. *See also* **Publishers; Royal Society.** *BriDem, ChrTho, CohAca, DigDém, RamCtw, VerMus.*

Denoyé, Jacques Antoine   Simple *contrafacta** apart, the tradition of reworking secular polyphonic pieces as sacred ones seems not to have interested French composers during the first half of the eighteenth century. Even in the second half, examples are relatively few: the best-known is probably Michel Corrette's adaptation of Vivaldi's* concerto *La primavera* as a *motet** *à grand chœur, Laudate Dominum* (1766). All the more surprising, then, that a recently discovered *Messe à grand chœur et symphonie* by Jacques Antoine Denoyé derives much of its thematic material from Rameau's secular music, which is treated with immense skill and imagination. We know little about Denoyé (he died in Strasbourg in 1759, where he had been a cathedral musician for about ten years), but he had clearly soaked himself in the Ramellian idiom to the extent that he could effortlessly manufacture new Rameau – and good Rameau, at that. The work is in effect a parody Mass, complete with a motto or head-motif drawn from the keyboard pieces 'Les Tendres Plaintes' and 'La Cupis'. From time to time Denoyé weaves further borrowings seamlessly into his own music, which is distinctive but stylistically complementary. Anyone who enjoys the game of 'spot the tune' will enjoy this challenge. *See also* **Requiem** *GesHom.*

Deshayes, Catherine-Thérèse Boutinon   Rameau's long association with the financier La Pouplinière* probably owes its origins to Thérèse Deshayes (1714–56). Grand-daughter of the playwright Florent Dancourt and daughter of the renowned actress Mimi Dancourt, she was one of Rameau's most talented pupils*, studying both harpsichord and music theory. In about 1734 she moved in with La Pouplinière, first as mistress and then as wife; it was doubtless she who persuaded her beloved teacher to transfer his allegiance from the prince de Carignan* to the La Pouplinière household in or around 1736. As an ardent champion of Rameau's music and theoretical writings, Thérèse ensured that her residence became 'a citadel of *ramisme*' (Cucuel) during the Lulliste-Ramiste* dispute. In 1737 she published a 14-page review in *Le Pour et contre* of Rameau's *Génération harmonique**, which reveals a thorough understanding of its significance. (Maret* wrongly believed this review to be by Madame de Saint-Maur, another Rameau pupil.) In 1740 Thérèse acted as godmother to Rameau's third child, Alexandre, named after her husband. Her marriage ended in 1748 in bizarre circumstances. Thereafter, Rameau's association with La Pouplinière became increasingly difficult, and he and his wife left the financier's household in 1753. *CucPou, DouRam, GirRam, MarÉlo, RamCtw, SadPat.*

Dessus   The treble member of each family of instruments was known in France as the *dessus*; hence the violin, strictly speaking, was the *dessus de violon*, though by the eighteenth century this term was usually shortened to *violon*. In the vocal context the French made little distinction between voice-types. The top choral line in operas and motets was generally an all-purpose *dessus* with a relatively limited compass, usually in the range *d'–a''*. Most solo roles in Rameau's early operas also fall within this range, though in later operas the highest note extends to *b''♭* or very occasionally higher. *CyrCho, RouDic.*

Destouches, André Cardinal One of the most talented and successful opera composers of the period between Lully* and Rameau, Destouches (1672–1749) also played a major role in the administration of the Académie Royale de Musique*. In 1713 he was appointed by Louis XIV to a newly-created post of *inspecteur général* to re-establish order at the Académie; the two sets of *règlements* drawn up under his authority in 1713 and 1714 were still officially in force during Rameau's operatic career. Destouches's extensive correspondence with prince Antoine I of Monaco from 1709 until after his retirement in 1730 provides precious insights into the running of a chronically debt-laden company and the challenges presented by insubordinate and temperamental performers. *DurAca, RosDes, TesCor, WooLul, WooSad.*

Deus noster refugium Soon after its establishment in 1713, the Académie des Beaux-Arts in Lyon* acquired a score and a set of fourteen parts of this *motet* *à grand chœur*, these being entered as no. 11 in the Académie's chronological inventory. The motet, a setting of Psalm 68, is thus believed to date from Rameau's years in Lyon between the summer of 1712 and March 1715. Although these Lyon sources are now lost, the work survives in two manuscripts in the Decroix* collection copied in the late 1770s, probably from material provided by the composer's son Claude-François Rameau*. The passage 'mota est in terra' includes Rameau's earliest surviving use of slurred* tremolo. In the final *récit*, 'Vacate et videte', the staves intended for the solo singer remain blank: as one of Decroix's scribes notes, this part was lacking in his source, which presumably consisted of separate part-books. *DurMot, DurRel, HerMot, MalMot, ValAca, ValLyo.*

Dialogue entre Lulli, Rameau et Orphée dans les Champs Elisées Published in 1774, this anonymous pamphlet has been attributed to Pierre Louis Moline (1740–1820) and, less plausibly, to Marmontel*. Despite its title, the pamphlet is a eulogy of the music of Gluck, thus illustrating the speed with which this Bohemian composer's operas, once they reached Paris, eclipsed those of his French predecessors. The text presents a dialogue between Lully* and Rameau, each of whom vaunts his own operatic style and disparages the other's. Orpheus, praising the superior achievements of Gluck, tells them that they must abandon the old rules if their works are to match Gluck's mastery and force of expression. The book's frontispiece shows Lully and Rameau in Elysium; Orpheus stands in front of them holding the score of Gluck's opera *Iphigénie en Aulide*. The depiction of Rameau is copied from the bust by Caffieri*, while that of Lully is modelled on the bronze attributed to Jean Collignon on the composer's tomb in the church of Notre-Dame des Victoires, Paris. *BarMus, GétPor, LagLul, MasOpé.*

Diane et Actéon An appendix to the third volume of the Rameau *Œuvres complètes* * includes a cantata with this title, transcribed from a manuscript said to have been in Rameau's papers at the time of his death. The work is actually by Joseph Bodin de Boismortier, first published as an independent cantata in 1732 with the title *Actéon*. *MalCan, MonCan, TunCan.*

Diatonique-enharmonique   *see* 'L'Enharmonique'

Diderot, Denis   Like most of his fellow *philosophes*, Diderot (1713–84) was an enthusiastic champion of Rameau, at least in his earlier years. One chapter of his novel *Les Bijoux indiscrets* (1748) gives an amusing account of the Lulliste-Ramiste* dispute in which the rival merits of 'Utmiutsol' (Lully) and 'Utremifasollasiututut' (Rameau) are compared; despite a veneer of even-handedness, Diderot's sympathies are clearly with the latter. Moreover, it was he who suggested the idea of bringing Rameau's theories to a wider public by publishing them in more accessible prose, a challenge first taken up by d'Alembert* in 1752; Diderot himself had already helped Rameau with the drafting of the manuscript 'Mémoire' that became the basis of *Démonstration du principe de l'harmonie* (1750), acknowledged as one of Rameau's most readable theoretical works. As co-editor of the *Encyclopédie*, Diderot invited the composer to contribute all the articles on music and must have been disappointed when his invitation was declined. However, the publication of Rameau's vehement attacks in *Erreurs sur la musique dans l'Encyclopédie* (1755) and related pamphlets led to an irretrievable breakdown in the relationship between the two men. Furthermore, Diderot could not accept what he described as the 'visionary gibberish and apocalyptic truths' in Rameau's final writings. The extent to which the attitude of the great French *philosophe* had changed towards his former friend may be judged from the malevolent, if fictitious, portrait of the composer in Diderot's novel *Le Neveu de Rameau*. *See also* **Rameau, Jean-François.** *BazDid, ChrDid, ChoPré, ChrTho, CohAca, DidLum, KafEnc, MasLul, PapDid, ThmDid, VerMus.*

Dijon   Rameau's native city was no backwater: at the time of his birth it enjoyed a rich musical and intellectual life. The collegiate church of Saint-Étienne, where Rameau's father was sometime organist, could evidently muster the forces to perform the elaborate Vespers for two choirs and orchestra by Pierre Menault (1642–94), *maître de chapelle* there from 1687, and this was not the only city church with an active choir school. At that time the town had no municipal theatre, though the Opéra de Lyon, whose repertoire included works by Lully*, Campra* and Desmarets, had a licence to tour its productions to other towns, Dijon among them. Moreover, the Collège des Godrans*, the Jesuit secondary school that Rameau attended, put on didactic productions which featured music and dance. Dijon was unusual for this period in showing a lively interest in Italian music. The tradition was evidently initiated by the parliamentarian Monsieur de Malteste (d. 1690), who organized concerts that included extracts from Venetian opera; it continued with Claude Nicaise (1623–1701), canon at the cathedral, whose taste for Italian music is revealed in his correspondence with other scholars, notably René Ouvrard. Nicaise had spent some time in Italy, as had Rameau's godfather Jean-Baptiste Lantin de Montagny, a Burgundian parliamentarian who organized a local academy of intellectuals. Rameau's youthful journey to Milan* may well have been stimulated by contact with such men. *See also* **Académie de Sciences, Arts et Belles-Lettres de Dijon.** *BreJeu, DouMus, EllDij, GarOrg, GirAut, GirRam, HénIdé, KocSer, PaqAsp, PisPar, QuiJeu, ZasApp.*

Diligam te, Domine   A score of Rameau motets in the Decroix* collection bears a note claiming that Rameau had 'also composed the motet *Diligam te*'. A setting of this psalm survives in a manuscript originating from the

Concert Spirituel*, but with the name of its composer torn off, and by the end of the eighteenth century the motet had been catalogued as anonymous. At some later stage the name 'Rameau' was added, and this attribution was accepted, with some reservation, when the work was published in the *Œuvres complètes*. On stylistic grounds, however, the attribution must be considered erroneous. *BouHer, LebFon.*

Dissertation sur les différentes métodes [sic] ***d'accompagnement***   Published by Boivin and Leclair in 1732, the *Dissertation sur les différentes métodes d'accompagnement pour le clavecin, ou pour l'orgue* was the first of Rameau's treatises to adopt an almost entirely practical approach; indeed, he announced that his method could be used 'even by those who cannot read music'. As early as 1724, in the preface to his *Pièces de clavessin*, the composer had stated his intention of publishing a complete system of harpsichord fingering that would be of particular value in 'accompagnement'* (continuo playing), and he had evidently prepared this by the start of his controversy with a 'second musician', possibly Montéclair*, in 1729. In the *Dissertation* Rameau criticizes the traditional manner of figuring the bass as being too complicated, and he proposes a drastic simplification, reducing the number of symbols from more than thirty to a mere seven. He also sets out a new method of connecting chords, whereby the right hand remains in a closed position and moves whenever possible in stepwise contrary motion, without use of the thumb. Yet although this method was admired by Jean-Jacques Rousseau*, it never caught on, and Rameau himself made no use of it in his autograph or published scores. Although he contemplated issuing a fundamentally revised version of the system, this never materialized. *See also* **Privileges**; **Publishers**. *ChrBas, ChrTho, HayNou, LesRam, RamCtw.*

Divertissement   For the fabulist Jean de La Bruyère (1645–96), the essential characteristic of French opera was not so much to plumb the depths of human experience as 'to hold the spirit, the eyes and the ears in an equal enchantment' (*Les Caractères*, 1688). This was a view echoed in the eighteenth century to justify the mixture of drama, spectacle, singing and dancing. To accommodate the competing demands of these and other elements, the French adopted from the outset a convention whereby the dramatic action would give way at some point in each act to a divertissement or *fête*, often signalled by an *annonce*. Whereas the *scènes d'action** unfolded predominantly in recitative, the divertissements comprised *ariettes**, dance* songs, choruses, extensive ballet sequences and stage spectacle, all integrated into continuous sequences occupying up to a third or even a half of each act. Far from being irrelevant distractions, well-managed divertissements could contribute to the drama in various ways. Quite apart from supplying the necessary spectacle (a peace-pipe ceremony in *Les Indes galantes*, IV; an athletics contest in *Naïs*, I; an occult ritual in *Zoroastre*, IV; a torture scene in *Les Boréades*, V), the divertissement could enhance a character's psychological profile, as when Pollux resists the alluring Celestial Pleasures in his resolve to rescue his brother (*Castor et Pollux*, II). Divertissements could generate an element of dramatic irony, as in *Hippolyte et Aricie* (Act III), where the audience knows that Theseus cannot vent his tortured emotions because of the unexpected arrival of his subjects to give thanks to Neptune for his safe return. The acts or entrées* of lighter genres such as *opéra-ballet** or *ballet héroïque** might even include two separate divertissements, the first a preparation for some major plot-development, the second a celebration of the happy outcome. In *Pigmalion**, the first divertissement occurs when the sculptor's beloved statue comes to life and must therefore be taught how to move, thus occasioning a 'pattern-book' of dance steps. The divertissement could also prepare what Aristotle calls *peripateia* (peripeties) – unexpected reversals of fortune, exemplified in *Les Fêtes de l'Hymen et de l'Amour* (Act II), when a sacrificial ceremony is interrupted by the overflowing Nile. Even so, *divertissements* only rarely include contributions from the principal characters and, in that sense, tend to be dramatically static; indeed, this is typically reflected in a work's modulatory character, which will be in a state of flux in the *scènes d'action** but anchored to one prevailing tonality in the divertissements. *AntFre, HarBal, MasOpé, NauDra.*

'Do do, l'enfant do'   During the Lulliste-Ramiste* dispute, the opera *Dardanus* came under particularly fierce attack from Rameau's detractors. Among their weapons was a series of satirical* engravings, two of which singled out the Act IV 'Entrée des Songes' (Dreams). This ballet sequence, with its *parodie** 'Par un sommeil agréable', had been vaunted by the Ramistes as superior to the renowned *sommeil** in Lully's *Atys*. An engraving reproduced by La Laurencie shows Dardanus asleep on the Gorgons' anvil. He is wrapped in swaddling clothes made of strips of music paper on which appear quotations from Rameau's harpsichord pieces – an allusion to the re-use of 'Les Niais de Sologne' and other borrowings in this opera. A further engraving depicts him in a cradle, surrounded by Ramoneurs* who rock him to sleep with the nursery rhyme 'Do do, l'enfant do'. The resemblance between this popular melody and Rameau's *sommeil* is mocked in *Dardanus*, a *parodie* by Favart and others, premiered at the Théâtre-Italien* on 14 January 1740 during the first run of Rameau's opera. The example below shows the final bars of Rameau's chorus and their equivalent in the *parodie*, together with the melody of 'Do, do, l'enfant do' – itself derived from François Couperin's 'Le Dodo ou L'Amour au berceau' (*Pièces de clavecin*, Book Three, 1722). When Rameau reworked *Dardanus* for the 1744 revival, he cut the entire scene – a decision which Favart later claimed was as a direct result of his *parodie*. *ClaCon, DacDar, DavHer, GétSat, LauRam, LauGen, LegVau, LegVoi, MalDar.*

(a) Rameau, *Dardanus*, 'Par un sommeil agréable', IV, 2

(b) Favart, Panard, Parmentier, *Dardanus*, sc. 13

(c) 'Do, do, l'enfant do'

Donzelague, Pierre The lid of a harpsichord made in 1716 by Donzelague (1668–c.1750) and now in the Musée Lyonnais des Arts Décoratifs, Lyon, was redecorated after Rameau's death to represent his apotheosis. A large medallion of the composer is mounted on an obelisk and crowned with a laurel branch (= *rameau*) by two cherubs. Other cherubs carry smaller medallions, said to represent Lully*, Corelli, François Couperin*, Handel*, Mondonville* and Boccherini. The medallion of Rameau, though painted in gold, is a careful copy of a terra cotta medallion by Dominique Chassel (d.1767), which in turn appears to have been copied from the etching of the composer by Saint-Aubin* issued in 1762. The presence of Boccherini among the above composers represented suggests a late date, since his music was not publicly performed in Lyon before 1767. The identity of the decorator is not known. *GétHer, GétPor.*

Double In the early eighteenth-century French keyboard repertory, individual pieces were often supplied with a single decorative *double*, or variation. However, only one of the sixteen harpsichord collections published between 1699 and 1722 includes pieces with more than one *double*. In the period 1724–30, by contrast, Rameau and Jean-François Dandrieu* between them produced no fewer than eight sets of extended pattern-variations*, thus stimulating a renewed French interest in this genre. The technical demands of Rameau's *doubles* are such that he felt it necessary to assure the reader that any which proved too difficult could be omitted (*Pièces de clavessin*, preface). Several later manuscript sources include additional *doubles* for 'Les Niais de Sologne' and the Gavotte with six *doubles*, as well as for such pieces as 'Les Cyclopes', 'Les Sauvages' and 'Les Triolets' which were not originally supplied with *doubles*; these added variations are not generally thought to be by Rameau himself, although this has never been definitely established. *BouHer, GusFul, SadHan.*

Doublé In his table of keyboard ornaments of 1724 (reproduced on p. 20) Rameau uses the term *doublé* to signify the ornament nowadays known as a turn, for which he employs the modern symbol (∼). Outside the keyboard repertoire he prefers to indicate the turn either with grace-notes or by writing it out in measured notation. *See also* **Double cadence.** *HerMor, NeuOrn.*

Double cadence Rameau's table of keyboard ornaments of 1724 (see the reproduction on p. 20) shows the *double cadence* as an unprepared upper-note trill with a two-note suffix or termination. The symbol for this occurs only in his harpsichord pieces; in his other music the composer indicates the termination of a trill with a pair of grace notes or full-sized notes. The adjective 'double' stems from the fact that the trill effectively ends with a turn, for which the composer's preferred term was *doublé**. *NeuOrn, NeuPer.*

Double clefs In movements requiring transposing instruments such as clarinets* and orchestral horns*, Rameau occasionally uses a system of double clefs. The example overleaf from *Acante et Céphise* is in D major, as is clear from the violin and bass parts on the lowest two staves. The clarinets, however, are in A, where a written C produces the sounding pitch A. Their parts must thus be written a minor third higher throughout, in F major, in order to sound in D major – hence the one-flat signature of the initial clef on the top staff. The horns, meanwhile, are in D, where a written C produces the note D, so their part must be written a whole tone lower – hence the 'open' C major signature of the first clef on the second staff. Presumably the individual orchestral parts for these players were written out in those keys. But in mid-eighteenth-century France the concept of transposing instruments would still have been unfamiliar to many music-lovers. For those purchasing this engraved score, therefore, Rameau supplied a second clef and a D major signature in each case. In so doing, he made explicit a score-reading technique subsequently taught to generations of music students, in which the player mentally supplies the appropriate clef and key signature while reading the transposed staves. *See also* **Andante.** *BouPri, FajAca.*

Rameau, *Acante et Céphise*, 1751 (Paris, Bibliothèque Nationale de France, Département de la Musique, Rés. Vm². 119), Act II scene 6, p. 80. Reproduced by permission.

Double emploi   Rameau considered that in certain circumstances a chord could have two roots. Thus in C major, the chord F, A, C, D could be interpreted either as a subdominant chord with an added sixth, if the D resolved upwards, or the first inversion of a seventh chord on D, if the C resolved downwards. This concept, first exposed in *Nouveau système de musique théorique* and elaborated in *Génération harmonique*, proved controversial. It nevertheless reveals Rameau's practical grasp of how the implications of chord progressions are differently perceived according to their contexts. *ChrTho, LesRam, LesThe, RamCtw.*

Ducharger, Jean-Jacques   When Rameau was finalizing the text of his *Observations sur notre instinct pour la musique*, he received a letter from a little-known provincial, 'Ducharger of Dijon', pointing out that his compositions did not always observe the principles set out in his theoretical writings. Rameau evidently promised the writer that such matters would be addressed in a forthcoming treatise. When Ducharger enquired when this would appear, he received the following reply (13 June 1754), brusque to the point of rudeness but not untypical of Rameau's correspondence in his last decade: 'Sir, the book in question is now in print. It is entitled *Observations sur notre instinct pour la musique*. I have neither time nor health to think or to reflect. Forgive me, sir, I am old, you are young, and I am your very humble and very obedient servant, RAMEAU.' The *Observations* include an unflattering dismissal of Ducharger's objections, without mentioning him by name. Stung by this, Ducharger published Rameau's letter in his *Réflexions sur divers ouvrages* *de M.ʳ Rameau* (Rennes, 1761), which also includes some sharp criticism of aspects of his music theory. Ducharger is otherwise remembered only for an amusing and informative account of concerts in his native Dijon*, *Entretien d'un musician françois avec un gentilhomme russe* (1773). ChrTho, DucRéf, LauDoc, GirRam, HénIdé, TalHab.

Dumoulin brothers   Few personal details are known about the three Dumoulin brothers, distinguished dancers at the Académie Royale de Musique* during the first half of the eighteenth century. Each enjoyed a career lasting well over forty years: François Dumoulin entered the Académie in 1700 and retired in 1748, while his younger brothers Pierre and David both entered in 1705, retiring respectively in 1748 and 1751. They were thus all active during much of Rameau's operatic career and created many roles in his operas. David Dumoulin was generally considered the most accomplished of the three: where his brothers were often allotted character roles, he was chosen for important solo entrées* and as a partner for such stars as Blondy*, Dupré*, Camargo* and Sallé*. Their half-brother Henri Dumoulin, a member of the Académie since 1695, retired in 1730. BouHer, ChsInt, FaiSty, SadDan.

Duphly, Jacques   Towards the end of his life Duphly (1715–89) had faded into such total obscurity that it was necessary to enquire in the press what had become of him. In his prime, however, he had been a renowned keyboard player and, according to Marpurg*, harpsichord teacher to 'the leading families'. Duphly's four volumes of *pièces de clavecin*, issued between 1744 and 1768, reveal a composer of refinement and sensibility. The second volume (1746) was reprinted by the London publisher Walsh* in 1764 alongside an edition of Rameau's *Pièces de clavessin* of 1724. He and Rameau occasionally chose the same subjects to portray, as in 'La Boucon'* and 'La Forqueray'*. At times, his idiom comes close enough to the older composer's for Saint-Saëns* to have included in the Rameau *Œuvres complètes* five unattributed pieces ('L'Orageuse', 'La Vanloo', 'La Victoire', 'La Villeroy' and a pair of menuets) that have since been identified as Duphly's. The composer presented his pupil Lord Fitzwilliam* with exemplars of all four of his harpsichord collections; the second includes manuscript instructions on keyboard fingering, signed 'Duphly', that were later praised in Jean-Jacques Rousseau's* *Dictionnaire de musique*; it turns out, however, that these were largely copied from Rameau's instructions in the 1724 *Pièces de clavessin*. CudFit, GusFul, LauDoc, MalPiè, MarHis, RouDic.

Duport   During preparations for *La Princesse de Navarre* in 1744, the duc de Richelieu*, who was in charge of the royal wedding preparations, became aware that Rameau was bandying Voltaire's* libretto about within the La Pouplinière* household. In an attempt to stop what he regarded as potentially damaging behaviour, the duke wrote to Président Hénault, enclosing a letter from a certain Duport to Rameau vouching for Voltaire's libretto. In a covering note the duke describes Duport as 'a good musician and intimate friend of Rameau'. In Richelieu's view, Duport was the person with the most influence on the composer's way of thinking and thus better placed than the duke himself to persuade Rameau of the virtues of Voltaire's libretto. Given that Richelieu describes Duport as a *huissier de la chambre du roi*, the latter can be identified as the 'very good' cellist and harpsichordist who is mentioned in court memoirs as early as 1738 and who composed the opera *Jupiter et Europe* for performance there in 1749. He may have been the father of the distinguished cellists Jean-Pierre (1741–1818) and Jean-Louis Duport (1749–1819). Nothing further is known of his friendship with Rameau. *BesVol, GreSou, RidVol.*

Dupré, Louis   The star male dancer at the Académie Royale de Musique* in the 1730s and 1740s was Louis Dupré (1697–1774). Having entered the Académie in 1714, he left in 1723 to work in Poland, returning in 1730 with his younger brother Jean-Denis. Known as 'le grand Dupré' on account of his height and his artistic stature, Louis was renowned in his earlier years for portrayals of violent and animated characters; indeed, his first role in a Rameau opera was as a demon in *Hippolyte et Aricie*. However, a leg injury in the 1730s forced him to specialize in less energetic parts. An inventory of 1738 describes him as one of the best dancers ever to have appeared at the Opéra, both for his grace and the lightness and refinement of his steps. The noble and elevated bearing of his deportment earned him the nickname 'le Dieu de la Danse'. He was especially renowned for his expansive and mesmerising 'attitudes', some of which he would hold for several bars. Casanova*, who saw Dupré dance in 1750 (a year before his retirement), left an amusing description of his somewhat idiosyncratic but still immensely popular dance-style. Dupré was evidently an inspiring teacher, who was responsible for training many future star dancers, among them Camargo*, Vestris* and Noverre*. *BouHer, CamAca, ChrInt, FaiSty, SadDan.*

Durand (scribe)   Considering the huge number of manuscript sources he prepared of music by Rameau and others, remarkably few biographical details about Durand have survived, not even his forenames or dates of birth and death. He was a pupil of Brice Lallemand*, the Académie Royale de Musique's* long-serving chief scribe (*copiste de musique*). When Lallemand began to go blind towards the end of the 1740s, Durand took over his duties, officially replacing his master in 1751 at a salary of 1200 *livres* – double the meagre sum paid to Lallemand, even without bonuses. (Durand's prior experience of what the job entailed must have strengthened his negotiating hand.) His duties were similar to Lallemand's: he was evidently expected to pay five or more assistants out of his own pocket, and the manner in which he prepared master copies, assigned parts to individual performers and revised or repaired scores and parts all follow the model of his predecessor. Lois Rosow's research on the sources of this period has revealed an extraordinary division of labour involving Durand and his assistants, one of whom might copy the clefs and key signatures, another the music and yet another the words, while the chief scribe would proof-read the result. The handwriting of some of Durand's pupils is remarkably similar to his own. In addition to numerous sources for use at the Académie itself, Durand copied performing material for productions at the royal court, on behalf of the Menus-Plaisirs*, and for private individuals such as the marquis de La Salle*. His name appears in the Académie's accounts for the last time in March 1773. *BouDen, BouHer, GreSou, RosLal.*

Durand (publisher)   *See* **Editions; Œuvres complètes**

Dynamic marks   Although some Rameau sources, particularly those copied after his death, include Italian dynamics, the composer himself generally preferred French. The most frequently encountered dynamic marks in his scores are *doux* (the equivalent of *piano* rather than *dolce* and abbreviated as *d.* or *dx*), *fort* and *à demi jeu** or *à demi* (*mezzo-forte*). As in Italian, these could be nuanced in various ways: *très fort, très doux* (= *fortissimo, pianissimo*); *un peu fort, un peu doux* (*poco forte* or *poco piano*); *plus fort, plus doux* (*più forte, più piano*). Very rarely, Rameau indicates *à demi fort* or *à demi doux*. There is some evidence that, in violin and bass lines doubled by oboes, bassoons and/or *petites flûtes**, the marking *doux* indicated a temporary end to the woodwind doubling, which resumed at the subsequent *fort*. During rehearsals* Rameau sought to ensure that his markings were observed: in a number of production* scores he adds comments for the *batteur de mesure**, as in the case of *Zaïs*: 'Make sure the *doux* markings in the first violin parts are observed: the players make a great error in not doing so. Please watch out for this' ('Faites observer les doux marqués aux p.^rs violons, ils ont grand tort de n'en rien faire. Je vous prie d'y prendre garde'). He indicates *crescendo** and *diminuendo* in various ways, including an early form of the hairpin signs. Interestingly, he never includes dynamic marks in parts for flutes* or *petites flûtes*; given the relatively limited dynamic range of these instruments, he preferred to adjust the level of intensity by altering the number of players on each line (e.g., *flûte seule, deux flûtes, toutes les flûtes*). Dynamics seldom, if ever, occur in the singers' lines. *See also* **Adoucissez; Crescendo and diminuendo; Enflez; 'La Poule'.** *GreSou, MasOpé, MilOrc, RosPer.*

Editions Of all the great eighteenth-century composers, Rameau has until recently been the least well served by reliable or complete editions. True, the majority of his works appeared in print during his lifetime, but usually in *partition réduite** format, in which most of the inner choral and orchestral parts were omitted. After the composer's death, Decroix* tried to persuade Louis XVI to institute a complete Rameau edition, but this suggestion fell on deaf ears. Towards the end of the nineteenth century, Théodore Michaëlis launched an ambitious series, *Chefs-d'œuvre classiques de l'opéra français* (1877–84), designed to address the dearth of monumental editions of France's musical heritage; the series included numerous operas of the Lully-Rameau period, including seven by Rameau. Michaëlis's scores, however, consisted of little more than transcriptions of the original *partitions réduites*. Given their inelegant presentation and lack of inner parts, these scores can have done little to enhance Rameau's reputation, still less encourage performance or scholarly curiosity. Between 1895 and 1924 the Parisian publisher Durand issued eighteen volumes of a Rameau *Œuvres complètes**. This project, lavishly produced and with long, informative prefaces but editorially flawed to the point of being almost unusable, was abandoned in the aftermath of the First World War. Two further initiatives were announced respectively in 1973 and 1983 – Marc Pincherle's Association pour la Publication des Œuvres de Rameau, and the Broude Brothers' *The New Edition of the Works of Rameau*; sadly, both foundered after the publication of only a single volume. By contrast, *Jean-Philippe Rameau: Opera Omnia* (OOR*), currently in progress under the general editorship of Sylvie Bouissou*, seems set to achieve its aim of being the first-ever complete and authoritative edition of Rameau's music. *See also* **Indy, Vincent d'; Publishers; Saint-Saëns, Camille.** *BouHer, EllEar, FosRam, SadVin, WolŒu, ZasNew.*

'L'Egiptienne' In Rameau's day the primary meaning of the adjective *égyptien(ne)* was 'gypsy'. Whether the title of this piece from his *Nouvelles* *suites de pièces de clavecin* refers to a specific individual (male or female) or to some aspect of gypsy life is not known. Rameau's piece, with its invention-like imitations of a broken-chord figure, its sudden eruption of triplet figurations and virtuosic left-hand octaves, may well reveal the influence of Domenico Scarlatti*, who was in Paris at about the time Rameau was beginning work on the *Nouvelles suites*. GirRam, SadSca, RpeKey .

Élémens de musique théorique et pratique suivant les principes de M.ʳ Rameau The dissemination of Rameau's music theory received a powerful boost in 1752 when d'Alembert* published his *Elémens de musique théorique et pratique*. Here, the master's theories are stripped of what d'Alembert considered were their more debatable features, and expounded with lucidity and elegance. The first part of d'Alembert's text is derived from the *Démonstration du principe de l'harmonie* (1750), while the second part subjects Rameau's rules of composition in *Génération harmonique* (1737) to a radical overhaul, reducing them to five primary and three secondary rules, each of which d'Alembert justifies by cross-reference to the first part of his book. The *Élémens* was an immediate success: it was reprinted at least five times and translated into English, German (by Marpurg*) and Italian (by padre Martini*). The *Mercure de France** of May 1752 contains an open letter in which Rameau touchingly acknowledges his deep gratitude to d'Alembert. Yet for all its undoubted value, the *Élemens* has been shown by Thomas Christensen to oversimplify and distort certain aspects of Rameau's music theory, and has been blamed for some misunderstandings of his ideas, particularly outside France. The revised second edition of 1762, as well as eliminating certain 'proofs' which d'Alembert no longer found tenable, includes a 'Discours préliminaire' in which the writer rejects Rameau's notion of the *corps sonore**. *See also* **Prose style.** ChoPré, ChrTho, DalElé, DidLum, KinRam, RamCtw, VerMus.

L'Endriague Within a year of settling definitively in Paris, Rameau embarked on the first of four collaborations with Alexis Piron* at the Théâtre de la Foire*, providing incidental music for *L'Endriague*, a three-act *opéra comique** premiered at the Foire Saint-Germain on 8 February 1723. Rameau's music, now lost, was extensive and included two dramatic monologues ('Malheureuse! je touche à mon dernier instant' and 'La barbarie est contre moi') for the 14-year-old singer Mlle Petitpas*, later to star in several of his first operas. A further air, 'Peuple coupable, écoutez-moi!' was sung by an invisible genie. Among the dance music was an 'Entrée des génies' and a tambourin*, the latter quite possibly reused in his *Pièces de clavessin*, published the following year. BouRam, CamSpe, ConPir, PirŒu, PorPri, ProPir, SadPir.

Enflez In indicating crescendos* Rameau sometimes employed an early form of the 'hairpin'; more often, however, he preferred to use descriptive words or phrases, among them *enflez* (literally, to 'swell out') and *en enflant le son* ('inflating the sound'). CyrSty, GreSou, MasOpé.

Enharmonic genre Both as a theorist and a composer, Rameau was excited by the potential of the enharmonic genre, in which one or more notes is 're-spelt' (e.g., D♯ as E♭). The resulting progressions could, where appropriate, inspire 'dread and horror', as in the second Trio des Parques* in *Hippolyte et Aricie*, or could allow greater freedom of modulation, especially when allied to the system of equal temperament* that he advocated in *Génération harmonique* (1737) and later writings. Rameau particularly admired the Italians' use of such progressions, and he cites an example by Ariosti* that can be seen to have influenced his own *Castor et Pollux*. *BarEnh, ChrTho, LegPou, RamCtw.*

'L'Enharmonique' Rameau devotes much of his prefatory 'Remarques' in the *Nouvelles suites de pièces de clavecin* (1729 or 1730) to a discussion of the enharmonic* genre in two pieces in the collection. Warning the player that this was an effect 'that may not at first be to everyone's taste', he points to its use in 'L'Enharmonique' in the two extracts below. In the first, the D♭ in bar 54 is an enharmonic re-spelling of the C♯ in the preceding bar, at the point where the key shifts from D minor to F minor. Rameau recommends that, in approaching this striking feature ('trait saississant'), the player should dwell increasingly on the preceding written-out appoggiaturas ('coulés'). Elsewhere in his theoretical writings, he describes a hybrid genre which he terms 'diatonique-enharmonique'. This may be seen in the second extract below, where pairs of diatonic semitones are juxtaposed (B♭-A and A-G♯ in bar 15; A♭-G and G-F♯ in bar 17) as the music shifts to unrelated keys – from G minor to A major in bars 15–16, and from F minor to G major in bars 17–18. *BarEnh, ChrTho, GirRam, LegPou, RpeKey.*

Rameau, 'L'Enharmonique', *Nouvelles suites de pièces de clavecin*

L'Enlèvement d'Orithie In a letter of 1727 to La Motte*, Rameau mentions a cantata called *L'Enlèvement d'Orithie* – presumably an absent-minded reference to his early cantata entitled *Aquilon et Orithie** in all surviving sources. *BouHer, DorCan, GirRam, MonBou, TunCan.*

L'Enrôlement d'Arlequin Rameau's second collaboration with Alexis Piron* at the Théâtre de la Foire* consisted of a divertissement* for this one-act *opéra comique**, premiered at the Foire Saint-Laurent on 3 February 1726. The music, now lost, included a number of unspecified dances and a *vaudeville*. *ConPir, PirŒu, PorPre, ProPir, SadPir.*

Entr'acte The curtain at the Académie Royale de Musique* usually rose during the overture* and fell only at the end of the final act. Scene-changes between acts were thus carried out in full view of the audience during an orchestral entr'acte. This normally consisted of a ballet movement from the act that had just ended, transposed where necessary to connect the tonalities of the two framing acts. From the mid-eighteenth century onwards, however, calls were made for newly-composed entr'actes that would bridge the gap more sensitively. In fact, Rameau, following the lead of some of his predecessors, had already begun writing specific movements for this purpose, albeit infrequently: the 1744 *Dardanus* includes a 'bruit de guerre pour entr'acte', covering an offstage battle between Acts III and IV, while several later operas include entr'actes representing battles or storms. In *Acante et Céphise* the second act is followed by two newly composed movements (one of them subtitled 'Plainte'), which match the mood of the preceding act. In *Naïs* the prologue* is followed by an 'Entr'acte à la place de l'ouverture', supplied by Rameau because the overture itself – representing the battle between the Gods and Titans – was unsuited to the customary repeat after the prologue. *GirRam, MasOpé, NovLet, RosEnt, RouDic.*

Entrée   In eighteenth-century opera this term had two distinct meanings. The first dates back to the previous century and denotes a movement during which one or more dancers make their entrance – e.g., the 'Entrée des Indiens et Indiennes' and 'Entrée des Mages (Magi)', *Zoroastre* (II, 4). The second meaning is found in the *opéra-ballet**, where in published librettos and scores the individual acts are labelled 'entrée': a useful distinction, since it draws attention to the fact that each entrée has an independent plot. The entrées from different *opéras-ballets* were often combined into composite spectacles known as 'fragments'*. *AntFre, MasOpé.*

'L'Entretien des Muses'   Rameau's 'Conversation of the Muses' first appeared in his *Pièces de clavessin* of 1724. Domenico Scarlatti* may well have encountered this newly published piece when he visited Paris in the mid-1720s: his B minor Sonata, ĸ87, reveals an uncanny similarity of mood – a sense of wistful introspection rarely found in his other sonatas; moreover, both pieces incorporate a similar device just before the final cadence of each section, where the unhurried forward motion is interrupted by several repetitions of a single bar. Rameau was to re-use the opening section of 'L'Entretien des Muses' in the second entrée* ('La Musique') of *Les Fêtes d'Hébé* (1739), where it introduces an *oracle figuré* – a mimed episode in which the Genii of Apollo, Mars and Victory enact the Oracle's pronouncement. *BouHer, CyrHéb, GirRam, RpeKey, SadBor, SadSca.*

'L'Épouse entre deux draps'   Until recently it has been accepted that this piece, a raunchy three-part canon also known as 'La Femme entre deux draps', was by François Couperin*. However, Sylvie Bouissou* has observed that only one of the surviving sources attributes it to Couperin and that this source is not entirely reliable in its other attributions; she further notes that the canon occurs in two sources with links to Rameau – first, a miscellany of items said to have been found among his papers, in which it appears on the reverse side of his duo 'Lucas, pour se gausser'; and second, the Recueil* Bresou, one of whose title pages reads 'Canons [...] attribués à Rameau'. Whether such evidence is enough to overturn the attribution to Couperin is debatable, since both sources include numerous pieces by other composers. It may also be objected that, whereas Couperin's production of canons includes further examples of such scatological humour, Rameau's does not. The piece is also found, without attribution, in volume 2 of La Borde's* *Essai sur la musique ancienne et moderne*, with a less salacious text beginning 'Où peut-on être mieux, | Amis, que dans ce lieux?', and with the augmented* mediant chord in bar 3 altered to a bland major triad. *BouCan, BouHer, ClaCon, LabEss, MonBou.*

Eremans, Mlle The forenames and date of birth of Mlle Eremans (or Heremance) are not known. She entered the Académie Royale de Musique* in 1721, where the lightness and flexibility of her voice, her striking appearance and her acting ability won admirers. An official document of 1738 describes her as a 'good actress, but with a very sensitive temperament'. For Rameau she created the roles of Diane (*Hippolyte et Aricie*), Hébé (*Les Indes galantes*), Minerve (*Castor et Pollux*), Sappho (*Les Fêtes d'Hébé*) and Vénus (*Dardanus*). In the 1743 revival of *Hippolyte et Aricie* she took the more dramatic role of Phèdre. Her husband was the *basse-taille* Le Page*. She retired from the Académie in 1743 and died in 1761. *BenMus, BouHer, PieCon, PouJél, SadInv.*

Erreurs sur la musique dans l'Encyclopédie Although he declined Diderot's* invitation to write the music articles in the *Encyclopédie*, Rameau offered to vet the texts when they were eventually written. He was doubtless piqued to find that the articles had been entrusted to Jean-Jacques Rousseau* and further piqued at not being asked to read them before publication; he nevertheless held his peace, even after the appearance of Rousseau's *Lettre à M. Grimm, au sujet des Remarques ajoutées à sa Lettre sur Omphale* (1752), which includes snide and dismissive remarks about his theoretical writings. When Rousseau launched a scathing critique of French opera in his *Lettre sur la musique française* (1753), Rameau issued an initial response in *Observations sur notre instinct pour la musique* (1754), followed by a blistering attack on Rousseau in *Erreurs sur la musique dans l'Encyclopédie* (1755) and *Suite des erreurs sur la musique dans l'Encyclopédie* (1756). While there is some substance in Rameau's criticism of certain articles, many of his comments are little more than quibbles. In fact, his two pamphlets, issued anonymously, are as much a response to the *Lettre sur la musique française* as to the *Encyclopédie* articles: Rameau contests Rousseau's concept of 'unity of melody' and other aesthetic notions that were discussed in the *Lettre* but not in the music articles; he also dismisses certain Italian practices vaunted by Rousseau. Inevitably, Diderot* and d'Alembert* were obliged to support their contributor in the *Avertissement* to the sixth volume of the *Encyclopédie* (1756). This provoked the composer's *Réponse de M.ʳ Rameau à MM. les editeurs de l'Encyclopédie sur leur dernier Avertissement* (1757), which initiated a further rancorous war of words. Rousseau's 'Du principe de la mélodie, ou Réponse aux erreurs sur la musique' and 'Examen des deux principes avancés par M.ʳ Rameau', drafted during this dispute, remained unpublished in his lifetime. *BazDid, ChrTho, DidLum, OliEnc, RamCtw, ThmDid, VerRam, WokEss.*

Euler, Leonhard On 30 April 1752 Rameau sent a copy of his recent *Nouvelles réflexions sur la démonstration du principe de l'harmonie* to Euler (1707–83), hoping to gain the approbation of this brilliant Swiss mathematician and physicist who was then working at the Berlin Academy of Sciences. In a reply dated 13 September 1752, Euler goes to considerable trouble to emphasize the extent to which his own views accorded with Rameau's; he nonetheless politely but firmly challenged the validity of Rameau's theory on the *identité des octaves**. This led Rameau to publish an open letter to Euler in the *Mercure de France** (December 1752), in which, writing in the third person, he robustly defends his position; a revised version of this letter was later published as *Extrait d'une réponse de Mr Rameau à M. Euler, sur l'identité des octaves* (1753). Such self-damaging behaviour in responding cantankerously to any perceived challenge to his authority as a scientist is, alas, typical of Rameau's final years. *ChrTho, JacNou, RamCtw, VerMus.*

Expressive markings Rameau once remarked that 'Lully needs actors, I need singers', a comment that has sometimes been interpreted as indicating that he was little interested in the dramatic projection of his vocal music. Yet his own printed and manuscript indications of tempo and expression, not to mention comments in his theoretical works, suggest quite the opposite. The list of annotations on his vocal lines is astonishingly varied: 'en colère', 'en joye', 'en pindarisant' (pretentiously), 'en plainte', 'en pleurs', 'en sentiment', 'en surprise', 'en tendre regret', 'hardiment ', 'ironique', 'pompeusement', 'posément' (calmly, deliberately), 'débité'* (declaimed), 'avec feu', 'avec précipitation', 'avec sentiment mais toujours un peu gai', 'avec toute la tendresse possible'. Often such annotations occur in series, as in *Naïs* (I, 6) – 'un peu passionné' (rather passionate) and 'encore plus passionné' (even more passionate) – or in *Les Paladins* (I, 3), where Orcan's part is initially marked 'brutalement', then 'tendrement'. This last work includes a comic scene where Nérine arrives out of breath ('comme essoufflé'), each of her first few lines being separated by three dots as she gets her breath back ('Nérine affecte de reprendre son haleine à chacque trois points', I, 4). Annotations added by the singers themselves or by their coach include 'grand trouble', 'sourire' and the enigmatic 'saisir'*. Occasionally rubrics of this sort appear on instrumental lines, as in *Les Sibarites*, where a *symphonie* in which Cupid escorts the god Mars is marked 'flutes avec sentiment'. Rameau was not alone among his French contemporaries in indicating such subtleties. This, together with evidence from reviews and memoirs, confirms that – whatever the deficiencies of some individual performers – opera at the Académie Royale de Musique* was by no means merely 'concert in costume'. Indeed, singers there are known to have studied acting under the direction of members of the Académie staff. *ChaRou, CyrEss, CyrSin, GirRam, GreSou, MasOpé, MilOrc, SawPig, SawNou.*

Exultet coelum laudibus The library catalogue of the Académie des Beaux-Arts in Lyon lists a score and seven performing parts of a motet of this name by Rameau. The work, now lost, was a setting of a hymn for Second Vespers in the Common of Apostles, scored for three voices with unnamed obbligato instruments. In requiring small forces, this work would nowadays be classified as a *petit motet*, though that term had not yet been coined. There is nothing in the Académie's catalogue to indicate the date of composition. *BouHer, BouRam, DurMot, DurRel, ValAca, ValLyo.*

Fair Theatres   *See* **Théâtre de la Foire.**

Fandango   Many features of this traditional Spanish dance may be found in 'Les Trois Mains' from Rameau's *Nouvelles suites de pièces de clavecin*. At that time the fandango was characterised by a moderate triple time with emphasis on the first and last beats; a minor tonality; a prevalent harmonic rhythm of one chord per bar; and alternation between tonic and dominant in consecutive bars. Rameau's piece shares all these characteristics with a fandango by Santiago de Murcia, thought to date from the 1720s. Both pieces, moreover, include a distinctive range of rhythmic and melodic traits that recur in later fandangos by Boccherini, Gluck and Mozart, as well as in two attributed to Domenico Scarlatti* and one to Soler. These include melodic cells in even quavers, starting after the first quaver of the bar; motifs of four semiquavers that emphasize the third beat; and cadential sequences of descending semiquavers with an upward skip of a third between each four-note cell (marked *x* in the example below). While 'Les Trois Mains' may not sound particularly Iberian, Rameau was clearly familiar enough with the fandango as a genre to have absorbed many of its characteristics. It may thus be no coincidence that the piece appeared only a few years after Scarlatti's visits to Paris in the 1720s. *SadSca.*

Rameau, 'Les Trois Mains', *Nouvelles suites de pièces de clavecin*

'Fanfarinette'   The title of this piece, from the *Nouvelles suites de pièces de clavecin*, may derive from *fanfaron*, which in modern French means 'braggart' but which in Rameau's day could also denote someone who feigned bravery. Neither meaning has any obvious rapport with the grace and elegance of this movement, however, and the title may, as Girdlestone suggests, merely refer to a nickname. *Boul ler, DicAut, GusFul, GirRam, RpeKey.*

Favart, Charles-Simon   *See L'Ambigu de la folie*; 'Do do, l'enfant do'; 'Les Niais de Sologne'.

La féerie   French ballet and opera had long cultivated a taste for the exotic, but it was not until 1725, when Louis Fuzelier* adopted what he called 'le Système fabuleux des Orientaux' in his libretto to Aubert's *La Reine des Péris*, that the Paris Opéra fully embraced Middle-Eastern mythology. The enchanted realm of *la féerie*, with its aerial beings and dualist system of good and evil, was further explored in the 1730s and 1740s by such composers as Brassac, Rebel* and Francœur. A thread running through several works of this type is the exploration of psychologically complex moral questions, often in the form of trial by ordeal. Rameau's first essay in the new genre was the entrée* 'La Féerie' in *Les Fêtes de Polymnie* (1745), to a libretto by Louis de Cahusac*. Two of Cahusac's later librettos for Rameau – *Zaïs* and *Zoroastre* – make more extensive use of *la féerie*, as does Marmontel's libretto for *Acante et Céphise* (1751) and Monticourt's for *Les Paladins*. *BucSup, ChaRou, GirRam, GirTra, MasOpé, RecGen.*

Fel, Marie   For most of his operatic career Rameau was served by two exceptionally gifted singers: the *haute-contre** Pierre Jéliote* and the soprano Marie Fel (1713–94). Marie made her debut at the Académie Royale de Musique* in November 1734, a year later than Rameau. In that same month her brother Antoine (c.1696–1771) joined the chorus as a *taille**. Her first roles were fairly small; indeed, it was not until 1745 that she sang a major dramatic part in a Rameau work, when she appeared as La Folie in *Platée*. Thereafter, until her retirement from the Opéra in 1758, she created almost all the principal female roles in his operas, notably Zélidie in *Zaïs*, Amélite in *Zoroastre* and the title roles in *Naïs* and *Acante et Céphise*. Contemporary reports emphasize Marie Fel's singing rather than her acting. As a pupil of Christina Somis (1704–83), she had learned an Italian style of singing. Her light, agile voice was perfectly suited to the vocalises of Italianate music, not only in *ariettes** but also in the Latin solo motets that she often sang at the Concert Spirituel. She was admired for her clear diction and precise ornamentation as well as for the ability to vary the vocal timbre. Throughout a long career her voice retained its silvery freshness and youth. A long-standing relationship with Cahusac* broke up in c.1759 when the two were on the point of getting married. A fine pastel portrait by her lover Quentin de La Tour* survives in the Musée Antoine Lécuyer, Saint-Quentin. *BouHer, CamAca, ChaRou, CyrEss, CyrSin, PieCon, ProFel, PouJél, RivFil, SadInv, VlaTed.*

'La Femme entre deux draps'   *See* **'L'Épouse entre deux draps'**.

Les Fêtes de l'Hymen et de l'Amour   Commissioned by Louis XV's court to celebrate the Dauphin's second marriage, to Maria-Josepha of Saxony, *Les Fêtes de l'Hymen, ou Les Dieux d'Egypte* was first performed in the Grande Écurie at Versailles on 15 March 1747. Though categorized in librettos and scores as a *ballet héroïque**, the work belongs to the genre defined in the eighteenth century as *opéra-ballet**, and comprises a prologue and three entrées*. With little time to execute this commission, Rameau and his librettist Cahusac* adapted an existing project, *Les Dieux d'Egypte*. Its theme proved fortuitously appropriate, since the three entrées – 'Osiris', 'Canope' and 'Asueris, ou Les Isies' – culminate in the marriage of one of the Egyptian gods, each of whom is revealed as a model of virtue and good governance. The work's revised title emphasizes the connection to the royal event, as does the newly-composed prologue. In this work Cahusac prided himself on giving new importance and relevance to the supernatural (*le merveilleux**) and to the use of spectacular stage machines; those for the overflowing Nile were long admired. Symptomatic of the librettist's desire to integrate dance and action, the opera contains no fewer than seven *ballets figurés**. *Les Fêtes de l'Hymen* is the first of the Rameau-Cahusac operas to allude unambiguously to tenets and rituals of freemasonry*, not only in its Egyptian setting but more specifically through the esoteric ritual in 'Canope' and the enlightening mission in 'Osiris'. That such allusions were recognized at the time is revealed by Poinsinet's *parodie** entitled *Les Fra-Maçonnes* (Foire Saint-Laurent, 1754), in which the plot of 'Osiris' is manipulated as a plea to admit women to masonic lodges. In Rameau's day *Les Fêtes de l'Hymen* was rightly regarded as one of his finest works. A revised version was transferred to the Paris Opéra in November 1748. The opera was revived in 1754 and 1765–66, achieving the remarkable total of 106 performances. 'Osiris' remained in the repertory until 1772, 'Asuéris' until 1776. *BouHer, BucSup, ChaRou, GirRam, GreSou, LecDiv, MalHym, MasOpé, SouFêt, SouHym.*

Les Fêtes de Polymnie The first of Rameau's collaborations with Cahusac*, this work celebrates the battle of Fontenoy and was first performed at the Académie Royale de Musique* on 12 October 1745. Described in surviving sources as a *ballet héroïque*, the work is in reality an *opéra-ballet**. Despite a first run of twenty-nine performances, it was revived only once, in 1753, though individual entrées* appeared in *fragments** in 1754 and 1765. The prologue ('Le Temple de Mémoire') represents a rare return to the panegyric of Lully's* prologues: in recognition of the French victory, the Arts erect a statue of Louis XV, while the Muses extol his virtues. To entertain the victors, Polymnie, Muse of lyric poetry, introduces her 'fêtes', each of which is based on a different lyric genre. Thus 'La Fable' is derived from the Greek legend of the courtship of Hebe by Alcides, 'L'Histoire' treats the true story of Seleucus, king of Syria, who generously allows the object of his love to marry his own son, and 'La Féerie' explores the world of Middle-Eastern mythology. Thomas Green has revealed that *Les Fêtes de Polymnie* was originally conceived as part of the royal celebration of the Dauphin's wedding earlier in 1745. A court connection is suggested by the involvement in the original production* score of scribes from the Menus-Plaisirs*, while Cahusac's libretto is dedicated to Louis XV, and each entrée includes flattering references to the king. Moreover, their plots are concerned not with victory but with the courtship and marriage of an idealized royal couple. However, a letter by Voltaire* indicates that this work was replaced in the Versailles schedule by François Collin de Blamont's opera *Jupiter vainqueur des Titans*. Thus it seems likely that *Les Fêtes de Polymnie* was only later adapted to the Fontenoy celebrations by the addition of a circumstantial prologue. *See also* **Debussy, Claude Achille.** *BesVol, BouHer, BucSup, ChaRou, GirRam, GreSou, MalPol, MasOpé.*

Les Fêtes de Ramire After the premiere of *La Princesse de Navarre**, Rameau and Voltaire* were instructed by the duc de Richelieu*, the court official in charge of the Menus-Plaisirs*, to revise their *comédie-ballet** by combining its three separate divertissements into a single *acte de ballet** with linking recitatives. But although Voltaire produced the necessary verse, Rameau claimed he was too busy completing *Le Temple de la Gloire*, another court commission. The task of making the necessary adjustments was therefore given to Jean-Jacques Rousseau*, even though he and Rameau were already on bad terms. Rousseau later complained that the task had been 'long and difficult', and his efforts were severely criticized by Rameau's pupil Thérèse Deshayes*, who used her influence with her lover, the duc de Richelieu, to ensure that the score was passed back for completion by Rameau. The latter nevertheless disowned the work when it was performed at Versailles on 22 December 1745. Rousseau claims to have composed the recitatives and an Italianate overture. The latter, as Julien Dubruque has shown, appears to have survived in all sources of *La Princesse de Navarre* and was long accepted as Rameau's. The air 'O mort, viens terminer les douleurs de ma vie' and several others may be Rousseau. In his *Confessions* the author states that he was never paid for his services, whereas the Menus-Plaisirs* accounts show that he received 792 *livres*. *BesVol, BouHer, BouRam, GirRam, MalPri, MasOpé, RidVol, RouCon, SawVol.*

Les Fêtes d'Hébé, ou Les talents lyriques   Premiered at the Académie Royale de Musique* on 21 May 1739, *Les Fêtes d'Hébé* was Rameau's second *opéra-ballet**. The anonymous libretto is reliably attributed to Gautier de Montdorge*, though several other writers are reported as having made revisions and additions, among them Bernard*, La Pouplinière* and the abbé Pellegrin*. Whereas *Les Indes galantes*, Rameau's first *opéra-ballet*, had been set mainly in the modern world, this one reverts to the stock classical Greek subject matter found in most *opéras-ballets* since the 1720s. *Les Fêtes d'Hébé* was often referred to by its subtitle, *Les talents lyriques*, which gives a better idea of the nature of the work, since each entrée* treats one of the 'lyric talents': poetry, music and dance. The libretto was initially much criticized, and the second entrée had to be radically revised, to the extent that one edition of the libretto describes it as a 'nouvelle entrée'. Rameau's opponents in the Lulliste-Ramiste* dispute seized on his reuse of music from the 1724 *Pièces de clavessin* (the musette*, tambourin* and 'L'Entretien des Muses'*) and from the cantata *Le Berger fidèle* as symptoms of an exhausted imagination. Despite these and other criticisms, *Les Fêtes d'Hébé* was an instant and lasting box-office hit, its success boosted in the early stages by the appearance of the athletic Italian dancer Barbarina Campanini* and her husband, for whom Rameau added at least four ballet numbers. After a first run of seventy-one performances, the work was revived in 1747, 1756 and 1764, while individual entrées remained in the Académie's repertory until 1777. *AntOpe, BouHer, ChaRou, CyrHéb, GirRam, GreSou, MasOpé, MalHéb, MelPar, SadBor, SadPat.*

Figurant   Mid-eighteenth-century lists of dancers at the Académie Royale de Musique* differentiate between the principal dancers, who appeared in solos or in *pas de deux*, and the 'danseurs figurants', who formed what is nowadays known as the *corps de ballet*. At this time the salary of a *figurant* was typically 400 *livres* or less, while the best of the principal solo dancers received 2,000 *livres* or more. The lists of dancers provided in contemporary librettos often distinguish typographically between the principal dancers and the *figurants* – a useful feature for modern choreographers wishing to recreate historical dance styles and practices. *BarPla, BouHer, BouLiv, ChsInt, SadDan, SadZo1.*

'Filles de l'Opéra'   The private lives of the female singers and dancers at the Académie Royale de Musique* excited an enormous amount of contemporary comment, mainly arising from their perceived moral laxity. Most of these women, known collectively as the 'filles de l'Opéra', were maintained by aristocratic or wealthy lovers. A few were even admitted to the Académie without salary on the understanding that they would soon find a powerful 'protector' – as in the case of the chorus member Mlle Desaigles; according to an official document of 1738, 'her lack of talent for the stage means that she has no work. By way of compensation, she knows how to pay for her holidays by other means. She was able to pluck the goose of M. Le Comte, former director of the opera'. Casanova* was amused when Marie Fel* proudly confided that each of her three children had a different aristocrat for a father. The dancer Marie Sallé* was so atypical in avoiding such amorous entanglements that she gained the nickname 'La Vestale'. Reactions to the off-stage adventures of these *filles* ranged from fierce condemnation in moral tracts to undisguised, if prurient, glee in innumerable satirical verses, many of them preserved in multi-volume 'chansonniers'. The fact that, on stage, such 'scarlet women' could be required to portray noble, chaste or divine personages created its own tensions and disparities. Predictably, the sexual proclivities of the male performers went largely unremarked. *CamAca, CowWom, RivFil, SadDan, SadSin, WooSad.*

Fitzwilliam of Merrion, Richard, 7th Viscount   For an Anglo-Irish nobleman of his era, Lord Fitzwilliam (1745–1816) was unusual in developing a passion for French music. In 1765, a year after graduating from Cambridge, he travelled to Paris to study harpsichord and continuo playing with Jacques Duphly*, one of the most fashionable teachers of the day. On subsequent visits to the city, Fitzwilliam accumulated a considerable collection of French keyboard music, motets and dramatic works. These last include seven full scores of Rameau operas, professionally copied on paper with a 1785 watermark and signed 'Fitzwilliam 1791'. The set, now in the Fitzwilliam Museum, Cambridge, includes all Rameau's *tragédies en musique** except *Les Boréades*, plus two *opéras-ballets: Les Indes galantes* and *Les Fêtes d'Hébé*. All were still in the Opéra repertory during the viscount's first visits to Paris, and he is known to have attended a performance of *Castor* there in 1778. The oddity in the collection is *Les Paladins*, which was remembered in 1791, if at all, only as a dismal failure; why Fitzwilliam would have chosen to have it copied is a mystery. He was impressed enough by *Castor* to organize two concert performances of the overture and various excerpts at the Academy of Ancient Music in February and March 1791. It was a sign of the times that the orchestra included added parts for horns and trombones. *BouHer, CudFit.*

Flageolet   Rameau occasionally found a use for the flageolet in the orchestra. His parts for this instrument are extremely simple: in the final *contredanse* of *Pigmalion* (1748), a single flageolet has a range of only a fourth; in *Platée* (II, 3), a comic depiction of the pandemonium (*charivari*) of a flock of frightened birds includes two flageolets, their ranges limited respectively to a fifth and a major second. The simplicity and restricted compass of these parts contrasts markedly with Rameau's virtuosic writing for *petites flûtes**, which were evidently transverse piccolos rather than fipple flutes. The production* score of *Hippolyte et Aricie* includes an annotation, probably added at one of the revivals, suggesting that a flageolet and *tambourin** should be added to the Act III 'Rigaudon en tambourin'. *BarPla, BouHip, SadOrc.*

Flute   Although the word 'flûte' could mean either transverse flute or recorder in Rameau's day, the composer appears to have made no specific use of the latter instrument. Listings of the Académie Royale de Musique* personnel between 1738 and 1764 indicate that the transverse flute and oboe parts were shared between a group of five or six players. While some of these, like Michel Blavet (1700–68), were primarily flautists, others were expected to play either instrument where required, as well as the *petite flûte**. Each Rameau opera demands at least four flautists, as becomes clear from his labelling system, which distinguishes carefully between singular and plural when the flutes divide ('première / deuxième' and 'premières / deuxièmes flûtes'). Contrary to his treatment of the other woodwind, Rameau does not include dynamic* marks in his flute parts; rather, he varies the number of players on each line, achieving gradations of volume by such annotations as 'flûte seule', 'deux flûtes', 'toutes les flûtes'. Nor does the composer normally combine flutes and oboes on unison lines, even in the context of woodwind doubling of the violins. The quantity of obbligato flute writing varies sharply from opera to opera, depending on the dramatic situation. In *Hippolyte et Aricie*, twenty-one movements call for independent flutes, compared with only seven in *Castor et Pollux*. Apart from some exceptional movements in B♭ or F minor, most of Rameau's flute parts from the 1730s stay close to the one-keyed flute's favourite keys of G, D or A and their relative minors, and they rarely exceed the compass *d′ – e‴*. From the 1740s onwards, notes as high as *g‴* become commonplace, as does the use of signatures with up to four flats, reflecting improvements in instrument design and technical advances on the part of the players. *GorOrc, GreSou, MasOpé, SadOrc, SpiZas.*

'La Follette' Sometimes the appropriate interpretation of the titles of Rameau's keyboard pieces is not the obvious one, as is the case with this movement from his *Pièces de clavessin* of 1724. At first sight, the word *follette* seems to derive from *follet* ('scatter-brained'), yet the piece includes none of the zany, mad-cap gestures suggested by this interpretation. Happily, Littré's *Dictionnaire de la langue française* (1872–77) reveals that a *follette* was 'a sort of head-scarf [*fichu*] fashionable around 1722'. Quite apart from its uncannily precise chronological link, Littré's definition – hitherto overlooked by commentators on this piece – is ideally suited to the undulating melodic lines and prolonged trills of Rameau's elegant rondeau (see the example below). A similarly flowing character is noticeable in 'La Follète' from Dandrieu's *Troisième livre de pièces de clavecin* of 1734. (Littré's other definition of 'follette' – as the common name for mountain spinach [*arroché*] – hardly seems apt.) *DicAut, FraDan, GirRam, GusFul.*

Rameau, 'La Follette', *Pièces de clavessin* (1724)

'La Forqueray' The fashion for naming pieces after members of the Forqueray family, set by François Couperin* (*Pièces de clavecin*, Book Three, 1722), was followed by Rameau (*Pièces de clavecin en concerts*, 1741), his son Claude-François* and Jacques Duphly*. The particular Forqueray honoured in Rameau's case was either Antoine (1672–1745) or his son Jean-Baptiste (1699–1782), both renowned viol players. The latter is perhaps the more likely: Jean-Baptiste's wife Marie-Rose Dubois (1717–87) was an equally skilled harpsichordist, and it is possible that 'La Forqueray' and the other pieces in Rameau's collection were conceived with these two performers in mind. Girdlestone even suggests that the piece was a wedding tribute to the couple, who were married in the year in which this volume was published. As a return compliment, perhaps, Jean-Baptiste included his own tribute, 'La Rameau', in the *Pièces de viole* [...] *mise en pièces de clavecin* (1747). Rameau's piece is headed 'Fugue', a term which in France often indicated a loosely imitative texture rather than the 'textbook'

fugue with its emphasis on imitation at the fourth or fifth. In this respect,
the composer may have been influenced by the very Handelian fugues in the
Pièces de clavecin (1734) by Pierre Février (1696–1760). Indeed, the subject of
'La Forqueray' bears more than a passing resemblance to the countersubject
of Février's B minor fugue. (In the example below, the Février extract is
transposed down a third, its note-values doubled and ornaments omitted.) In
keeping with its fugal character, Rameau's piece is through-composed – the
only such movement in his entire keyboard output – but is marked to be played
twice. *BouHer, GirRam, GusFul, HerMor, RpeKey.*

(a) Rameau, 'La Forqueray', *Pièces de clavecin en concerts* (1741)

(b) Février, Fugue, *Pièces de clavecin [...] premier livre* (1734), countersubject

Fragments   As a way of boosting box-office takings, the Académie Royale
de Musique* management hit on the idea of devising composite spectacles
known as *fragmen(t)s* or *spectacles coupés*. The practice began with *Les Fragmens
de Monsieur de Lully*, compiled in 1702 by Danchet and Campra*, but became
especially popular with the Opéra management after the middle of the century.
The individual components were usually entrées* from popular *opéras-ballets*,
but sets of *fragments* sometimes included independent *actes de ballet** (e.g.,
the 1754 *Anacréon*, revived in 1766 as part of *Les Fêtes lyriques* with works by
Louis-Joseph Francœur and Niel) or even abandoned prologues (e.g., the one
to *Les Indes galantes*, included in various *fragments* in 1770 and 1772). To add
an element of novelty, the management occasionally premiered a new work as
part of the mixture, as in the cases of *Pigmalion, La Guirlande* and *La Naissance
d'Osiris*. Such composite spectacles were a popular choice with the Académie's
singers for *capitation** performances. *ChaRou, LajBib, MasOpé, SerOpé.*

Francœur, François   *See* **Rebel, François.**

Freemasonry   The importance of freemasonry in pre-Revolutionary France has
long been recognized. During the mid-eighteenth century, this order attracted a
huge following, especially among writers, artists and musicians, and there can
be no doubting its appeal to those of a liberal or reformist temperament. Its
aims were both philosophical (with emphasis on the enlightenment that comes
from initiation) and philanthropic (the encouragement of good works and the
propagation of virtue). A number of Rameau's later operas, notably *Les Fêtes de
l'Hymen, Zaïs, Zoroastre, Acante et Céphise* and *Les Boréades*, have been shown
to contain masonic themes and symbols, among them initiation, voyages of
discovery, purification by the elements and the use of talismans. In the 1730s
and 1740s the order was regarded with some suspicion, and police raids on
masonic lodges continued until 1745, only a few years before the appearance
of most of the above operas. Hence the masonic allusions in these works tend

to be veiled and involve standard elements that could be taken at face value by the uninitiated. That this masonic orientation was nevertheless recognized in Rameau's day is illustrated by a *parodie** of *Les Fêtes de l'Hymen** entitled *Les Fra-maçonnes* and by the wording of several reviews of *Zoroastre* written by freemasons. The librettists of these works, Cahusac* and Marmontel*, had known masonic associations, while Rameau was 'outed' as a mason in a satirical poem by Travenol*. *CotMaç, JacEnl, KinRam, LauVal, SadFre, SadZaï, SadZor.*

French violin clef   Dating back no further than the mid-nineteenth century, this term indicates a G clef on the lowest line (G^1). It is nevertheless a misnomer. In France, music for most treble instruments, whether wind or strings, was traditionally notated in this clef, which could accommodate the standard ranges of these instruments with no more than a single leger line below and above the staff. Given that seventeenth-century French violin music made little use of the lowest string and did not normally exceed first position, it fell neatly within the confines of this clef. When the violin's lowest string was required, the soprano clef (C^1) was temporarily substituted. Throughout Rameau's career, G^1 remained the standard clef for violin and upper woodwind parts, despite the considerable expansion of instrumental tessituras during that period. In a few exceptional pieces (e.g., the *Cantate pour le jour de la Saint-Louis**) Rameau notated an instrumental obbligato in the treble clef (G^2). *CyrSty.*

Fundamental bass   *See **Basse fondamentale**.*

Fuzelier, Louis   It was probably during his collaboration with Alexis Piron* at the Théâtre de la Foire* in the mid-1720s that Rameau first came into contact with Fuzelier (1674–1752), one of his future librettists. Fuzelier had established his reputation at the Fairs and remained active there, though his output of more than two hundred stage works includes plays for all the major Parisian theatres. As a librettist, he reveals an innovative turn of mind: *Les Fêtes grecques et romaines* (1723), set by Collin de Blamont, established the genre of *ballet héroïque**, breaking new ground in treating events from ancient history rather than from myth or legend. His libretto for Jacques Aubert's *La Reine des Péris* (1725) introduced the genre of *la féerie**, later exploited in Rameau's *Zaïs, Acante et Céphise* and other works. Fuzelier's one libretto for Rameau, *Les Indes galantes**, is similarly inventive in being based on topical subjects, these being culled from press reports, travellers' tales, recent books or personal experience. *AntFre, BloAme, BouHer, BouRam, DuaInd, GirRam, GreSou, MalInd, MasBal, MasOpé, SavAme, VenCom, WolInd.*

Gamaches, Étienne-Simon de (abbé)   Among the clergy at Sainte-Croix de la Bretonnerie* when Rameau was organist there in the 1730s was the abbé de Gamaches (1672–1756), a distinguished member of the Académie Royale des Sciences* and future author of *Astronomie physique* (1740) and *Les Agrémens du langue réduits à ses principes* (1757). In *Génération harmonique* (1737) Rameau acknowledges the abbé's help in resolving a knotty theoretical problem. Gamaches was one of three Académie members commissioned to examine the manuscript of this treatise; the short but positive report, signed on 1 January 1737, survives in the archives of the Institut de France. *ChrTho, GirRam, RamCtw.*

Garrick, David   In 1751 the renowned actor, playwright and impresario David

Garrick (1717–79) visited Paris for the first time. His travel diary includes many brief remarks on the various theatrical entertainments he attended. On 26 May he saw Mouret's *Le Ballet des sens* at the Opéra: 'a very *raw* Entertainment to me: ye scenes were well conducted & had a good Effect, ye habits seemingly rich, the singers & dancers very numerous; but ye singing abominable to *me*, & ye dancing very indifferent'. Two days later he returned to the Opéra to see Rameau's *Les Indes galantes*: 'y^e *Shew* is great but ye singing execrable, there was spirit of expression in ye musick & ye dancing very well; ye best *actor* I have seen hitherto is *Chassee**, ye bass singer. I was disappointed in *Dupré** (tame Grace)'. Garrick did not return to the Opéra until 14 June: 'liked it worse than before, half a sleep, got a headAch, went home & in a bad humor all ye Evening'. Such largely negative responses to French opera are not untypical of English visitors at that time, who were more accustomed to *opera seria* and Italian singing styles and were largely unfamiliar with the French manner of singing. *ChaRou, GarDia.*

Gautier-Dagoty, Jean-Baptiste-André   Son of a distinguished engraver, the painter Gautier-Dagoty (1740–86) is renowned for his portraits of Marie-Antoinette and others. His *Galerie françoise des hommes et des femmes célèbres qui ont paru en France* (1770) includes a ten-page biography of Rameau, preceded by a mezzotint portrait designed and possibly engraved by the author, though the engraver's name is now illegible. Unlike many engraved depictions of the composer, this genial if slightly wistful portrait does not seem to have been copied from the bust by Caffieri*. Curiously, Gautier-Dagoty's mezzotint was replaced in the 1771 edition by Restout's* engraving of the composer. *GétPor, GirRam.*

Gavotte with six doubles   Resemblances have been noted between this piece from Rameau's *Nouvelles suites de pièces de clavecin* (1729 or 1730) and the Air and five *doubles** from Handel's* D minor harpsichord suite (HWV428), published in London in 1720. Not only do the two themes share the same length and phrase structure, but Rameau clearly modelled the figuration in each of the first three *doubles* on the equivalent motifs in Handel's first three. Thereafter, the two sets diverge sharply: while Handel moves from simple to compound metre at the fourth *double*, Rameau maintains the metre and semiquaver movement but introduces various *batteries** and hazardous leaps, in a display of astonishing virtuosity: having absorbed elements of Handel's keyboard technique in the first three *doubles*, Rameau evidently wished to demonstrate his own technical prowess in the remaining ones. He may also have been influenced by the structure and some of the figuration of Domenico Scarlatti's* A minor set of variations, K61. *See also* **Pattern variations**. *GirRam, GusFul, LocVar, RpeKey, SadHan, SadSca.*

Gélin, Nicolas   Appointed as a choral *basse-taille** and understudy at the Académie Royale de Musique* in 1750, Gélin (1726–1810) rapidly established a reputation as a soloist, his sonorous and elegant voice making him a natural successor to Chassé*. He sang in many Rameau revivals and also created several notable roles, including Oromasès in the 1756 *Zoroastre* and Anselme in *Les Paladins*; he would also have created the role of Borilée in *Les Boréades**, had the scheduled performance taken place. He continued to sing at the Académie until 1779, creating major roles in operas by Dauvergne, Gluck and Gossec. *See also* **Balbastre's harpsichord**. *BouBor, BouHer, CyrCho, PieCon.*

Génération harmonique, ou Traité de musique théorique et pratique   As befits a treatise dedicated to the members of the Académie Royale des Science*, Rameau's *Génération harmonique* (1737) begins with a series of propositions and experiments in imitation of Newton's *Opticks* (1704), the clearest manifestation to date of his endeavour to raise music to the level of a scientific discipline. From these experiments Rameau deduced that a single vibrating body (*corps sonore**) generated not only the major but also the minor triad. (In later writings he acknowledged the latter deduction to be false.) This treatise borrows and manipulates Mairan's* concept of the elasticity of air in order to explain the harmonic overtones audible in the *corps sonore*. Rameau also extends his application of the triple geometric* progression: whereas his *Nouveau systême** had attempted to show that this proportion generated all the notes of a mode, he now uses it to link the tonic, dominant and subdominant triads in a defining harmonic relationship. Rameau's discussion of the tonal attraction of these triads reveals a familiarity with Newtonian ideas, stimulated no doubt by his association with Maupertuis*, his friendship with Mairan* and recent collaboration with Voltaire*. By now, however, the composer had become aware of inconsistencies in his derivation of mode from the triple geometric progression; to get round these, *Génération harmonique* further elaborates the concept of *double emploi**, first framed in the *Nouveau systême*. *Génération harmonique* includes Rameau's first discussion of the enharmonic* genre, where he alludes to his own use of this device in the *Nouvelles suites de pièces de clavecin* and the Trio des Parques* from *Hippolyte et Aricie*. In a discussion of temperament*, Rameau now rejects the mean-tone tuning he had earlier advocated, in favour of equal temperament. From this treatise we learn that the composer's interest in music theory began during his early youth: by the age of only 'seven or eight' he had already instinctively realized that the interval of a tritone should be resolved outwards onto a sixth. *See also* **Publishers.** *BarEnh, BurCor, ChiGén, ChrBas, ChrCor, ChrTho, CohAca, CohDis, FerEvo, HayGen, HayNou, RamCtw.*

Geometric progressions   Soon after publishing his *Traité de l'harmonie* (1722), Rameau learned from Castel* the significance of geometric progressions for his theoretical work. These could be related to the three fundamental overtones generated by a vibrating body (*corps sonore**) – i.e., the second, third and fifth partials, which equate respectively to the octave, twelfth (compound fifth) and seventeenth (compound major third). When expanded geometrically, the values 2, 3 and 5 produce the double progression (1–2–4–8 ...), triple progression (1–3–9–27 ...) and quintuple progression (1–5–25–125 ...). Rameau used the double progression as proof of octave equivalence (*identité des octaves**), whereby intervals greater than an octave are perceived as compound intervals. By means of the triple progression he derived the diatonic scale, the progression of fifths and, subsequently, the tonal relationship of tonic, dominant and subdominant triads. From the quintuple progression came the chromatic and enharmonic* genres. Such use of geometric progressions came in for criticism, particularly from d'Alembert*, who considered them unnecessary and omitted them from his exposition of the master's theories in *Elémens de musique théorique et pratique suivant les principes de Mr Rameau**. *ChrCor, ChrTho, RamCtw.*

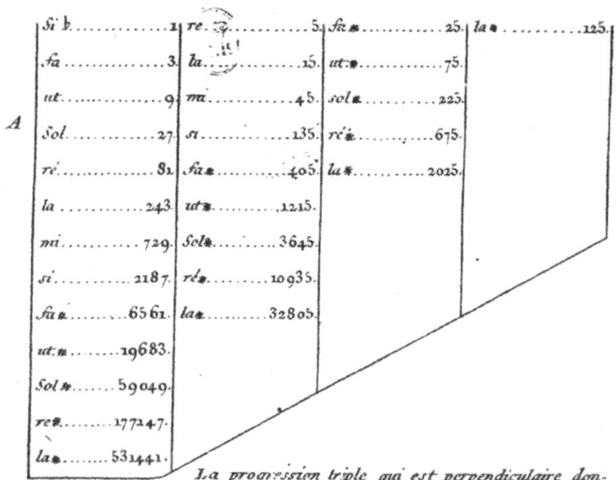

Rameau, *Démonstration du principe de l'harmonie*, 1750 (Paris, Bibliothèque Nationale de France, V-25152), p. 247. Reproduced by permission.

Gianotti, Pietro   A native of Lucca, the composer Gianotti (d. 1765) settled in Paris, where his first set of violin sonatas was published in 1728. From 1742 until his retirement in 1757, he was a member of the Paris Opéra orchestra, first as a *haute-contre de violon**, then as a *contrebasse*. Here, he came into frequent contact with Rameau and may already have enrolled at his School of Composition*. Gianotti was evidently a talented enough pupil for Rameau to entrust him with his manuscript textbook *L'Art de la basse fondamentale** in the hope that his protégé would transform it into a publishable state – an opportunity the composer had earlier offered to d'Alembert*. Gianotti eventually took up this suggestion: his primer *Le Guide du compositeur* (1759) is in effect a reorganized, abridged and lucid exposé of Rameau's ideas on the teaching of composition. *ChaPol, ChrArt, ChrTho, GiaGui, GorOrc.*

Gilles, Jean   When Rameau was appointed to a temporary post as music director at Notre-Dame des Doms, Avignon*, on 14 January 1702, it was to deputize for Gilles (1668–1705), who had been offered the position of *maître de musique* some six months earlier but had not taken it up. In the event, Gilles never relinquished his post at the Cathedral of Saint-Étienne in Toulouse, where he would remain until his death. If he ever visited Avignon during Rameau's time in the city, there is no record that two men ever met. Some six decades later, however, the names of Gilles and Rameau were again associated. Soon after Rameau's death in September 1764, three memorial* services were organized in Paris. Two of these featured performances of Gilles's *Messe des morts*, which had become the standard work performed at the funerals of distinguished public figures. For the Rameau commemorations, this Requiem was subjected to considerable revision, with inserted *contrafacta** based on music from *Castor et Pollux* and with other modifications; indeed, it may have been for this reason that, later that same year, Michel Corrette (1707–95) published the work in a version more faithful to Gilles's intentions. *BreJeu, HajGil, HamMem, PraGil, QuiJeu, ZasApp.*

Girdlestone, Cuthbert M. Professor of French at what is now the University of Newcastle, Girdlestone (1895–1975) was a perceptive and engaging writer on music. His life-and-works study of Rameau, the first of its kind in English, did much to enhance the composer's reputation among Anglophone readers; it remains a thoroughly readable and inspiring introduction to the composer and his music, enlivened by copious music examples. Girdlestone's study of the *tragédie en musique** as a literary genre, though now rather dated in its approach, is notable for its abundant insights into the dramatic character of specific works. *GirRam, GirTra, GirVol.*

Glissando On keyboard instruments, a glissando is usually achieved by sliding the nail of a finger or thumb rapidly over the keys; the technique thus differs from portamento* (sometimes also referred to, justifiably, as glissando), which entails a gliding between notes without distinguishing the intervening pitches. While the use of portamento was not uncommon in music for voice or strings in Rameau's day, keyboard glissando was extremely rare in France; it is specified for the first time, to my knowledge, in Moyreau's *Pièces de clavecin* (1753) and later by Balbastre* and Michel Corrette. However, Siegbert Rampe has suggested that the scales at the end of each section of 'Les Trois Mains'* from Rameau's *Nouvelles suites de pièces de clavecin* are 'obviously intended to be taken as glissandi with the thumb' (see the example below). Rapid keyboard scales on the natural keys could certainly imply glissando, although this is more likely when the scales are slurred, as in Bach's Concerto for two harpsichords (BWV 1061), than when they are unslurred, as here. Yet Rampe's hypothesis gains support from the known presence of Domenico Scarlatti* in Paris in 1724 and 1725, the period when Rameau was beginning to compose his *Nouvelles suites*. In view of Scarlatti's well-known use of glissando, it may be no coincidence that Rameau seems to have adopted the technique so soon after the Italian's visits – and in a piece that includes characteristics of the fandango*. This of course assumes that Scarlatti had already adopted the technique: impossible to prove but not implausible, given the presence of a glissando in Sonata III of Azzolino della Ciaia's near-contemporary *Sonate per cembalo* of c.1727. *RpeKey, SadSca.*

Rameau, 'Les Trois Mains', *Nouvelles suites de pièces de clavecin*

Goethe, Johann Wolfgang von One of the more unexpected tributes to Rameau was paid by the 26-year-old Goethe (1749–1832), who contributed a eulogy on the composer to Johann Caspar Lavater's *Physiognomishe Fragmente, zur Beförderung der Menschenkenntniss und Menschenliebe* (Leipzig, 1775). This work, as its title suggests, examines the extent to which a person's character can be deduced from facial characteristics. Goethe assesses Rameau's nature from an engraving by Sturm copied from Saint-Aubin's* medallion, itself based on Caffieri's* bust of the composer. The writer is struck by Rameau's pure intellect and by the look in his eye that suggests attentiveness only to inner feeling. In later writings Goethe was to maintain a positive attitude towards Rameau and his achievement. Whether he knew much of the composer's music is, however, doubtful. He was later to publish a German translation of Diderot's* satire *Le Neveu de Rameau* (as *Rameaus Neffe*, 1805). *FosRam, GauJug, GétPor, RamCtw.*

Graffigny, Madame de Françoise d'Issembourg Du Buisson d'Happoncourt (1695–1758), generally referred to after her marriage as Madame de Graffigny, is increasingly regarded as one of the major French writers of the mid-eighteenth century. She achieved instant fame with her epistolary novel *Lettres d'une Péruvienne* (1747), while the sentimental comedy *Cénie* (1750) was one of the most successful plays of its day. The recent publication of her voluminous correspondence has brought to light, *inter alia*, numerous details about Rameau and his family, whom she encountered at social gatherings. Proud to consider herself a Ramoneuse*, Madame de Graffigny frequently attended performances and rehearsals* at the Opéra, and her letters often comment entertainingly on her experiences there. Thanks to this correspondence, we are now much better informed about Rameau's principal librettist, Louis de Cahusac*, an inner member of the Graffigny circle, in which he was known – ironically, no doubt – by the nicknames La Carpe, La Douceur and Le Doux. *DaiCor, SadPat, SouFêt, SouHym.*

Grand chœur From the beginnings of French opera, the chorus and orchestra were both divided into a *grand chœur* and a *petit chœur**. Contrary to the practice in the chorus*, where the members of the *petit chœur* were drawn from the full ensemble, the two orchestral 'choirs' remained to a large extent separate entities, combining in only a minority of movements. The orchestral *grand chœur* at the Académie Royale de Musique* remained fairly stable during Rameau's operatic career, though contemporary listings reveal a gradual increase in overall numbers:

Grand chœur of the Académie Royale de Musique

Instrument	1738	1750	1756	1760
flutes / oboes	5	5	6	6
bassoons	5	4	5	4
trumpet	–	1	1	1
horns	–	–	–	2
violins	12	16	16	15
violas (*hautes-contre* & *tailles*)	5	6	6	6
cellos	8	7	7	8
Total	35	39	41	42

The *grand chœur* included no continuo players, who all belonged to the *petit chœur*. More surprising is the absence of a double-bass instrument. The Académie's single *contrebasse** player belonged officially to the *petit chœur*, though he also took part in certain fully-scored movements involving the *grand chœur*. Instruments such as the *timbales**, *tambourin** and *musette* were played when required by members of the string section, as were the horn* and trumpet in the earlier part of this period.

The expression 'à grand chœur' is found in two specific contexts: to distinguish the *motet** *à grand chœur* from smaller-scale sacred genres; and to denote an orchestra in which the string section included two or more viola parts. *FavMot, GorOrc, GreDou, SadCan, SadInv, SadKey, SpiZas.*

Graun, Carl Heinrich   *See* **Telemann, Georg Philipp.**

Grimm, Frederich Melchior, baron von   A native of Regensburg, the German writer Grimm (1723–1807) settled in Paris in 1749, where he established the newsletter *Correspondance littéraire* (1753–73) for which he is now widely remembered. During his early years in France, Grimm was a staunch admirer of Rameau. His *Lettre sur Omphale* (1752), though comprising a withering critique of Destouches's* 51-year-old *Omphale* on the occasion of its fourth revival, is extravagant in its praise of Rameau's music and its 'variety of inspiration and expression'; the *Lettre* may thus be regarded as a belated contribution to the Lulliste-Ramiste* dispute. Yet in his *Petit prophète de Boehmischbroda* (1753), the pamphlet that launched the Querelle des Bouffons*, Grimm includes Rameau in his overall attack on French opera – a cynical *volte face* prompted, no doubt, by the Querelle's political sub-text. Thereafter, all Grimm's references to the composer are laced with heavy sarcasm; his obituary in the *Correspondance littéraire* is particularly negative, describing Rameau as avaricious and lacking any human sentiment, and his music as 'gothic'. *GrmCor, KafEnc, OliEnc, SclOtt.*

Guignon, Jean-Pierre   The virtuoso Italian violinist Giovanni Pietro Ghignone (1702–74), known in France as Jean-Pierre Guignon, made his Paris debut in 1725 at the newly founded Concert Spirituel*. In 1730 he joined the service of the prince de Carignan* and must therefore have met Rameau when the composer came under the prince's patronage between 1733 and 1736. Guignon, who was appointed *ordinaire de la musique du roi* in 1733, is one of two royal musicians whom Rameau names in *Génération harmonique* during the course of a discussion of tuning systems: Rameau cites Guignon's statement that the best string players tempered the fifths of their open strings in order to 'soften the harshness' of the interval formed by the lowest and highest strings – evidence the author uses to bolster his argument in favour of equal temperament*. *See also* **Caix, de.**   *ChrTho, LauÉco, RamCwt, SadPat.*

Guimard, Marie-Madeleine   After making her debut at the Académie Royale de Musique* in 1762, Mlle Guimard (1743–1816) established herself as the star female dancer of her generation, best remembered for her participation in Gluck's Parisian operas during the 1770s. Although she created no roles for Rameau, she took part in numerous revivals of his operas. Noverre praised the charm, simplicity and impeccable taste of her dancing. *BouHer, CamAca, NovLet.*

La Guirlande, ou Les fleurs enchantées   This *acte de ballet**, the second of Rameau's four collaborations with Marmontel*, was first performed at the Académie Royale de Musique* on 21 September 1751 in a triple bill that included 'Les Sauvages' from *Les Indes galantes* (1736) and Rebel* and Francœur's *Les Génies tutélaires*, the latter also receiving its premiere. This composite spectacle constituted the Académie's first celebration of the birth of the duc de Bourgogne, though nothing in the present work suggests that it had been designed for that purpose. The opera was well received, achieving a respectable total of twenty-two performances on its first run and a further twenty when it was revived in 1762. It has the distinction of being the first Rameau opera to be revived in 'modern' times, being performed in 1903 at the Schola Cantorum, Paris, when the audience included Debussy*. *BouHer, GirRam, GreSou, MasOpé.*

Handel, George Frideric   According to Sir John Hawkins (*A General History of the Science and Practice of Music*, 1776), 'Mr. Handel was ever wont to speak of [Rameau] in terms of great respect'. From the context of this remark, Handel (1685–1759) was referring to his French contemporary as a theorist rather than a composer. Nevertheless, his library included not only Rameau's 'various treatises on the art' but also the scores of his harpsichord pieces and unspecified operas. Handel seems to have borrowed uncharacteristically little from Rameau, though a resemblance has been noted between the opening of 'La Forqueray'* and a passage in the overture to Handel's *Joseph and his Brethren*, and also between the chorus 'Que jusqu'aux cieux s'élèvent nos accords' in *Les Fêtes d'Hébé* and the start of 'And the Glory of the Lord' in *Messiah*. Rameau's pieces had been published respectively two and three years before the premieres of these Handel works. Rather more significant is Rameau's debt to Handel. One movement in *La Princesse de Navarre* (1745) shares two themes with the aria 'Honour and arms' in *Samson* (1743), while the A minor Gavotte* with six *doubles* is closely modelled on Handel's D minor keyboard variations (HWV 428) and helped stimulate a new trend for multiple pattern-variations* in the French harpsichord repertory from the mid-1720s onwards. *ChaHib, GilRam, SadHan.*

Haute-contre   In French opera of the Lully-Rameau period the *haute-contre* was the heroic voice par excellence – the voice-type to which the leading male roles were usually assigned. Exhaustive research has confirmed that this voice-type is not at all the equivalent of 'countertenor', if by that term is meant 'falsettist'. Rather the solo *haute-contre* was a high tenor who did not make use of the falsetto register. In this respect it was quite distinct from the contemporary Italian *tenore*, whose range was extended upwards by as much as a fifth with the aid of falsetto. Surprisingly, perhaps, contemporary descriptions reveal that the *haute-contre* was generally considered a more powerful voice than the *tenore*. At the beginning of Rameau's operatic career, the standard range of solo parts was *f* to *b'* (the approximate equivalent of *e♭* to *a'* at modern concert pitch), but by the 1750s this had been extended upwards by at least a tone. The relative importance of the *haute-contre* also grew during those years. In 1738 a list of 'acteurs des rôles' included three *hautes-contre* (to use the correct form of plural), one *taille** (tenor) and six *basses-tailles** (baritone); by 1760 the balance had shifted, with six *hautes-contre*, one *taille* and only three *basses-tailles*. Such an evolution was encouraged by the powerful and effortless singing of Pierre Jéliote*, the most celebrated *haute-contre* of the entire era. Only after his retirement from the Académie Royale de Musique*, in 1755, do we encounter criticism that some inferior singers now used falsetto for the highest notes, a practice which the French found disagreeable. In choruses at the Opéra and elsewhere, the 'alto' line was assigned to *hautes-contre*, who mainly used their chest voices. *CyrHau, CyrEss, ParFal, ZasEni.*

Haute-contre de violon   By the 1720s the standard French orchestra was based on a four-part string section comprising two viola parts – the *haute-contre de violon* and *taille de violon**. The *hautes-contre* operated within the upper end of the instrument's compass; their part was normally written in the soprano clef (C[1]), which had the advantage of avoiding leger lines above the staff, much of their music being written in first position. (Only from the 1740s onwards did the use of higher positions become more common). In Rameau's scores this part is often abbreviated 'h.c.'. When the two viola parts played in unison, their line was labelled *parties**. *LemHip, MasOpé, GorOrc, RosOrc, SadOrc, SpiZas.*

Hippolyte et Aricie   Rameau's first opera, on a libretto by Simon-Joseph Pellegrin*, was premiered at the Académie Royale de Musique* on 1 October 1733, six days after the composer's fiftieth birthday. To many opera-goers Rameau was previously known, if at all, more as a learned theorist than as a creative artist. The boldness of this *tragédie en musique** sharply divided public opinion and set in motion the long-running Lulliste-Ramiste* dispute. Although many people gradually warmed to the emotional power of Rameau's music, this opera had a troubled early history. The technical inadequacy or insubordination of certain performers led to the abandoning of the celebrated enharmonic* passage in the second Trio des Parques*, while public criticism forced some major restructuring of the opera. The first two scenes of Act V were cut because they infringed the conventional unity* of place; thus audiences never learned subsequently of Phaedra's tragic fate or of Theseus's divine punishment for initiating his son Hippolytus's apparent death. The powerful *air de monologue** 'Cruelle mère des Amours' at the start of Act III was replaced by a shorter and blander movement. Even more damaging was a revision of Pellegrin's inspired positioning of the Act III divertissement*, originally situated at the point where Theseus has just witnessed an apparently incestuous assault on Phaedra by his son and is about to make his tragic decision to avenge this outrage. A divertissement at that point was nevertheless thought too unconventional, and it was moved to a weaker position the end of the act. These and other changes, made against Rameau's better judgement, severely blunted the work's impact. Although *Hippolyte et Aricie* was successfully revived in 1742, 1757 and 1767, this work never enjoyed the level of esteem enjoyed by *Castor et Pollux* or *Dardanus*. Nowadays, restored to its original state, it is regarded as one of Rameau's towering achievements. *See also* **Montéclair, Michel Pignolet de.** *BouHer, BouHi1, BouHi2, BucSup, BurHip, CazHip, DilIma, DilMon, GirRam, GirTra, GreSou, KinPoé, MalHip, NorPhe, RosScè, SadHip, ThoAes, WooSad, VerDra, VerRec.*

Horns   Not until 1759 were horn players regularly included in listings of the Académie Royale de Musique* orchestra. Before that date, horns had been played by various members of the string section or occasionally by supernumeraries. Rameau initially used the traditional hooped *cor de chasse* in D in scenes associated with the hunt; in his first opera, *Hippolyte et Aricie* (1733), the horn part never divides and is limited to simple hunting fanfares. In *Les Fêtes d'Hébé* (1739) the instrument is no longer linked with the hunt; moreover, horns in F and D are required: the former in Act I, the latter in three dances added to Act II for the Italian ballerina Barbarina Campanini* as the 'Génie de la Victoire'. From the 1740s onwards, Rameau calls for horns in a wider variety of keys – E and G in *Le Temple de la Gloire* (1745), C, D, F, G and A in *Les Paladins* (1760) and C, D, F and E♭ in *Les Boréades* (1763). While it is has been assumed that such instruments were the new German orchestral horns with crooks, there is evidence that multiple horns in different tonalities were now being made in France: in 1753 the duc d'Aumont commissioned seven pairs of horns pitched respectively in C, D, E, F, G, A and B♭, which were used in opera performances at court and elsewhere; moreover, an inventory of 1767 reveals that the Académie Royale de Musique owned five pairs of horns in different keys. Whatever the intended instrument, Rameau became increasingly fond of horns, using them from the mid-1740s onwards in a wider range of contexts and exploiting their role as sustaining instruments. Moreover, the technical demands of his horn parts steadily increases, eventually requiring some hand-stopping. One curious feature of Rameau's designation of horn parts is apparent in his autograph and engraved scores: whereas his labelling of other instruments meticulously distinguishes between singular and plural ('premier / premiers', 'deuxième / deuxièmes'), divided horns are invariably labelled 'premier cors / deuxième cors'. Given that only one player per part is ever required, the composer clearly thought of the word 'cors' as singular. Thus the rubric 'cors seul' on the horn line in *Hippolyte et Aricie* was Rameau's idiosyncratic way of indicating that a single instrument was required. *See also the music example in* **Double clefs**. *BouBor, BouPri, DubTem, GorOrc, SadInv, SadOrc.*

Identité des octaves   To Rameau, it seemed self-evident that all intervals larger than an octave were merely octave doublings of the equivalent smaller interval: hence the ninth was a compound second, the tenth a compound third, and so on. It was thus necessary for him to devise the concept of *supposition** to explain such chords as the ninth and eleventh. His belief in octave identity eventually brought him into conflict with Leonhard Euler*, who countered his assertion that octave duplications were identical to the unison with arguments that Rameau was unable to refute. *ChrTho, JacCtw, LesThe.*

L'Impatience   According to Maret*, this cantata was composed during Rameau's time in Clermont* – presumably the second period (1715–22) rather than the first (1702–05), since the *cantate françoise** as a genre had barely established itself by then. Given that the work is a soliloquy addressed by an impatient lover to his beloved Corinne, it may be sung by a *haute-contre** even though the vocal line is notated in the treble clef (G^2), as was the convention in such cases. The technically demanding obbligato line calls for a seven-string *basse de viole*. *BouHer, CyrCan, CyrChr, CyrEss, CyrPer, DorCan, MarÉlo, MonBou, TunCan.*

In convertendo Dominus   When this *motet* à grand chœur* was given three performances at the Concert Spirituel* in March and April 1751, the *Mercure de France** reported that it had been composed 'almost 40 years ago'. This would place its composition during Rameau's years in Lyon* between July 1712 and March 1715. The Académie des Beaux-Arts in Lyon* acquired a score and sixty parts of the work, probably some years after the composer had moved to Clermont*. The text is taken mainly from Psalm 125 of the Vulgate, though one verse ('Laudabo nomen Dei') comes from Psalm 68 and may once have formed part of a now-lost setting of *Salvum me fac Deus**. The principal source of *In convertendo* is an autograph score prepared for performance at the Concert Spirituel in 1751. This score, written on paper dating from no earlier than 1742, includes many second thoughts. Whereas some movements are relatively untouched, others have been revised so extensively that little trace of the original remains.

It is even possible, as Thomas Green suggests, that these revisions were made after the 1751 performances, in response to widespread criticism of the motet. The Lyon Académie acquired a score of this revised version by May 1754, and the work was performed there in February 1771. *BouHer, DurMot, DurRel, FavMot, GreSou, HerMot, MalMot, PieCon, ValAca, ValLyo.*

Inclina Domine   A setting of this text with an attribution to Rameau survives in the Bibliothèque Nationale de France. The work is a solo *motet** for *basse-taille** accompanied by flutes, violins, bassoons and continuo. Mary Cyr has shown that the attribution to Rameau dates from the nineteenth century and that the piece was actually composed by François Martin* and first performed in 1751 at the Concert Spirituel*. The surviving score is evidently in Martin's own hand. *CyrEss, CyrInc, FavMot, LebFon.*

Les Indes galantes   The production score of Rameau's second opera bears the title 'Les Victoires galantes', though the present title had been adopted by the time of the premiere. Scores and librettos classify *Les Indes galantes* as a *ballet* or, more often, a *ballet héroïque**, although it belongs to the genre that aestheticians of Rameau's day categorized as *opéra-ballet**. The librettist Louis Fuzelier* modelled the work on the specific kind of *opéra-ballet* pioneered by La Motte* and Campra* in *L'Europe galante* (1697) which is peopled by modern rather than mythological characters. Fuzelier's libretto can, indeed, be seen as a direct counterpart to La Motte's: where *L'Europe galante* presents stereotypes of love as found in four European countries, *Les Indes* treats attitudes to love in four regions of the 'Indes' – at that time a convenient term for almost any exotic, non-European location. The plots of the four entrées* unfold respectively near a Peruvian volcano; on an island in the Indian Ocean; in a Persian flower market; and in a North American forest. The topicality of Fuzelier's situations may be judged from the fact that some were derived from published reports of recent events or from personal experience. When *Les Indes galantes* was premiered at the Académie Royale de Musique* on 23 August 1735, it consisted of only the prologue and two entrées, 'Les Incas du Pérou' and 'Le Turc généreux'. The entrée 'Les Fleurs' was added at the third performance but was then heavily revised after criticism of the perceived absurdity of disguising the hero as a woman. In response to public dissatisfaction with the work's dramatic dialogue, Rameau took the unusual step of publishing the prologue and three entrées without recitative and reconstituted as 'Quatre grands concerts'*. An additional entrée, 'Les Sauvages', was added on 10 March 1736. Despite the various criticisms, the opera's first production ran to sixty-three performances, and the work was thereafter frequently revived either as a whole (with the entrées rearranged in varying permutations) or as separate entrées. *See also* **Fragments**. *BloNat, BouHer, DuaInd, GirRam, LecDiv, MalInd, MasOpé, MelPar, SavAme, WolInd.*

'L'Indifférente'   Commentators have noted similarities between the titles of several pieces by Rameau and Dandrieu*, among them this one, which Dandrieu used a year or so before Rameau, in his *Second livre de pièces de clavecin* (1728). The deliberately ambiguous title of the latter's short piece, from the *Nouvelles suites de pièces de clavecin* (1729 or 1730), would have conveyed as many meanings to an eighteenth-century player or listener as it does today:

impartial, unconcerned, apathetic, insensitive to love... *DicAut, GirRam, GusFul, FraDan, RaySav, RpeKey.*

'L'Indiscrette' The deliberately ambiguous title of this rondeau from the *Pièces de clavecin en concerts* (1741) could refer to an indiscreet action or individual, someone incapable of keeping secret, or the tell-tale glances that betray one's private thoughts. This last meaning may be hinted at in Rameau's rondeau refrain, with its contrast of outward calm (the even quavers in the violin and bass viol parts) and inner turbulence (a swirling harpsichord accompaniment of quintuplet semiquavers). In his arrangement for solo harpsichord included in the 1741 volume, Rameau drastically simplifies the refrain, stripping away the quintuplets and leaving the harpsichord with just the even quavers of the original violin and bass viol lines. *BouHer, DicAut, HerMor, GirRam, RpeKey.*

D'Indy, Vincent As director of the Schola Cantorum from 1900, Vincent d'Indy (1851–1931) was active in the promotion of early music in France; his many concert performances there included three Rameau operas: *La Guirlande* (1903), *Castor et Pollux* (excerpts, 1903) and *Dardanus* (1907). For the Rameau *Œuvres complètes** he edited *Hippolyte et Aricie* (1900), *Dardanus* (1905) and *Zaïs* (1911). Unfortunately, these editions are marred by countless unreported 'improvements' to the orchestration and voice-leading. Such editorial liberties, evidently motivated by d'Indy's extreme political and religious beliefs, make his editions largely unusable, though the prefaces by Charles Malherbe* remain essential reading. *See also* **Editions**. *EllEar, FosRam, PauInd, SadSaë, SadVin.*

Io There is no evidence that this *acte de ballet** was ever performed in Rameau's lifetime. It was once suspected of being the composer's last work, on the grounds that all surviving sources break off before the final divertissement*. But *Io* includes a duet whose text and music are found in a more polished form in *Les Fêtes de Polymnie*, while the music also appears in *La Princesse de Navarre*. As both these works were premiered in 1745, *Io* must presumably have been written by then. There is, however, no reason to believe that the librettist of either work, respectively Cahusac and Voltaire, was responsible for the *Io* libretto. *BouHer, BouRam, GreSou, MasOpé, SadBor.*

Jacobi, Erwin R. A noted specialist in the history of music theory, Jacobi (1909–78) wrote extensively on the contributions of Rameau and his contemporaries to this field. His facsimile edition of Rameau's complete theoretical writings (1967–72) includes numerous ancillary documents, including contemporary reviews and reports; these, along with his own meticulous prefaces to the six volumes in this series, provide an unrivalled resource for the study of the development of Rameau's theories and their reception. In the course of his research, Jacobi published newly discovered correspondence between Rameau and other European scholars, including Bernouilli*, Euler* and Martini*. Jacobi, who was also a keyboard player, produced the first reliable modern edition of Rameau's solo harpsichord music (1966). *See also* **'La Dauphine'**. *JacMar, JacNou, JacPiè, JacVér, RamCtw.*

Jacobins The Dominican monastery in Lyon where Rameau was organist from 1713 until 1715 was known colloquially as the Jacobins ('Les Pères Dominicains dits Jacobins'). Although his official contract dates from December

1713, it is possible that the composer took up this post in the previous May or June, soon after a new organ by Julien Tribuot had been installed. This four-manual instrument consisted of fourteen stops on the *grand orgue*, two (a *jeu de trompette* and five-rank *cornet*) on the *récit*, four on the écho, ten on the *positif* and three on the *pédale*. Rameau's salary was 200 *livres* per year. *BreJeu, GirRam, KocSer, MonBou, QuiJeu, ValLyo, ValRam.*

'Le Jardinier et les ciseaux'   *See* **Leclair, Jean-Marie.**

Javillier family   Several members of this family of dancers were members of the Académie Royale de Musique* during Rameau's time. Claude (Javillier *père*) entered the Académie in 1701 and had become ballet master of the Académie's dance school by 1738. His three sons, often referred to as Javillier 1, 2, and 3 (or *l'aîné, le cadet* and *le jeune*), were active during the 1730s and 1740s and created many dance roles in the Rameau operas of those years. *BouHer, CamAca, SadDan.*

Jean-Philippe Rameau: Opera Omnia   *See* **OOR.**

Jéliote, Pierre   Recruited at great expense from Toulouse, where he had been a choirboy, Jéliote (1713–97) made his debut at the Académie Royale de Musique* in 1733, only a few months before the premiere of Rameau's first opera, *Hippolyte et Aricie*. Among his first roles was that of Amour in the prologue of this work. The fact that the part is written in the treble clef has led to speculation that his voice had not yet broken. However, it is more likely that the role was allotted to him at the last minute, a conclusion supported by the fact that the other part he sang in this work (Première Parque [Fate]) is written in the alto clef normally used by *hautes-contre**. Within a few years Jéliote was playing all the leading *haute-contre* roles. Those he created for Rameau include the title roles in *Dardanus, Platée* (at court but not in the 1749 and subsequent revivals at the Opéra), *Zaïs, Pigmalion* and *Zoroastre*. An inventory of Académie employees in 1738 describes him as having 'one of the most beautiful voices for clarity and ornamentation [*cadences*]'. His upper register, which ascended to *d''* (approximately *c''* at modern pitch), was remarkable for its flexibility and heroic character. He retired from the Académie in 1755 but continued to sing in concerts, in productions at court and at the Concert Spirituel*. In contemporary documents his name is variously spelt Jéliote or Géliotte (with or without an accent) but never in the form '[de] Jélyotte' adopted in many modern writings. *BouHer, BouHip, CamAca, PieCon, PouJél, SadInv, VlaTed, WooSad.*

'Je suis un fou'   The earliest known source of this playful three-part canon at the unison is a manuscript collection of drinking songs and canons in the municipal library at Châlons-en-Champagne (Ms. 282) dated 1720, in which it is unattributed. The piece is attributed to Rameau in a manuscript in the Santini collection in Münster. It also appears in the Recueil Bresou* and in a manuscript miscellany in the Decroix* collection said to have been found among Rameau's papers; in the latter it is written on the reverse side of a copy of Rameau's duo 'Lucas pour se gausser'. *BouCan, BouHer, MonBou.*

Jeu de théâtre   Widely used in contemporary reviews and assessments of stage performers, this term denotes the actor's gestures, attitudes and demeanour. *BarAct, DicAut, WaeGes.*

'Journal de l'Opéra'   When Charles Nuitter (1828–99) was appointed archivist at the Académie Royale de Musique*, he undertook to compile a ledger listing the daily repertoire of the Opéra from its foundation in 1671 onwards. His reconstruction of the early period, in the manuscript 'Journal de l'Opéra', was based on press reports, diaries and material from the Académie's archives, some of which no longer exist. Each opening of the 'Journal' is devoted to a specific month: the right-hand side lists the dates of each performance, together with the box-office takings (where known), while the facing page provides details of associated events that took place on that day – the visit of some dignitary; the titles of competing events at other theatres; the debut, retirement or death of an Académie singer or dancer, and so on. This manuscript, which was continued long after Nuitter's death, is still held by the Bibliothèque Nationale de France (Bibliothèque-Musée de l'Opéra), and may now be consulted online.

Journal de Trévoux   Officially entitled *Mémoires pour l'histoire des sciences & des beaux-arts*, this erudite if conservative monthly journal was generally known as the *Journal* [or *Mémoires*] *de Trévoux*, after its original place of publication. It was founded by the Jesuits with the aim of providing the public with an up-to-date account of developments in the sciences and arts. Among its most faithful contributors was Louis-Bernard Castel*, whose extensive reviews of the *Traité de l'harmonie* and *Nouveau systême de musique théorique* were the first to bring Rameau's theoretical works to widespread public notice throughout Europe. Castel's later reviews of Rameau's writings proved more critical, and his assessment of *Génération harmonique* provoked a sharp rebuttal from the composer, entitled 'Remarques [...] sur l'extrait qu'on a donné de son livre intitulé *Génération harmonique*, dans le *Journal de Trévoux*, décembre 1737'. This proved too strong for the Jesuits, and the riposte eventually appeared in the free-thinking *Le Pour et contre*. *ChrTho, RamCtw, SgaDic.*

'La Joyeuse'   The jubilant character of this gavotte-like rondeau from the *Pièces de clavessin* (1724) is expressed in the many carillon-like scales in close canon, one involving a continuous descent of three octaves. These canons feature both in the refrain and in the two *couplets**, though the latter both begin with a contrasting hurdy-gurdy-like melody over a drone. The title became popular in French keyboard publications of the 1730s and 1740s. *BouHer, GirRam, GusFul, RpeKey*

Key characteristics   During the transition from modality to modern tonality, several French theorists attempted to pinpoint the emotive character of individual keys. Rameau's contribution to this development appeared in his *Traité de l'harmonie* (1722), in the wake of listings by Jean Rousseau (1691), Marc-Antoine Charpentier* (c.1692) and Charles Masson (1697). For Rameau, the major keys of C, D and A were suitable for songs of jubilation and rejoicing ('chants d'allegresse & de rejoüissance'), F and B♭ for storms, furies and such-like ('tempests, [...] furies & autres sujets de cette espece'), G and E for 'tender and cheerful pieces' ('chants tendres et gais') and D, A and E for grandeur and magnificence ('le grand et le magnifique'). The minor keys of D, G, B and E expressed sweetness and tenderness ('la douceur & [...] la tendresse'); C and F minor were suited both to tenderness and to plaints ('convient à la tendresse & aux plaintes'), while F and B♭ minor were suitable for funereal pieces ('chants lugubres'). Such subjective listings were influenced by various factors, foremost among them the effect of the unequal tuning systems still in general use. As Rameau put it: 'the major third, which moves us naturally to joy [...], impresses upon us ideas even of fury when it is too large. The minor third, which brings us naturally to sweetness and tenderness, saddens us when it is too small' (*Nouveau système de musique théorique*, 1726). Thus the more flats or sharps in a signature, the more extreme the emotional state. Although major keys were generally associated with cheerful, positive emotions, and minor ones with tenderness or sorrow, Rameau considered the flat keys to be intrinsically darker in colour than the sharp ones, hence his choice of E♭ major to express the intense pathos of Télaïre's air 'Tristes apprêts' (*Castor et Pollux*, II, 4). Key-character was also influenced by the construction and capabilities of wind instruments. The 'rejoicing' associated with C and D major was partly conditioned by the fact that French trumpets were built in those keys, while the 'tenderness' of G major and the simple minor keys is doubtless linked with the character of the newly developed Baroque flute and recorder, which – at least in the early days – sounded best in those tonalities. Associations with instrumental colour may also explain one apparent oddity – the association of F and B♭ major with storms and furies. Following the lead of Charpentier, who also characterizes F major as 'furious and quick-tempered' ('furieux et emporté'), Rameau frequently uses these 'darker' major keys for this purpose, partly for the practical reason that the oboes and bassoons that invariably doubled the outer string parts in such contexts could more comfortably negotiate rapid semiquaver runs in these keys. In the *Traité* Rameau states that keys other than those listed 'are not in general use', yet by the 1740s his operas include modulations to keys as extreme as G♯ major. By that time, he had come to advocate equal temperament* and renounced his earlier opinions on key-character. *SteKey.*

La Borde, Jean-Benjamin de   *See* 'La Laborde'.

La Bruère, Charles-Antoine Le Clerc de   An amateur writer of noble birth, Le Clerc de La Bruère (1715–54) began his literary career at the age of nineteen with the comedy *Les Mécontents* (1734). When his patron the duc de Nivernais was appointed ambassador to the Papal Court in 1743, La Bruère followed him to Rome. His first libretto was the *opéra-ballet** *Les Voyages de l'Amour* (1736) with music by Boismortier. Although this work enjoyed little success, Voltaire praised the libretto for its grace and wit. La Bruère is presumed to have met Rameau at the dining club known as the Caveau*. Their first collaboration, in the late 1730s, did not initially lead to success; La Bruère's libretto for *Dardanus**, despite a high-minded political theme, was savaged by the critics: the marquis d'Argenson* described the plot as 'a potpourri of ill-matched supernatural incidents, from which all interest is banished'. The fundamentally revised version prepared for the 1744 revival was somewhat more successful. When *Dardanus* was further revived in 1760 it had come to be regarded as one of French opera's chief glories. La Bruère's one other collaboration with Rameau was on the ill-fated *Linus**. *ArgNot, BesVol, ButCho, DacDar, DavHer, DilMon, GirRam, MalDar, MasOpé, VerDra.*

La Condamine, Charles-Marie de   *See* **Maupertuis, Pierre-Louis.**

La Laurencie, Lionel de   In his late thirties La Laurencie (1861–1933) abandoned an administrative career to devote himself to musicology, specializing in French music from Lully* to Gluck. His writings on Rameau include a short but perceptive biography (1908) and several articles reporting major archival discoveries relating to the composer's family, his financial affairs, his use of clarinets and much else. *LauCla, LauDoc, LauÉco, LauGen, LauLet, LauRam, LauSai, LauTel, MélLau.*

La Motte, Antoine Houdar de   An influential aesthetician of French theatre and a leading 'modern' in the quarrel between the Anciens and Modernes, Houdar de La Motte (1672–1731) was also a prolific dramatist. His libretto for Campra's* *L'Europe galante* of 1697 established the genre of *opéra-ballet**, while his librettos in this and other formats greatly expanded the role of the divertissement*. In 1727 La Motte evidently rejected Rameau's request for a libretto, seemingly on the grounds that Rameau had no experience of writing opera and that he was really only a theorist. On 25 October the composer sent a spirited reply countering these charges: he declares that only a 'school musician' would be so absorbed in theory as to sacrifice 'common sense, wit and feeling'; he confirms that he has 'studied Nature before having painted her' (La Motte was a strong advocate of the concept of imitation of nature) and invites the poet to come and hear how his compositions characterize a wide range of moods and emotions. Rameau's letter, found among La Motte's papers, was published in the *Mercure de France** in 1765. In La Motte's defence it should be said that by 1727 he was blind and crippled with arthritis, while his days as a librettist were already two decades behind him. He may even have supplied Rameau with a cantata text in response to the composer's admission that he lacked suitable words: it may be no coincidence that *Le Berger fidèle**, described as a 'cantate nouvelle', was publicly performed only a year later. Eventually, Rameau did get to set part of a La Motte libretto – the entrée* 'La Sculpture', heavily adapted as *Pigmalion**. *AntFre, GirRam, KinPoé, MarÉlo.*

La Pouplinière, Alexandre-Jean-Joseph Le Riche de   In the mid-1730s, several years after his first opera, Rameau came under the protection of the weathly tax-farmer (*fermier général*) Le Riche de La Pouplinière (1693–1762). It was long believed that Rameau joined the financier's circle as early as 1731, but the re-dating of Voltaire's correspondence reveals that this did not happen until some time between November 1735 and August 1736. Evidence to the contrary – an anecdote first recounted some twenty-five years after the event and a description of a society wedding in which La Pouplinière is said to have 'loaned' Rameau to the financier Samuel Bernard in 1733 – is unreliable or, in the latter case, forged. In fact, the composer's patron between December 1733 and 1735 is known to have been the prince de Carignan*, La Pouplinière's arch-rival. In or about 1734 the latter took as mistress and later married Thérèse Deshayes*, a devoted pupil of Rameau, and it may well have been she who persuaded her future husband to invite the newly-fashionable composer into his household.

Rameau's association with La Pouplinière, which lasted from about 1736 until 1753, was of the utmost importance to his career. According to Grimm*, the financier's home was 'a meeting-place for all classes. Courtiers, men of the world, literary folk, artists, foreigners, actors, actresses, *filles de joie*, all were assembled there. The house was known as the menagerie and the host as the sultan'. Yet little is known about the terms of Rameau's appointment or, before 1751, the size and constitution of his patron's musical establishment. In 1741 La Pouplinière took over some of the prince of Carignan's players, including the violinist Joseph Canavas and possibly the flautist Michel Blavet and violinist Jean-Pierre Guignon*. Singers and dancers from the Paris Opéra were frequent dinner guests and took part in concerts and theatrical entertainments. In the later 1740s La Pouplinière was to import from Germany and Bohemia virtuosos of the clarinet* and orchestral horn*. These instruments were then new to France, and Rameau was the first to use them at the Paris Opéra. *See also* **Marmontel**; **'Paroles qui ont précédé le Te Deum'**. *BesVol, BouRam, CucPou, DaiCor, HenAri, SadPat.*

La Salle, marquis de An important source of music by Rameau and his contemporaries originates from the extensive library of Marie-Louis Caillebot, marquis de La Salle (1716–1798). This collection, confiscated during the Revolution, included some 460 music books, scores and part-books, now preserved in the Bibliothèque Nationale de France (Bibliothèque-Musée de l'Opéra and Département de la musique), Paris. The marquis was a keen amateur violinist and singer. From 1747 to 1750 he participated in Madame de Pompadour's Théâtre des Petits Cabinets*, taking the roles of Le Temps and Linus in the original version of Rameau's *Les Surprises de l'Amour* (1748). He also organized numerous private performances of operas. Among the materials prepared for these events are ten sets of part-books of Rameau operas. These are derived from authoritative sources, since some of them include corrections and revisions by scribes from the Académie Royale de Musique*, including Lallemand* and Durand*, and others from the Menus-Plaisirs*. Their principal value to the modern editor is as a reliable source of the inner choral and orchestral parts, which are often lacking in other sources. *BouDen, BouHer, GreSou, LemHip.*

La Tour, Maurice Quentin de In 1911 Théophile Eck explored the possibility that a pastel 'Sketch for a portrait of a man' by Quentin de La Tour (1704–88) was a depiction of Rameau. The two men must surely have known each other through their close association with La Pouplinière*, who happens to be the subject of one of La Tour's portraits. Still, there is little else to support Eck's hypothesis, and the pastel, in the Musée Antoine Lecuyer at Saint Quentin, is now catalogued as 'Portrait d'inconnu'. *EckRam, GétPor, LauGen.*

'Laboravi clamans' Published by Rameau in his *Traité de l'harmonie** as an example of fugal procedures, this piece is headed 'Quinque', a Latin term that Brossard's *Dictionaire* (1703) defines as a quintet for solo voices. In Rameau's day, an ensemble of this kind would normally be found only in a *motet** *à grand chœur*. Given that the text of 'Laboravi' and one movement of *In convertendo** are from the psalm *Salvum me fac Deus**, it has plausibly been suggested by Jean Duron that both movements originated in a now-lost setting of this psalm. *BouHer, BroDic, DurMot, DurRel, GirRam, MalMot.*

'La Laborde' It is widely assumed that the title of this movement from the *Pièces de clavecin en concerts* (1741) refers to Jean-Benjamin de La Borde (1734–94), an aristocrat who later distinguished himself as a composer and writer on music. True, La Borde had barely reached the age of seven when this piece was published, but he was something of a prodigy: having studied harmony and composition with Rameau, he produced his first *opéra comique**, to considerable acclaim, when he was only fourteen. *BouHer, GirRam, GusFul, HerMor, MarÉlo, RpeKey.*

Lalande, Michel-Richard de   As *surintendant* of the royal chapel, Lalande (1657–1726) established the classic 'Versailles' *motet** *à grand chœur*, developed as a sacred counterpart to the Lullian *tragédie en musique**. These genres being regarded as twin statements of France's national musical identity, Lalande was dubbed 'the Latin Lully' by his pupil Collin de Blamont. Rameau's motets, like most others of the period, adopt the structural model of Lalande's. As a symptom of Rameau's familiarity with the older composer's motets, the mourning chorus 'Que tout gémisse' in *Castor et Pollux* quotes the opening of Lalande's *De profundis*. Rameau's chorus was in turn adapted to the words 'Kyrie eleison' for performance during the memorial* services after his death. *See also* **'Paroles qui ont précédé le Te Deum'**. *AntFre, DurMot, FavMot.*

Lallemand, Brice   For much of Rameau's operatic career at the Académie Royale de Musique*, the *copiste de musique* (chief scribe) was Brice Lallemand. Born in 1684 or 1685, Lallemand entered the Académie in c.1708 and still held this post some four decades later. His annual salary was 600 *livres*, much the same as that of a chorus member or rank-and-file orchestral player. He regularly earned a further 350 *livres* for overtime and a supplement of 200 *livres* for work related to the Concert Spirituel* during the period when this series was administered by the Académie (1734–49). In addition to numerous sources copied for use at the Académie itself, Lallemand's hand can be identified in performing materials prepared for productions at the royal court and for private individuals such as the marquis de La Salle*. Towards the end of the 1740s Lallemand went blind, and from November 1749 a proxy was obliged to sign documents on his behalf. From about that time his eventual successor, Durand*, had begun to take over his duties, though Lallemand officially retained the title of *copiste* until 1751. He died some time between 1754 and 1756. As chief scribe, Lallemand was in charge of the Académie's copying shop in the Magasin* de l'Opéra, where he supervised the work of at least five assistants; these were evidently paid out of his very modest salary. He would typically prepare a master copy of each choral and orchestral part, farming these out to his assistants to prepare multiple copies. He was also responsible for repairing manuscripts and performing parts, for incorporating revisions when operas were revived, and for assigning specific part-books to individual singers and players. *BouDen, BouHer, GreSou, RosLal.*

Lany family   Several members of this family of dancers were members of the Académie Royale de Musique* in Rameau's day. Jean-Barthélemy Lany (1718–86) entered in 1740 but moved three years later to the court of Frederick II of Prussia. He returned to Paris in 1748, serving as solo dancer and ballet master* at the Académie until his retirement in 1769, his responsibilities thus including the choreography of Rameau's operas from *Naïs* onwards. Noverre*, hardly an impartial commentator, considered him a mediocre choreographer; it was nevertheless during Lany's years as ballet master that the use of *ballet figuré** and *pantomime** became more widespread, leading to a closer integration of dance and plot. In 1762 he was appointed Louis XV's *maître des ballets*. His sister and pupil Louise-Madeleine Lany (1733–77) appeared as a child prodigy at the Opéra-Comique* in *L'Ambigu de la folie*, a *parodie* of *Les Indes galantes* that was evidently conducted by Rameau himself. She went on to enjoy a brilliant career at the Académie from 1748 to 1767. Noverre was one of many who praised her dazzling technique. Two further members of the family, identified in librettos as Lany *le cadet* and Lany 3ᵉ, danced in revivals of several Rameau operas between 1763 and 1770. *BouHer, CamAca, ChrInt, NovLet, PorNov, PorPre.*

'La Lapoplinière' The dedicatee of this movement from the *Pièces de clavecin en concerts* (1741) is generally agreed to be La Pouplinière*, Rameau's principal patron since the mid-1730s, something of whose character may be captured in the capricious thematic changes, grandiose pauses and ostentatious hand-crossings. *CucPou, GirRam, HerMor, RpeKey, SadPat.*

'Le Lardon' In the eighteenth century the word *lardon* was not yet used as a familiar term for a child or 'kid'; rather, it commonly denoted something inserted: strips of salted pork for interlarding a joint, for example, or a loose-leaf insert into a newspaper ('feuillet qui sert de supplément à une gazette'). 'Le Lardon', from Rameau's *Pièces de clavessin* of 1724, literally embodies the physical insertion of the fingers of one hand between the other, a technique required for the detached chords at the opening and elsewhere. In this little menuet, the connection between title and music is only fully apparent in live performance; it might indeed be intended as a private joke for the performer's benefit. *DicAut, GirRam, GusFul, RpeKey.*

Larrivée, Henri While working as an apprentice wig-maker, Larrivée (1737–1802) was talent-spotted by François Rebel* and recruited to the Académie Royale de Musique* chorus in 1755 as a *basse-taille*. He began taking solo roles and soon established himself as a star singer and a skilful actor. His career lasted more than thirty years, extending well into the era of Gluck's Parisian operas. Blessed with good looks and a full, flexible if somewhat nasal voice, Larrivée was admired for the clarity of his diction and the liveliness of his declamation. His participation in Rameau operas was mainly in revivals, though he created the role of Artole in *Les Sibarites* and Orcan in *Les Paladins*, and would have created those of Adamas and Apollon in *Les Boréades*, had the planned premiere taken place. In 1762 he married the soprano Marie-Jeanne Lemière*. *BouHer, CamAca, PieCon.*

Larrivée, Marie-Jeanne *See* **Lemière, Marie-Jeanne.**

Le Gros, Joseph The leading *haute-contre* at the Académie Royale de Musique* during the two decades after Rameau's death, Le Gros (1730–93) was recruited from Laon Cathedral by Rebel* and Francœur, who had heard of the exceptional quality of his voice. Le Gros's debut in 1764 came too late for him to create any roles for Rameau, but as the natural successor to Jéliote* he took the male lead in many revivals. He is best remembered today as the creator of major roles in Gluck's operas, including Achille (*Iphigénie en Aulide*), Orphée (*Orphée et Euridice*) and Admète (*Alceste*). In 1777 he became director of the Concert Spirituel*. *BouHer, CamAca, PieCon.*

Le Maure, Catherine-Nicole Although she was one of the two finest French dramatic sopranos of her generation, Mlle Le Maure (1704–86) was endowed with a volatile temperament that led to several premature 'retirements' from the Académie Royale de Musique*, of which she had been a member since about 1716. Such absences allowed more time for concert appearances, as when she gave the premiere of Rameau's *Le Berger fidèle** in 1728. One regrettable consequence of her final prolonged absence from the Académie (1735–40) was that she missed the opportunity to create any role for Rameau. She did, however, take the parts of Aricie at the 1742 revival of *Hippolyte et Aricie*, Émilie and Zima at the 1743 revival of *Les Indes galantes* and Iphise in the revised 1744 version of *Dardanus*. Her rivalry with the soprano Marie Pélissier*, which began in the 1720s, created two factions: the 'Mauriens' and the 'Pélissiens'. For Voltaire*, these two singers appealed to the public in different ways: 'Pélissier par son art, Le Maure par sa voix', which was strong and pure. *BenVer, BouHer, PieCon, PouJél, RivFil, SadInv, VlaTed.*

Le Page, François Having been admitted to the chorus of the Académie Royale de Musique* in 1735, Le Page (1709–82) was promoted to 'acteur des rôles' two years later. Between then and his retirement in 1751 he proved a versatile *basse-taille**, second in esteem only to Chassé*. Major roles he created for Rameau include Isménor and Teucer (*Dardanus*), Cithéron (*Platée*), Canope (*Les Fêtes de l'Hymen*), Cindor (*Zaïs*) and La Vengéance (*Zoroastre*). He was married to the soprano Mlle Eremans*. His younger brother Joseph entered the Académie in 1741 as a *basse-taille*, singing in the chorus until 1764. *BouHer, CamAca, CyrCho, PouJél, SadInv.*

Le Valois d'Orville, Adrien-Joseph Son of the state treasurer in Rouen, Le Valois d'Orville (1715–80) was an amateur playwright who collaborated in numerous comedies at the Théâtre-Italien* and Théâtre de la Foire*. Although he is sometimes credited with the libretto of *Platée**, based on a play by Jacques Autreau*, it seems that Autreau himself was largely responsible for adapting his own play, perhaps with help from La Pouplinière*. Elizabeth Bartlet suggests that Le Valois d'Orville's contribution was limited to the restructuring of Act III and to minor revisions made during rehearsals. *BarPla, GirRam, GreSou, GirRam, LegPla, MasOpé.*

Leclair, Jean-Marie *l'aîné* Although Rameau and Leclair (1697–1764) were the two outstanding French eighteenth-century composers in their respective fields, there is little in their biographies to link them directly. In 1730 Leclair married Louise Roussel, the engraver of Rameau's *Pièces de clavessin* (1724), *Nouvelles suites de pièces de clavecin* and *Cantates à voix seule* (1729 or 1730). From 1733 to 1737 he was appointed *ordinaire de la musique du roi* and may thus have taken part in *Hippolyte et Aricie* and other Rameau operas performed in the Concerts de la Reine*. Although Leclair spent long periods away from Paris, he frequently appeared at the Concert Spirituel* as a virtuoso violinist. He must also have frequently attended the Académie Royale de Musique* in preparation for the premiere in 1746 of *Scylla et Glaucus*, his only *tragédie en musique** and one of the few operas of the period to rival those of Rameau in dramatic power and musical invention. However, he can surely not have been happy that, within weeks of the premiere, the Académie management mutilated its tragic ending by adding a *pantomime**, 'Le Jardinier et les ciseaux', performed to the overture of Rameau's *Hippolyte et Aricie* by dancers carrying gardening shears. *See also* **'Musette en rondeau'**. *LauÉco, SadZas, ZasScy.*

Lemière, Marie-Jeanne After making her debut in 1750 at the Académie Royale de Musique* and at the Concert Spirituel*, Marie-Jeanne Lemière (1733–1786) established herself as one of the leading lyric sopranos of her day. At the Académie she created numerous roles, among them Nérine in *Les Paladins*. In 1762 she married Henri Larrivée* and was thereafter referred to in librettos and press reports as Mme Larrivée. She retired in 1777. *BouHer, CamAca, PieCon, PouJél.*

Letters of Nobility Only a handful of eighteenth-century French musicians – Collin de Blamont (1750), François Rebel* (1760), Rameau, Francœur, Blanchard (1764) and Dauvergne (1786) – were accorded *lettres de noblesse* by the king. The award was purely honorific. In Rameau's case it was belated, to say the least, having been granted less than a year before the composer's death. His coat of arms is described as 'an azure shield with a silver dove holding in its beak a golden olive branch [*rameau d'olivier d'or*: a pun on his name]. This shield is surmounted by a helmet in profile, decorated with gold, azure and silver lambrequins.' (The official image, designed in 1765, is reproduced on the cover of each volume of *RCT**.) In December 1763, Bachaumont reported that Rameau had also received the cordon of the Ordre de Saint-Michel, the necessary fees having been provided by Louis XV. *BacMém, BenMus, BouHer, LauDoc, MacMus.*

Lille According to Decroix*, Rameau left Paris after his defeat in the Saint-Paul* competition, to become organist at Saint-Étienne in Lille. This is unlikely, as the composer was in Paris for the baptism of his son Claude-François on 3 August 1727, only three months after the contest, and his subsequent publications in the late-1720s give Paris addresses. In any case, Decroix's placing of the Saint-Paul competition – before Rameau's arrival at Clermont* in 1715 – is far too early. Yet the claim cannot be ignored: Decroix, a native of Lille, was in frequent contact with Claude-François Rameau* after the composer's death and had access to sources unavailable to other biographers. Unfortunately, the relevant church archives were destroyed in 1792. Much later, during Raparlier's* time as director of the Société des Concerts de Lille, the town was to become an active centre for the performance of Rameau's operas. *BreJeu, DecBio, QuiJeu, SouRéc.*

Linus All that remains of this five-act *tragédie en musique** are two manuscript copies of La Bruère's* libretto and two of the violin part. This material, now in the Bibliothèque Nationale de France, derives from the Decroix* and Soleinne* collections, both assembled after Rameau's death. The libretto had been substantially completed by October 1749, and there was talk of having it set by a Roman composer or, as La Bruère himself wished, by Mondonville*. By April 1750, however, Rameau had agreed to take on the project. The music, completed before November of that year, was rehearsed in the marquise de Villeroy's* private theatre on 10 May 1751. The comte de Stainville, future duc de Choiseul (1719–85), who oversaw the gestation of this project, considered the first four acts to have been generally successful, although Rameau himself felt that many revisions were needed. Everyone present agreed that the words and music of the fifth act were seriously deficient, and Collé* later maintained that Rameau never quite completed the music after La Bruère had made the necessary changes. Many years later, the composer's son Claude-François Rameau* told Decroix that, soon after the rehearsal, the marquise de Villeroy was taken seriously ill and that, in the resulting confusion, the score and all the other parts were lost or stolen. (Claude-François was almost certainly referring to his own father's grave illness, widely reported in 1751.) The surviving violin part reveals two self-borrowings from *La Princesse de Navarre*. *ButCho, BouHer, BouRam, ColJou, GreSou, LebDec, SadBor.*

Lisis et Délie   According to the printed libretto (Paris, 1753), this *acte de ballet** was intended for performance on 6 November 1753 during the court's annual *voyage* to Fontainebleau, as an afterpiece to *Les Hommes*, a one-act *comédie-ballet** by Saint-Foix and Giraud. However, the *Mercure de France** and other sources make clear that the performance never took place. The subject matter of Marmontel's* libretto – love disguised as friendship – was judged to be too similar to that of Rameau's *Daphnis et Églé*, also scheduled for performance during that year's entertainments at Fontainebleau. All that survives is the libretto. *BouHer, GirRam, GreSou, MasOpé, RicFon.*

Livre de caricatures   The Rothschild collection at Waddesdon Manor, an English country house near Aylesbury, includes a collection of some four hundred caricatures by Charles-Germain de Saint-Aubin (1721–86), designer of embroidery and lace to Louis XV. The drawings, executed over a period of almost forty years from about 1740, include numerous satirical portrayals of prominent figures in contemporary political, intellectual and artistic circles. (These may be accessed online at http://www.waddesdon.org.uk/collection/special-projects/st.-aubin.) Several images depict Rameau or allude to his works. Drawing 675.240, entitled 'Avez vous Jamais vü le Celebre R', is clearly based on the 1764 caricature* by Carmontelle. (In the illustration overleaf, the composer's name has been completed by Pierre-Antoine Tardieu (c.1784–1869), who inherited the *Livre* in the 1820s.) The titles of the books on which Rameau stands are given as 'hipolitte | aricie', 'basse | fondamentalle', 'PLATÉE', 'castor | pollux' and 'vacarmini'. This last was the name or, more likely, the nickname of a virtuoso Italian violinist who played in Paris in 1733, doubtless included here to exploit the pun on the French word *vacarme* (din, racket). The subtitle 'Si le difficile est le beau' quotes a satirical poem 'Contre la moderne musique', launched during the Lulliste-Ramiste* dispute, which includes the couplet 'If the difficult is beautiful, | Rameau is a great man'. Interestingly, a satirical engraving that circulated during this same dispute likewise features a Damoclean sword.

The previous drawing, 675.239, shows a plinth from which a dozen mice or rats try to dislodge an open score labelled 'LULLY', in an attempt to replace it with one entitled 'Vacarmini | RAMEAU'. The drawing's title, 'Ils auront bien de la peine' ('They'll have a hard job'), reveals the artist's sympathies. The subtitle 'Triomphe de Lully sur les partisans de Rameau' was added by Tardieu in the nineteenth century. Less appropriate, perhaps, was his annotation 'Rameau' on drawing 675.56, entitled 'Devinés Qui' ('Guess who?'). This shows a comical figure dressed in sheets of manuscript paper and surrounded by flames. Nothing else in the image suggests a link with Rameau, however, unless the flames and the man's sooty cheeks are intended to evoke the *ramoneurs** (chimney sweeps), the composer's supporters. Tardieu makes an equally tenuous link in drawing 675.177, 'Le meritte ne se mesure plus a la taille' ('Worth is no longer measured by height'), which depicts an elongated oriental man, complete with pigtail. Given the lack of musical imagery in the drawing, Tardieu's annotation 'Satyre contre Rameau' seems to have been based solely on the man's unnatural height. (He would not have known that the final act of Rameau's *Les Paladins* has a Chinese setting.) No such doubt surrounds drawing 675.63. Entitled 'Découverte de la basse fondamentalle | Par ramikisof, japonois, en l'an 997784396', it shows an exotic bird upon which is mounted an oriental man and a monkey, both playing fantastical

Charles-Germain de Saint-Aubin, 'Avez-vous Jamais vü le Celebre Rameau', c.1740–1775, in *Livre de Caricatures tant bonnes que mauvaises*; watercolour, ink and graphite on paper; 187 x 132mm ; Waddesdon, The Rothschild Collection (The National Trust); acc. no. 675.240. Photo : Imaging Services Bodleian Library © The National Trust, Waddesdon Manor.

brass instruments. Behind the bird is a second oriental, presumably Ramikisof (Rameau), who conducts with a scroll of paper. His nose is positioned uncomfortably close to the first man's naked buttocks – the 'fundament', we assume, from which the discovery of the *basse fondamentale* was made. Such scatological imagery is typical of this *Livre de caricatures*, which was affectionately known in the Saint-Aubin family as 'The book of arses'. *GétSat, JonLiv*

Livret   Anglophone specialists in the music of the Lully-Rameau period, when referring to the poem of an opera, often use the French term *livret*. While this word did exist in Rameau's day, it was not used in that particular sense until the second half of the nineteenth century. Rather, the booklet containing the text of an opera, on sale at the opera house door, was called the 'livre de paroles' (word-book); the text itself was usually referred to as the 'poème' or the 'paroles', while the librettist was known as 'le poète'. Quite why the use of *livret* in this context has gained such wide currency in modern English-language publications is not clear. The word 'libretto', though originally Italian, is now the standard English term for an opera text, whatever language this happens to be written in. If a French synonym is required, it would be better, perhaps, to use terms from the period than a modern anachronism. *BouHer, BouLiv, DicAut, DidLiv, RouDic.*

'La Livri'   Whether the title of this movement from the *Pièces de clavecin en concerts* (1741) relates to a place or an individual is not clear. Of the many French settlements with this name, Rameau would have been most familiar with the village of Livry-sur-Seine, not far from Fontainebleau on the route from Paris. More convincingly, perhaps, the piece has been linked with Louis Sanguin, comte de Livry (1679–1741), principal patron of the playwright Piron*. Although Piron was later to disown Rameau, the two men were still on friendly terms in the 1730s, hence some association between the composer and Piron's benefactor is possible. There is, moreover, circumstantial evidence that Livry was a freemason* and may thus have encountered Rameau at masonic gatherings. It may therefore be no coincidence that a reworking of 'La Livri' as a Gavotte en rondeau appears in *Zoroastre* (1749) during a ritual with obvious masonic significance. However, the idea that the original piece, with its seemingly elegiac character, was a posthumous tribute to the count, who died in July 1741, is undermined by the fact that Rameau's score was at press by March of that year. The same volume also includes an arrangement of 'La Livri' for solo harpsichord. *GirRam, GusFul, HerMor, RpeKey, SadBor, SadZo1.*

Louré   French theorists in Rameau's day generally, if not unanimously, understood this term to indicate a mild form of rhythmic inequality, where a dotted note on the first quaver of a pair is made a little longer. *See also* **Andante**; **Notes inégales**. *GreSou, GreGen, HefRhy, MasOpé.*

'Lucas, pour se gausser de nous'   First published in the February 1707 issue of Ballard's* *Recueil d'airs sérieux et à boire*, this drinking song for soprano, bass and continuo proved one of Rameau's most popular pieces, surviving in at least five printed and twenty-nine manuscript sources. Ballard's edition is headed 'Air à boire de Monsieur Rameau. Deux paysans', and the two singers appropriately adopt a Burgundian peasant dialect as they threaten the hapless Lucas with blows to his potbelly, to stop his amorous advances toward their young neighbour. A second version, scored for three voices (two sopranos and bass), circulated from as early as 1717. Rameau probably submitted the original version to the Ballard printing house soon after his arrival in Paris in about 1705. If Jean-Baptiste Christophe Ballard's claim is to be believed that he commissioned Rameau's *Traité de l'harmonie*, the first contact between these two men may well date from this period. *BouHer, GirRam, GouRec, MasBac, MonBou.*

Lulliste-Ramiste dispute   The huge impact of Rameau's operatic debut may be judged from the fact that the shockwaves it generated continued to reverberate for almost twenty years. Soon after the premiere of *Hippolyte et Aricie* (1733), the composer came under sustained attack from conservative opera-goers, who saw his music as a threat to the traditional style of opera established by Lully* some sixty years earlier. This faction, dubbed the Lullistes and led by the librettist Roy*, is said to have included the composers Lalande, Mouret, Couperin* and Leclair*. Rameau's growing band of defenders, known as Ramistes or Ramoneurs*, included such literary figures as Voltaire* and Diderot* and the composer's patron La Pouplinière*. The Lullistes maintained that Rameau's music was over-complex, excessively forceful, noisy and dissonant – in a word, *baroque** – and that it was lacking in sentiment and expression. In this respect, Rameau's formidable reputation as a music theorist proved an impediment, since some critics detected in his harmony 'a geometric quality that frightens the heart' (Cartaud de la Vilate, 1736). While the Ramistes could acknowledge the strengths of the Lullian tradition, their opponents refused to concede any merit in Rameau's music. The Lulliste assaults, directed as much at the composer's person as at his music, came in various guises: open letters to the press, defamatory poems (among them Roy's *Marsias allegorie** and Jean-Baptiste Rousseau's* 'Distillateurs des accords baroques'), satirical* engravings – even, in the case of Campra's *Achille et Déïdamie**, an entire prologue. In reality, many opera-goers belonged to neither faction. As Diderot put it in *Les Bijoux indiscrets* (1747): 'the ignorant and the greybeards all supported [Lully]; the young and artists of talent (*virtuoses*) supported [Rameau]; whereas persons of taste, whether young or greybeard, held both composers in great esteem'. Indeed, none of the Rameau operas under attack suffered at the box office, suggesting that the Lullistes were more strident than numerous. By the mid-1740s much of the force had gone out of their campaign, although as late as 1749 they mounted a rearguard action in organizing a cabal during performances of *Zoroastre*. *See also* '**Triomphe de Rameau**'. *AntFre, CowOri, CowWom, GétSat, GirRam, IshDal, MasLul, SadPat, SadZo1.*

Lully, Jean-Baptiste   As the *de facto* founder of French opera in the 1670s, Lully (1632–87) created the *tragédie en musique**, a genre that not only dominated his own output but would bear his imprint for many decades to come. Lully's thirteen *tragédies*, all but two to librettos by Quinault*, established the dramatic and, in important respects, the musical tone of opera in France for the best part of a century. They proved immensely popular at many levels of society and were frequently revived, to the extent that audiences at the newly-created Académie Royale de Musique* got to know them by heart and sometimes joined in with the singers. At the time of Rameau's operatic debut (1733), most of the Lully *tragédies* remained in the repertory and were still regarded, some five or six decades after their creation, as yardsticks against which all new works of this kind were judged. They soon began to suffer, however, by comparison with Rameau's; although many of them continued to be revived in the 1740s, 1750s and beyond, they became increasingly regarded as outmoded, especially during the Querelle des Bouffons*. By now, too, they were subjected to ever-more-swingeing cuts, reorchestrations and substitutions. Many opera-lovers blamed this perceived corruption of taste on Rameau; he himself nevertheless maintained that he had 'always respected Lully as a great master' and had 'never cited him except to praise him'. *See also* **Lulliste-Ramiste dispute; Trio des Parques**. *AntFre, GorLul, MasLul, RosArm, SchRam, WooSad.*

Lyon In a review of the *Traité de l'harmonie* in 1722, Castel* described Rameau as being 'well known in Dijon, Clermont and especially in Lyon'. Rameau's move to this city is now known to have occurred about a year earlier than previously believed: on 1 September 1712 he signed a legal document before a city notary in which he is described as 'organiste à Lyon', and there is reason to believe that he had established himself there some two months earlier. On 13 July 1713 he was described as 'maistre organiste et musicien de cette ville' when the Lyon authorities paid him 250 *livres* for organizing a concert to celebrate the Peace of Utrecht; sadly, the event never took place. In December of that year he was officially appointed organist at the monastery of the Jacobins*. A self-confessed opera lover since the age of twelve, Rameau attended the newly established Opéra de Lyon, whose repertoire in the mid-1710s included works by Campra*, Desmarets and Destouches*; as he himself recalled in 'Réflexions sur la manière de former la voix' (1752), it was in the *parterre* of this theatre that he heard an 'artisan in a harsh and rough trade' ('un Artisan d'une profession dure et grossière') instinctively singing the *basse fondamentale* rather than the tune or bass of the music being performed. Moreover, the conception of the *Traité de l'harmonie* (1722), which was evidently the fruit of ten years' meditation, presumably dates from Rameau's time in Lyon. A major event in the city's cultural life was the founding in 1713 of the Académie des Beaux-Arts de Lyon, and it was probably for this concert society that Rameau composed *Deus noster refugium* and several other motets. On 17 March 1715 the arrival of the new archbishop was celebrated in the Chambre du Conseil with 'one of the best concerts ever heard', the music being by Rameau. A month later he took up his second appointment as organist at Clermont cathedral. *See also* **Bergiron du Fort-Michon; Bollioud-Mermet, Louis; Christin, Jean-Pierre.** *BreJeu, BouRam, CleAct, GirRam, HerMot, KocSer, PaqAsp, QuiJeu, ValLyo, ValRam, ValSiè, ZasApp.*

Magasin de l'Opéra In 1715 the Académie Royale de Musique* took possession of new premises to store its scenery and costumes and to house ancillary activities. Situated on the rue Saint-Nicaise, a short distance from the Palais-Royal* theatre, the Magasin de l'Opéra (as it was known) was funded by revenue raised at the Académie's public Balls. The Magasin provided space not only for storage and rehearsals but also for the costume and set designers, machinist, tailor, harpsichord tuner and chief cashier; by the middle of the century it also housed the Académie's singing and dance schools and the music-copying workshop, together with residential premises for four Académie personnel. *GorDc, GorOpé, RosLal, SemBal, SerOpé.*

Mairan, Jean-Jacques Dortous de Rameau may not have known Dortous de Mairan (1678–1771) when, as official censor, this distinguished mathematician approved publication of his *Pièces de clavessin* in January 1724, though the two men had become friends by the later 1720s. In *Génération harmonique* (1737) Rameau was to incorporate Mairan's hypothesis on the elasticity of air into his attempt to explain harmonic overtones. Mairan was one of the team appointed by the Académie Royale des Sciences* to write a report on this publication, and he later defended the treatise and its author against the abbé Desfontaines's hostile comments. In the 'Mémoire' that became the basis of his *Démonstration du principe de l'harmonie* (1750), Rameau still makes use of Mairan's sympathetic resonance theory. In the course of revising his manuscript for publication, however, he became aware of flaws in this hypothesis and substituted an alternative (less convincing) explanation. Although Mairan was again on the Académie's reporting panel, he was probably not shown these revisions. *BreJeu, ChrTho, CohAca, GirRam, RamCtw.*

Malherbe, Charles   Rameau scholarship owes a huge debt to the work of Malherbe (1853–1911). Trained as a lawyer and later as a composer, he was appointed assistant archivist at the Bibliothèque de l'Opéra in 1896, becoming archivist there three years later. Between 1894 and 1911 he contributed prefaces to the first sixteen volumes of the Rameau *Œuvres complètes**. His magisterial 'commentaires bibliographiques', seldom fewer than seventy pages and often well over one hundred, still make essential reading. Those on the individual operas are especially detailed, providing information on the work's genesis, its contemporary reception, costumes and sets, revivals, box-office takings, cast-changes, and much besides. His huge collection of manuscripts, which included two of Rameau's autographs, was bequeathed to the Paris Conservatoire and is now housed in the Bibliothèque Nationale de France. *EllEar, FosRam, GreSou, SadVin.*

Malter family   Of the many eighteenth-century dancers and dance teachers named Malter, those most closely associated with Rameau are the brothers François-Antoine, François-Louis and Jean-Baptiste, whose father René was a member of the Académie Royale de Danse. They entered the Académie Royale de Musique* respectively in 1714, 1722 and 1734, and participated in numerous Rameau operas from the 1730s onwards. They were often identified by their nicknames: François-Antoine as Malter le Diable, because he excelled in Furies' dances; François-Louis as Malter l'Oiseau, because of the amazing lightness of his steps; and Jean-Baptiste as Malter l'Anglois, because he accompanied Marie Sallé* on her visit to London in 1733–34. In 1748 François-Antoine choreographed the dances in *Zaïs*. A further family member, François Duval, known as Malter *le jeune*, took part in Rameau revivals between 1766 and 1778. *BouHer, CamAca, NovLet, SadDan.*

Mangot, Jacques-Simon   When Rameau married Marie-Louise Mangot*, her brother Jacques-Simon (or Siméon) was a member of the royal wind-band (Grande Écurie du Roi), in which he held the post of 'musette et hautbois de Poitou' from 1718 to 1738. He subsequently devoted himself mainly to opera as singer, composer and impresario, holding the privilege of various theatres in southern France, among them those in Bordeaux, Marseille and (from 1749) Lyon, where he also directed the Académie des Beaux-Arts. During his time at the Opéra de Lyon, Mangot scheduled productions of *Les Indes galantes* and *Les*

Fêtes d'Hébé, along with his own *ballet héroïque* *Le Triomphe de Vénus* (1749). In 1756 he moved to Italy as *maestro di cappella* at the court of Parma. Jacques-Simon remained in contact with his sister, who sent him 1,500 *livres* in 1752, and he later acted as intermediary during a lengthy correspondence between Rameau and padre Martini*. He was doubtless also responsible for the decision to perform Rameau's *Castor et Pollux* at Parma, with the libretto translated into Italian. A *Duo de M. Mangot* forms part of a manuscript miscellany said to have been found among Rameau's papers. Jacques-Simon's other compositions, which included motets, have not survived. *BédMan, BoyFam, BoyTur, CyrTra, JacMar, LauGen, RamCtw, ValLyo.*

Mangot, Marie-Louise   In 1726, at the age of forty-two, Jean-Philippe Rameau married the 19-year-old Marie-Louise Mangot (1707–85), a member of a family of musicians originally from Lyon. Her father, Jacques, was a *symphoniste* (instrumentalist) in the Musique du Roi; her brother Jacques-Simon Mangot* had been a member of the royal wind band since 1718. Marie-Louise, who had probably been one of Rameau's pupils*, was a talented singer and harpsichordist. Though not a professional, she was skilled enough to take solo roles in concert performances of her husband's works at the Concerts de la Reine*. In 1734 she sang the part of Aricie in *Hippolyte et Aricie*, after which 'the queen highly praised her voice and her tasteful manner of ornamentation'. Marie-Louise again participated in this concert series in 1736 (*Les Indes galantes*), 1738 (*Castor et Pollux*) and 1740 (*Les Fêtes d'Hébé*). In the 1730s and 1740s there are scattered reports of her performing at private gatherings. Teding* van Berkhout, for example, describes her singing at the home of Jacques Autreau*, while Madame de Graffigny* recounts a visit to Passy, the country residence of La Pouplinière*, where 'Rameau played the harpsichord divinely; his wife sings very well'. The couple appear to have enjoyed a happy relationship and, at least until the 1750s, an active social life. Marie-Louise gave birth to four children – Claude-François* (1727), Marie-Louise* (1732), Alexandre (born 1740; died in childhood, in or soon after 1745) and Marie-Alexandrine* (1744). After 1768 Mme Rameau moved to her son-in-law's residence at Andrésy, near the Seine to the west of Paris, where she remained until her death. *BoyFam, CucPou, DaiCor, LauDoc, LauGen, SchFam, VlaTed.*

'La Marais'   The dedicatee of this movement from Rameau's *Pièces de clavecin en concerts* (1741) could be one of several musicians – Marin Marais (1656–1728), of course, renowned both as composer and virtuoso viol player, or one his four children who took up the viol. Of these, the most likely is Roland Marais (c.1685–1750), who published two books of *pièces de viole* (1735, 1738) and whose excellence as a player was praised by Marpurg*, among others. Roland was evidently a freemason and may thus have come into contact with Rameau at masonic gatherings. *See also* **Travenol, Louis-Antoine.** *BouHer, GirRam, GusFul, HerMor, MilGor, RpeKey.*

Marchand, Louis   When Rameau first arrived in Paris in 1705 or 1706, he is said to have lodged opposite the Grands Cordeliers (Franciscans), a monastery in the Latin Quarter, in order to experience the organ playing of the foremost French organist of his day, Louis Marchand (1669–1732). By the time Rameau's *Premier livre de pièces de clavecin* was published in 1706, he had succeeded Marchand as organist at the Collège Louis-le-Grand*. Rameau may well have acceded to this post as a result of his mentor's influence. By now, however, he had moved lodgings to the 'Vieille ruë du Temple [...] chez un Perruquier' (wig-maker) in the Marais district, a considerable distance from Marchand's quarter – which may lend credence to Maret's* claim that Marchand had become jealous of his young admirer's organ* compositions. Yet Burney, who met Rameau in 1764, attests to the composer's continued high regard for Marchand, quoting him as saying that 'the greatest pleasure of his life was hearing Marchand perform; that no one could be compared to him in the management of a fugue; and that [...] no musician ever equalled him in extempore playing'. Whether or not Rameau was taught by the older composer, his *Premier livre de pièces de clavecin* adopts the model established in Marchand's two books of *pièces de clavecin* of 1699 and 1702. *BreJeu, GirRam, GusFul, MarÉlo, QuiJeu.*

Maret, Hugues   One of the most informative early biographies of Rameau is the *Éloge historique de M.ʳ Rameau* (1766) by Dr Hugues Maret (1726–86), permanent secretary of the Académie des Sciences, Arts et Belles-Lettres de Dijon* and a distinguished physician. The *Éloge* is a published version of a eulogy delivered at the Académie the previous year. Although Rameau had been a member of this society, Maret evidently knew little about him and thus set out to assemble as much detail as possible from those who had had dealings with his eminent subject. Among these were: the playwright Piron*; the composer Balbastre*; père Gaultier, a former classmate; Michel Pélissier de Féligonde (1729–87), permanent secretary of the Académie de Clermont; Charles-Marie de La Condamine (1701–74), a mathematician who had been a member of Maupertuis's* circle; and the painter Nicolas Vennevault*. The resulting *Éloge*, though by no means error-free, is a methodical and carefully documented account of Rameau's life and achievements. Many details of the composer's first forty years are known only from this source. *BreJeu, GirRam, MarÉlo, QuiJeu.*

Marmontel, Jean-François   Widely remembered in opera circles both for his prominent role in the Gluckiste-Piccinniste dispute of the 1770s and his librettos for Grétry, Piccinni and others, Marmontel (1722–99) began his theatrical career with the tragedy *Denis le Tyran*, performed at the Comédie-Française in 1748 to considerable acclaim. Soon afterwards, he joined La Pouplinière's* entourage at the financier's country home at Passy, where he frequently came into contact with Rameau. In his *Mémoires* Marmontel recalls that, having seen the composer working on poor librettos, he resolved to do better, despite not having previously attempted the task of libretto writing. *La Guirlande* and *Acante et Céphise* were first performed during the celebrations for the birth of the duc de Bourgogne in 1751, though neither seems originally intended for that purpose. Marmontel's last-known collaboration with Rameau comprised two *actes de ballet**, *Lisis et Délie** and *Les Sibarites*, intended for performance during the court entertainments at Fontainebleau in 1753. The former was ignominiously dropped from the schedule at the last minute; the latter had more success and was later absorbed into the 1757 reworking of *Les Surprises de l'Amour*. It is just possible that Marmontel was librettist of *Les Paladins**. His *Éléments de littérature* (1787), a compilation of the articles he contributed to the *Encyclopédie*, devotes considerable space to the genres and aesthetics of French opera. *ChaRou, CucPou, GirRam, GreSou, MasOpé, RicFon.*

Marpurg, Friedrich Wilhelm   In 1746 the German critic and composer Marpurg (1718–95) travelled to Paris, where he met many of the leading intellectuals and musicians, among them Rameau. A lifelong Francophile, he adopted an overtly French style in his *Pièces de clavecin*, a set of five suites published in Paris in c.1748. Marpurg's *Der critische Musicus an der Spree* (1749–50) is the first of his many writings to praise Rameau's compositions, while his *Historische kritische Beyträge zur Aufnahme der Musik* (1755) includes the earliest comprehensive survey of the Frenchman's music theory. Marpurg's translation of d'Alembert's* *Elémens de musique théorique et pratique* (1757), though not free of inaccuracy, became the principal means by which Rameau's music theory was disseminated in Germany. *ChrTho, GauJug, GirRam, LesThe, MarHis, MarRam, MarVer, RamCtw.*

Marsias allegorie   One notorious event during the Lulliste-Ramiste* dispute involved a public scuffle between Rameau and the writer Pierre-Charles Roy*, leader of the Lulliste faction. The altercation took place in August 1737 in the courtyard of the Louvre, where Rameau threatened his opponent with a beating, and the two men had to be separated when Roy drew his sword. The immediate cause was the appearance of a defamatory anonymous poem, *Marsias allegorie, ou Le nouveau Carizelly*, which circulated widely and was generally attributed to Roy. The poem takes as its starting point the legendary contest between Apollo and the satyr Marsyas. Apollo represents music that is 'sweet, harmonious and touching', whereas the satyr, being half-man and half-beast, can only imitate the roaring of lions and hissing of snakes. Before being flayed alive, Marsyas fathers a gruesome offspring, a 'modern Marsyas' (Rameau) with an 'ostrich's neck, puckered eyebrows, dried-up legs [and] a mouth for biting but not for laughter'. This monster, 'in addition to his raucous music, has a mania for the written word' (music theory). His one concern is noise: 'all calmer music makes this fool grind his teeth'. Marsyas-Rameau is seen as a threat to the decorum and good taste of the French operatic tradition: 'Tremble, Quinault!* Tremble, Lully!* He is going to plunge you into oblivion'. The poem's short preface alludes to the Italian composer Cariselli, who had come to France with the ambition of supplanting Lully. By implication, Rameau (the 'new Carizelly' of the poem's subtitle) was consumed with the same ambition. *BloNat, DilIma, RivFil, SadPat.*

Martin, François   Best remembered as a pioneer of the symphony in France and as an innovative composer of chamber music, Martin (c.1727–57) was a cellist in the orchestra of the Académie Royale de Musique* from 1746. He frequently appeared as cello soloist at the Concert Spirituel*, for which he also composed numerous motets. Among these is an attractive solo motet *Inclina Domine* long thought to have been by Rameau. *AquSiè, CyrEss, CyrInc. PieCon.*

Martinecourt, Claude de   Jean-Philippe Rameau's mother, Claude, was the daughter of a well-connected notary whose family (according to Jean-François Rameau*, at least) could trace its lineage back to the Crusades. She was born in 1651 at Gemeaux, a village some thirteen miles north-east of Dijon. In 1671, she married Jean Rameau*, bearing him twelve children within the space of twenty-one years. Her death in 1697, when Jean-Philippe was still only thirteen, may have contributed to his decision to leave the Collège des Godrans* before completing his studies. *BouRam, BreJeu, KocWil, LauDoc, QuiJeu.*

Martini, Giovanni Battista (padre)   At the beginning of 1759 Rameau sent the Academia delle Scienze dell'Istituto in Bologna a manuscript entitled 'Réflexions sur le principe sonore', a work eventually published in a revised version (entitled 'Nouvelles réflexions...') as part of his *Code de musique pratique* (1760). Among the members deputed to report on his findings was the academy's distinguished music theorist padre Martini (1706–84). Rameau, now aged seventy-five and all too aware that time was running short, clearly hoped for a rapid response. Martini, however, felt the need to commission Italian translations of all Rameau's published theoretical writings; furthermore, he seems to have been in no hurry to present a report, perhaps because Rameau's ideas ran counter to traditional Italian concepts of music theory. The extensive correspondence between the two men continued over a two-year period. Martini did indeed prepare a 16-page critique of Rameau's theories, but this had not been delivered to the academy by April 1761 and probably never was. In it, the writer acknowledges the merit of some of Rameau's ideas, among them the *basse fondamontale*, but cannot accept his ideas on acoustics or metaphysics. *See also* **Mangot, Jacques-Simon.**   *CanLet, ChrTho, JacMar, LesThe, RamCtw.*

Masson, Paul-Marie   As a musicologist, Masson (1882–1954) is best remembered for his masterly doctoral thesis *L'Opéra de Rameau*, published in 1930. Written with elegance, clarity and enormous musical insight, this is still the most detailed stylistic analysis of Rameau's operas ever undertaken. In other publications Masson made important contributions to the composer's biography, including the discovery of an autograph letter, while his studies on the Lulliste-Ramiste* dispute and on the *ballet héroïque* remain essential reading.   *MasBac, MasBal, MasLul, MasOpé, MasPol, MélMas.*

Mattheson, Johann   The earliest writer to express hostility in print towards Rameau's music theory was the German composer, critic and theorist Mattheson (1681–1764). His review of the *Traité de l'harmonie*, published in the periodical *Critica musica* in 1725, is especially disparaging of the concept of the primacy of harmony over melody, a notion the author ridicules by quoting Rameau out of context. Ten years later Mattheson returned to the attack: in *Kleine Generalbass-Schule* (1735) he creates spurious links between unrelated elements in the *Traité* and *Nouveau système*, finally declaring roundly that amongst the 'deliberate hairsplitting' and 'tiresome fads and eccentricities' in Rameau's voluminous writings, he could find only 'two ounces of sound judgement and barely a drachm [*Quintlein*] of good taste'. Mattheson was scarcely more complimentary about Rameau's musical style, his knowledge of which was limited to the keyboard pieces. He relished the task of translating into German Jean-Baptiste Rousseau's* satirical poem 'Distillateurs d'accords baroques' (as 'Höckrichter Klänge Wasserbrenner', in *Beyträge zur Histoire des Theaters*, 1750), and he later dismissed Rameau as an infatuated, pedantic and affected imitator of Lully* (*Philologisches Tresospiel*, 1752). Such was Mattheson's influence in Germany that his outspoken attacks on Rameau's music theory were undoubtedly responsible for the initially negative reaction towards it on the part of many Germans, not least Johann Sebastian and Carl Philipp Emanuel Bach.   *ChrTho, DesJug, LesThe, RamCtw.*

Maupertuis, Pierre-Louis Moreau de   In the 1720s the mathematician Maupertuis (1698–1759) established a 'Société des arts', to which, according

to Grandjean de Fouchy who chronicled its foundation, 'the sciences would also be admitted, but [...] only to assist artists or to respond to their questions'.
Among the group's first members was Rameau. This little-known fact assumes some significance when we recall that Maupertuis was one of the first in France to embrace the theories of Sir Isaac Newton (1642–1727), at a time when these were not widely accepted outside England. For his part, Rameau, in *Génération harmonique* (1737), reveals an awareness of Newtonian ideas that has hitherto been attributed to his friendship with Mairan* and recent collaboration with Voltaire*, but may already have been stimulated by contact with Maupertuis. Rameau's correspondence with the mathematician Johann II Bernouilli* in Basel and the physicist Sir Hans Sloane in London may likewise have been inspired by Maupertuis: the former was a close friend, while the latter was president of the Royal Society*, of which Maupertuis had been a member since 1728. Furthermore, Rameau's final theoretical work, 'Vérités également ignorées et interressantes'*, is indebted to the mathematician's own writings. Another founder member of Maupertuis's society was Charles-Marie de La Condamine (1701–74). Until now, there has been little if anything to link Rameau with this distinguished mathematician, but the fact that the two men belonged to Maupertuis's group may have been known to Maret*: hence his decision to contact La Condamine for factual details to include in his *Éloge historique de Mr Rameau*. BeeMau, ChrTho, DouRam, MarÉlo, MilRoy, SchVér.

Maxim air   From its beginnings, French opera found a place in the recitative for many 'airs-maximes' – song-like *petits airs** whose text, usually sung by a confidant, expresses some aphoristic observation on the dramatic situation. In the early days, the glib or lascivious nature of such pronouncements was criticized by moralists, though not, it seems, by most opera-goers. If the number of maxim airs had dropped considerably by Rameau's day, they do occur, particularly in the lighter genres of *opéra-ballet** and *pastorale héroïque**, and even in the *tragédie en musique**. *Castor et Pollux*, for instance, includes numerous examples, some of them sung by principal characters; see, for example, Télaïre's reaction to the death of her beloved Castor ('Quelle faible victoire', I, 2), which includes the couplet 'La vengeance se plait à la gloire, | Mais ne console pas l'amour' ('Vengeance may boast its fame, but does not comfort a lost love'). AntFre, MasOpé, WooLul.

Médée   In his *Éloge historique*, Maret* claims that Rameau had written a cantata with this title during his second period in Clermont*; but despite the efforts of Decroix* and others to trace the work, it has never been found. GirRam, MarÉlo, MonBou, SchFam.

'Mémoire où l'on expose les fondemens du Système de musique théorique et pratique de Mr Rameau',   See *Démonstration du principe de l'harmonie*.

Memorial services   Within the first few months after Rameau's death on 12 September 1764, no fewer than three memorial services were organized in Paris, while others were arranged in various provincial towns, among them Orléans, Avignon*, Marseille and (possibly) Dijon* and Rouen. The first, organized with remarkable speed by the Académie Royale de Musique*, took place on 27 September in the Église de l'Oratoire (now the Temple Protestant de l'Oratoire du Louvre) on the rue Saint-Honoré. Between 1500 and 1600 invitations were issued in the name of Rameau's widow and their son Claude-François*. Almost 180 musicians from the Opéra, the Musique du Roi and various Paris churches took part in what was evidently a moving ceremony. As was often the case on these occasions, Gilles's* *Messe des morts* was performed, the second Kyrie being replaced by a *contrafactum** of the chorus 'Que tous gémisse' from *Castor et Pollux* (I, 1), a movement that had already been adapted to a different sacred text in the 'Paroles qui ont précédé le Te Deum'* of 1744. The service also included Rebel's* *fauxbourdon* setting of the *De profundis*, now lost. A second service, organized by Philidor*, took place at the Carmelite Church (Saint-Joseph-des-Carmes) on 10 October. The music, all of it by Philidor himself, included a *Messe de requiem* and a *De profundis*, also lost. This was evidently a smaller event and elicited mixed reviews. The third service, on 16 December, was funded by subscription, the takings of which were intended to finance a statue of Rameau. Like the first, it was held at the Oratoire and involved at least as many performers. Gilles's *Messe des morts* and Rebel's *De profundis* were again performed, along with a *Dies irae* by Guilleminot Dugué, *maître de musique* at the neighbouring church of Saint-Germain-l'Auxerrois. The score and performing parts of Gilles's *Messe* used at this service (and probably at the first one) survive. They include not only the second Kyrie derived from *Castor et Pollux* but two further *contrafacta*: the second Gradual, 'Quemadmodum desiderat cervus', is a reworking of Castor's soliloquy 'Séjour de l'éternelle paix' from the same opera (IV, 1), while John Hammond has revealed that the 'Pie Jesu' is based on the aria 'Caro sposo' by Domenico Alberti*. Gilles's score had been revised in line with current taste, with extensive adaptation of the phrase lengths and scoring, and the addition of parts for two horns and obbligato bassoons. *HamMem, LauDoc.*

Menus-Plaisirs Established in 1627, the Menus-Plaisirs du Roi was the organization responsible for all official entertainments at the French court, these 'lesser pleasures' including not only special festivals and celebrations but also the regular productions of plays and operas. Rameau's contacts with the Menus-Plaisirs increased markedly from the mid-1740s, when he received the first of a series of court commissions. Between 1741 and 1748 a new building was constructed in Versailles to house the *intendant* and his administration, and to provide storage and working space for, among others, the court music copyists. This building, on the Avenue de Paris, is now the headquarters of the Centre de Musique Baroque de Versailles. *BenMus, BouDen, LemMen, SerOpé, SouSlo.*

Mercier, Louis Sébastien In his witty and sharply observed *Le Tableau de Paris*, published during the 1780s, Mercier (1740–1814) provides two memorable pen-portraits of Rameau, whom the writer claims to have met in his youth. 'He was a tall man, dry and thin, who had no stomach and who, since he was bent, always walked in the Palais-Royal [gardens] with his hands behind his back to keep his balance. He had a long nose, a pointed chin, flutes instead of legs, a hoarse voice. He appeared to be of a difficult temperament. In the manner of poets, he spoke nonsense about his art.' This physical description accords well with surviving portraits* and caricatures* of Rameau. Elsewhere in *Le Tableau*, Mercier characterizes the composer's working relationship with Voltaire*: 'Rameau could never make Voltaire listen to a note of music, and the other could never make him understand the beauty of any of his verses; such that, when working together on an opera, they nearly came to blows, yet all the while speaking of harmony.' These reports, entertaining though they are, must be read in the knowledge that they appeared some two decades after Rameau's death and that, in respect of the second one, Mercier's attitude towards Voltaire was generally antipathetic. *MerTab.*

Mercure de France   Between 1724 and 1778 the gazette that had begun life as *Le Mercure galant* was renamed the *Mercure de France*. It appeared monthly, sometimes with a second issue in June and/or December, and included a miscellany of articles, poetry, anecdotes, news and reviews. As a semi-official publication intended to keep the upper echelons of society in touch with developments at court, the *Mercure* adopted a deferential tone towards the powers that be, and its reviews were generally bland. For the music historian, as for many others, it is nevertheless an invaluable source, providing factual information on productions or revivals at the Opéra and other theatres, on the publication of new books and music, and on the performers and repertoire at the Concert Spirituel* and Concerts de la Reine*. It is remarkable how many of Rameau's librettists – the abbé Pellegrin*, Fuzelier*, La Bruère*, Marmontel* and Piron* – had some input into the gazette, whether as reviewers, editors or both. *SgaDic.*

Le merveilleux   When used as a noun, this term was understood in the eighteenth century to mean 'the supernatural' rather than merely 'the marvellous' – an important distinction. From the beginnings of French opera, *le merveilleux* constituted an essential component, since the rational Gallic mind found the concept of all-sung drama easier to accept if it took place in a world inhabited by gods, magicians and allegorical or legendary figures. Use of the supernatural was nevertheless governed by rules that applied to opera as much as to spoken tragedy: *nécessité*, whereby each aspect of a work must justify itself as 'necessary' by the criterion that its removal or displacement would damage the harmonious disposition of the work; *propriété* or *convenance*, whereby each element must receive only those attributes that were 'appropriate' or 'suitable' to it; and *vraisemblance*, whereby such elements must be managed in a way that did not offend the audience's sense of what was 'probable' or 'likely'. In opera, the 'necessity' of *le merveilleux* to justify sung drama had been established at the outset. This did not, however, give the librettist free rein: recourse to the supernatural was thought justifiable only when all human means had been exhausted. Under the rule of 'propriety', the attributes and conduct of gods, magicians and heroes had to conform to what was known about them, or could be inferred, from classical sources; moreover, supernatural beings must behave in keeping with their status. The 'credibility' (*vraisemblance*) of the supernatural might seem hardest to justify but was at least as important. Although audiences wanted to see marvels at the Opéra, they could not be expected to accept anything. Supernatural events, once justified by the law of *nécessité*, would thus seem more credible if their execution conformed to natural laws – hence the preponderance of storms, earthquakes, shipwrecks and dream-sequences. By the same argument, the descent of a god was considered more acceptable if it took place either in a 'natural' manner (e.g., on a cloud) or in a way that did not stretch the audience's credulity (on a chariot supported by winged beings). *BouCri, BucSup, CahDan, GirTra, KinPoé, KinRam, MasOpé, NauDra.*

'Mes chers amis, quittez vos rouges bords'   The second volume of La Borde's *Essai sur la musique ancienne et moderne* (1780) is the only known source of this piece, identified as a 'Canon à six parties de Rameau' (see the illustration below). As La Borde was one of Rameau's composition pupils*, the attribution seems plausible, particularly in view of the older composer's known interest in canons*. Headed 'Cadran Harmonique' (harmonic sundial), the piece appears in two cryptic notations, both set out as a perfect circle. The upper circle has bar lines but no time signature; a treble clef is placed, not on the staff but at the centre of the circle, in such a way as to indicate the starting point. The lower circle has a ¢ time signature at the centre, again pointing to the start; this time, however, all the melody notes are written on the middle line, the pitches being changed by a succession of different clefs (G^1, C^3, G^2, C^4, C^1, F^3 etc.). The downward scale in the first phrase of the melody alludes to the 'carillon of the dead' mentioned in the mock-serious text. *BouCan, BouHer, LabEss, MonBou.*

Mesuré   In French opera, the *batteur de mesure** did not normally conduct during the recitative, so as to allow the singers a degree of rhythmic freedom in declaiming the dialogue. From time to time, however, especially at moments of

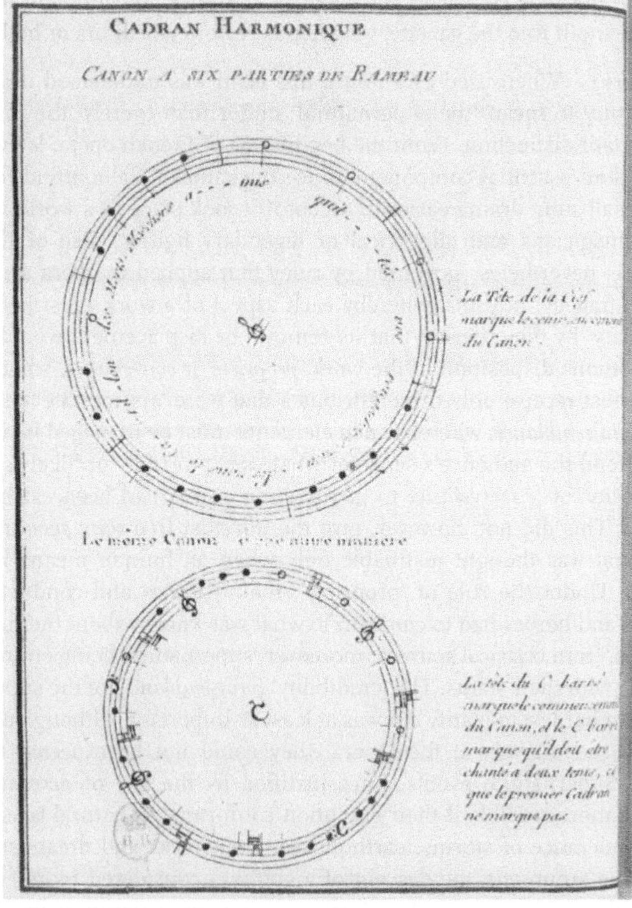

Jean-Benjamin de La Borde, *Essai sur la musique ancienne et moderne*, 1780 (Paris, Bibliothèque Nationale de France, Département de la Musique, 4-Vm. 231), vol. II, after p. 51. Reproduced by permission.

heightened expression or of lyrical expansion, Rameau and his contemporaries would mark a passage *mesuré* to indicate that it should be sung in tempo. The indication 'récitatif' after such a passage marks the return to a freer rhythmic interpretation; indeed, the isolated and otherwise inexplicable appearance of this word in the middle of a dialogue is usually a clue that the preceding passage was intended to be performed *mesuré*. *ChaRou, CyrEss, CyrSin, GreSou, MasOpé.*

Michaëlis, Théodore, *See* **Editions.**

Milan The earliest suggestion that Rameau undertook a trip to Italy occurs in the obituary published in the *Mercure de France** a month after his death. According to Decroix*, the visit took place when the composer was eighteen, while Maret* supposed that it was before his twentieth year. The most likely date is 1701, since Rameau was working at Avignon* in January 1702 and took up a permanent post at Clermont* four months later. The journey is said to have been brief, and he evidently never travelled further than Milan. In later life Rameau confided to Chabanon* his regrets at not having stayed longer in Italy, where he believed he might have 'refined his taste'. Frustratingly, there are no documents to substantiate this visit, so we have little by which to judge what he saw or heard. Yet the musical experiences offered by a city like Milan, not to mention the northern Italian towns through which Rameau passed, must have been astonishing to a young musician from the French provinces, and there can be little doubt that his lifelong admiration for the best of Italian music and musical practice was heightened by this formative experience. *See also* **Arnaud, abbé François.** *BouRam, BreJeu, ChaÉlo, DecBio, QuiJeu, MarÉlo, ZasApp.*

Mirthis The title *Nélée et Mirthis* by which this work is nowadays often known is first found in Decroix's* posthumous copy of Rameau's autograph. Yet the composer himself entitled the piece *Mirthis*. There is no evidence that this *acte de ballet** was ever performed in the eighteenth century. It was designed as one entrée* in a projected *opéra-ballet* Les Beaux Jours de l'Amour**; we may therefore assume that the libretto is by Louis de Cahusac*, author of the other entrées. When this project was abandoned, Rameau apparently stopped work on *Mirthis*, leaving the final divertissement* incomplete. Thomas Green has revealed shared characteristics between this opera and the Rameau-Cahusac *Anacréon* (1754). Both librettos are concerned with the tensions between feigned love and real love; unusually, both protagonists are actual Greek poets, depicted in a teacher-pupil relationship. Equally unusual for this date, neither work makes use of the supernatural, suggesting that they were conceived for a theatre that lacked stage machinery – possibly Madame de Pompadour's Théâtre des Petits Cabinets*. *BouHer, GirRam, GreSou, MalPri, MasOpé, RicFon.*

Modulating canon Of Rameau's small surviving corpus of canons*, at least two are of the modulating variety most familiar today from the 'per tonos' canon in Bach's *Musical Offering*. 'Avec du vin, endormons-nous', a three-part canon at the fourth, appeared in the November 1719 issue of Ballard's *Airs sérieux et à boire**. It was reprinted in the *Traité de l'harmonie* (1722), along with another modulating canon, 'Ah! loin de rire, pleurons', a four-part canon at the fifth. A further modulating canon at the fifth, the three-part 'Si tu ne prends garde à toi', appears in the *Essai sur la musique ancienne et moderne* (1780) by Rameau's pupil La Borde; although no composer's name is given, the fact that this piece appears alongside Rameau's two authentic modulating canons has been accepted as evidence that this, too, is by him. Given that modulating canons were rare in France in Rameau's day, this may well be so, though the piece is similarly anonymous in all other sources. In these three canons, the melodic line is designed in such a way that each repetition begins at a higher pitch. Those in 'Ah! loin de rire, pleurons' and 'Avec du vin' are respectively a major and minor third higher, and in 'Si tu ne prends garde à toi' a tone higher. In performance, the singers thus gradually reach the top of their ranges, at which point, according to a rubric beneath the 1719 score of 'Avec du vin', they may continue an octave lower. Some forty years later, Rameau incorporated this same canon into a drinking scene in the entrée* 'Anacréon'*; a fragment, adapted to the text 'Avec Bacchus, endormons-nous' and written in score with the necessary changes of key-signature, survives in an early version of the work. *BouCan, BouHer, BouSu2, GosTre, LabEss, MonBou.*

Mondonville, Jean-Joseph Cassanéa de   'If I were not Rameau, there is no one I would rather be than Mondonville'. So wrote d'Aquin du Château-Lyon, son of the composer Louis-Claude Daquin*, in 1754. His remark illustrates the near-parity of esteem in which these two composers were held: while Rameau was generally thought to have the edge in opera, his younger contemporary was judged superior in the *motet* à grand chœur.* Mondonville (1711–72) was associated with La Pouplinière's* circle and may even have directed the financier's orchestra briefly after Rameau left the household in 1753. Yet few documents survive to link the two composers directly. One senses an element of rivalry: according to Collé*, Rameau was mortified at the public's preference for *Le Carnaval du Parnasse* over his own *Platée* in 1749; the diarist thought Mondonville's music 'a hundred notches' ('cent piques') below Rameau's. Favart later claimed, improbably, that the duc de Choiseul had commissioned Mondonville and Rameau to write military marches for the Swiss Guard, but that when the duke was dissatisfied with the results, Favart recommended Hasse and Gluck. In 1748 Mondonville married Rameau's pupil Anne Jeanne Boucon, a talented harpsichordist and probable dedicatee of 'La Boucon'*. *AquSiè, ButCho, ColJou, CucPou, MacMon, PieCon.*

Mongeot, abbé   On 29 May 1744 Rameau replied to a young provincial musician named Mongeot, who had sought his advice on how to succeed as an opera composer. Unlike his brusque messages to Ducharger*, Casaubon* and others, Rameau's response is quite detailed and has become justly famous in encapsulating his own early experience. He suggests to Mongeot that, in addition to a good knowledge of the theatre, the opera composer must have undertaken a lengthy study of nature 'in order to paint it as truthfully as possible'; he should be sensitive to ballet and its movements, and must know about the practicalities of acting and voice production. He suggests that it would be wise to start with ballet* rather than *tragédie**. Yet before such a major undertaking, the novice should compose some smaller-scale pieces – 'cantatas, divertissements and a thousand such "bagatelles", which feed the mind, foster the spirit and gradually make it capable of greater things. I have attended the theatre [*spectacle*] since I was twelve; I first worked for the Opéra only at fifty, and even then I did not think myself capable of doing so; but I took the risk, I had some success and I continued.' As far as we know, Mongeot never did compose an opera. He is probably the 'abbé Mongeot' whose motet *Cantate* was performed at the Concert Spirituel* in 1752, in which case this is his only known composition. He became music master to the princesse de Guéménée and her family at Versailles. After Rameau's death, Mongeot had the letter published in the *Mercure de France** (June 1765), at the suggestion of the composer's son Claude-François Rameau*. *GirRam, LauDoc, PieCon, SadPir.*

Monnet, Jean   After a dissolute early life, including a prison sentence for publishing scurrilous literature, Monnet (1703–85) began a career as an impresario in Paris and Lyon*. In his colourful and entertaining memoirs (*Supplément au Roman comique, ou Mémoires pour servir à la vie de Jean Monnet*, London, 1772) he describes how, in 1743, he bought from the Académie Royale de Musique* the *privilège* to run the Opéra-Comique*, which had fallen into a pitiful state. His efforts to put this enterprise on its feet proved so successful that the Académie, fearing loss of revenue, forced it to close in 1745. Among Monnet's first productions was a restaging of Piron's *Le P[ucelage], ou La rose**, retitled but probably retaining some of Rameau's music. Rameau himself was evidently recruited briefly to the Opéra-Comique to direct the music of Favart's *L'Ambigu de la folie**. *CamFoi, PorPre, SadPir, ValLyo.*

Monologue,   *See* **Air de monologue.**

Montdorge, Antoine-César Gautier de   The financier, writer and painter Gautier de Montdorge (1701–68) was a member of La Pouplinière's* circle, where he is presumed to have met Rameau. He is known to have written the libretto of *Les Fêtes d'Hébé*, though his name never appeared in any published edition of this work. The preface includes an unsigned letter from the author to Rameau in which he vainly hopes to forestall the criticism of 'connoisseurs': with disarming modesty, he claims merely to have supplied scenes which would lend themselves to music and spectacle but which are not intended to be read, their versification being 'considerably different from that which succeeds nowadays'. A fascinating glimpse into his working relationship with Rameau is provided by *Réflections d'un peintre sur l'opéra** which, though published anonymously, is securely attributed to him. Montdorge's only other foray into the world of opera was as author of the unsuccessful *comédie-ballet* L'Opéra de société*, set by Giraud in 1762. His other writings include three articles in the *Encyclopédie* on engraving techniques. *BouHer, CucPou, CyrHéb, GirRam, GreSou, KafEnc, MalHéb, MasOpé, MorPoè.*

Montéclair, Michel Pignolet de   In a review of the 1761 revival of the opera *Jephté* by Montéclair (1667–1737), the *Mercure de France** claimed that Rameau had been so struck by this work at its first appearance in February 1732 that he finally made up his mind to compose an opera, convinced by the 'noble and distinguished' character of *Jephté* that French opera was capable of 'a new force and new beauties'. In his theoretical writing Rameau singled out the chorus 'Tout tremble devant le Seigneur' (*Jephté*, I, 4) for special praise.

Montéclair is often said to be the 'second musician' who clashed with Rameau on the subject of music theory on 8 May 1729, probably at the home of Étienne Boucon, whose daughter later inspired the keyboard piece 'La Boucon'*. This meeting was reported in the *Mercure*, which also published the ensuing exchange of seven open letters between Rameau and the second musician over a period of two years. The debate touched on a number of issues but was mainly concerned with the teaching of *accompagnement** (continuo realization). The second musician stoutly defended the *règle de l'octave**, widely used as an aid to continuo realization, against Rameau's assertion that this had been superseded by his newly-developed concept of the *basse fondamentale**. The second musician also took against what he saw as the arrogant tone of his opponent's claims. The identification of Montéclair as the second musician stems from an eighteenth-century annotation on one exemplar of the *Mercure*'s report of the debate. This attribution has been questioned, however, on the grounds that Montéclair's theoretical publications contain nothing on *accompagnement*. Among the alternatives that have been proposed are François Campion (c.1685–1747), the first public advocate in France of the *règle de l'octave*, and Jacques de Bournonville (c.1675–1753), described by La Borde as the best *accompagnement* teacher of his day. *AntFre, ChrTho, FajPré, GirRam, GreSou, LabEss, RamCtw, VlaTed.*

Monticourt, Duplat de   *See **Les Paladins**.*

Montpellier   In 1730, during his polemic with a 'second musician' (possibly Montéclair*), Rameau admitted that at the age of twenty he had learned the *règle de l'octave** from a certain 'M. Lacroix of Montpellier'. This has been widely interpreted as an indication that the composer visited this city in the early 1700s, perhaps between his temporary appointment at Avignon* (1702) and his first period in Clermont*. While that may be so, the 'second musician' states that Rameau learned the rule of the octave when he was 'about 30' (i.e., the early 1710s, probably at Lyon) and provides the address of the man who taught him; from this, it becomes clear that the Lacroix in question was organist of Saint-André des Arts in Paris from 1716 to 1736. Given the conflict of dates and the uncertainty that Lacroix was still in Montpellier when he taught Rameau the rule, the composer's presence in the city remains no more than a possibility. *BreJeu, GirRam, QuiJeu, ZasApp.*

Motet   For the past century or so, it has been customary to divide the French Baroque motet repertory into two categories – the *grand motet*, an extended composition requiring solo singers, chorus and orchestra, and the briefer *petit motet*, scored for one or more solo singers and continuo, with or without *symphonie**. In Rameau's time, however, works in the former category were referred to as *motets à grand(s) chœur(s)*, a term that has the advantage of stressing the all-important choral component. There was no standard term for the latter category, such pieces being labelled according to the forces required: 'motet à voix seule', 'motet à deux voix avec symphonie' and so on. For the performance of the *motet à grand chœur*, few French ecclesiastical establishments other than the Chapelle Royale could muster the large forces required from their own resources, and additional performers had to be bought in as required. Such motets were thus reserved for special occasions, many of them connected with royal or state events. With the formation of concert-giving organizations like the Académie des Beaux-Arts in Lyon* or the Concert Spirituel* in Paris, motets 'à grand chœur' formed the core repertoire of their programmes – hence the emergence of the 'concert motet', written specifically for such programmes. Indeed, all of Rameau's surviving motets are of this type. *DurMot, FavMot, HerMot, MalMot, PieCon.*

Multiple stopping   Rameau was not, as is sometimes claimed, the first to introduce this technique at the Paris Opéra, but he made it a powerful feature of his style. In his earliest operas multiple stopping is limited to two main contexts: (a) forceful passages such as the *tonnerre* in *Castor et Pollux* (V, 4), where the lower notes are almost entirely open strings; and (b) passages of recitative accompanied by a rich web of sustained strings, marked 'à 2. cordes'. For Decroix*, this latter kind of accompaniment sounded as if it were played by a single instrument 'plus parfait encore que l'orgue'. Appropriately, such writing was reserved for particularly solemn or intense moments. During the later 1740s Rameau greatly expanded his use of both types of multiple stopping. The forceful type is less reliant on open strings and is used in a wider variety of contexts. In *Naïs* (I, 7), for instance, it represents the sparring of competing athletes; in *Platée* it evokes the braying of an ass (II, 3) and later the hurdy-gurdy (II, 5). As for the sustained variety, such accompaniments were no longer limited to strings. Following the lead of Mondonville and other younger contemporaries, Rameau enhances the double stoppings with sustained woodwind: flutes first appear in this context in the 1744 *Dardanus* (IV, 2), flutes plus bassoons in *Zoroastre* (e.g., III, 9). By now Rameau was also making extensive use of multiple-stopped chords played pizzicato*. *MasOpé, SadOrc, SadZo1.*

La Musette   The third volume of the Rameau *Œuvres complètes** includes a cantata with this title, scored for voice and continuo. The work is now known to be by Pierre de La Garde (1717–92), published in or before 1766, with obbligato parts for musette, violin and bassoon. *MalCan, MonBou, TunCan.*

Musette en rondeau   Among the best known of Rameau's many *musettes* is the one that first appeared in his *Pièces de clavessin* of 1724. According to the preface, this movement could be transposed to C and played 'together with a viol' – a clue that it had been conceived in this format, possibly as part of Rameau's incidental music to *L'Endriague** (1723). Rameau was later to rework the piece into a sumptuous and extended *parodie**, 'Suivez les lois', in *Les Fêtes d'Hébé* (1739). The melody was further parodied as 'Quel désespoir | D'être sans esprit à mon âge!' in *La Chercheuse d'esprit* (1741), an *opéra comique** by Charles Favart, and as the masonic chorus 'Chantons en chœur | Chantons notre maçonnerie' in *La Lire maçonne* (1775). An anonymous *parodie*, 'Beauty and Musick', appeared in John Welker's *Clio and Euterpe, or British Harmony* (London, c.1760), with a newly-composed obbligato and with the drone replaced by a freely invented bass. Intriguingly, Rameau's harpsichord musette bears a striking resemblance

Upper staff: Rameau, 'Musette en rondeau', *Pièces de clavessin* (1724)
Lower staff: Leclair, 'Musette', *Premier livre de sonates* (1723)

to one in Sonata VIII of Leclair's* *Premier livre de sonates* (1723). In the example on p. 137 (upper staff), Rameau's melody is transposed to G major to make comparison easier. The resemblance, more obvious in performance than on the page, raises the question of who got there first: Leclair arrived in Paris in 1723, but possibly not early enough to have attended the February premiere of *L'Endriague* – in which case, we should probably conclude that this is one of Rameau's rare 'borrowings' from other composers. *CyrVio, LegVau, SadBor, SadPir.*

Mute *e*   In spoken French the unstressed *e* is often not pronounced, as in 'donne', 'parlent' or the first *e* in 'logement'. This so-called mute *e* (*e muet* or *e caduc*) was, however, traditionally sounded in poetry, unless followed by another vowel, in which case the two vowels were elided (as in 'puissance est' in the line quoted below). If a line ended with a 'feminine' rhyme (e.g., 'ter-ri-ble') the mute *e*, though pronounced, was not included in the syllable count that determines line-length. Thus the twelve-syllable alexandrine has an uncounted thirteenth syllable when it ends with a feminine rhyme: 'De sa vas-te puis-sance_est l'i-ma-ge ter-ri-ble.' In vocal music, feminine rhymes could produce unwelcome stresses, since it was customary for a final cadence to end on the first beat of a bar. This aspect of word setting came in for criticism during the Querelle des Bouffons*, and Voltaire later drew attention to the way in which words like 'gloire' and 'victoire' often became 'gloir-*eu*' and 'victoir-*eu*'. It was for this reason, he claimed, that Rameau encouraged librettists to end each section with a masculine rhyme. *See also* **Versification**; ***Colla parte* doubling**. *BesVol, KasVer, MasOpé, RosDec, RosMet, WilAna.*

Naïs   First performed at the Académie Royale de Musique* on 22 April 1749, *Naïs* is a three-act 'opéra pour la Paix' on a libretto by Cahusac*. Though categorized in some sources as a *ballet héroïque**, the work belongs more logically to genre of *pastorale héroïque**. The 'peace' of the subtitle was the Treaty of Aix-la-Chapelle that concluded the War of the Austrian Succession (1740–48). It provides the subject matter of the allegorical prologue 'L'Accord des dieux' ('The Gods' Agreement'), where the war is represented as an attempt by the Titans to storm Olympus. A victorious Jupiter (Louis XV) magnanimously shares jurisdiction over the Universe with Pluton and Neptune, the latter representing France's former enemy, King George II. (Nobody remarked on the incongruity of making Neptune the hero of the ensuing drama: Rameau and Cahusac may indeed have added this celebratory prologue to a work already in progress.) The opera demonstrates particularly well Cahusac's skill at using 'local colour' to motivate the divertissements*: that of Act I, for example, depicts the onstage wrestling, boxing and racing of the Isthmian Games, over which the nymph Naïs presides and during which her courtship by the incognito Neptune continues. *BouHer, DenNaï, EmmNaï, GirRam, GreSou, LecDiv, MasOpé.*

La Naissance d'Osiris, ou La fête Pamilie   Described as a 'ballet allégorique', this *acte de ballet** celebrated the birth of the duc de Berry (the future Louis XVI), who is represented as the newborn Egyptian god Osiris. It was first performed on 12 October 1754 during the French court's annual *voyage* to Fontainebleau. It seems, however, that Rameau and his librettist Cahusac originally conceived the work as part of an *opéra-ballet** entitled *Les Beaux Jours de l'Amour**, in which case the royal birth to which the libretto alludes must have been that of the duc de Bourgogne, Dauphin of France, in 1751. (As early as April 1750, Rameau is known to have been working on an unnamed opera in preparation for a possible royal birth.) *La Naissance d'Osiris* seems never to have been revived in the eighteenth century. *BouHer, ButCho, GirRam, GreGen, GreSou, LecDiv, MasOpé, RicFon, SadBor, SawPig, SawNou.*

Nélée et Mirthis   See Mirthis.

Nemeitz, **Joachim Christoph**   After extensive travels around Europe, the German lawyer Nemeitz (1679–1753) published his *Séjour de Paris*, first in German (1717) then in French (1727). This delightful book, an early example of the literary genre of travel writing, provides the class-conscious tourist with tips on how to make the most of a trip to Paris, which Nemeitz had visited in 1713–14. The author devotes much space to music, since some ability in this area was, in his view, a way of gaining a foothold in polite society. He also provides an informative section on the dos and don'ts of attending the Opéra. Although Nemeitz's remarks refer to the time of his Paris visit almost a decade before Rameau settled there, most of what he has to say about behaviour and attitudes still held true in the 1720s and beyond. *LagThé, NemSej, WooSad.*

'Les Niais de Sologne'   The title of this movement from Rameau's *Pièces de clavessin* – literally 'the simpletons from Sologne', a marshy region near Orléans – borrows a traditional expression to describe someone who is not as daft as he looks. In the present context, the phrase encapsulates the deceptive nature of Rameau's rondeau. Initially the melody has the jaunty character of a popular tune; yet it soon becomes clear that its motivic organisation is far more sophisticated than that of most such tunes. While the running bass begins innocently enough, it gradually extends over a two-and-a-half-octave compass and introduces technical challenges, among them hazardous leaps and rotation of the hand over the thumb. Indeed, the latter was a technique that had never previously appeared in a French keyboard publication. Moreover, this 'simple' statement of the rondeau is followed by two *doubles** of increasing virtuosity.

Rameau recycled 'Les Niais de Sologne' as an elaborate *parodie** movement in *Dardanus*. The text, beginning 'Paix favourable, | Paix adorable | Viens, descends des cieux' ('O sweet and auspicious Peace, descend from the heavens'), refers to the controversial Treaty of Vienna (1738) which ended the War of the Austrian Succession. When *Dardanus* was parodied by Favart, Pannard and Parmentier at the Théâtre-Italien* in 1740, a reference to 'Paix pitoyable [pitiful]' had to be cut by the censor. The melody of 'Les Niais' later appeared in *Les Amours de Bastien et Bastienne* (1753), a *parodie** by Marie-Justine Favart and Harny de Guerville of Jean-Jacques Rousseau's* *Le Devin du village*, at the point where the eponymous lovers are reconciled – an example of the way in which such *parodies* could exploit inter-textual associations: in this case, the 'niais' (simpletons) and the 'paix favorable'. *DicAut, GirRam, LegVau, LocVar, RpeKey, SadBor, SadHan.*

Noblemen and Gentlemen's Catch Club   In 1763, at the age of eighty, Rameau sent the manuscript of a 'Méthode pour faire les canons' to this recently founded London club. He had evidently heard (possibly from one of its members, the duc de Nivernais, patron of Rameau's one-time librettist La Bruère*) that the club proposed to offer a prize for the best catches, canons* and glees submitted for consideration. The club's minute book reveals that Rameau's manuscript was translated into English, probably with the title 'Treatise on Musical Canons', and that 15 copies were made. In 1764 these were offered by subscription at £2 6s per copy, eleven of which were purchased by named members of the club. Attempts to locate one or more of these copies have so far proved unsuccessful, though the search continues. *BouCan, GlaNob, RobCat.*

Notes inégales   The French practice of performing certain evenly written notes unequally was so ingrained by the mid-eighteenth century that there was seldom need to specify it in scores or performing parts. Occasionally, Rameau's scores include the rubrics 'piqué' (i.e., unequal, in this context), 'un peu pointé' and 'louré'* (slightly unequal) or, in one case, 'un pointé gracieux' (with a graceful lilt; *Les Boréades*, I, 5). Rameau's use of the phrase 'à la françoise' in *Les Paladins* (I, 5) undoubtedly has much the same meaning. More often, we find the directions 'notes égales' or 'croches égales' at points where the convention was to be avoided. In the music example below, the annotations distinguish between the duplet quavers, to be played unequally, and the triplets, played as written. In certain pieces the cautionary direction 'égales' was added during rehearsals: sometimes by Rameau himself, sometimes by the *batteur de mesure** or *maître de musique*. Several such instances are found in movements marked Andante*, thus confirming that, in France at least, this Italian term normally indicated that the note-values were to be interpreted as written. Needless to say, the presence of an isolated direction 'égales' in the course of a piece reveals that the preceding passage was to be interpreted with unequal rhythms. Rameau also used the peculiarly French convention of adding superscript* dots or vertical* strokes in a passage to which inequality did not apply. *See also* **Articulation.** *GreSou, HefRhy, MasOpé, SadZo1, WolPal.*

Rameau, *ariette*, 'Aimez-vous sans cesse', *Zoroastre*, II, 4

Nourrir   Annotations in several of Rameau's opera scores include the term 'nourrir' (to nourish). The illustration below, from the production* score of *Hippolyte et Aricie*, bears an autograph note to the *batteur de mesure** alongside the bassoon obbligato: 'Recommendez aux Bassons de nourir [*sic*] les Sons, sans

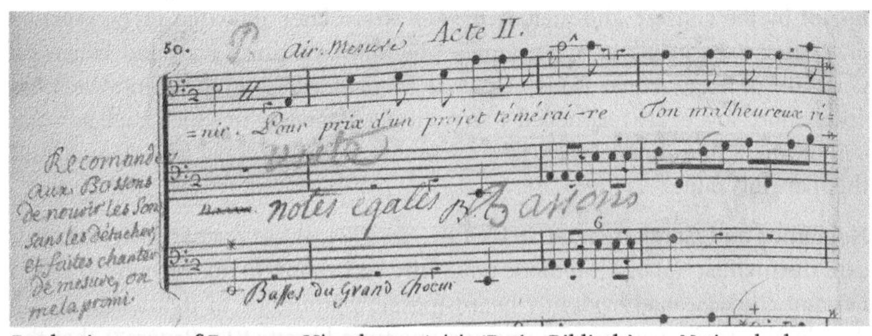

Production score of Rameau, *Hippolyte et Aricie* (Paris, Bibliothèque Nationale de France, Bibliothèque-Musée de l'Opéra, A. 128. a), Act II scene 2, p. 50. Reproduced by permission.

les détacher [...]' ('Advise the bassoons to sustain the sounds without detaching them'). Jean-Jacques Rousseau* confirms that 'nourrir les sons' means 'to sustain them exactly for their full value, rather than letting them die away before that value has expired, as is often done'. The term is found in two other Rameau production scores: at one point in *Les Sibarites*, scene 1, the violin parts are marked 'à demi et bien nourri' ('mezzo-forte and well sustained'), while in the prologue to *Le Temple de la Gloire* the multiple-stopped pizzicatos* bear the autograph indication: 'Nourir les arpèges depuis le bas' ('Sustain the arpeggios from the lowest note'). *See also* **Articulation.** *GreSou, MasOpé, MilOrc, RosHip, RouDic.*

Nouveau systême [sic] de musique théorique Rameau designed the *Nouveau systême* (1726) as an introduction to his first theoretical publication, the *Traité de l'harmonie* (1722). It is, however, much more than that, since his own thinking had meanwhile been influenced by the work of other scientists. Chief among these was Joseph Sauveur (1653–1716), whose discovery of the overtone series was seized on by Rameau in order to demonstrate that the intervals of a perfect major triad could actually be heard as upper partials or harmonics: the triad was hence founded in Nature. From Castel* he had learned the significance of the triple geometric* progression, which could be used to generate all the notes of a mode. Partly through this discovery, Rameau became aware of the fundamental importance of the subdominant chord: indeed, it was in the *Nouveau systême* that he coined the term *sous-dominante*, showing by means of the triple progression that the tonic is the central note in a sequence of fifths (e.g., F–C–G) comprising two 'dominants', one a fifth below the tonic, the other a fifth above. A further, related concept is that of *double emploi**, by means of which he argued that a chord could sometimes have two roots. The *Nouveau systême* includes an extended analysis of what for Rameau were flaws in the continuo figuring of Corelli's* sonatas. There is also a section on mean-tone tuning, which at this stage he considered to be the best form of temperament*. *ChdNou, ChrBas, ChrTho, CohCor, FerEvo, LesRam, LewTra, LesThe, LesRam, MacÉga, RamCtw.*

Nouvelles à la main At times of press censorship, there is a demand for ungagged sources of news, hence the vigorous circulation of clandestine *nouvelles* [or *gazettes*] *à la main* during the reign of Louis XV (1715–74). These manuscript newsletters, generally written by unidentified journalists or police agents, were sent in monthly instalments to a variety of subscribers, whose political, artistic or sociological interests tended to influence the nature of the news provided. The gazettes often include comment on theatrical events and gossip about authors, composers or performers; they are thus an entertaining source of information on the many scandals and quarrels of this period, among them the Lulliste-Ramiste* dispute and the Querelle des Bouffons*. Much of the content of the gazettes is based on hearsay (often introduced with the words 'on dit que ...') and must be treated with caution; they nevertheless provide a lively snapshot of public opinion on the artistic and other events of the day. *DacDar, DufNou, GétSat, MouRép, ProMus, SadPat, WooSad.*

Nouvelles réflexions de M.ʳ Rameau sur sa 'Démonstration du principe de l'harmonie' This short treatise, which appeared in 1752, is ostensibly a postscript to Rameau's *Démonstration*, published two years earlier. It nevertheless marks a radical shift in Rameau's thinking about the *corps sonore**. In that same year, the architect Charles Briseux (c.1680–1754) published a *Traité du beau essential dans les arts* in which he used the evidence of Rameau's discoveries to demonstrate that architecture was based on the principles of harmony. Rameau seized on this corroboration of his theories, which confirmed his growing belief that the principles derived from the *corps sonore* were 'common to all those arts of taste that have our senses for object and proportions for rules'. By now, too, he had discovered the 'sensationalist' psychology of John Locke (1632–1704), which held that all knowledge is acquired primarily through the senses. Rameau could thus validate the *corps sonore* by empirical means, in showing that it was 'drawn from nature and perceptible to three of our senses' (hearing, sight, touch). This elevation of experience over reason prompted Rameau to adopt as his watchword the aphorism *superbissimum auris judicium** ('the judgement of the ear is best'), which appears for the first time in these *Nouvelles réflexions*. He set great store by this publication, sending copies to the Swiss mathematicians Jean II Bernouilli* and Leonhard Euler* and the Italian philosopher Francesco Maria Zanotti (1692–1777) with a request for their opinions of it. *CanLet, ChrTho, CohGif, GirRam, RamCtw.*

'Nouvelles réflexions sur le principe sonore' *See* **Code de musique pratique; Académie Royale des Sciences.**

Nouvelles suites de pièces de clavecin The title page of Rameau's third collection of harpsichord pieces is undated, and the volume was long thought to have been published in or about 1728. A recent attempt by Siegbert Rampe to redate it to 1726–27 fails to take into account that this work was, from the outset, on sale at Jean-Pantaléon Leclerc's music shop on the rue du Roule, an enterprise that was not established until the autumn of 1728. Neal Zaslaw proposes the more plausible dating of 1729 or 1730, on the following grounds: the engraver signs herself Mlle Louise Roussel, hence the volume pre-dates her marriage in September 1730 to the composer Jean-Marie Leclair* (after which she signed herself Mme Leclair); meanwhile Johann Gottfried Walther's* 'Rameau' article in his *Musicalisches Lexicon* (1732) shows that the book had not appeared before the end of 1728, when Boivin published his 1729 catalogue, now lost.

In this collection Rameau follows the general plan of his *Pièces de clavessin* of 1724: it comprises two suites, of which the first (in A minor and major) includes a majority of dance movements and only three character* pieces, while the second (in G major and minor) consists almost entirely of pieces with character titles. On 25 October 1727 Rameau wrote to La Motte*, inviting the writer to come and hear how he had characterized the titles of seven of his harpsichord pieces. Only one of those named ('Les Sauvages') is from the *Nouvelles suites*, all the rest being from the 1724 collection, which suggests that the remaining character pieces in the present volume had not yet been written. Rameau's prefatory 'Remarques sur les Piéces de ce Livre, & sur les differens genres de Musique' include advice on tempo and other practical matters, and a lengthy discussion of his use of the enharmonic* genre in two of the movements. Later self-borrowings* include four pieces from this collection: 'Les Sauvages' in *Les Indes galantes* with the *parodie** 'Forêts paisibles'; the first Menuet in *Castor et Pollux* with the *parodie* 'Naissez, dons de Flore'; the second Menuet in *La Princesse de Navarre*; and the Sarabande in *Zoroastre*. *BarEnh, BouHer, BroCla, EllKey, GilRam, GirRam, GusFul, JacPiè, MalPiè, RpeKey, SadBor.*

Noverre, Jean-Georges   The visionary role played by Noverre (1727–1810) in the reform of ballet during the later eighteenth century is indisputable, and his *Lettres sur la danse* (1760) remain among the most eloquent and inspiring reflections on the subject ever written. As an observer of current practice at the Académie Royale de Musique* in Rameau's day, however, Noverre is less reliable. It is not widely appreciated that he spent remarkably little time in Paris during that period: apart from his debut appearance at the Opéra-Comique* in 1743 and a further season there in 1753–54, he worked almost entirely abroad (Berlin, London, Stuttgart) or in distant provincial cities (Marseille, Strasbourg, Lyon). Moreover, Noverre was a consummate self-publicist and claimed the credit for many reforms that had already been initiated by others, among them Sallé*, Dehesse* and Cahusac*. Undoubtedly, much remained to be achieved in the reform of choreography at the Paris Opéra, yet Noverre's dismal picture of a dysfunctional establishment is contradicted by independent evidence of communication and collaboration between composer, librettist and choreographer. To what extent his account is coloured by his recent failure to secure a position there as ballet master can only be surmised. *See also* **Pantomime.** *ChaRou, HeaEur, MasOpé, NovLet, PorNov.*

Oboe   Listed indiscriminately as 'MM. [Messieurs] les Fluttes' or 'MM. les Hautbois' (in line with the peculiarly French custom of referring to players by the name of their instrument), the five or six upper woodwind players at the Académie Royale de Musique* in the mid-eighteenth century played both oboe and flute, though some specialized more in one instrument than the other. Rameau's operas each require a minimum of four oboes, their roles differentiated by such rubrics as 'hautbois seul', 'premiers / deuxièmes hautbois', 'tous les hautbois'. The oboe's main function was still to double the violins, for which the standard indication was 'tous'*. A temporary end to this doubling is often implied by the dynamic mark *doux**. For most of his output Rameau keeps the oboe within the compass $d' - d'''$. In his later operas he takes increasing care to indicate alternatives for the oboes when the violins have tremolandos or descend below d'. Compared with the flute, independent passages for one or more oboes tend to be fewer, especially in the earlier operas, when the extent of this independence was still largely dependent on the number of scenes featuring shepherds, huntsmen or sailors. From the mid-1740s, however, the sound of the solo oboe is increasingly employed for its own sake, as in the plaintive obbligato in Clarine's air 'Soleil, fuis de ces lieux' in *Platée* (I, 6). In a chorus in this same opera (I, 3), Rameau memorably represents the frogs' croaking with a repeated, syncopated low $c'\sharp$, a note not strictly available on the Baroque oboe. *GorOrc, MasOpé, SadInv, SadOrc, SpiZas.*

Observations sur notre instinct pour la musique   Printed in 1754, this treatise was Rameau's response to the *Lettre sur la musique françoise*, Jean-Jacques Rousseau's* frontal assault on French music published a year earlier at the height of the Querelle des Bouffons*. The *Observations* represents the clearest statement of Rameau's aesthetic views. In challenging Rousseau's belief in the primacy of melody, Rameau reiterates his conviction that harmony alone, being rooted in the *corps sonore**, is capable of moving the passions. He reveals a growing awareness of the role of instinct in experiencing the agreeable sensations that result from certain relationships between notes; instinct is thus seen to support reason in confirming the *corps sonore* as the natural source of musical expression. In the latter part of the volume Rameau defends the French operatic tradition by means of a line-by-line rebuttal of Rousseau's critique of Lully's* renowned monologue 'Enfin il est en ma puissance' (*Armide*, 1686). In a ground-breaking analysis, Rameau draws attention to implied chromaticisms, each of which hints at a modulation and thereby contributes to the emotional flux demanded by the dramatic situation. *See also* **Publishers.** *BarRam, ChrTho, CohGif, DidDév, DilLul, VerDev, VerMod, VerRam.*

Œuvres complètes   Established in 1894, the Rameau *Œuvres complètes* was published by the firm of A. Durand & fils under the general editorship of Camille Saint-Saëns*. The edition was originally intended to include thirty-three volumes, but in the aftermath of the First World War, and with the death of Saint-Saëns (1921), the project foundered: after volume 18, no further volumes appeared, leaving eight of the operas unpublished. The list of editors makes interesting reading, not least for the number of composers it contains: Saint-Saëns himself, Vincent d'Indy*, Paul Dukas, Auguste Chapuis, Reynaldo Hahn, Alexandre Guilmant, Henri Büsser, George Marty and Claude Debussy*. The *Œuvres complètes* is a luxurious edition, with masterly contextual prefaces by Charles Malherbe* and others, together with descriptions of sources, critical notes and appendices of important variants. Unfortunately, nowhere is it made clear that certain editors took considerable liberties with the music. Not all editors are guilty: the volumes prepared by Büsser, Guilmant, Hahn, Marty and Debussy, while falling short of today's standards, do not for the most part seriously misrepresent Rameau's intentions. By contrast, those by Dukas, Chapuis and, above all, d'Indy are seriously flawed through including countless unreported 'improvements' to Rameau's idiosyncratic harmony and orchestration. The re-scorings include the addition of sustained Classical-style divided woodwind to most of the choruses, octave wind doublings, alterations of the composer's string layout, double-stopped tremolandos and much else. The volumes in question include many of Rameau's best-known operas: *Les Indes galantes* (Dukas), *Castor et Pollux* (Chapuis) and *Hippolyte et Aricie, Dardanus* and *Zaïs* (d'Indy). Yet as late as the 1980s and 1990s these editions were still being used for performances and recordings, some even performed on instruments of Rameau's period. This edition is rapidly being superseded by the Rameau *Opera Omnia* (OOR*). *OC, EllEar, FosRam, GreSou, PauInd, SadSaë, SadVin.*

OOR   Established in 1991 by Sylvie Bouissou*, *Jean-Philippe Rameau: Opera Omnia* (generally abbreviated as OOR) is designed to be the first-ever critical edition of Rameau's entire musical output. The first five volumes were published by Gérard Billaudot Éditeur between 1998 and 2002. Since 2003 OOR has been under the aegis of the Société Jean-Philippe Rameau*, with Bärenreiter as worldwide distributor. When complete, it will comprise six series, devoted respectively to instrumental music (three volumes), sacred music (one volume), secular vocal music (one volume), dramatic music (thirty-one full scores plus piano reductions), incomplete works and fragments (two volumes) and 'érudition' (the five-volume *Rameau Catalogue thématique**), and a further six devoted to the autograph manuscripts, watermarks, pedagogical and aesthetic texts, and iconography. Each volume includes a substantial preface in French and English and a full critical apparatus. *See also* **Editions**.

Opéra comique Throughout its history, this term has conventionally denoted a stage work in which music is interspersed with spoken dialogue. In the first half of the eighteenth century it was applied to spoken plays punctuated by *vaudevilles** – usually well-known melodies to which new words were fitted. Some of these so-called 'opéras comiques en vaudevilles' also included a certain amount of original music, as is the case with those by Alexis Piron* to which Rameau contributed. In the 1750s a newer type of *opéra comique* emerged, designated *comédie mêlée d'ariettes*, in which the quantity of new music was significantly greater. *CamSpe, ChaRou, GroCom, VenCom.*

Opéra-Comique Although the theatres at the two big Paris fairs are collectively referred to as the Théâtre de la Foire*, they were officially designated in 1715 as the Théâtre de l'Opéra-Comique. In 1743 the privilege to run the Opéra-Comique was acquired by Jean Monnet*, assisted by the playwright Charles-Simon Favart (1710–92). Monnet's revitalizing of the repertoire proved so successful that within two years the theatre had been suppressed by the Académie Royale de Musique*. Not until 1752 did the Opéra-Comique reopen, in the theatre that Monnet had built at the Foire Saint-Laurent. *See also* ***L'Ambigu de la folie.*** *BouRam, CamSpe, FraOpé, GroCom, PorFoi, PorNov, SadPir, VenCom.*

Opéra, Paris *See* **Académie Royale de Musique.**

Opéra-ballet The terminology applied to different operatic genres during the eighteenth century is nowhere more inconsistent than in the case of the *opéra-ballet*. This term was adopted by Marmontel* and other aestheticians around the middle of the century to denote a genre which, unlike the *tragédie en musique**, did not have a continuous action spread over several acts; rather, it comprised several separate acts or entrées*, each with a self-contained plot, whose subject matter was nevertheless linked to some collective idea hinted at in the work's title (e.g., *Les Éléments* or *Les Muses*). Unfortunately, the term *opéra-ballet* had not been coined at the start of the century when the new genre was emerging. Hence librettos and scores of what are *de facto* 'opéras-ballets' confusingly employ such less specific or ambiguous terms as 'ballet'* or 'ballet héroïque'*, both of which were also applied to works with a continuous plot. A modern critical edition must, of course, retain the appellation found in the principal sources. At the same time, it should also categorize the work according to which of the standard eighteenth-century genres it more logically belongs to. *AntFre, AntOpe, BouHer, ChaRou, GirRam, MasBal, MasOpé.*

Opera-going, experience of Voltaire* captured the special appeal of opera-going, a vital part of the Parisian social scene in Rameau's day: 'We must go to this magical palace | Where fine verse, ballet, music, | The art of deceiving the eye with colour | And that most happy art of seducing our hearts | Turn a hundred pleasures into one single pleasure' (*Le Mondain*, 1736). For many bejewelled occupants of the tiered boxes at the Académie Royale de Musique*, the experience was primarily social. As one fictional fop put it, there was nothing duller than listening to opera 'like some corner shopkeeper or newly-arrived provincial. We men of some style come here to see and be seen by women.' But others, especially those in the *parterre**, paid rapt attention to the evolving music drama. Many would follow the libretto*, which they could buy at the door and could read because the house lights were not extinguished. Casanova* admired the silence of the audience: 'such a novelty for an Italian'. Yet although the best productions at the Opéra could hold audiences spellbound, conditions at its Palais-Royal* theatre were far from ideal. The auditorium was unanimously judged to be too small, and there are many complaints about the overcrowding, the heat and the smell. Even so, there was a real sense of intimacy in the theatre, and most spectators were only a short distance from the stage, which projected in front of the proscenium. With acoustics that were evidently good, the performers can have had little difficulty in communicating even the most delicate passages, while the impact of a chorus* of around forty and an orchestra of up to fifty players (and sometimes more) must often have seemed almost overwhelming. *SerOpé, WooSad, ZasOpe.*

'L'Orageuse'   *See* **Duphly, Jacques**.

Orchestras   We know little about the orchestras Rameau encountered in his early years in the provinces. In 1715, during his time in Lyon*, the orchestra of the Académie des Beaux-Arts included forty players; according to a German traveller, they were all amateurs, mostly merchants, but the performance standard was good. Soon after Rameau settled in Paris in 1722, he began composing music for the Théâtre de la Foire*; while we have no statistics from the period of his activities there (1723–26), the theatre orchestra in 1721 comprised six violins, three *basses de violon** and one bassoon. The orchestra with which he was most closely associated from 1733 onwards was that of the Académie Royale de Musique*, whose numbers during those years ranged from forty-seven to fifty players. (The internal disposition of this orchestra is discussed under *grand chœur** and *petit chœur**.) In about 1736, several years after his operatic debut, Rameau joined the retinue of La Pouplinière*, whose private orchestra he directed until 1753; unfortunately we have no breakdown of the composition of this ensemble during that period. *See also* **Concert Spirituel**; **Concert Français**. *CucPou, GorOrc, HerMot, PorPre, SadInv, SadPir, SpiZas.*

Organ music   Despite the fact that Rameau held an organist post of some kind for a total of almost thirty years, not a single organ piece by him is known to survive. According to Maret*, the young composer showed Louis Marchand* some 'pièces d'orgue' in 1706. Yet Maret was writing at second hand some six decades after the event, and the music in question could well have been Rameau's first harpsichord suite, published that year. The 'troisième livre d'orgue de M.ʳ Rameau' purchased in 1761 by the chapter of Embrun Cathedral was almost certainly the *Pièces de clavecin en concerts*, while vague references to his 'pièces d'orgue en manuscrit' in assorted nineteenth-century writings are all unsubstantiated and probably stem from a belief that Rameau 'must have' composed something for his instrument. Decroix*, who spent many years trying to locate everything the composer had written, found nothing of this kind. In fact, Rameau probably preferred to exercise his skills in extemporisation, an art traditionally venerated by organists. Interestingly, his *Code de musique pratique* (1760) includes a 'Méthode pour le Prélude' (i.e., improvisation), which discusses the techniques by which 'the greatest organists' and other players are instructed. *BreJeu, DecBio, KocSer, MarÉlo, QuiJeu, ZasApp.*

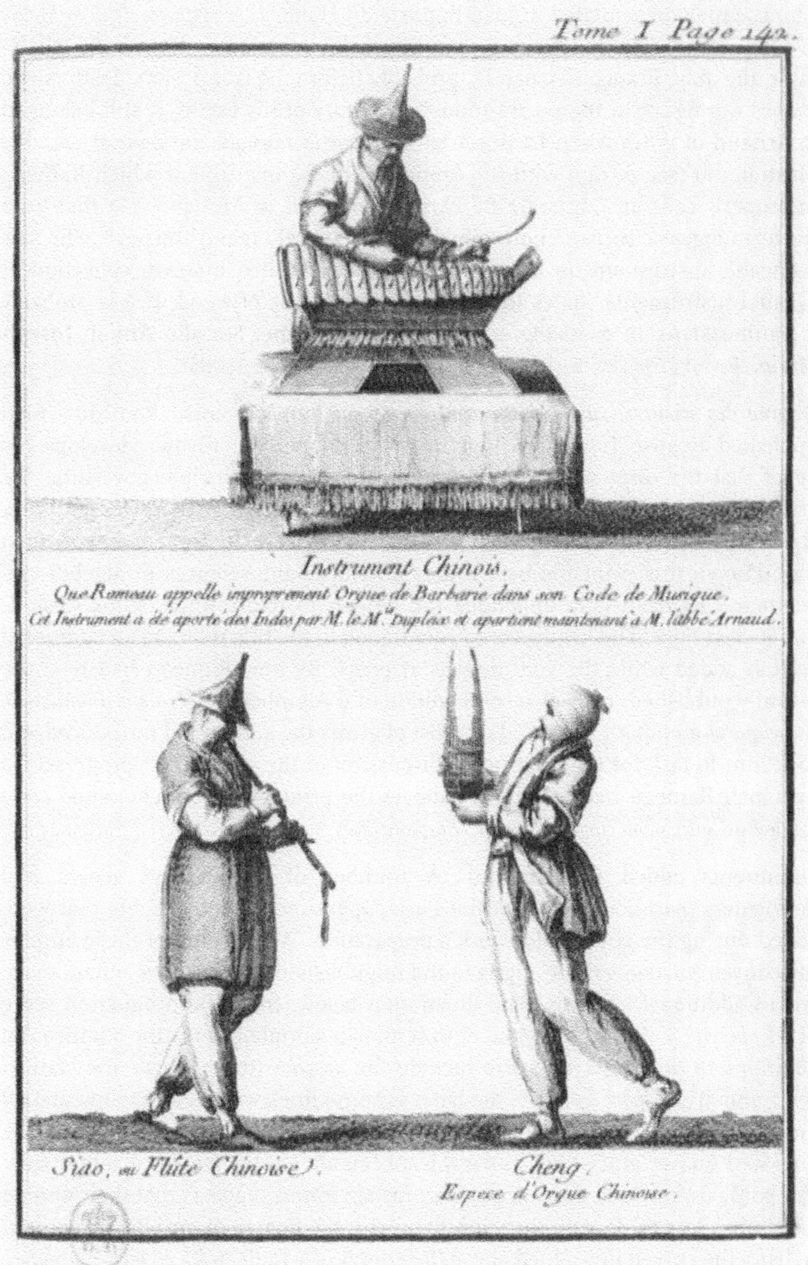

Jean-Benjamin de La Borde, *Essai sur la musique ancienne et moderne*, 1780 (Paris, Bibliothèque Nationale de France, Département de la Musique, 4-Vm. 231), vol. I, after p. 142. Reproduced by permission. *See* **Orgue de barbarie.**

Orgue de barbarie   Some time in the late 1750s, the marquis de Dupleix (1697–1763), a former governor-general of the French establishments in India, gave Rameau an instrument which he had come across at the Cape of Good Hope. The composer was later to describe it as an 'orgue de barbarie' (*Nouvelles réflexions sur le principe sonore*, an addition to his *Code de musique pratique*, 1760), and it was on this pentatonic instrument that he evidently tried out all the Chinese melodies notated in Jean-Baptiste du Halde's *Description de l'empire de la Chine* (1735). The instrument was eventually acquired by Rameau's collaborator, the abbé François Arnaud*, probably before the composer's death, since it does not figure in the posthumous* inventory of his estate. It still belonged to Arnaud in 1780, when La Borde's* *Essai sur la musique ancienne et moderne* illustrated it (see p. 147) with the caption 'Chinese instrument which Rameau improperly calls an Orgue de Barbarie in his *Code de Musique*'. (At that time, the term *orgue de barbarie* normally denoted a barrel organ.) Burney*, who saw Rameau's instrument on a visit to Paris and who had his own collection of oriental instruments, states that the bars were made of wood. It was probably a south-east Asian *gambang*, a species of xylophone. *See also* **Amiot, Joseph-Marie.** *BurHis, ChrTho, GirRam, LabEss, RamCtw, SavAme, SchBar.*

Origine des sciences, suivie d'une controverse sur le même sujet   Rameau's final published treatise (1762), written in the third person, further develops his belief that the *corps sonore** represented a universal principle governing the arts and sciences. From Jean-Etienne Montucla's recent *Histoire des mathématiques* (1758), he mistakenly deduced that the priests of Ancient Egypt must have known this principle before they developed the sciences of algebra and geometry. Rameau later appended the *Origine* to re-printings of his *Code de musique pratique*. The 'controversy' mentioned in the title refers to an additional section added while the volume was at press. By now Rameau had read the recently published, revised second edition of d'Alembert's* *Élémens de musique théorique et pratique**; he rattled off a list of errors the author had introduced and took him to task for eliminating all discussion of the geometric* progressions by which Rameau had sought to validate the principle of his cherished *corps sonore** *BurCor, ChrTho, LesCon, LesThe, RamCtw.*

Ornaments added in rehearsal   A number of production* scores and performers' part-books used at the Paris Opéra include ornaments that were added during the course of a work's preparation. While some of these employ the conventional *agrément** signs found in published opera scores, others make use of additional symbols. The illustration below, from the production score of *Hippolyte et Aricie*, shows a representative sample. Here, the manuscript additions to the engraved score include the *accent** (the ⋀ above the staff in bb. 2 and 5) and *port de voix**; the latter is sometimes written as a conventional grace-note (bb. 3 and 9) but elsewhere as a small minim (bb. 3 and 6), while the engraved quaver grace-note in bar 5 has been altered by hand to a semiquaver. The contexts in which these appoggiaturas are found suggests that their written length has less to do with duration than with the degree of emphasis required. In bar 7 the curved line added above the engraved + indicates a *cadence** *appuyée*, while the added ornament sign over the semiquaver in b. 6 signifies a *cadence feinte* (or *brisée*), a very short trill after the written-out appoggiatura. The on-staff vertical* lines or strokes in bars 1, 4, 5, 7 and 9 are breath-marks, which are

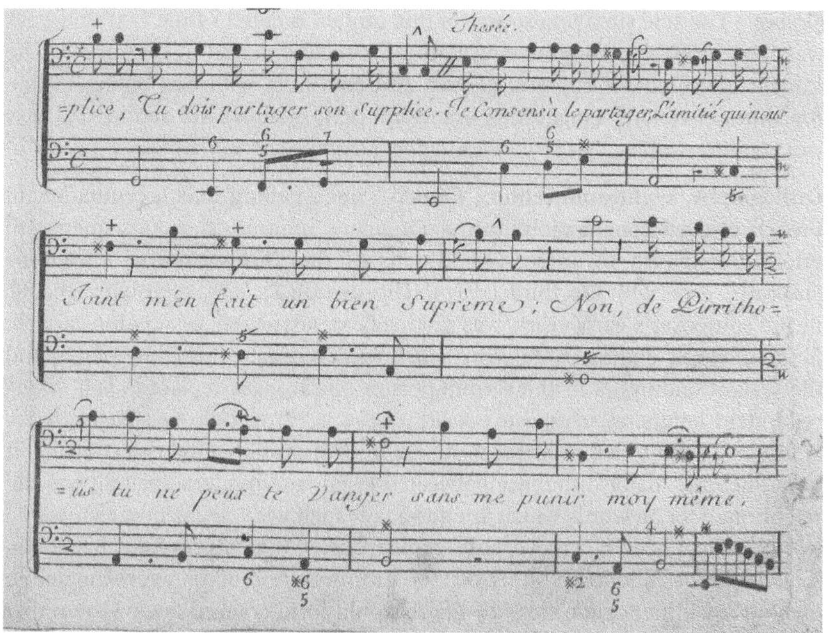

Production score of Rameau, *Hippolyte et Aricie* (Paris, Bibliothèque Nationale de France, Bibliothèque-Musée de l'Opéra, A. 128. a.), Act II scene 2, p. 47. Reproduced by permission.

often positioned so as to suggest that the singer should end the sound with a gasp. These added symbols are not always included in modern editions. *CyrEss, GreSou, McGSpa, SawNou, WilAna.*

Orphée aux Enfers   The intriguing claim that Rameau once considered a setting of the Orpheus myth is made in an anonymous volume entitled *Lettres d'Eurydice à Orphée*, published in 1763 and devoted to the subject of reciprocal love beyond the grave. In his preface, the author states that as a young man he had written a libretto entitled *Orphée aux Enfers*, which he 'had the vanity to read to the celebrated Rameau'. The composer evidently expressed approval of certain passages, notably the denouement and scenes involving the three Fates (Parques). 'Then, whether in truth or out of courtesy, he promised to set my opera to music as soon as he had picked up the theatrical lyre once again [dès qu'il reprendrait la lyre théâtrale], which he had abandoned because of certain dissatisfactions'. If this account is reliable (and it does have an authentic ring), the episode presumably belongs to the early 1740s, since at no other time could Rameau be said to have 'abandoned the theatrical lyre'. It thus adds weight to the hypothesis that the composer had fallen out with Thuret* and the management of the Académie Royale de Musique* in the period immediately following *Dardanus*. Frustratingly, the writer does not reveal the nature of these 'dissatisfactions', though they may well have had to do with financial matters: the composer long maintained that he had not been adequately recompensed by the management, considering the revenue his works brought in. Had things worked out differently, however, we might have had an Orpheus setting by Rameau to place alongside those of Monteverdi and Gluck. *LauLet, SadPat.*

Orphée The sole surviving source of this cantata is dated 1 June 1721; the work was thus probably written during Rameau's second period in Clermont*. The cantata is scored for soprano (*dessus*) and continuo, with one obbligato line for 'flutes et violons' (suggesting orchestral performance) and another for bass viol. *BouHer, CyrCan, CyrChr, CyrEss, DorCan, MonBou, SadCan, TunCan.*

Orthography, eighteenth-century French The spelling and accentuation of French evolved considerably during Rameau's lifetime as a consequence of reforms proposed in successive editions of the *Dictionnaire de l'Académie Française*, especially the third (1740). The use of accents, seemingly chaotic in the composer's early years, was gradually standardized, as was the variable plural of words ending in *-ent* (thus *talens* was eventually ousted by *talents*) and the variant ending *-és* in the second-person plural (*allez* replaced *allés*). Many redundant letters, as in *sçavoir* (*savoir*), *escript* (*écrit*) or *chacque* (*chaque*), were eliminated. With the appearance of the fourth edition of the dictionary in 1762, the only major difference between 'period' and modern spelling was the retention of 'oi' in words which are nowadays spelt with 'ai' (as in *connoisseur*, a word that had been taken over into English before the current French spelling *connaisseur* was adopted). Moreover, the pronunciation of 'oi' approximated to 'ouai' or 'oué', hence the frogs in *Platée* would have croaked 'kwé, kwé' rather than the 'quoi, quoi' of modern French. The extent to which the above reforms were adopted by individual writers depended on their age and level of education. Rameau, whose schooling pre-dated many of these changes, was somewhat old-fashioned in his orthography, while letters from his wife and daughter-in-law, discovered by Herbert Schneider, are typical of female writers of the time in adopting a largely phonetic spelling; indeed, some passages have to be read aloud before their meaning becomes clear. *DicAut, SchFam.*

Overture In his first operas Rameau adopted the traditional form of French overture, with its dotted first section and fugato second, though with some sophistications: in the overture to *Hippolyte et Aricie*, for example, the fugato unusually presents the subject and its inversion in free alternation and, in the final bars, combines it with a reminiscence of the opening of the first section. Several of Rameau's overtures from the mid-1740s onwards adopt the general form – or even, to some extent, the style – of the contemporary Italian *sinfonia*, in which two fast movements frame a slower one. The final movements in several of his later overtures, while not in conventional sonata* form, include tonally contrasted subject-groups, modulatory development sections and at least partial recapitulations. Rameau was instrumental in transforming the overture from an isolated introductory movement into one closely connected with the ensuing drama. Though briefly anticipated in *Castor*, this idea did not gain ground until the late 1740s. From that time, several of his 'programme' overtures contain tone-paintings that foreshadow the action (*Pigmalion, Zaïs, Zoroastre* and *Acante et Céphise*); others are linked musically to a later scene (*Platée, La Naissance d'Osiris* and *Les Paladins*). Some fall into both categories (*Les Fêtes de Polymnie, Les Surprises de l'Amour, Naïs* and *Les Boréades*). In this development, Rameau anticipated Gluck by several decades. The overture was normally repeated as an entr'acte* after the prologue or, once the prologue had been abandoned, after the first act. *GreSou, GirRam, MasOpé, RicFon.*

Les Paladins Identified in the libretto as a *comédie-ballet**, this opera is better classified as a *comédie lyrique**, since it lacks spoken dialogue. Of all Rameau's major works, it was the least successful. Premiered at the Académie Royale de Musique* on 12 February 1760, it was taken off after only fifteen performances, when the box-office takings had fallen to a derisory 724 *livres*. No eighteenth-century revival is recorded. The autograph score and the full set of performing parts used in the 1760 production (the latter only recently discovered) bear the title *Le Vénitien*, replaced by the time of the premiere. Doubts exist as to the identity of the librettist: the *Spectacles de Paris* (1761) tantalizingly suggests 'Mar...' (perhaps Marmontel* or Lefèbre de Marcouville, *b.* 1722); Collé* flatly refutes the ascription to Bernard* or the abbé Voisenon, though the former authorship is supported both in a later footnote by Collé (1780) and in an annotation on Decroix's* copy of the score. The attribution to Jean-François Duplat de Monticourt (dates unknown), accepted in many modern reference works, derives from Beffara*; but whether such an innovative libretto could be the work of a total unknown is questionable; furthermore, Monticourt is not identified as the librettist by his friend Collé. Reasons for the opera's abject failure evidently stemmed mainly from the libretto: based on a *conte* by La Fontaine (itself derived from canto xviii of Ariosto's *Orlando furioso*), it was considered inept, and its mixture of comic and serious elements contravened the proprieties of eighteenth-century French theatre. Perhaps also the performers were unable to do justice to such a zany score, which often seems way ahead of its time. There is reason to believe that Rameau had begun work on the project in the mid-1750s, during or soon after the Querelle des Bouffons*: certainly, many procedures and stylistic elements in the opera reflect an engagement with, and reaction to, the newly fashionable Pergolesian *opera buffa*. *BouHer, ChaRou, ColJou, GirRam, GorOrc, GreSou, LecDiv, MasOpé, ProMus, WolAut, WolInt, WalPal.*

Palais-Royal theatre The theatre occupied by the Académie Royale de Musique* almost from its beginnings until a year before Rameau's death was scarcely the imposing building we might expect such a royal institution to possess. Situated in the present Palais-Royal on the rue Saint-Honoré, it was very small compared with Italian theatres of the period. A plan dating from 1724 shows that the interior measured only 35 x 17 metres, with a stage area 9 metres wide and 17 deep. When Lully* took over the theatre in 1674, he had the interior redesigned, with the auditorium configured in a horseshoe layout. Although the decor was occasionally refurbished during the ensuing nine decades, this basic structure remained unchanged. The orchestra enclosure in front of the stage measured 7.5 x 3 metres, which, for an ensemble of almost fifty players, must have been extremely cramped. The remaining floor area was divided into the *parterre**, where spectators stood, and the *amphithéâtre*, where they sat on benches. Around the horseshoe were two tiers of fifteen boxes and, above these, the *paradis*. It has been estimated that the theatre, in its early years, could accommodate up to 1,300 spectators – though fewer in Rameau's day, as seating had by then been introduced in the *paradis*. An archival document of 1744 listing possible improvements describes the cramped staircases, insanitary conditions ('we must get rid of the buckets') and unbearable heat and stench. The theatre eventually burnt down in 1763, at which point the company was temporarily housed in the much larger but acoustically poor Salle des Machines in the Tuileries. *See also* **Opera-going, experience of**. *CoeThe, LagThé, SerOpé, WooSad, ZasOpe.*

Pandore   Undeterred by the collapse of his *Samson** project in the mid-1730s, Voltaire* returned to libretto writing, completing the text of what he described as an 'opéra philosophique' by the end of January 1740. At first, he considered Rameau unsuited to this work because of the extensive recitative required. When the composer was sent the libretto, he declined it, having temporarily withdrawn from opera composition in the wake of a breach with Thuret* and the Opéra management. Rameau may equally have been wary of taking on another opera with an unconventionally didactic theme. Set against a power-struggle between the gods and Titans, the libretto reworks the myth in which Pandora is tricked into releasing the forces of evil into the world, which allows Voltaire to point the moral that the cause of her downfall – hence that of mankind – is not a desire for knowledge but her credulity in trusting the gods. The latter are moreover depicted in an unflattering light, none more so than Jupiter, who would inevitably be seen as an allegory for Louis XV. By 1744 Voltaire had offered the libretto to Royer*, and the work was eventually scheduled for performance the following year as part of the Dauphin's wedding festivities. It was as a result of Royer's failure to complete this score that Rameau's *Platée** was drafted in at the last minute. *BesVol, BouRam, GirTra, GreSou, KinVol, RidVol.*

Pantomime   The mid-eighteenth century witnessed a resurgence of interest in expressive mime, led in France by such dancers and choreographers as Sallé*, Dehesse* and Noverre*, and encouraged by the writings of Cahusac* and others. Rameau clearly relished the opportunity this provided to forge a closer link between opera and ballet. Most of his operas include *ballets figurés** (whether or not identified as such) featuring a mimed action related to the plot. Many movements in his later works are entitled 'Pantomime' to denote the inclusion of some such mime, the nature of which is sometimes but not necessarily indicated in a stage direction. Thomas Green presents evidence from the autograph manuscripts which suggests that Rameau often composed the music for such *pantomimes* with a draft scenario before him; the score of *Zéphire* includes a note, thought to be in the hand of Cahusac, the presumed librettist, that provides a lengthy outline of the choreography, beginning: 'After the ariette, an air during which a nymph will flee from a zephyr. A cupid will stop this nymph by showing her his torch. The zephyr will take advantage of the nymph's surprise; he will run after her, and during this piece that comprises different tempi, the cupid, nymph and zephyr will dance a first *pas [de trois...]*'. That Rameau was realizing a further scenario in *Zéphire* is evident in the *Air vif* (scene 5), where the relationship of the dancers' movements is indicated by means of a three-letter code – F, O and E signifying, respectively, 'fuite' (flight), 'opposition' and 'ensemble'; from this it becomes clear that a group of nymphs at first resist the advances of the zephyrs but then succumb. The composer's role in devising or modifying such scenarios is illustrated by an autograph note in *Les Paladins* (II, 3): 'A noise must come from backstage to indicate that [Atis's pilgrims] try to hold on to Orcan, who escapes at the sign + then runs from one side of the stage to the other like a madman'. *BerPan, BouLiv, CahDan, ChaRou, HarBal, HarTou, GreSou, LawGes, LecDeh, MasOpé, NovLet, WaeGes.*

'La Pantomime'   The title of this 'loure vive' from Rameau's *Pièces de clavecin en concerts* refers either to a mime artist or to a mimed episode, both denoted by the word *pantomime**. The latter interpretation is perhaps more plausible, given the music's many contrasts of mood and gesture. The title had already been used by François Couperin (fourth book of *Pièces de clavecin*, 1730) and would be reused by later keyboard composers, notably Jean-François Rameau*, the composer's eccentric nephew; sadly, his 'Pantomime: la Muse italienne ou les furets' (*furets* could be 'ferrets' or 'nosey parkers') is now lost. The present piece is an early example of Rameau's use of an embryonic sonata* form. He later included a reworking of it as the third movement of the overture to *Les Surprises de l'Amour* for the 1757 revival. In this revised version, Rameau adopts a standard binary structure, thus raising the question of whether he had deliberately eliminated the more forward-looking features of his sonata structure or whether the 'new', orchestral version preserves the form of an even earlier one. *DicAut, GirRam, GusFul, HerMor, RpeKey, SadBor, SadLec.*

Parodie   French librettists were often required to adapt words to existing dance movements. The composer would provide the poet with a *canevas**, or outline, indicating the number of syllables per line and the position of musical accents. The resulting dance* song was known as a *parodie*, a word which, in this sense at least, had no pejorative connotations. The practice of 'parodying' led to a diversification of the rhyme structure of French poetry. In the *parodie* of a gavotte in *Castor et Pollux* – 'Renais | Plus brillan-*te*, | Paix charman-*te*, | Sois constan-*te*, | Tu fais | Mon atten-*te*' – five of the seven lines have feminine endings with the same rhyme, thereby infringing a convention of French versification* that masculine and feminine rhymes should alternate. This same term was also used in a satirical sense for the *parodies* of plays and operas presented at the Théâtre de la Foire*, the Théâtre-Italien* and the Opéra-Comique*. *Les Indes galantes*, for example, was the subject of at least six *parodies* – four by Favart (*La Foire de Bezons, L'Ambigue de la Folie*, Les Indes dansantes* and *Les Amours champêtres*) and two by Denis Carolet (*La Grenouillière galante* and *Les Amours des Indes*). The power of these 'critiques chantantes' should not be underestimated: Rameau and his librettists, in reviving operas for revivals, would often cut passages or correct dramaturgical weaknesses that had been singled out for ridicule in this way. (For a typical example, see **'Do do, l'enfant do'**.) At the same time, *parodies* could also stimulate public interest in a given work, since knowledge of the model was essential to an enjoyment of the satire. *See also* **Dardanus**. *FraOpé, LegPar, LegVoi, MalInd, MasOpé, MelPar, NoiHip, VenCom.*

'Paroles qui ont précédé le Te Deum'   On 30 September 1744, to celebrate Louis XV's recovery from illness, the company of *fermiers généraux* (tax-farmers) organized the performance of an unnamed *Te Deum* at the Augustinian church on the Place des Victoires, Paris. This work was preceded by two *contrafacta**, published in an engraved score and described as 'texts that preceded the *Te Deum*'. Two Latin texts, *Qui gemitus, quae lachrimae* and *Sperate non in vanum*, are set, respectively, to the music of 'Que tout gémisse' from *Castor et Pollux* and 'Clair flambeau du monde' from *Les Indes galantes*. It seems likely that Rameau himself had a hand in preparing these *contrafacta*. Not only does the score include new music linking the two movements, but his patron La

Pouplinière* is also known to have been involved in the event and doubtless expected Rameau to participate in such a high-profile display of the tax-farmers' financial largesse. Georges Cucuel's suggestion that the *Te Deum* in question was by Lalande* is unfounded. The 'Paroles' were evidently performed at the Concert Spirituel three months later. *CucPou.*

Parterre   At the Palais-Royal* theatre, as elsewhere, the *parterre* or pit was the sloping area below stage-level immediately in front of the orchestra and stage. Here the admission price was the lowest in the house, because spectators had to stand rather than sit. Yet paradoxically this was where the stage perspective could be seen at its best and the music experienced at its most immediate. For this reason the *parterre* was popular not just with those unable to afford more expensive tickets but with the most discerning of opera-goers. Moreover, people in this area were free to come and go at will. By extension the term *parterre* was applied to the spectators who stood in this area. Because the *parterre* was composed primarily of opera-lovers rather than those who merely wished to be seen in their finery, their prevailing judgment could prove decisive in the relative success of a production, and the collective reaction of 'the parterre' was often reported in *nouvelles à la main** and elsewhere. However, the extent to which the *parterre*'s opinion could be divided is evident from such notorious episodes as the Lulliste-Ramiste dispute* and the Querelle des Bouffons*. *LagThé, WooSad, ZasOpe.*

Parties   Seventeenth-century orchestras at the French court and at the Académie Royale de Musique* included a five-part string section, the three inner parts being played by instruments of different sizes and tuned like the modern viola. By the mid-1720s the lowest of these, the *quinte de violon*, had been eliminated, leaving the *hautes-contre de violon** and *tailles de violon**. Rameau inherited this four-part string division, which forms the basis of much of the orchestral music in his first operas and may still be found in his final works. But from the 1740s onwards he increasingly combines the violas in unison, either for short sections or for whole movements. In such passages the unison violas are usually labelled 'parties', a shorthand for the term *parties de remplissage* ('filling-in parts') by which the inner lines had traditionally been known. These lines are normally written in the mezzo-soprano clef (C^2), though this was often replaced in posthumous sources by the alto clef (C^3). Whereas Lully* had evidently farmed out the composition of the *parties* to his secretaries, Rameau invariably wrote his own inner parts, as was now the norm. In his first operas these never extend above *f″* and could thus be played in first position. From the 1740s onwards the violas were required to play in higher positions. Moreover the degree of melodic independence of their lines increases, to the extent that they can no longer be regarded as mere 'fillers'. During the second half of the century, the term 'alto' was adopted for the viola parts. This may be found in posthumous sources of Rameau's works but not in those which date from the composer's lifetime. *BouHer, GorOrc, MasOpé, RouDic, SadOrc, SpiZas.*

Partition réduite   Beginning in 1679, the publisher Christophe Ballard* issued a series of full scores (*partitions générales*) of the operas of Lully* and his successors. To many amateur musicians, these folio-sized volumes must have seemed daunting, requiring the user to read ten or more staves simultaneously. It was with this amateur market in mind that Ballard and other French publishers began issuing what were known as *partitions réduites* (reduced scores), produced in a more user-friendly oblong format. Here the music appears on two or occasionally three staves, a reduction achieved mainly by eliminating the inner choral and orchestral parts (*parties de remplissage*) in all but a few places. This development proved popular, especially with opera composers, who benefited from the reduced production costs. The engraved scores of Rameau's operas, produced under his supervision and at his own expense, are all *partitions réduites*. By now, the reduction process was less drastic, and it was not uncommon for such scores to include passages laid out on four or five staves; indeed, some movements in the later Rameau operas include systems of up to ten, the maximum available in the oblong format. Moreover, the engraving process allowed a considerable amount of detail to be crammed in. Yet although a growing number of passages include some or all the inner parts, the vast majority of these nowadays have to be retrieved from authoritative manuscript sources or, in the last resort, supplied by the modern editor. The *partition réduite* format was not restricted to opera publications: it was sometimes adopted in sources of French orchestral suites and cantatas. Indeed, a case may be made for regarding the surviving scores of Rameau's *Aquilon et Orithie* and possibly some of his other cantatas as being *partitions réduites* and thus in need of some editorial completion. *ChrPub, CyrSty, GreSou, MapRam, MasBac, SadCan.*

Pastorale héroïque   From its beginnings, French opera cultivated the lighter genre of *pastorale héroïque* alongside the *tragédie en musique**, from which it is distinguished by its exclusively bucolic subject matter and its construction in three acts rather than five. (An exception is Rameau's one-act *Daphnis et Églé*, better classified as an *acte de ballet**). The genre acquired its 'héroïque' tag not because it necessarily involves heroic deeds but rather because the characters include one or more heroes, gods or, in the case of those set in the world of *la féerie**, genies. The emphasis is on love in an idealized rural setting, in which the hero/god competes with one or more rivals for the love of a shepherdess. Despite their less weighty character, Rameau's three essays in the genre, *Acante et Céphise*, *Naïs* and *Zaïs* (the last two being *pastorales héroïques* in all but name), variously explore moral questions relating to social rank, fidelity and the abuse or renunciation of power. *AntFre, ChaRou, FajOpé, GirRam, MasOpé, PowPas.*

Patronage   Rameau seems generally to have distanced himself from aristocratic patronage. Only two of the dedications* of his numerous published works are addressed to a member of the nobility. Although he briefly enjoyed the protection of the prince de Carignan* at the start of his operatic career, he was soon to change his allegiance to La Pouplinière*, a wealthy tax-farmer descended from the *haute bourgeoisie*. After his break with La Pouplinière in 1753, he accepted no further patronage. *CucPou, HenAri, SadPat.*

Pattern-variations   Rameau's 'Les Niais de Sologne'* and Gavotte* with six *doubles* exemplify a style of keyboard variation where the harmonic structure of the theme is maintained, and where each variation exploits a particular figuration involving the development of a short motif or motifs. The renewal of interest in this kind of variation in the French harpsichord repertory from 1724 onwards, instigated by Rameau and Dandrieu*, was evidently stimulated by the example of Handel's* keyboard suites, which circulated widely in France in the early 1720s. *FraDan, GusFul, SadHan*

Pélissier, Marie   Soon after her debut at the Académie Royale de Musique* in 1722, Marie Pélissier (1706/7–49) moved to Rouen to sing in her husband's theatre. After his bankruptcy, she returned to the Académie in 1726, to great acclaim. Sensing danger, Mlle Le Maure* returned from one of her 'retirements', and a fierce rivalry developed between these singers and their respective supporters, the 'Mauriens' and 'Pélissiens'. In 1734 Pélissier was dismissed after a scandal involving her lover Dulis. She fled to London but returned to sing at the Opéra in 1735, remaining there until her retirement in 1741. Among the many roles she created were five of Rameau's finest: Aricie in *Hippolyte et Aricie*, Émilie in *Les Indes galantes*, Télaïre in *Castor et Pollux* and Iphise in both *Les Fêtes d'Hébé* and *Dardanus*. Pélissier's voice was small and, initially at least, somewhat forced. Nevertheless, in the emotional power of her declamation, the clarity of her diction and the eloquence of her gestures and facial expressions, she was regarded as an heir to (if not quite the equal of) Lully's* legendary soprano Marthe Le Rochois. *BenMus, BenVer, ChaRou, RivFil, PouJél, SadInv.*

Pellegrin, Simon-Joseph (abbé)   Rameau's first opera librettist, the abbé Pellegrin (1663–1745), led a colourful early life, serving as a naval chaplain in the eastern Mediterranean. In 1704 he embarked on a literary career. Although his prolific output includes an abundance of religious poetry, spoken tragedies and pieces for the Théâtre de la Foire*, he is nowadays best remembered for the librettos he provided for Destouches*, Desmarets, Montéclair* and, especially, Rameau. Almost universally reviled by his fellow writers as a mere versifier, Pellegrin was nevertheless a librettist of some distinction. He had a penchant for reworking the subject matter of existing tragedies, among them Corneille's *Médée* (for Salomon's *Médée et Jason*) and Racine's *Phèdre* (for Rameau's *Hippolyte et Aricie*); the choice of such themes allowed Pellegrin to present serious moral issues that transcend the obligatory amorous intrigues of the libretto. The same is true of the subject of *Jephté* (set by Montéclair in 1732), the first work on a Biblical subject to be staged at the Opéra. Indeed, if the *Mercure de France** (1761) is to be believed, it was the 'noble and distinguished character' of this work that inspired Rameau to begin his belated operatic career. Although Pellegrin is not otherwise noted as a theorist, his justificatory preface to the libretto of *Hippolyte et Aricie* is an important document in defining aspects of contemporary dramaturgy and the treatment of *le merveilleux** in opera. *BreJeu, BouHer, BouHi1, BouRam, BurHip, CazHip, DilIma, DilMon, GirRam, GirTra, GreSou, KinPoé, MalHip, MorHip, RecGen, SadHip, VerDra, WooSad.*

Pères de la Mercy   From the title page of Rameau's *Premier livre de pièces de clavecin* (1706) we learn that the composer was organist at the Collège Louis-le-Grand* and at the 'Pères de la Mercy' – i.e., Notre Dame de la Merci et de la Rédemption des Captifs (Mercedarians), a monastery on what is now the rue des Archives in the fashionable Marais district. Rameau's annual salary was a meagre 120 *livres*, for which he was expected to play at High Mass on all Sundays and feast days except during Advent and Lent, a total of more than eighty days per year. The instrument, installed in 1674, was not large: it consisted of two cases, one above the other, containing 'two bourdons, two flutes and other stops, with two wind-chests and two manuals'. The composer was still credited as organist at the Pères de la Mercy on the title page of the 1708 edition of his *Premier livre*. *BreJeu, GirRam, QuiJeu.*

Petit chœur   From the beginnings of French opera, the chorus and orchestra were both divided into a *grand chœur** and a *petit chœur*. In choral movements, the latter was responsible for sections with reduced scoring (usually trio passages for divided sopranos and *haute-contre**, but other combinations were possible), and some entire movements were assigned to the *petit chœur*. Brossard, in 1703, stated that this group comprised 'the best singers' of the full chorus; they were not, in other words, a separate group.

At the Paris Opéra the orchestral *petit chœur* consisted primarily of the continuo players, though in the early decades of the eighteenth century it also included two flutes and two violins, these melody instruments being responsible for the more delicate obbligato accompaniments. By 1738, towards the beginning of Rameau's operatic career, the flutes had been eliminated, whereas the number of violins had grown to four. The remaining instruments formed the continuo group, comprising four *basses* – three cellos and one *contrebasse** – and a single harpsichord. (By now the continuo section no longer included a theorbo*.) This disposition of the *petit chœur* remained constant for the rest of Rameau's lifetime, except that at some point between 1738 and 1750 the four violins were excluded. Orchestral listings always show the *batteur de mesure** as belonging to the *petit chœur*. *BroDic, CyrBas, CyrCho, CyrSty, GorOrc, SadInv, SpiZas.*

Petite reprise   *See **Reprise**.*

Petites flûtes   Around 1742 Michel Corrette* noted that instrument makers in Paris were nowadays producing 'petites Flutes Traversieres à l'Octave' – in other words, side-blown piccolos. Most of Rameau's parts for the *petites flûtes* remain within the compass *d''–d'''* (or *g'–d'''* in his earliest operas); at this stage they stay close to the keys of C, G, D and E. By contrast, the parts in *Le Temple de la Gloire* (1745) require a quite different range: *c''–g'''*. Two spectacular bird-song movements from the late 1740s make different demands again. In *Zaïs* (prologue, scene 2) the range is *f'–b''♭* and the key B♭; in *Naïs* (II, 6), *c''–c'''* and F major. Rameau's first opera makes no use of *petites flûtes*, at least before the 1757 revival; in the remaining operas of the 1730s these instruments appear only sporadically and are restricted almost entirely to dance movements. From the 1740s Rameau makes more liberal use of them: they appear four times in *Platée, Les Fêtes de l'Hymen* and *Zaïs*, and nine in *Naïs*. By now they are also used to add brilliance to choruses and solo vocal items. In movements with two independent parts, Rameau's meticulous markings reveal that often a minimum of four players is required. This more ambitious use of *petites flûtes* continues in the later operas. It is noticeable, however, that they are less prominent in the *tragédies* of this final period: they occur only twice in the 1756 *Zoroastre*, once in *Les Boréades* and not at all in the 1754 *Castor et Pollux*. *See also* **Flageolet**. *MasOpé, SadOrc.*

Petitpas, Mlle   At the age of 14, Mlle Petitpas (c.1709–1739, forenames unknown) made her debut at the Théâtre de la Foire* in *L'Endriague**, an *opéra* *comique** by Piron*, in which she sang two dramatic monologues specially composed for her by Rameau. In 1727 she entered the Académie Royale de Musique*, where she excelled in light, decorative roles: her performance of the 'Air du rossignol' in *Hippolyte et Aricie* (1733) was ecstatically received. She later travelled clandestinely to England but resumed her appointment at the Opéra from April 1734 until her premature death, creating the parts of Amour and Fatime in *Les Indes galantes* and three minor roles in *Dardanus*. She also sang at the Concert Spirituel* between 1731 and 1734 *BouHer, CamSpe, PieCon, PouJél, RivFil, SadInv, SadPir.*

Petits airs   In operas of the Lully-Rameau period, the dialogue scenes (*scènes d'action**) are delivered mainly in recitative; unlike in Italian opera, they do not include elaborate solo vocal movements, at least before the 1740s. Even so, French declamatory recitative was relieved from time to time by *petits airs*, in which a character might express a more intense emotion or, in the case of maxim* airs, deliver some aphorism, Such *airs*, also known as *airs de mouvement* to indicate that they were sung in strict time, were accompanied by continuo, occasionally with obbligato instruments. They are usually cast in simple binary, ternary or rondeau forms, though some are through-composed and others are so short and unstructured that the term *air* can indicate little more than an alternative to the indication *mesuré** (in strict time). *AntFre, BouRam, ChaRou, GirRam, GreSou, MasOpé, VerRec.*

'Les Petits Marteaux'   One of the two independent manuscript sources of this short harpsichord piece is headed 'Les petits marteaux. de Mr Rameau'. While this might initially be taken to mean 'Mr Rameau's little hammers', David Fuller notes that the full stop after 'marteaux' changes the sense to 'The little hammers, by Mr Rameau'. The second source merely has 'Les petits marteaux', suggesting that this was indeed the full title. The attribution evidently derives from Rameau's pupil Balbastre*. The piece exploits various *batteries** associated with Rameau, including the kind of hand-crossing* which he claimed to have invented. The title may allude to the distinguished harpsichord player Madame Du Hallay (c.1717–c.1750): according to d'Aquin de Château-Lyon, Rameau 'used to call her fingers his little hammers.' *AquSiè, BouHer, FulMar, GusFul, RpeKey, VlaTed.*

Philidor, François-André Danican   There is little to link Rameau directly with François-André Philidor (1726–95), at least during the older man's lifetime. Yet within a month of Rameau's death on 12 September 1764, Philidor – best known to his contemporaries as a chess player and composer of *opéra comique** – had organized and written the music for a memorial* service commemorating the event. According to Restout*, this was in gratitude for the esteem that Rameau had shown towards Philidor and in particular towards one of his *opéras comiques*, *Le Maréchal ferrant* (1761). Restout's comment has a ring of truth: Rameau is known to have admired the newer type of *opéra comique* which emerged in the wake of the Querelle des Bouffons* and of which Philidor was a leading exponent. He also praised Philidor's contributions to Jean-Jacques Rousseau's* opera *Les Muses galantes*.

Rameau's memorial service, held at Saint-Joseph-des-Carmes near the Palais du Luxembourg on 10 October, included Philidor's own *Messe de requiem* and

De profundis, both now lost. Whether these works already existed or had been composed during the few weeks since Rameau's death is not known. Philidor's music for the event divided opinion. The *Avant-coureur* drew attention to the 'many passages full of sparkle and genius', while Palissot was struck by 'la majésté de l'élévation'. But Bachaumont considered that Philidor had 'not displayed anywhere the majestic and awesome composition that the subject demands; almost throughout we hear the composer of *opéra comique*'. Perhaps chastened, Philidor thereafter wrote little sacred music. BacMém, LauDoc, HamMem, PalRam, ResGal.

'Pièce sans titre'   Two unidentified pieces copied into an eighteenth-century harpsichord anthology were accepted by the editors of the *Œuvres complètes** as being possibly by Rameau, each of them published as 'pièce sans titre'. One has since been shown to be 'La Vanloo' from the *Second livre de pièces de clavecin* (1748) by Duphly* and the other a pair of minuets from the same collection. GusFul, LauDoc, MalPiè.

Pièces de clavecin en concerts   Rameau's final collection of harpsichord pieces, published in 1741, belongs to the newly-fashionable genre of accompanied* keyboard music. It was published by subscription, to forestall pirated editions. The five *concerts** are scored for obbligato harpsichord with 'accompanying' lines for violin and *basse de viole**. The score indicates ways in which the violin line may be adapted for flute. The bass viol part lies so frequently in the upper register that Rameau was able to supply an alternative for second violin with remarkably little adaptation. The word 'concerts'* reflects the fact that the specified instruments are of different families. In this context at least, it has no connection with the term 'concerto', although the London publishing house of Walsh* was evidently unaware of this when it issued an edition entitled *Five Concertos for the Harpsichord* [...] *Accompanied with a Violin or German Flute or Two Violins or Viola* [sic] (1750). Rameau's own *Avis aux concertants* ('Advice to the players') states that the pieces were published in score rather than as separate parts so that the violinist and bass viol player could distinguish thematic material from mere accompaniment, 'in order to play even more softly' in the latter case. In spite of the ensemble nature of the *concerts*, Rameau claims that 'these pieces, played on the harpsichord alone, leave nothing to be desired'. He provides detailed guidance on how keyboard players could adapt them in order to maximise their effect as solos; this advice, largely ignored until recently, proves remarkably effective in practice. For the five movements where such adaptation was too complicated to be left to the player, Rameau provided written-out solo arrangements.

In this collection, the traditional dance movements are almost entirely supplanted by character* pieces: of the nineteen movements, all but the two menuets and tambourins* have character titles. By now Rameau's approach to titles had also evolved, in that nine pieces are named after pupils*, patrons, fellow composers or other individuals, a fashion he had hitherto ignored. The link between title and piece may not, however, be strong: according to the *Avis*, many titles were suggested by 'persons of taste and skill', but only after the pieces were composed. Several movements originated in the operas *Castor et Pollux* and *Dardanus*, while others would be re-cycled in later operas. To judge from the number of surviving exemplars, the volume sold well, and Rameau issued a second edition in 1752. *See also* **Six Concerts** [...] *en symphonie*; **Avison, Charles**. *BouHer, BroCla, EllKey, FulAcc, GusFul, GutPié, HerMor, KidSon, MalCon, RpeKey, SadBor.*

Pièces de clavessin Although the title page of Rameau's second collection of harpsichord pieces bears no date, the *privilège** was granted on 9 January 1724. The volume includes two suites: the first, in E minor and major, is somewhat old-fashioned in consisting mainly of dance movements, with only two character* pieces; by contrast, the second suite, in D major and minor, is made up entirely of character pieces. Alongside the table of ornaments (see illustration on p. 20) is a C major 'Menuet en rondeau', intended to illustrate the advice on fingering in Rameau's prefatory essay 'De la méchanique des doigts sur le clavessin'. This essay discusses other technical devices, including *batteries** and *roulements**, and indicates that 'several pieces' in the volume, among them the Musette en rondeau and two Rigaudons, could be transposed, which suggests that these pieces may have been conceived in other keys. Further editions were published in Paris in 1731 and 1736, and by Walsh in London in 1764. At least forty-six exemplars of the French editions have survived; many are printed on paper manufactured after 1741, while some include advertisements dating from the 1760s, thus demonstrating the sustained popularity of this collection. Among those evidently influenced by it were J.S. Bach and Domenico Scarlatti*. Rameau reused several movements – the Musette and 'Tembourin' [*sic*], 'L'Entretien des Muses', 'Les Niais de Sologne' and 'Les Tendres Plaintes' – in his operas and ballets. *BroCla, CyrVio, EllKey, GilRam, JacPiè, MalPiè, RpeKey, SadSca, WilAnx.*

Pigmalion According to the *Mercure de France**, Rameau wrote this *acte de ballet** in less than a week in an attempt to help the Académie Royale de Musique's* new management out of debt. While the opera never achieved that well-nigh impossible task, the *Mercure*'s claim seems plausible, given that the premiere on 28 August 1748 took place only three months after Tréfontaine's* appointment as *directeur*. Moreover, the production* score of this work shows signs of being prepared in haste. *Pigmalion* nevertheless proved immensely popular: by the time of its final eighteenth-century revival in 1781, it had notched up more than two hundred performances at the Académie or at the French court. The librettist, Ballot* de Sovot, borrowed the subject and about one-third of the text from La Motte's* entrée* 'La Sculpture' from *Le Triomphe de l'Amour*, an *opéra-ballet** originally set by La Barre in 1700. This was a new development: while the practice of resetting existing librettos was common in Italy and elsewhere, not until *Pigmalion* was it adopted at the Paris Opéra (quite possibly at the suggestion of Charles de Brosses*); even then, the librettist was criticized as the 'correcteur' of La Motte. This work illustrates how cleverly the all-important divertissement* could be integrated into the plot: when Pigmalion's statue is brought to life by Cupid, she has to be taught how to move; appropriately, with the help of Cupid and the Graces, she learns the characteristics of the standard dance-types, each dance more animated than the last. The idea for this may have been borrowed from Marie Sallé's* ballet-pantomime on the Pygmalion story, danced in London and later given in Paris at the Théâtre-Italien* in 1734. Rameau's overture*, which was said to depict the sound of Pygmalion's chisel, became a great favourite at

the Concert Spirituel* in an organ arrangement by Balbastre*. *See also* **Rebel,
Jean-Féry.** *BerPyg, BouHer, BucSup, ChaRou, EmmPyg, GirRam, GreSou, HyeSig,
LawGes, MasOpé, OpdPig, SawPig, SawNou.*

Pillot, Jean-Pierre Regarded as a natural successor to Pierre Jéliote*, whose
retirement from the Académie Royale de Musique* in 1755 coincided with
his own debut there, Pillot (1733–after 1789) took many of the leading *haute-
contre** parts during Rameau's final years. He created the *travesti* role of the
fairy Manto in *Les Paladins* and sang the part of Castor in the 1764 revival of
Castor et Pollux. His likeness may thus be depicted, with that of other singers
in this production, on the lid of one of Balbastre's* harpsichords. Pillot retired
in 1771, having been overshadowed from the mid-1760s onwards by Joseph Le
Gros*. *CamAca, GétPor.*

Pincé A mordent, an oscillation between the main note and the note
below, was known in France as a *pincé* or *martellement*. In his keyboard
music (see the ornament table on p. 20), Rameau employs d'Anglebert's
symbol, a curved bracket following the note. The keyboard *agréments** are not
encountered in the engraved scores of his operas, where the sign for a *pincé*,
particularly the later works, is a chevron (⁺⁺). In performing parts used by
Rameau's singers, a vertical* stroke above the note signifies a *pincé*. Whatever
the repertory or the symbol used, this ornament was often preceded by a
rising appoggiatura (*port de voix**), to form a composite *port de voix et pincé*.
Indeed, it was common practice in vocal and instrumental music for a *pincé*
to be added to a *port de voix*, whether or not the former was indicated in the
score. In Rameau's 1724 table, the *pincé* and *port de voix et pincé* are both
shown with multiple oscillations, though whether this convention applied to
other repertories is not known. *See also* **Pizzicato.** *McGSpa, NeuOrn, NeuPer,
SawNou, WilAna.*

Piron, Charles Alexis Like Rameau, Alexis Piron (1689–1773) was a native
of Dijon*. After studying law, he moved to Paris in 1719, where his *Arlequin
Deucalion* was staged at the Théâtre de la Foire* in 1722. This three-act
*opéra comique** brilliantly circumvented the restriction on spoken dialogue
imposed by the Comédie-Française and established Piron as one of the leading
playwrights at the Fair theatres. Many of his subsequent *opéras comiques**
included newly-composed music alongside traditional *vaudevilles**, as in those
with contributions by Rameau – *L'Endriague**, *L'Enrôlement d'Arlequin**, *La
Robe de dissension** and *Le P[ucelage], ou La rose**. By 1728 Piron had turned his
attention to the Comédie-Française, for which he wrote a series of tragedies
and other plays. These included a final collaboration with Rameau, *Les Courses
de Tempé** (1734). The playwright, often described as 'le rubicond Piron', was
a founder member of the convivial literary club known as the Caveau*. In
later life, however, he became embittered, especially after Louis XV vetoed
his election to the Académie Française because of his obscene *Ode à Priape*, a
youthful indiscretion. Piron gradually withdrew from public life and began to
write increasingly misanthropic letters and epigrams. This doubtless explains
the tone of his extraordinary response when Maret* requested information for
a Rameau obituary. Piron, despite his lengthy collaboration with the composer,
claims: 'we did not see each other in all for more than the space of a single

day'. Yet he had earlier referred to Rameau as 'mon cher compatriote', who had composed his incidental music 'for my sake' ('pour l'amour de moi'). It is in this light that we should read his harsh and unsympathetic comments on the composer, which Maret preferred not to include in his *Éloge historique de M.ʳ Rameau*. BouRam, ConPir, GirRam, HenAri, PirŒu, ProPir, SadPir.

Pitch, performing   During Rameau's lifetime there were two prevailing pitch standards in France, the *ton de l'Opéra* and the *ton de la chambre du roi*. A further pitch, the *ton de chapelle*, was for much of this time quite similar to the first of these. Research by Bruce Haynes and others has established that the *ton de l'Opéra* was approximately $a' = 392$ Hz – about a whole tone lower that the modern concert pitch of $a' = 440$ Hz. That this 'Opéra pitch', in use at the Académie Royale de Musique*, remained stable throughout Rameau's operatic career is confirmed by the lack of fluctuation in vocal tessituras of the period; to have changed the pitch significantly would, after all, have required the Académie's wind instruments to be rebuilt, a colossal and needless expense. Haynes calculates that the *ton de la chambre* was in the range 404–409 Hz, hence more than a semitone below $a' = 440$ Hz and perceptibly lower than the modern so-called 'Baroque pitch' of 415 Hz. We may assume that Rameau's cantatas and keyboard music were conceived with this 'chamber pitch' in mind. Both pitches have obvious implications for the performance of vocal *haute-contre** parts, which are dauntingly high when performed at $a' = 440$. CyrSty, HayPit.

Pizzicato   Although the technique of plucking bowed stringed instruments had long been cultivated in Europe, the French took little interest in it before the mid-eighteenth century. A rare example in opera occurs in the entrée* 'Les Sérénades et les Joueurs' in Campra's* *Les Festes vénitiennes* (1710), in which all the *basses de violon** are directed to pluck during Léandre's air 'Jaloux de régner seul' – part of his on-stage serenade. Rameau first used the technique as a sound effect in the 1744 version of *Dardanus* (IV, 3), where approaching footsteps are represented by a halting pizzicato for the cellos of the *petit chœur**. In subsequent operas he rarely exploited this 'linear' pizzicato, though he borrows Vivaldi's* idea of using it to represent rain, both in *Platée* (I, 6) and in the *sommeil** in 'Anacréon' (*Les Surprises de l'Amour*, 1757 version), and it evokes a ticking clock in *Les Boréades* (IV, 4). By contrast, Rameau makes extensive use of multiple-stopped plucked chords for the whole string section; indeed, these occur so frequently in his later operas as to make nonsense of Jean-Jacques Rousseau's* claim that pizzicato was 'almost unknown' in France. Rameau's plucked chords usually have some descriptive purpose – to represent on-stage instruments such as the lyre (*Platée, Le Temple de la Gloire* and others) or sailors' guitars (*Naïs*, I, and the 1757 version of *Hippolyte et Aricie*, III), or the clinking of the jailer's keys (*Les Paladins*, I, 1). In the last instance, Rameau experiments with some players plucking the chords and others bowing them as multiple stops. In French scores of the period, *pizzicato* is indicated by the direction *pincé** and cancelled by a phrase such as *avec l'archet*. See also **Nourrir**. MasOpé, MilOrc, RouDic, SadOrc.

Platée   Along with *La Princesse de Navarre*, this work was commissioned by Louis XV's court to celebrate the Dauphin's wedding. It was given a single performance, to round off the festivities, on 31 March 1745, in a temporary theatre in the Grande Écurie, Versailles. While the original sources of *Platée* describe it as a 'ballet bouffon' or a 'comédie-ballet'*, the work is nowadays generally classified as a *comédie lyrique** and comprises a prologue ('La Naissance de la comédie') and three acts with a single continuous plot. Jacques Autreau's* libretto, derived from the ancient Greek writer Pausanius, was adapted for the Versailles performance by Le Valois d'Orville*. Its subject – the mock marriage between Jupiter and a vain and credulous marsh nymph – seems ill-suited to the occasion: many spectators must have found Platée's grotesque representation by a male singer in drag insensitive, given that the new Dauphine was apparently no beauty. This aspect of the work seems to have excited little comment, however, though Voltaire* described the opera as the most detestable show he had ever seen, and the King, when asked repeatedly if he would like to hear the work again, did not deign to reply. As it happens, *Platée* (subtitled *Junon jalouse*) had not been conceived for this occasion; but when Royer failed to produce the planned setting of Voltaire's *Pandore**, the organizers drafted in Rameau's work-in-progress, seemingly oblivious to its incongruity. The composer evidently expected *Platée* to be rapidly transferred to the Paris Opéra, since he had already sent the score to be engraved. In the event, the work had to wait four years to be staged there. The 1749 production, with revisions to the libretto by Ballot* de Sovot and considerable reworking by Rameau, was criticized in literary circles but proved popular with the public. Revived in 1754 at the height of the Querelle des Bouffons*, *Platée* came to be widely regarded as one of Rameau's finest works and a model for future developments in French opera. It was again successfully revived between 1759 and 1761. Thereafter, however, only the prologue was performed, appearing for the last time in 1773. *BarPla, BesVol, BouHer, ChaRou, CowWom, GirRam, GreAri, GreSou, LegPla, MasOpé, ThoPla.*

Polyrhythms Rameau sometimes makes simultaneous use of duple (or quadruple) and triple metre, usually in brief passages but occasionally for whole movements. An example of the latter is the turbulent 'Chœur des esprits malfaisans et cruels' in *Zoroastre* (I, 6), barred in **2** with a predominantly semiquaver accompaniment but with choral parts that are noted as if in 6/8 throughout. In some pieces, the possibility arises that rhythms in one metre should be assimilated to those of another. In the example below, from 'Les Niais de Sologne', the engraver seems to have made a deliberate attempt to align the second of each duplet with the third of the corresponding triplet, though not perhaps consistently enough to tip the

Rameau, 'Les Niais de Sologne', *Pièces de clavessin* (1724) (Paris, Bibliothèque Nationale de France, Département de la Musique, Vm⁷. 1873)

balance in favour of assimilation. Elsewhere, an audible conflict of metres is certainly intended, as in the 'charivari' of frightened birds in *Platée* (III, 3), where two flageolets* have triplet quavers against the violins' semiquavers, slurred in pairs, or the 'Gavotte pour les Heures et les Zephirs' (*Les Boréades*, IV, 4), in which the combination of triplets for the *petites flûtes** and duplets for the bassoons evokes the sound of a ticking clock. Several movements in the *Pièces de clavecin en concerts* (1741) make prominent use of polyrhythms, including passages of four against three in 'La Laborde', eight against six in 'La Pantomime' and, most unusually for the period, five against two in 'L'Indiscrette'. *BarPla, RpeKey, SadZor.*

Pompadour, Jeanne Antoinette Poisson, marquise de   *See* **Théâtre des Petits Cabinets**.

Port de voix   In his keyboard music Rameau indicates the *port de voix* (rising appoggiatura) with a curved bracket before the note; in all other genres it is shown as a grace note. The latter appears as a quaver in Rameau's opera scores, whereas ornaments* added in rehearsal to the parts used by his singers include *ports de voix* notated either as a semibreve or a minim, the latter sometimes with a flag or hook. Given that these 'long' grace notes often precede notes as short as a quaver, they may well indicate emphasis rather than duration. Rameau's illustration of the *port de voix* in his table of keyboard ornaments, reproduced on page 20, shows that it was to be interpreted as a 'super-legato', the appoggiatura being released only after the resolution had been sounded. In vocal and instrumental music the rising appoggiatura was frequently terminated by a *pincé** (mordent), whether or not the latter was indicated in the source. The example below shows two versions of a passage from *Les Indes galantes*, the first using the ornament symbols commonly found in opera scores, the second (from the 'Quatre grands concerts'*) notated with keyboard-style *agréments**. Each rising appoggiatura in the former (bb. 5, 7 and 8) is shown in the latter as a *port de voix et pincé* (indicated by the curved brackets before and after the note). *CyrEss, GreSou, McGSpa, NeuOrn, NeuPer, SawNou.*

Rameau, *Les Indes galantes*, 'Prélude pour l'adoration du soleil', II, 5:

(a) manuscript production score, *F-Po*, A.132.1

(b) notated with keyboard *agréments* in 'Quatre grands concerts'

Portamento   The device of portamento – gliding from one note to another without distinguishing the intervening pitches – had emerged as a vocal technique by the early seventeenth century. The first evidence of its use in France appears in Mersenne's description of the *port de voix** in his *Harmonie universelle* (1636), while the *Pièces a une et a deux violes* by Marin Marais* (1686) includes a symbol for the *coulé de doigt* ('sliding of the finger'). Such portamenti were generally limited to movement between adjacent notes, whereas Rameau's *Platée* (1745) makes more ambitious use of the technique for comic effect, as shown in the example below. As Momus presents the eponymous nymph with Cupid's 'gifts' (tears, sorrow, cries, languor), the violin line is marked: 'sliding the same finger and making audible the two quarter-tones between *e′* and *f′*. By implication, the chromatic descent in the following bar is also performed as a portamento. When *Platée* was first performed at court, this effect elicited no known reaction. However, it evidently proved too strong for Parisian audiences when the work was given at the Opéra in 1749, since this passage was cut soon after the premiere. *See also* **Glissando**. *BarPla, CyrSty.*

Rameau, *Platée*, III, 4

Portraits   Numerous images have at one time or another been said to depict Rameau's likeness. Most of these (engraved medallions, caricatures*, decorated* harpsichord lids and the like) can be shown to derive from just three sources – a watercolour by Carmontelle*, a caricature by the same artist, and a bust by Caffieri*. The lid of one of Balbastre's* harpsichords is decorated with a portrayal of Rameau surrounded by scenes from *Castor et Pollux*. A celebrated oil painting variously attributed to Aved* and Chardin* has long been accepted as a portrait of Rameau, though serious questions remain about the identity of both the artist and the sitter. A further five images fall into the category of rejected* portraits. As for the satirical* engravings, any resemblance to Rameau is generally believed to be fortuitous. *GétPor.*

Posthumous inventory   On 19 September 1764, one week after Rameau's death, an inventory was drawn up of his estate, which was valued at 199,426 *livres*. It reveals that the composer's apartment on the rue des Bons-Enfants comprised ten rooms and a cellar. Rameau's study looked out over the Palais-Royal gardens, where he had long enjoyed a daily stroll. Among other things, the inventory itemizes the composer's modest furnishings and mainly threadbare wardrobe, which included two wigs but only one pair of shoes. It records an unidentified oil portrait of the composer, which his widow later offered to Decroix*, two engraved portraits and a copy of what must be the Caffieri* bust. Also listed are numerous exemplars of his published scores and treatises, for which his house was a point of sale, 2,016 engraved plates of his scores valued at 3,024 *livres*, and '20 bundles of [manuscript] music not worth listing'. At the time of his death, Rameau owned a single dilapidated musical instrument: 'un vieux clavecin à un clavier en mauvais état' (perhaps one of the harpsichords he inherited from his father Jean Rameau*). In the cellar were two barrels and fifty bottles of red Hérissé wine from his native Burgundy. Money bags in a writing desk in his wife's room contained coins to the value of 40,584 *livres*. KocWil, LauDoc.

'La Poule'   Rameau's evocation of a barnyard hen in the *Nouvelles suites de pièces de clavecin* (1729 or 1730) has become one of his best-known character pieces*, thanks in part to Respighi's arrangement, as 'La gallina', in his suite *Gli uccelli*. The inspiration for 'La Poule' may date back to the time soon after Rameau arrived in Paris in 1722, when he was befriended by Castel*. This Jesuit mathematician claims to have sketched 'the outline of pieces that imitate the voice of Nature' and recommended that the composer study the bird-song notated in Kircher's *Musurgia universalis* (1650): there he would find, among others, 'the cry of the hen calling her chickens'. Although Rameau does not copy the hen-calls in *Musurgia universalis*, he follows Kircher in placing onomatopoeic syllables (in this case 'Co co co co co co co dai') beneath the opening notes. His extensive use in this piece of repeated left-hand chords in quavers – a style of accompaniment almost unprecedented in French keyboard music – may betray the influence of Domenico Scarlatti*, who had visited Paris in the mid-1720s. By that time, 'La Poule' had probably not been completed, since Rameau does not mentioned it in the letter to La Motte* of 25 September 1727 in which he names several other keyboard pieces as examples of his ability to characterize. 'La Poule' is one of the earliest French harpsichord pieces to use dynamic* marks to indicate manual changes. BouHer, GirRam, RamCtw, RpeKey, SadSca.

Premier livre de pièces de clavecin   Rameau's first collection of harpsichord pieces – his earliest publication – appeared in 1706 and follows the model established by his mentor Louis Marchand* in 1699: it comprises a single suite in which a partly unmeasured* prelude introduces a sequence of eight dance movements and a single character* piece, 'Vénitiénne' [*sic*]. (A similar title is found in Gaspard Le Roux's *Pièces de clavecin*, 1705, while La Barre's *La Vénitienne* was performed at the Paris Opéra in May and June of that year.) Rameau's title page has led to some misunderstanding about the publication date. The engraving recycles a decorative *cartouche* that had been used for several earlier publications. While the date of Rameau's volume is clearly given as 1706, another date – 1705 – is visible above the inside lower edge of the *cartouche*. The latter evidently relates to the engraving of the *cartouche*; it can also be seen, for instance, on one exemplar of Charpentier's* *Motets melêz de simphonie*, published in 1709. There can be little doubt that Rameau's volume appeared in 1706. It is not listed in Foucault's catalogue for the years 1705–1706, and was thus probably issued by Foucault at the end of 1706. A second edition (now lost) was published in 1708 by Christophe Ballard, who had evidently acquired the engraved plates. His son Jean-Baptiste Christophe* issued a further edition in 1741. *BouHer, BroCla, EllKey, FulPor, GilRam, GirRam, GusFul, JacPiè, MalPiè, RpeKey.*

Préramiste   As a convenient shorthand for the period between Lully's last opera (1686) and Rameau's first (1733), the term *préramiste* is sometimes applied in a purely chronological sense to denote Rameau's predecessors and their music. More usefully, however, the notion of *préramisme* has come to define departures from the Lullian norm, and especially those which anticipate important stylistic developments in Rameau's operas. By extension, the term is sometimes applied to his immediate precursors in the field of music theory. *AntFre, FadInv, FajPré, VerDra.*

La Princesse de Navarre   For the lavish celebrations surrounding the wedding of the Dauphin, Louis XV's son, to Maria Teresa of Spain, Rameau received his first commissions to compose for the court – *La Princesse de Navarre* to open the festivities and *Platée* to conclude them. The former work, a three-act *comédie-ballet** to a libretto by Voltaire*, was first performed on 23 February 1745 in a specially constructed theatre in the Grande Écurie at Versailles. The king was pleased enough with the production to command a second performance, though the new Dauphine, whose Spanish upbringing had not prepared her for French music and theatre, was unimpressed. Rameau's overture* is lost: the tripartite overture in surviving sources is evidently the one composed by Rousseau for *Les Fêtes de Ramire**. The ensuing divertissements*, one at the end of each act, are only loosely connected with the plot of the spoken play, though the final one relates directly to the dynastic marriage: as the Pyrenees are seen to collapse, the scene is transformed into a magnificent Temple of Love. A commemorative engraving by Cochin* shows in great detail a scene from this final divertissement. The music of *La Princesse de Navarre*, recycled by Jean-Jacques Rousseau* and entitled *Les Fêtes de Ramire**, was presented at court later that year. The original work, with a new prologue by Voltaire, was revived in Bordeaux in 1763. By that time, Rameau had reused much of the ballet music in subsequent works. *BesVol, BouHer, BouThé, GirRam, JacVol, MalPri, MasOpé, RidVol, SadBor, SawBor.*

Privileges   To protect their work from piracy, French authors and composers could apply to the Syndicat de la Librairie for 'lettres de privilèges' valid for between three and twenty years. Rameau is known to have taken out five privileges: on 1 February 1724, for eight years, in respect of his cantatas and instrumental pieces; on 15 November 1731, for three years, for the *Dissertation sur les différentes métodes d'accompagnement*; on 19 September 1733 for six years, for any vocal or instrumental work; on 12 August 1741, for twelve years, to cover his music 'without words'; and on 31 May 1754, for three years, for his

Observations sur notre instinct pour la musique. See also **Publishers.** *BouHer, BreLib, DevPre.*

Le Procureur dupe sans le savoir The unidentified scribe who copied out the anonymous text of this *opéra comique** noted that it had been extracted 'from a score found in the papers of the famous composer Rameau'. He considered that the piece had been written for some private theatre in about 1758, a date suggested by the play's allusion to a comedy by Céron performed that year. The idea that Rameau, now in his mid-seventies, should have collaborated in such a project is all the more intriguing in view of the fact that the text makes several references to the recent Querelle des Bouffons*. However, most of the vocal items were evidently intended to be sung to *vaudevilles**, whose *timbres** are indicated in the text. It is thus not clear what contribution Rameau made to the piece, if any. *BreJeu, BouHer, RolVau.*

Production score This term has come to be used for scores prepared for use during performances at the Académie Royale de Musique* or at court. Some twenty production scores of Rameau operas survive, mostly in the Bibliothèque Nationale de France (Bibliothèque-Musée de l'Opéra), Paris, which houses what remains of the Académie's library. While some of them are in manuscript, the majority consist of exemplars of the published score or recycled proofs, the latter including corrections in Rameau's or other hands. The advantage of proofs in this context was that their wide margins were ideal for indicating revisions. Given that many production scores were reused for successive revivals over a period of three decades or more, they present the modern editor with a challenge – how to distinguish the many archaeological layers of revision: insertions of new material; autograph and other modifications on *collettes**; cuts ranging from a few bars to whole scenes; undated annotations by Rameau and others; cues in red crayon added by the *batteur de mesure**; and much else. In several of the production scores used after Rameau's death, some of his music was replaced with pieces by Berton* and others – a symptom of the rapid posthumous decline in popularity of his music. Invaluable as they are, the production scores often lack inner choral and orchestral parts. If, as is often the case, the production score is necessarily the principal source, such missing material must be taken from authoritative secondary sources or, in the last resort, reconstructed by the editor. *BouHer, GreSou.*

Prologue Until 1749, virtually every opera performed at the Paris Opéra or at court included a substantial prologue, the original function of which was to glorify the monarch and his achievements, real or imaginary. By the early-to-mid eighteenth century, the function of the prologue had diversified. While a number of Rameau's prologues are in praise of the monarchy, these occur mainly in works such as *Les Fêtes de Polymnie, Le Temple de la Gloire* and *Les Fêtes de l'Hymen et de l'Amour*, commissioned by Louis XV's court to celebrate royal events. Several prologues nevertheless allude to political matters: *Castor et Pollux* refers to the Peace of Vienna, while *Naïs* marks the Treaty of Aix-la-Chapelle with a prologue entitled 'L'Accord des Dieux'. In the case of the *opéras-ballets**, the prologue serves to introduce the general idea linking the component entrées*; thus in *Les Fêtes d'Hébé* (subtitled *Les talents lyriques*), Hebe and her attendant deities descend to the banks of the

Seine to celebrate the 'lyric talents', these being poetry, music and dance, each of which becomes the subject of one of the entrées*. The prologue could sometimes be appropriated to make a specific point: in *Hippolyte et Aricie* it is used to justify liberties in the treatment of the classical subject-matter; in Campra's* *Achille et Déïdamie** it takes a stand in the Lulliste-Ramiste* dispute. Rameau's *Zoroastre* (1749) was the first French opera deliberately to abandon the prologue, which is replaced in this and some later works by a programmatic overture*. Thereafter, new operas were given without prologues, as were many older ones when they were revived. Some prologues, once abandoned, gained a second life in composite spectacles known as *fragments**. *GirRam, HarPro, MasOpé, NauDra.*

Prose style Rameau's decision to leave the Collège des Godrans* without completing his education left its mark on his style of writing. According to Maret*, the youthful composer took steps to improve his linguistic skills after being reproved by a woman with whom he had fallen in love. Yet anyone who has struggled with the *Traité de l'harmonie* and later treatises will know how clumsy and long-winded his prose can seem. After the appearance of *Génération harmonique* (1737), Diderot* suggested that 'someone should extract [Rameau's] admirable system from the obscurities that enshroud it and put it within everyone's reach', a suggestion adopted to good effect by d'Alembert* in his *Élémens de musique théorique et pratique** (1752). Meanwhile, Diderot himself helped Rameau draft the *Démonstration du principe de l'harmonie** (1750). Rameau several times expressed gratitude to those who had assisted him in this way. To Castel* he admitted in 1736 that 'I can only say things, but you are able to give them light and colour'. After the appearance of d'Alembert's *Élémens*, Rameau touchingly acknowledged that the author had reworked his ideas with 'a simplicity to which I considered them susceptible, but which I could have given them only with much more difficulty, and perhaps less successfully than he'. *See also* **Arnaud, François (abbé)**. *ChrTho, GirRam, MarÉlo, RamCtw.*

Publishers In choosing publishers, Rameau's policy for his music differed from that for his theoretical writings. All his printed scores were self-published in association with the firm of Boivin and its commercial partners or successors; the composer's home address thus appears on the title pages as one of several points of sale. With his theoretical works, by contrast, Rameau changed publishers frequently. The *Traité de l'harmonie* (1722) and *Nouveau système* (1726) were both printed by Ballard*, who by 1730 had also begun type-setting the *Dissertation sur les différentes métodes d'accompagnement*. But this work, doubtless as a result of some dispute between author and publisher, was eventually issued two years later by Boivin and Le Clerc. Between 1739 and 1741 Ballard nevertheless took the unusual step of issuing full scores of five Rameau operas in manuscript but with printed title pages. Meanwhile, *Génération harmonique* (1737) and *Observations sur notre instinct pour la musique* (1754) were published by Prault *fils*, while the two intervening works, *Démonstration du principe de l'harmonie* (1750) and *Nouvelles réflexions* (1752), were entrusted to Durand and Pissot, publishers of the *Encyclopédie*: indeed, the choice of this distinguished publishing house must have been at the suggestion of Diderot*, Rameau's collaborator in the *Démonstration* and Durand's principal editor. Having later crossed swords with Diderot* and the Encyclopedists in *Erreurs sur la musique dans l'Encyclopédie* (1755), Rameau could no longer use this publisher, and the *Erreurs* and related pamphlets were issued by Sébastien Jorry. Rameau's final published treatises, *Code de musique pratique* (1760) and *Origine des sciences* (1762), were granted the exceptional honour of being issued by the royal press (Imprimerie Royale) in the Louvre. Even so, Jean-Jacques Rousseau's* jibe that Rameau's treatises 'had the singularity of becoming famous without being read' is supported by the fact that, unlike his scores, only one of the composer's theoretical works appeared in a second edition: as a result, the general perception of his theories in the years after his death was mainly based on second-hand, not always accurate, accounts. *BouHer, ChrTho, DevLes, DevPre, GusFul, MapRam.*

Le P[ucelage], ou La rose   This one-act *opéra comique**, the third of Rameau's collaborations with Piron*, was completed by July 1726 and passed by the censor, but subsequently banned by the chief of police because its subject matter was judged to be obscene. Rameau's music, now lost, included a da capo air, 'Le jour ne luit qu'à peine encore', a representation of the dawn chorus featuring the song of the nightingale, a musette and several 'danses légères et galantes'. On 5 March 1744 the play was eventually staged by Jean Monnet* at the Opéra-Comique* with the less salacious title *Le Jardin de l'Hymen, ou La rose*; this production probably included some of Rameau's music. In 1752 it was restaged as *La Rose, ou les Festes de l'Hymen* with alterations by Charles-Simon Favart (1710–92); while the libretto again preserves the text of Rameau's da capo air, the divertissement* was cut, and it seems unlikely that any of the original music was used; however, one of the airs was sung to the melody of 'À l'Amour rendez les armes' from *Hippolyte et Aricie*. *BouRam, ConPir, PirŒu, ProPir, SadPir.*

Pupils   Despite the fact that much of Rameau's professional life was given over to teaching*, relatively few of his pupils have been identified. Among those who studied the harpsichord with him were a number of talented women: Marie Louise Mignot (1712–90), the future Madame Denis and best known as Voltaire's* niece and mistress, had developed a style of playing that, according to Madame de Genlis's *Mémoires*, 'transports us back in spirit to the time of Louis XIV'. Anne-Jeanne Boucon, who later married the composer Mondonville* and is almost certainly the dedicatee of 'La Boucon'* in Rameau's *Pièces de clavecin en concerts*, proved a particularly gifted player. Equally gifted was Thérèse Deshayes*, mistress and eventually wife of La Pouplinière, her interests also extending to music theory. It is probable that Rameau's wife Marie-Louise Mangot*, a harpsichordist as well as a singer, had once been his pupil. Those who studied harmony and theory include Madame de Saint-Maur, née Alion (c.1695–1774) and the composers Antoine Dauvergne (1713–97), Claude-Bénigne Balbastre*, Jean-Benjamin de La Borde (the probable dedicatee of Rameau's 'La Laborde'*), Marpurg* and Pietro Gianotti*; indeed, Gianotti later published what is essentially a digest of his teacher's composition course. In 1756 Rameau stated proudly that he had taught one of the editors of the *Encyclopédie* (d'Alembert* rather than Diderot*, as sometimes claimed) 'everything he wanted to know about music theory'. Thomas Green suggests that Jean Rollet, Rameau's preferred copyist and author of a *Méthode pour apprendre la* *musique* (c.1760), was also a pupil. *See also* **'Les Petits Marteaux'**. *ChrTho, CucPou, GreSou, LauDoc, MorPed, QuiAnn, RamCtw, ZasApp.*

Puvigné, Mlle   Neither the forenames nor the dates of birth and death of this dancer are known, though it seems likely that she was born in c.1736. The daughter of a dancer ('Puvigné *mère*') and a pupil of Dehesse*, she created a sensation as a child prodigy when she danced in 1743 at Monnet's* newly-refurbished Opéra-Comique* alongside the young Noverre* and Mlle Lany* in a *pas de trois*. She later performed in ballets at Madame de Pompadour's Théâtre des Petits Cabinets*. Described by Madame de Graffigny* as 'le petit chef-d'œuvre de la nature', she entered the Académie Royale de Musique* in 1743, often dancing the graceful roles originally created by Marie Sallé*, to whom she was considered the natural successor. Her most individual roles were as the Statue in *Pigmalion* and a shepherdess in *Naïs*, both of which required her to sing as well as dance. *BouHer, CamFoi, DaiCor, FaiSty, PorNov.*

Quam dilecta   The inventory of the Académie des Beaux-Arts de Lyon lists a score of this *motet* *à grand chœur*, which has led to the assumption that the work dates from Rameau's years in Lyon* between 1712 and 1715. While this may be so, it should be noted that the chronological inventory catalogues the work as no. 113 – an indication that it was acquired some considerable time after the Académie's foundation in 1713. (By way of comparison, a score of Rameau's *In convertendo*, listed as no. 219, did not enter the library until the 1750s.) Although the Lyon score of *Quam dilecta* is now lost, the motet survives in two manuscripts in the Decroix* collection dating from the late 1770s and probably prepared from material sent by the composer's son Claude-François Rameau*. *DurMot, DurRel, GirRam, HerMot, MalMot, ValAca, ValLyo.*

'Quatre grands concerts'   When *Les Indes galantes* appeared in 1735, the Lulliste-Ramiste* dispute was in full swing. Reacting to criticism of the *scènes d'action** (dramatic dialogue) in this work, Rameau decided not to publish the complete score. Instead, he took the unusual step of issuing only the instrumental movements and vocal set-pieces (solos, ensembles and choruses), regrouping these into 'Quatre grands concerts', or concert suites. An even more unusual feature of this publication is the manner in which the instrumental pieces are presented. Rameau's preface states that 'the *symphonies** are even arranged as harpsichord pieces, and the ornaments in them are consistent with those in my other harpsichord pieces'. This last remark refers to his use of the characteristic French *agrément** signs associated exclusively with keyboard music. His published opera scores, by contrast, follow standard practice in indicating the ornaments mainly by written-out grace notes and the multi-purpose + sign. The distinction between these two traditions of ornament symbols is, indeed, apparent in this same publication, which also includes 'Les Sauvages', an entrée* added to *Les Indes galantes* in 1736. Not only is this entrée published with opera-style ornament symbols rather than keyboard *agréments*, but the orchestral writing shows no sign of having been adapted for keyboard. In any case, Rameau's preface makes clear that his remarks about harpsichord arrangements do not apply to 'Les Sauvages'. The arrangements in the 'Quatre grands concerts' nevertheless served a dual purpose, to be played either as solos or as accompanied* keyboard music; thus Rameau generally avoided the kind of keyboard figuration that could not easily be adapted by the other players. *See also* **Concert**. *BouHer, GilRam, RpeKey, SadInd.*

Querelle des Bouffons   Though ostensibly a dispute between the rival merits of French serious opera and Italian *opera buffa*, this notorious pamphlet-war may be seen to have an important political dimension, hence the extensive literature it continues to generate. Its immediate cause was the arrival, in September 1752, of an Italian troupe directed by Eustachio Bambini (1697–1770) and their performances of Pergolesi's *La serva padrona* and other *opere buffe* (hence the troupe's nickname of Bouffons) at the Paris Opéra. The underlying cause, however, was the political unrest generated during a long-running dispute between Jansenists and Jesuits concerning the papal bull *Unigenitus*. When the largely Jansenist *parlement* found its judgments repeatedly thwarted by the king's council in the early 1750s, the parliamentarians mounted a challenge to royal authority that led to their exile in May 1753. Meanwhile, in February 1752 the king had suppressed the first two volumes of the *Encyclopédie*, and leading intellectuals such as Grimm* and Jean-Jacques Rousseau* were seeking a pretext to mount a comparable challenge. They hit on the idea of attacking what they saw as the outmoded repertory of the Académie Royale de Musique, using this institution's 'royal' status to question state control not merely of opera but also, more broadly, of thought and speech: hence the intertwining of musical, aesthetic, religious and political issues in many of the pamphlets issued during the Querelle, notably Grimm's *Le Petit Prophète de Boehmischbroda* (January 1753), the broadside that marks the true start of hostilities. In all, some sixty pamphlets were exchanged between the *coin du roi* (the partisans of French music) and their opponents, the *coin de la reine* or *bouffonistes*. Much the most inflammatory was Rousseau's *Lettre sur la musique française* (November 1753), which sought to undermine the entire basis of French vocal music. (The author was subsequently burned in effigy by members of the Opéra orchestra.) Rameau's main contribution to the quarrel, the *Observations sur notre instinct pour la musique** (1754), is a measured and detailed response to Rousseau's *Lettre*, though his subsequent attacks on Rousseau in the *Erreurs sur la musique dans l'Encyclopédie** and related pamphlets were to become increasingly strident. *ChaRou, ChrTho, ChoPré, CooQue, CowOri, FabBou, IshDal, IshQue, LayQue, VerMus, WebWan.*

Quinault, Philippe   As Lully's* principal librettist, Philippe Quinault (1635–88) played a crucial role in the creation of the *tragédie en musique** during the 1670s and 1680s. His librettos, though initially criticized, came to be regarded in the eighteenth century as models of their kind: indeed, Charles de Brosses*, Noverre* and others were to suggest that Rameau should reset them, though without necessarily replacing Lully's recitative. Unlike in Italy and elsewhere, however, it was not yet the custom in France to reset existing librettos (Rameau's *Pigmalion** of 1748 is the earliest example given at the Paris Opéra); moreover, Rameau must have known that conservative opera lovers would have regarded the idea of supplanting the music of their revered Lully as near-sacrilege. *AgaLet, AntFre, DidLiv, KinPoé, NovLet, WooLul.*

Quinque   *See* **Laboravi clamans**.

Quittard, Henri   A music historian with wide-ranging interests, Quittard (1864–1919) is particularly valued by Rameau scholars for his detailed study of the composer's early life, undertaken contemporaneously with a similar study by Michel Brenet*. In uncovering many new documents and correcting errors in earlier biographical accounts, these scholars greatly enriched our knowledge of what was hitherto a murky period in the composer's biography. *QuiJeu.*

Rameau, Claude Bernard   Jean-Philippe's younger brother Claude was born in Dijon* in 1689. In 1715 he married Marguerite Rondelet (c.1682–1736), who was said to have been Jean-Philippe's first love. She gave birth a year later to Jean-François Rameau*, the notorious nephew of Diderot's* satire *Le Neveu de Rameau.* Claude held a succession of organist posts, principally at Notre-Dame and Saint-Étienne in his native Dijon, before settling in Autun in 1755 as cathedral organist, where he remained until his death in 1761. Maret* decribes him as less erudite (*savant*) than his brother but a better player. At the age of sixty-seven, a year after his move to Autun, Claude remarried. The first of his children by his new wife was Lazare (b. 1757), another 'neveu de Rameau' almost as eccentric as the first. Claude was by all accounts a violent, undisciplined character, prone to gambling. In 1736, when the Dijon confraternity of mercers failed to pay for his services as organist, he took revenge with a cacophonous improvisation involving the most disagreeable combinations of stops. This well-documented incident may well be the origin of a similar anecdote told about his elder brother in relation to his time at Clermont*. Jean-François *le neveu* gave Mercier* a lurid account of his father's early life, in which Claude was hanged for looting but cut down at the last moment by passing soldiers – a tale that is surely the product of an overactive imagination. Claude enjoyed a close relationship with his brother that endured even after the latter settled in Paris. In 1727 he acted as godfather to Jean-Philippe's first child, Claude-François*, and in 1752 published a sharp riposte to an anonymous writer who dared to criticize aspects of his brother's theories. His only surviving composition, a *cantatille* 'Le Buveur devenu amoureux' ('The Drinker turned Lover'), dedicated to his brother, was published in Paris by Mme Boivin in c.1750. *GarOrg, GirAut, GirRam, KocRel, KocSer, KocWil, MasPol, MarÉlo.*

Rameau, Claude-François   Jean-Philippe's eldest child was born in 1727. He was an amateur composer of some ability, to judge from the keyboard part of a 'premiere suitte' which is all that survives of an ensemble work by 'Mr Rameau fils'. In his youth, Claude-François evidently acted as messenger-boy in his father's dealings with Voltaire* and others; he was also occasionally used by Jean-Philippe as an amanuensis: a recently discovered letter dating from 1752 and evidently addressed to the comte d'Argenson* is one of several mainly in Claude-François's hand but signed by his father. In 1755 Rameau *père* helped him purchase the much-prized title of *valet de chambre* in the king's service, in providing 17,500 of the necessary 21,500 *livres*. When Jean-Philippe died in 1764, Claude-François inherited his manuscripts, printed books and more than two thousand engraved plates of the published scores. He did little, however, to promote his father's posthumous reputation. True, he lent Decroix* a number of books and scores, including one autograph manuscript, but Decroix had to write four letters before he received a response; and while

Claude-François evidently supported the notion of a complete Rameau edition, he was lackadaisical in producing the necessary material: while he repeatedly stated, for instance, that he could not locate Rameau's correspondence with Voltaire and other distinguished people, these were soon tracked down among his possessions after his death. In 1772 Claude-François married Marie-Françoise-Suzanne Dubois and had a son, Louis-Antoine, the following year. Soon after he died in 1788, his widow offered Decroix a 'portrait du grand Rameau'. Unfortunately her letter does not name the artist, so we do not know whether this was the oil painting variously attributed to Aved* and Chardin* (the subject of some controversy) or some other portrait that has not survived. *BouHer, GirRam, GreSou, GusFul, LauDoc, LauGen, RamCtw, SadLet, SchRam, WisVer.*

Rameau, Jean   The lineage of Jean Rameau (1638–1714), father of Jean-Philippe, has been traced back at least as far as the 1550s; his ancestors, mainly from the region west of Dijon*, included agricultural workers, wine makers and administrative officials. Jean, born in Dijon itself, was the son of a church official and evidently the first member of the family to make music his profession. In 1660 he was appointed organist at the collegiate church of Saint-Étienne in Dijon and subsequently held two other concurrent organ posts in the city, at the abbey of Saint-Bénigne from 1672 and at Saint-Pierre from 1682. In 1671 he married Claude de Martinecourt*, daughter of a well-connected notary from the nearby village of Gemeaux. The couple had twelve children, born on an almost annual basis, of whom only five survived into adulthood. In 1690 Jean was appointed organist at Notre-Dame, Dijon, a post he held until 1709, when he resigned in favour of his son Jean-Philippe. Rameau *père*, though disputatious by nature and unpolished in his language and manners, gave his children a sound musical education. His will reveals that he owned numerous instruments, including a chamber organ, a large two-manual harpsichord decorated in the Chinese style valued at 180 *livres*, a one-manual harpsichord (60 *livres*), a large spinet (50 *livres*), a spinet by 'Rucairs', i.e., Ruckers (40 *livres*), another by Breton (40 *livres*), a small spinet (20 *livres*) and a *dessus* de viole* (25 *livres*). Different codicils to Jean's will divide these instruments variously between his children Jean-Philippe, Claude-Bernard* and Marie-Claude*, seemingly on the basis of which of the offspring was in or out of favour. *BreJeu, GirAut, GirRam, KocRel, KocSer, KocWil, MarÉlo, QuiJeu.*

Rameau, Jean-Baptiste   On his baptismal record the future composer is named Jean-Philippe Rameau, yet a number of legal documents from various stages of his life identify him as Jean-Baptiste (in one case as Jean Baptiste Philippe). The former style even occurs on the captions of several engraved portraits, as in the illustration opposite, which also manages to get his year of birth wrong. A clue to this discrepancy is found in early documents where the composer signs himself 'J. Rameau fils' or 'J. Rameau fils esne' (*fils aîné*: eldest son), thereby implying that at this stage he had adopted Jean as his only forename. According to Tiénot, it was the custom in Burgundy at that time for boys called Jean to be referred to as 'Jean-Baptiste' or even 'Baptiste'. In press reviews and reports, as in his own published works and manuscripts, the composer is always identified merely as 'Rameau', his surname usually preceded by Monsieur or its equivalent, 'le Sieur'. *BreJeu, GétPor, KocSer, LauDoc, MarRam, QuiJeu, TiéRam.*

Anonymous etching, 'Jean-Baptiste Rameau' (*sic*), after Carmontelle (Paris, Bibliothèque Nationale de France, Département de la Musique, Est. Rameau J.P. 032). Reproduced by permission.

Rameau, Jean-François Immortalized in Diderot's* satire *Le Neveu de Rameau*, Jean-François Rameau (1716–77) is much the most eccentric character in Jean-Philippe's biography. The eldest son of the composer's brother Claude Bernard Rameau*, Jean-François was mistreated by his father and left the family home in Dijon* in 1736 when his mother died. After enrolling in the army, he returned to his native city in 1739, where he took minor orders. His father disinherited him in 1746, by which time he had arrived in Paris in an attempt to establish a musical career in the shadow of his illustrious uncle. An early sign of his fiery temperament revealed itself in 1748, when he was jailed for three weeks for insulting one of the directors at the Académie Royale de Musique*. The warrant for his imprisonment describes him as unsociable and difficult to control. This disturbance, in the foyer of the Académie, occurred on the day of the Paris premiere of his uncle's opera *Les Fêtes de l'Hymen et de l'Amour*. Three weeks later, Jean-Philippe wrote to the comte de Maurepas, secretary of state, to have his nephew deported to the Caribbean. In his reply, Maurepas sympathizes that Jean-François had not profited more from the good education his uncle had provided, but makes clear that deportation was beyond his powers. The nephew was released three weeks later. Jean-Philippe, who had been allowed to suggest the length of the jail sentence, later excluded him from any inheritance. Jean-François did not learn his lesson: in 1753 he caused another disturbance at the Opéra by slow-handclapping a speech by the city official in charge of this august institution.

For all that, Jean-François remained fiercely loyal to his uncle. Proud of his surname, he always referred to himself as 'Rameau le neveu'. During the Querelle des Bouffons* he took a pro-French, Ramiste position. His autobiographical poem *La Raméïde** (1766) adopts a similarly generous stance. Jean-François had earlier published his 'Œuvre I', the *Nouvelles pièces de clavecin en six suites* (1757), now lost; press reviews describe in some detail its component movements, among them 'Les Trois Rameaux', a sequence of pieces portraying uncle, father and nephew. For the *Mercure de France** (June 1757), this publication revealed 'a great fire of the imagination and the courage to avoid the commonplace and risk everything in order to be original'. An orchestral piece by him, also lost, was performed at the Concert Spirituel* in 1758. His texts for several romances and *vaudevilles* survive, but all that is left of his music is the melodic line of two pieces. Towards the end of his life Jean-François went into a general decline, and in 1769 his sister requested his arrest for misconduct. He was sent to the monastery of Bons-Fils at Armentières, a lunatic asylum and place of detention, where he died eight years later. *GirAut, GirRam, GusFul, LauDoc, MagNev, ProNev.*

'La Rameau'　While it seems likely that this movement from the *Pièces de clavecin en concerts* (1741) is a self-portrait, the dedicatee could be any one of the musical members of Rameau's family – wife, brother, sister, son, nephew... Indeed, Girdlestone suggests that the piece was a family joke, reflecting the keyboard practice that went on in the Rameau household. Jean-Baptiste Forqueray was to entitle one movement 'La Rameau' in his *Pièces de viole* [...] *mise en pieces de clavecin* (1747) – doubtless returning Rameau's compliment in naming a piece in the present collection 'La Forqueray'*. Jean-François Rameau*, the composer's nephew, included a group portrait, 'Les Trois Rameaux', in his *Pièces de clavecin* (1757), now lost. *BouHer, GirRam, GusFul, HerMor, RpeKey.*

Rameau, Marie-Alexandrine　The youngest of Jean-Philippe's four children, Marie-Alexandrine was born in 1744 when the composer was 60. The following year, Rameau took out an annuity of 1,200 *livres* on her life and, in 1758, another of 1,000 *livres*. Collé* recounts a conversation that may reveal the state of Marie-Alexandrine's relationship with her aged father. A year before he died, Rameau attended a performance of Collé's comedy *Dupuis et Desronais* (1763), in which the heartless and domineering Dupuis, fearing that his daughter would abandon him once she married, swears that her wedding will not take place during his lifetime. After the performance, Rameau said to Collé: 'je suis Dupuis'. This suggests that, unless he was teasing or Collé was being more than usually malevolent towards him, the composer had issued a similar ban in his own daughter's case. And sure enough, less than three months after Rameau's burial, Marie-Alexandrine's marriage contract was drawn up and later signed in the presence of a glittering array of witnesses, including five dukes, seven marquis or marquises and seven counts or countesses. The wedding was celebrated the following January in the Rameau family's parish church of Saint-Eustache*. The groom, François Marie de Gaultier (1728–1801), was a musketeer in the king's first company and of noble rank ('écuyer'). When he died, in Münster, Westphalia, he is described as 'émigré', having escaped from France in 1792 during the Revolution. Whether Marie-Alexandrine went with him is not known. She died in Mazan, her husband's birthplace in the Vaucluse region, in 1808. *BouRam, ColJou, GirRam, LauDoc, LauGen.*

Rameau, Marie-Claude [Catherine]   In his *Éloge historique de Mr Rameau* (1766) Hugues Maret* states that Jean-Philippe had a sister named Catherine who 'died in 1762, a good harpsichord player. For a long time she taught music in Dijon, but for several years before she died her infirmities prevented her from working, and her brother [...] made her an allowance which he always paid punctually'. Maret, himself a Dijonnais, doubtless knew her. No archival record relating to the composer's siblings mentions a Catherine Rameau, but since Maret mentions her date of death, this must be Marie-Claude (1681–1762), one of Jean-Philippe's seven elder sisters. That she was a musician is confirmed by her father's will, different codicils to which divide his collection of musical instruments variously between Jean-Philippe, Claude Bernard* and Marie-Claude, but not his other children. *GirAut, GirRam, KocRel, KocWil, MarÉlo.*

Rameau, Marie-Louise   Jean-Philippe's second child was born in 1732 and given the same forenames as her mother. In 1745 Rameau invested in a tontine (a collectively funded annuity) on her behalf. During a visit to La Pouplinière's* country house with her father in 1748, she evidently met Madame de Graffigny*, who remarked on her close resemblance to him. Two years later Marie-Louise entered the convent of the Dames de la Visitation de Sainte-Marie in Montargis, some seventy miles south of Paris; there she became known as 'Sister Louise Julie' and served as a *dame de chœur*. Although she received a dowry from her father at that time, he did not attend the veiling ceremony. She died at Montargis in 1777 and is buried in the crypt of the convent. *BouRam, DaiCor, GirRam, LauDoc.*

Rameau, Pierre   Little is known of the life of Pierre Rameau (1674–1748), who was active in the early eighteenth century as a dancing master. In 1725 he published two influential treatises on French court dance: *Le Maître à danser* and *L'Abbrégé* [sic] *de la nouvelle méthode*. The first includes a clear explanation of the execution of French dance-steps, together with numerous comments on posture and the use of the arms, while the second proposes a modification of Raoul-Auger Feuillet's dance notation. As far as we know, Pierre was no direct relative of Jean-Philippe Rameau. The identity of these two men seems to have been confused by Decroix*, however, when he claimed that in 1702 the composer joined a theatrical troupe touring the south of France. Neal Zaslaw has shown that the troupe in question must have been the Lyon* Opéra, of which Pierre was a member at that time. *LanBel, ValLyo, ZasApp.*

RCT (Rameau Thematic Catalogue) Published by the Centre National de la Recherche Scientifique (CNRS), the Rameau *Catalogue thématique des œuvres musicales* is currently being prepared by Sylvie Bouissou* and Denis Herlin with the participation of Pascal Denécheau. This monumental undertaking represents a huge advance in Rameau scholarship. To date, three volumes have appeared: 'Musique instrumentale, musique vocale religieuse et profane'; 'Livrets' (librettos); and the first volume of 'Musique dramatique'. A second volume of 'musique dramatique' is in preparation, and the catalogue will be completed by a fifth volume comprising archival and bibliographical sources, indexes of scribes, engravers, concordances and other matters. *BouHer.*

La Raméïde In 1766 Jean-François Rameau*, Jean-Philippe's notorious nephew, published a long autobiographical poem entitled *La Raméïde*, in which he exposes his misfortunes and appeals for the public charity to which he felt the glorious name of Rameau entitled him. Despite mistreatment by his father and rejection by his uncle, the author refers warmly to both men and reveals a genuine love and admiration of Jean-Philippe's music. He also shows himself to be an ardent supporter of the French national style. For all its literary short-comings, the poem reveals a complex psychology and a wealth of biographical detail. *La Nouvelle Raméïde*, a sequel published the same year under his name, was actually written by his friend Jacques Cazotte (1719–92). *GirRam, MagNev.*

Ramoneur During the Lulliste-Ramiste* dispute, Rameau's supporters were known both as Ramistes and, by 1737, as Ramoneurs. The latter label, though originally pejorative (*ramoneur*: chimney sweep), became a badge of pride to the composer's supporters. In 1739, for instance, Madame de Graffigny* recorded her impressions of a rehearsal of *Dardanus*: 'I was enchanted with it and immediately discovered myself to be a Ramoneuse'. (Occasionally the variant *ramonat* is found.) An anonymous arrangement of a tambourin* from *Les Fêtes d'Hébé* (I, 5) is entitled 'La Ramoneuse' in a *Deuxième recueil de contredanses*, published in the 1740s or 1750s by Mme Boivin; here, the title is doubtless used in an ironic sense, since the tambourin was a type of dance that never appeared in the operas of Lully*. *DacDar, DaiCor, MasLul, SadPat, SemBal, WooSad.*

Raparlier Numerous sets of performing parts of Rameau operas bear the stamp 'Raparlier', the name of a musician and impresario active in northern France in the later eighteenth century. Few details of Raparlier's biography survive. In 1759 he became director of the Société des Concerts in Lille and directed the town's theatre from 1771 to 1776. His informative treatise, *Principes de musique: les agréments du chant et un essai sur la prononciation, l'articulation et la prosodie de la langue française*, was published in Paris (1769) and Lille (1772). Raparlier's sets of performing parts were mainly copied for use in the Lille region; many bear the names of local amateur players, among them abbés and women. The majority of these parts reflect a local performing tradition considerably different from that of the Académie Royale de Musique* in distinguishing the string players of the 'symphonies'* (i.e., *ripieno*) from those of the 'accompagnements' (*concertino*), in including lines for third violon and in the use of organ continuo. Some sets are based on published *partitions réduites**, hence lack many inner choral and orchestral parts. While they are of some sociological interest, they are of little use for establishing authoritative texts of Rameau's music. *BouHer, LebDec, LebFon, SouRéc.*

'Le Rappel des oiseaux' In the title of this piece, from the *Pièces de clavessin* of 1724, the word *rappel* is probably used in a military sense, as in the term *battre le rappel*: to call the troops to the flag. The fanfare-like opening figures and *batteries** in both hands certainly support such an interpretation, though in this case the 'troops' are a flock of evidently unruly birds. An alternative interpretation linked to the art of falconry has been proposed by Françoise Petit, who notes that the terminology for the signal that summoned a bird to the falconer's fist varied according to the species of bird. Whereas a goshawk was recalled by a *réclame*, a falcon was summoned by a four-note *rappel* sung or shouted by the falconer. It is thus conceivable that the four-note anacrusis figure that dominates 'Le Rappel des oiseaux' is derived from such a *rappel*. *GirRam, GusFul, PetFau, RpeKey.*

Rebel, François, and François Francœur The careers of François Rebel (1701–75) and François Francœur (1698–1787) are so closely intertwined that they may conveniently be considered together. Known as the *petits violons* for reasons that are not hard to guess, the two men rose through the ranks of the Académie Royale de Musique*, first as members of the violin section, then as officials: Rebel became *batteur de mesure** and Francœur *maître de musique* in 1739, the former being responsible for rehearsals and performances, the latter for the training of the soloists and chorus. Alongside these duties, they collaborated as composers in a series of stage works, notably *Pirame et Thisbé* (1726), *Scanderberg* (1735) and *Zélindor, roi des sylphes* (1745), in which Rebel is said to have composed the 'morceaux de force' and Francœur the 'morceaux de sentiment'. In 1743 they were appointed *inspecteurs* at the Académie, but resigned their posts after complaints of low performing standards during the 1753 court production of Rameau's *Daphnis et Églé**. They nevertheless returned as joint *directeurs* in 1757, when they instituted a process of regeneration at the Académie that continued until their retirement in 1767. Scattered remarks suggest that their relationship with Rameau was not an easy one: Balbastre told Maret* that they 'often made the composer revise the scores of pieces to which he had been extremely attached'. A police record of 1753, reporting a disturbance at the Opéra caused by Claude-François Rameau*, mentions 'the hatred towards Rebel and Francœur on the part of the Rameau family'. Another report of the same year states that 'Rebel and Francœur, as musicians, were very jealous of Rameau, and practically never had his operas performed'. This last remark, at least, is unjustified, since Rameau's operas featured prominently in the Académie schedules during Rebel and Francœur's period as *directeurs*. *ArgMém, CesReb, ChaPol, ChaRou, GreSou, LabEss, MarÉlo, ProNev, RosDes.*

Rebel, Jean-Féry One of the most distinguished of Lully's* successors at the Académie Royale de Musique*, Jean-Féry Rebel (1666–1747) is particularly noted for his opera *Ulysse* (1703) and for the invention of the *symphonie chorégraphique*, a genre of ballet which, unusually for the period, included no singing. One such work, *Les Caractères de la danse* (1715), juxtaposes fragments of the standard ballet movements to create a vehicle for the star dancer Françoise Prévost, an idea borrowed by her pupil Marie Sallé* for the ballet *Pigmalion* (1734) and imitated in the first divertissement* of Rameau's own *Pigmalion**. As *batteur de mesure** at the Académie between 1714 and 1738, Rebel conducted the premieres of Rameau's first four operas. The experience seems to have rubbed off on him, since the first movement of *Les Éléments*, his final *symphonie chorégraphique*, published in 1738, includes a fairly blatant borrowing from Rameau's *Castor et Pollux*, premiered the previous year. (See the example below.) This passage occurs in the opening movement, 'Cahos', where it is marked *Frémissement* (shuddering) and includes the characteristic notation associated with slurred* tremolo. A decade later, Rameau would include his own 'representation of Chaos' in the overture to *Zaïs* (1748). *CesReb.*

(a) Rameau, *Castor et Pollux* (1737), 'Que tout gémisse', I, 1

(b) Rebel, 'Cahos', *Les Éléments* (1738)

Récit This term, not to be confused with *récitatif*, denotes any passage performed by a solo voice or instrument. Outside the contexts of organ music and court ballet, it is most often encountered in the *motet** *à grand chœur*, where it distinguishes solo passages from those for the choir. A *récit* might thus be a full-scale da capo aria, as in the first movement of Rameau's *In convertendo*, or a short solo interjection within a chorus. The fourth movement of *Quam dilecta* ('Beati qui habitant in domo tua') exemplifies a favourite type, the *récit et chœur*, in which the soloist begins with a substantial aria, after which the chorus reworks the same material, with solo interpolations. No doubt the word *récit* was used in this repertory to avoid the secular associations of such terms as *air* or *ariette**. Organs of the Rameau period included a *récit* division comprising a small number of solo stops, these being played from a short-compass manual whose lowest note was usually middle C. *See also* **Collège Louis-le-Grand; Jacobins**. *AntFre, DurMot, FavMot, RouDic.*

Recueil Bresou A manuscript of assorted rounds and canons in the Bibliothèque Nationale de France (Département de la Musique, Rés. F. 1212) has come to be known as the 'Recueil Bresou', as it bears the annotation 'à Monsieur le Conseiller Bresou à Lille'. The manuscript, entitled 'Canons à trois, quatre, cienq [*sic*], et six parties', is of some interest to Rameau scholars, since a second title, upside down on the final page, reads 'Canons à trois, quatre, et six parties attribués à Rameau'. A later annotation – 'Ah! mais non' by 'BW' (probably Jean-Baptiste Weckerlin, a librarian at the Paris Conservatoire where the manuscript was long preserved) – reflects the fact that several of these canons can be securely attributed to other composers. Still, the Bresou collection includes all of the composer's published canons, as well as several contained in a miscellany in the Decroix* collection that is said to have been found among Rameau papers. Whether this evidence is enough to authenticate the Rameau attributions is, however, debatable, especially as many items in the Decroix miscellany can also be shown to be by other composers. *See also* **Traité de la composition des canons en musique**. *BouCan, BouHer, MonBou, SadLet.*

Réflections d'un peintre sur l'opéra A rare insight into Rameau's working relationship with one of his librettists is revealed in this small book, published anonymously in The Hague in 1743 but securely attributed to Montdorge*, author of *Les Fêtes d'Hébé*. The book quotes at length a letter to an unnamed poet-friend from an unnamed composer. Given that the letter reveals identifiable stages in the revision process of *Les Fêtes d'Hébé*, there can be no doubt that the poet is Montdorge himself and the composer Rameau, even if details of their collaboration have doubtless been embroidered in the interests of a 'good read'. The letter presents the relationship between composer and librettist as that of tyrant and slave. The composer peremptorily demands changes, as much for musical as for poetic reasons; the poet, meanwhile, is frustrated to discover that the new material he provided at the composer's request is subsequently abandoned. Montdorge's 'poet' has particular trouble in constructing verses on the composer's *canevas**. The musician disputes that this task is difficult: he claims that his own *canevas* for a Gigue ('Nos cœurs | Trompeurs, | Douceurs, | En ces retraites, | La douce Musette | Répette | Les ardeurs | En fureur [...]') had taken only half-an-hour to write. Among the poet's other concerns is Rameau's habit of reading the libretto publicly in a café frequented by poets (perhaps the Caveau* or the Café Procope). All these frustrations are echoed by Voltaire* and Collé* in their accounts of collaboration with Rameau. Sadly, we only ever get the poets' side of the relationship. While the composer was undoubtedly a difficult man to work with, none of these writers is known to have had any musical expertise, and it may well be that they were incapable of understanding the special requirements of writing verse for setting to music. *BesVol, CyrHéb, GirRam, GreSou, MorPoè.*

Règle de l'octave First popularized in France by the theorbist François Campion (c.1685–1747) in his *Traité d'accompagnement* of 1716, the 'rule of the octave' was a useful expedient for continuo players, in prescribing one specific chord to play on each note of the rising and falling major and minor scales. Root position chords were assigned to scale degrees I and V, while the remaining degrees took sixth chords of various kinds. By memorizing the chord associated with each scale degree, the player could harmonize any diatonic scale progression. In theory, the pattern had to be learned for each of the twenty-four major and minor keys, though in practice most players would have limited themselves to those with up to four sharps or flats. During a heated polemic in the early 1730s with a 'second musician', possibly Montéclair*, Rameau argued that his concept of *basse fondamentale** provided a simpler alternative to the *règle*. *ChrTho, ChrRèg.*

Rehearsals   It was common practice in Rameau's day for spectators to attended rehearsals at the Académie Royale de Musique*. In 1739 Madame de Graffigny* reported seeing more than 150 people there at a rehearsal of *Dardanus* directed by Rameau himself. During the Lulliste-Ramiste dispute*, the *nouvelles à la main** recorded rival opinions on Rameau's operas, bandied about by those who had already seen them in rehearsal. In the 1740s attempts were made to exclude the public from these events, not altogether successfully. Dress rehearsals took place in the Palais-Royal* or the court theatres, while preliminary rehearsals were held in the Magasin* de l'Opéra or at the homes of various individuals, among them the prince de Carignan*, Marie Fel* and the marquise de Villeroy*. According to the Académie's statutes, rehearsals were to take place within a two-week period, beginning at the point when the popularity of the current work in the schedule showed signs of declining. The statutes stress the need for punctual attendance, with a fine of 6 *livres* for the first infringement, a month's salary for the second, and dismissal for the third. Rameau, who throughout his operatic career lived within walking distance of the Palais-Royal, was assiduous in attending rehearsals; moreover, numerous documents provide details of his temporary accommodation at Versailles or Fontainebleau during the rehearsal period for court productions. Even without this evidence, the many autograph annotations on the production* scores reveal that, even in his final years, he remained vigilant over matters of accuracy. Maret* tells how the composer would sit alone in the auditorium, where he 'picked out the merest dissonance that was foreign to the work, and pointed directly to whichever of the musicians was responsible for it'. *DacDar, DaiCor, GreSou, MarÉlo, SadPat.*

Rejected portraits   While the task of authenticating eighteenth-century portraits can be notoriously difficult, it is often easier to discredit existing attributions or identifications. At one time or another, visual images by Jean Charles Delafosse*, Quentin de La Tour*, Jean Bernard Restout*, Jean-Baptiste Van Loo* and François Voyez* have been said to represent Rameau's likeness, but such claims are nowadays impossible to maintain. Despite their spuriosity, these images continue to appear on websites and in CD liner notes. *GétPor.*

'Remarques [...] sur les differens genres de musique'   *See **Nouvelles suites de pièces de clavecin**.*

Reprise   Any section of a French composition that was intended to be repeated was known as a *reprise*. The term is frequently encountered at the start of the second section of a binary-form piece, as a visual guide to where the repeat begins. It is used in a different sense in rondeau movements, to indicate the intervening *couplets**, these being labelled where necessary 1re / 2de / 3me *reprise*, or similar. (An example is shown in 'La Follette'*.) The technical demands of several of the *reprises* (i.e., *couplets*) in Rameau's rondeaux are such that the composer felt the need to assure performers that any which proved too difficult could be omitted (*Pièces de clavessin*, preface). The final bars of a binary piece are sometimes marked *petite reprise*, to indicate that these bars are repeated after the *reprise* of the second section. Occasionally, as in 'La Boucon'* from the *Pièces de clavecin en concerts*, Rameau writes out the *petite reprise* in full, since it is not a literal repeat of the final bars. Many production* scores of operas bear handwritten annotations such as '1 commencement, 2 fins'; these clarify the number of repeats of each section, presumably in the light of decisions agreed between the composer, choreographer and *batteur de mesure*.

Requiem   Rameau himself never composed a Requiem Mass. At memorial* services after his death, an adaptation of the *Messe des morts* by Gilles* was used, in which extracts from *Castor et Pollux* were adapted to the text of the Kyrie and Gradual. Two other *contrafacta** of his music to the Requiem text have survived, both preserved in the Bibliothèque Nationale de France. The earlier of the two, which has only recently come to light, borrows passages from this same opera, these being interspersed with music by an unidentified composer. The extracts are well chosen: the opening 'Requiem aeternam', for instance, is based on the chorus 'Que tout gémisse' and on Télaïre's monologue 'Tristes apprêts', both originally sung around the tomb of Castor, while the 'Lux aeterna' includes the *ritournelle* of Castor's soliloquy 'Séjour de l'éternelle paix', set in the Elysian Fields, and continues with an adaptation of 'Voici des dieux l'asile aimable' written for one of the 'Plaisirs célestes'. Music from the scene at the entrance to Hades is reused in the 'Libera me'. Watermark evidence and the fact that all the borrowed music derives from the 1754 version of *Castor* suggest that this *contra-factum* was made in the later 1750s, possibly for performance in the Toulouse region. Another anonymous *contrafactum*, entitled 'Requiem de Rameau' and dating from the early nineteenth century, comprises a single movement in which the text of 'Requiem aeternam' is set to the music of 'Du Destin le vouloir suprême', the first Trio des Parques* in *Hippolyte et Aricie*. BouHer.

Restout, Jean Bernard   Son of the more famous Jean II Restout (1692–1768), noted for his historical and religious paintings, Jean Bernard Restout (1732–97) won the Prix de Rome in 1758 and later became an Academician. He designed a portrait of Rameau, now apparently lost, which formed the basis of an etching by one of the Benoist family of engravers; this appeared in the 1771 edition of Gautier-Dagoty's* *Galerie françoise des hommes et des femmes célèbres*. Rameau is portrayed in half-profile within an oval medallion. This and the supporting cartouche were evidently copied from the engraving of Rameau by Augustin de Saint-Aubin*, while the likeness itself appears to have been inspired by the bust by Caffieri*. Among rejected* portraits of Rameau is one formerly attributed to Restout in the Musée des Beaux-Arts, Dijon. This is now believed to be an anonymous portrait of Ponce Denis Écouchard Lebrun-Pindare (1729–1807). GétPor.

'Réveillez-vous, dormeur sans fin'   First published in the *Traité de l'harmonie* in 1722, this short five-part canon at the unison illustrates Rameau's discussion of how to write a simple perpetual canon. The piece appears in two guises:

the first with the text set syllabically in minims and crotchets; the second with added 'inessential' notes designed to make the melody more elegant. In the latter version the word 'relindindin' is set to rapidly repeated semiquavers, representing the alarm clock that wakes up the sleeper mentioned in the title. *BouCan, BouHer, GosTre, MonBou, RamCtw.*

Richelieu, Louis Ferdinand Armand du Plessis, duc de   As Louis XV's *premier gentilhomme de la chambre* from 1744, the duc de Richelieu (1696–1788) had control of the Menus-Plaisirs* during the period when Rameau was most active as a composer for the court (1745–54). Numerous references in Voltaire's correspondence throw light on the duke's part in the Versailles productions of *La Princesse de Navarre** and *Le Temple de la Gloire**. Richelieu's affair with Thérèse Deshayes*, which came to light when a secret doorway was discovered connecting his property to Thérèse's bedroom, caused the collapse of her marriage to La Pouplinière*, an event that marked the beginning of the end of Rameau's relationship with his patron. *See also* **Duport**; *Les Fêtes de Ramire*. *BarPla, BesVol, CucPou, DubTem, GirRam, LemMen.*

Ritournelle   Contrary to the most common meaning of the Italian 'ritornello' from which it is derived, the French term *ritournelle* seldom indicated a 'return' of earlier material during the course of a larger movement. From the time of Lully* onwards, the *ritournelle* was more often a prelude than a recurrent section. As such, it was used to preface individual entrées* of *opéras-ballets** or acts of *tragédies*, as in the 1754 *Castor et Pollux* (Acts I and V). Such extended movements often play a psychological role in conveying the state of mind of the characters who are about to enter. In the entrée 'L'Enlèvement d'Adonis' from *Les Surprises de l'Amour*, the framing ritornellos in the chorus 'Chantons l'Amour' (scene 10) are nevertheless labelled *ritournelle* in acknowledgement of Italian practice. *AntFre, MasOpé, RouDic.*

La Robe de Dissension, ou Le faux prodige   This two-act *opéra comique**, premiered at the Foire Saint-Laurent on 7 September 1726, was Rameau's final collaboration with Alexis Piron* at the Théâtre de la Foire*. The composer contributed two divertissements*, one at the end of each act, which between them comprised a considerable amount of music, now lost. Among the vocal items was the air 'Dans la flamme et les airs', introduced by Arlequin as 'quelque petite maxime d'Opéra', while the ballet music included a 'Danse d'Esprits élémentaires' and an 'Entrée des quatre nations différentes' – possibly the prototypes of similarly named dances in *Zaïs* and *Les Indes galantes*. *ConPir, PirŒu, ProPir, SadPir.*

Romainville, Mlle Rotisset de   Having established herself as a singer at Louis XV's court from 1738, Mlle Romainville (d.1752) entered the Académie Royale de Musique* in 1743, where her good looks and pretty voice proved popular. She created three roles in *Zaïs* and the female lead in *Acante et Céphise*. In or about 1752 she retired, having caused a scandal by accepting large sums of money, jewellery and a sumptuous mansion from a certain M^r. de Maisonrouge, whom she then married two months after his wife's death. *BouHer, PieCon, PouJél.*

Rondeau   *See* **Couplet; Reprise; Suite.**

Rondement   Of the eighteen separate movements in the *Pièces de clavecin en concerts* (1741) no fewer than seven are marked 'rondement', a direction that is otherwise rare in Rameau's music. At that time the word meant 'smoothly', 'equally' or (in a figurative sense) 'without artifice'. Its use in a musical context would thus seem to have more to do with character than with tempo. Admittedly, one modern sense of the word is 'to conduct business briskly and efficiently', but there is no evidence that it had yet acquired this meaning in Rameau's day. *DicAut, SawDou.*

Roulements In his essay 'De la méchanique des doigts sur le clavessin' in the *Pièces de clavessin* of 1724, Rameau uses the term *roulements* to describe rapid scales on the keyboard. These could be performed by 'passing the thumb under whatever fingers you wish or to pass one of the other fingers over the thumb'. Alternatively, the scales could be shared between the hands, as in 'Les Tourbillons'* in this same volume. Rameau stresses that such hand-divisions should be as smoothly executed 'as if they had been played by the fingers of the same hand.' *HolBac, SadSca, WilAnx.*

Rousseau, Jean-Baptiste In a musical context, Jean-Baptiste Rousseau (1671–1741) is mainly remembered as the poet who, in the first decades of the eighteenth century, established the *cantate françoise** as a genre. Despite considerable respect in literary circles, he gained notoriety as the author of libellous and sometimes obscene verses, often issued anonymously; this led to his prosecution for defamation of character in 1712, as a result of which he was sentenced to permanent exile. On 17 November 1739 he aimed a satirical* poem at Rameau, 'Distillateur d'accords baroques', that has become one of the best-known products of the Lulliste-Ramiste* dispute: 'You who distil the bizarre harmonies | With which so many idiots are smitten, | Take your coarse operas | Among the Thracians and Iroquois. | Despite your heterogeneous art, | Lully remains the sole support | Of the lyric stage. | Flee! Grant him his due, | And flay no longer the ears of honest folk'. The question nevertheless arises about how much of Rameau's music the poet knew. Once in exile, the only time he spent in Paris was a clandestine few months in the winter of 1738–39, a period when no Rameau opera was staged. The poem, written in Brussels, is mainly an attack on *Dardanus*, which he had not seen but whose 'fate' he had learned (presumably from those who had attended the rehearsals*, since the premiere did not take place until the following month). The reference to 'Iroquois' must, however, be a dig at the 'sauvages' in *Les Indes galantes*, which he likewise never saw. *See also* **Baroque; Mattheson, Johann.** *BloNat, DacDar, DorCan, GirRam, MasLul, TunCan.*

Rousseau, Jean-Jacques Much has been written about the turbulent relationship between Rameau and Rousseau (1712–78), two of the towering figures of their age. When Rousseau arrived in Paris in 1741, he was a huge admirer of Rameau the composer and theorist. This attitude was to change abruptly after an encounter in La Pouplinière's* salon in 1745, when an excerpt from Rousseau's *opéra-ballet** *Les Muses galantes* was tried out. In his *Confessions* the composer was later to admit that he had been helped by Philidor* with some of 'the accompaniments and connecting parts' of this work. Rameau soon realized that the music was not all the work of one man: according to Rousseau, he declared that 'part of what he had heard was by a great master of the art and the rest by an ignoramus who did not understand music'. This public humiliation, which according to one set of *nouvelles à la main* caused Rousseau to 'cry like a child', sowed the seeds of his undying hatred of Rameau. Even so, in his music articles for the *Encyclopédie*, Rousseau showed respect towards Rameau's theoretical writings, at least in the early volumes; any hint of criticism was toned down by the editors, Diderot* or d'Alembert*, who were both staunch Rameau supporters at that time. But in his *Lettre à M. Grimm, au sujet des Remarques ajoutées à sa Lettre sur Omphale* (1752), Rousseau could not resist including snide and supercilious remarks about Rameau's writings. This, and Rousseau's subsequent *Lettre sur la musique française* (1753), eventually provoked a response from Rameau in his *Erreurs sur la musique dans l'Encyclopédie**, the first of several increasingly vituperative pamphlets that caused the final rift between the composer and the editors of the *Encyclopédie*. In view of Rameau's maladroit handling of these disputes, most accounts of his relationship with Rousseau have been more sympathetic to the latter. Rameau's position, however, was based on his assessment of Rousseau as being 'devoid of ear, feeling and experience'; and, indeed, Rousseau was an untutored musician who found score reading difficult, believed that the inner parts contributed little if anything of value to a piece, and evidently had problems in following two simultaneous contrapuntal lines. For a consummate practical musician like Rameau, such weaknesses invalidated the younger man both as composer and critic. *See also* **Les Fêtes de Ramire.** *CanPhi, ChaPol, ChaRou, ChrTho, ChoPré, CucPou, DidLum, DucVal, JacVol, KafEnc, KinPoé, KinRam, LeiRou, RidVol, RouCon, SawVol, VerMus, WokEss.*

Roy, Pierre-Charles   Regarded as one of the most talented librettists of his generation, Roy (1683–1764) collaborated with all the major French opera composers of the day except Rameau. The poet had developed a deep-seated aversion to this composer, and during the Lulliste-Ramiste* dispute he became the ringleader of the Lulliste faction. Among his attacks on Rameau was a scurrilous poem, *Marsias allegorie**, in which he ridicules Rameau's appearance and his 'discordant' music. The widespread circulation of this poem led to a public brawl between the two men in 1737, after which Rameau was advised by his friends not to carry a sword. More generally, regrets were expressed that the two men never collaborated, since Roy could surely have provided Rameau with better librettos than many of those he set. 'Ah! Monsieur Roy,' wrote d'Aquin de Château-Lyon, 'instead of wasting your time criticizing Rameau, why did you never work with him? Your work would live for ever'. *AquSiè, BloNat, DilIma, GirTra, MasLul, SadPat.*

Royal Society, The   Rameau's first attempt to gain recognition for his theoretical work began in or soon after 1726, when he sent a copy of the *Nouveau système de musique théorique* to the Royal Society in London; the aim was to draw his discoveries to the attention of what was then the foremost scientific institution in Europe and to gain its official approbation for his latest publication. While Rameau's letter does not survive, the society's archives include a review by the mathematician Brook Taylor (1685–1731) that was read at a meeting on 18 January 1728. Taylor, who had also perused the *Traité de l'harmonie*, describes Rameau's system as 'reasonable and natural' and praises the author for reducing 'the confused variety of intricate and difficult rules in this art to so few and so simple principles'. There is, however, no record of further action by the Royal Society other than a note dated 20 January 1728 that Rameau was to be thanked for sending his 'Tract'. Undeterred, Rameau wrote on 12 August 1737 to the society's president, Sir Hans Sloane (1660–1753), enclosing a copy of *Génération harmonique* and summarizing its content. The letter was read at a meeting on 3 November; but although James Hamilton, Earl of Abercorne (1686–1744), was asked to review the treatise, he evidently failed to do so. On 26 February 1750, still undaunted, Rameau sent the society his recent *Démonstration du principe de l'harmonie*, again with a brief summary of its content, together with another copy of *Génération harmonique*. Although his letter was read to the society on 10 May, and Johann Christoph Pepusch (1667–1752) was asked to examine the two treatises, no review was forthcoming. On 19 November 1750, having heard nothing from the society for nine months, Rameau sent a twelve-page letter explaining his theories. (This, as Leta Miller points out, anticipates certain aesthetic concepts included two years later in his *Nouvelles réflexions de Mr Rameau sur sa 'Démonstration du principe de l'harmonie'*.) A translation and review were once again commissioned, but neither survives. While this whole episode does little for the reputation of the Royal Society, it illustrates Rameau's extraordinary persistence in seeking out international recognition for his writings. *See also* **Maupertuis, Pierre-Louis Moreau de**. *ChrTho, CohAca, MilLet, RamCtw.*

Royer, Joseph-Nicolas-Pancrace   A native of Turin, Royer (c.1705–55) settled in Paris in 1725 and won a reputation as a talented composer of opera and keyboard music. He held the post of *maître de musique* at the Académie Royale de Musique* from 1730 until 1733, a period that witnessed the premieres of his own first opera, *Pyrrhus*, and Rameau's first, *Hippolyte et Aricie*. From 1748 until his death Royer was director of the Concert Spirituel*, where he raised the performing standards and introduced new or unfamiliar works, including Rameau's *In convertendo**. In 1753 he was appointed *inspecteur général* at the Académie. Two harpsichord pieces, 'La Sensible' and 'La Zaïde', which survive in unattributed manuscript copies, were published in the Rameau *Œuvres complètes** but have since been shown to come from Royer's *Pièces de clavecin, premier livre,* of 1746. Barbier reports a violent quarrel between Royer and Rameau in October 1742, during which Royer's companion Pierre Simard, a former director of the Concert Spirituel, had to be restrained from giving Rameau 'twenty kicks in the stomach'. *See also* **Pandore**. *BarChr, GirTra, HamMem, JacVol, LauDoc, MacMus, PieCon, ProPri, RidVol.*

Saint-Aubin, Augustin de   A member of a respected family of artists, Augustin de Saint-Aubin (1736–1807) gained a reputation as an engraver and book illustrator. In 1762 he issued a fine etching entitled 'J. Ph. Rameau', copied directly from the Caffieri* bust of 1760. The composer is depicted in profile within a circular medallion supported by a cartouche. Beneath the medallion are two olive branches, a visual pun (*rameau*: 'branch'). This engraving was widely imitated, though with decreasing fidelity, as in an anonymous oil painting that belonged to the Galleria Filarmonica of padre Martini* and is now in the Museo Internazionale e Biblioteca della Musica, Bologna. A watercolour by Saint-Aubin's older brother Gabriel-Jacques (1724–80) provides much the best visual representation of the interior of the Palais-Royal* theatre in Rameau's day. A *Livre de caricatures** by Charles-Germain de Saint-Aubin (1721–86), the eldest of the three brothers, includes irreverent depictions of Rameau (see illustration on p. 120). *See also* **Goethe, Johann Wolfgang von**. *GétPor, GétSat, ZasOpe.*

Sainte-Croix de la Bretonnerie Some time after his failure to gain a post at the church of Saint-Paul* in 1727, Rameau was appointed organist at Sainte-Croix de la Bretonnerie, the monastery of the brothers of the Holy Cross, situated on the road that bears its name in the Marais quarter in Paris. The first evidence of Rameau's appointment is found in the 1732 volume of Valhebert's *Agenda du voyageur*, where we learn that 'music-lovers go there to hear the organ played by an excellent master to whom the public is grateful for a learned *Traité de l'harmonie* and a *Nouveau systême de musique* [...] M.ʳ Rameau'. He held this post until at least 1738. (Was it a coincidence that the abbé de Gamaches*, a canon at Sainte-Croix, was appointed by the Académie Royale de Sciences* to appraise the manuscript of Rameau's *Génération harmonique* in 1737?) All that survives of the monastery, largely destroyed during the Revolution, is a section of cloister linking the rue Sainte-Croix de la Bretonnerie and the rue des Archives. *BouRam, BreJeu, ChrTho, GirRam, RamCtw, ValVoy.*

Sainte-Marie-Madeleine-en-la-Cité Soon after his arrival in Paris in 1705 or 1706, Rameau secured concurrent organist posts at the Collège Louis-le-Grand* and the monastery of the Pères de la Mercy*. He evidently regarded these as provisional, however, since on 12 September 1706 he was short-listed for the post at Sainte-Marie-Madeleine-en-la-Cité, a church on the Île de la Cité not far from Notre-Dame; this had become vacant on the departure of François Dagincourt (1684–1758) for Rouen cathedral. Because of the large number of applicants, a competition was held on 1 November between Rameau and five other players: a blind organist named Gilliers (Dagincourt's deputy); Manceau, organist of Notre-Dame de Bonne Nouvelle; Morel, organist at the convent of the Saint-Sacrament; Corneil, assistant organist at Notre-Dame; and Louis Antoine Dornel (c.1685–1775), who had no current appointment. Among the jury were Nicolas Gigault (c.1627–1707), organist of Saint-Nicolas-des-Champs; Claude Rachel de Montalan (1646–1738), organist of Saint-André des Arts; and Jean-François Dandrieu (c.1681–1738), organist of Saint-Merry. After a contest lasting more than two hours, the post was awarded to Rameau. Yet despite the fact that the conditions of employment, published in advance, stipulated that the successful candidate should hold no other concurrent organist position, Rameau refused to relinquish his existing posts, so the appointment was offered instead to a grateful Dornel. *BreJeu, GérEgl, GirRam, KocSer, QuiJeu.*

Saint-Eustache During his final decade, Rameau lived on the rue des Bons-Enfants in the parish of Saint-Eustache, close to the Palais-Royal* theatre. It was in this church that he was buried, one day after his death on 12 September 1764, in the presence of his son Claude-François Rameau* and a certain Edme Charles le François de Villeneuve. No other member of the family is recorded as being present. Today, the composer is commemorated, along with Franz Liszt (an unlikely pairing), in one of the side-chapels, which houses a copy of the Caffieri* bust and a plaque erected in 1883 by the Société des Compositeurs de Musique. The claim made in 1912 that Rameau played the Saint-Eustache organ at a grand society wedding in 1733 has been shown to be a forgery. *BouHer, GirRam, LauDoc, SadPat.*

Saint-Paul   By the time Rameau settled permanently in Paris in 1722, he had already served as organist at Clermont* Cathedral for a total of about eleven years. It would nevertheless be the best part of a decade before he secured an organist post in Paris. His first-known attempt to do so was unsuccessful. On 28 April 1727, a competition was held at the church of Saint-Paul in the Marais district to find a replacement for the recently deceased Jean-Baptiste Buterne (1650–1727), an organist at the royal chapel. The other candidates were Edme Vaudry, one of Louis Marchand's* successors at Saint-Benoît; 'Coprin', i.e., Nicolas Couperin (1680–1748), cousin of François Couperin* and his eventual successor at Saint-Gervais; and the organist and composer Louis-Claude Daquin* (1694–1772). Among the jury members were Lully's* one-time secretary, Jean-François Lallouette (1651–1728), *maître de musique* at Notre-Dame, and Edme Foliot (d. after 1752), master of the choristers at Saint-Paul. Some of Rameau's early biographers mistakenly claimed that Marchand, his former mentor, was also on the panel. The post was awarded to Daquin, for whom Rameau nevertheless maintained a high regard. Decroix's* suggestion that the disappointed Rameau moved to a church post in Lille* is unlikely but not impossible. *BreJeu, GirRam, QuiJeu.*

Saint-Saëns, Camille   The gradual rehabilitation of Rameau in the nineteenth century received a boost in 1894, when Saint-Saëns (1835–1921) established the editorial board of a projected Rameau *Œuvres complètes**. In addition to acting as general editor, Saint-Saëns prepared the first five volumes, comprising the keyboard music, cantatas and motets. As a lifelong admirer of Rameau, Saint-Saëns took an active part in performing his music, regarding him as the greatest musical genius France had ever produced. *See also* **Editions; *Samson.*** *EllEar, EllSai, FosRam, JacVol, SadSaë.*

Saisir   Surviving part-books used by mid-eighteenth-century singers at the Académie Royale de Musique* include annotations relating to performance, most of them added by the Académie's *maître de musique** or other officials. Among these is the term *saisir* (literally, 'to seize'), which normally occurs after a breath mark or pause and often at a change of sentiment. Dictionaries of the period reveal that this word could be used figuratively in the sense of 'to discern, or to grasp an idea' and that 'to be seized' is to be affected by an emotion such as displeasure or sorrow. From the contexts in which it is used in the part-books, *saisir* would thus seem to indicate a sudden inspiration, probably accompanied by some physical gesture. *BarAct, CyrEss, CyrSin, DicAut, McGSpa, SawPig, SawNou.*

Sallé, Marie   Daughter of a fairground acrobat and niece of the renowned Harlequin known as Francisque (c.1695–1760), Marie Sallé (1707–56) first appeared as a child dancer at the Théâtre de la Foire*. At the age of nine she danced with her brother Francis at Lincoln's Inn Fields Theatre, the first of many performances in London theatres during the next three decades. In 1721 she took part in Campra's* *Les Fêtes vénitiennes* at the Académie Royale de Musique*, as understudy to her teacher Françoise Prévost. Mlle Sallé made her formal debut at the Académie in 1727. Her graceful and poetic dancing soon provoked a lively dispute between her growing band of supporters and those of Mlle Camargo*, these two dancers being unrivalled exponents respectively of the *danse basse** and *danse haute**. Although she exploited a traditional style of ballet, Sallé was an innovator: in 1729 she and Antoine Laval* performed Jean-Féry Rebel's* *Les Caractères de la danse* in modern dress and without the hitherto obligatory masks. On an extended visit to London in 1733–34 she choreographed and danced a *pantomime** entitled *Pigmalion*, in which she appeared as the Statue in a simple muslin costume, without corset, panier or underskirt. Her incomparably expressive dance-style and skills in mime inspired the first role Rameau that created for her – an elaborate nine-movement 'ballet des fleurs' (a *ballet figuré** in all but name). Here, as La Rose, she is assaulted by Borée, god of the North Wind, but resists him and is later revived by Zéphire. Her later involvement in Rameau operas includes the star roles of Hébé (*Castor et Pollux*) and Terpsichore (*Les Fêtes d'Hébé*). She retired from the Académie in 1740, although until 1752 she occasionally took part in court productions. *BeaDan, BouHer, CahDan, ChaHib, ChrInt, FaiSty, HarBal, McCEng, McCSal, NovLet, SadDan, TesCor.*

Salvum me fac Deus   There is good reason to believe that Rameau composed a *motet** *à grand chœur* on the text of Psalm 68, *Salvum me fac Deus*. An isolated setting of verse 4 of this psalm survives as the solo quintet *Laboravi**, which the composer included in his *Traité de l'harmonie* (1722) as an example of fugal procedures. Moreover, his motet *In convertendo* includes a further verse from the same psalm, 'Laudate nomen Dei', in what is otherwise a setting of Psalm 125. *In convertendo* currently survives only in a heavily revised version of 1751 or 1752, and it is possible that Rameau decided at that stage to incorporate a movement from his earlier Psalm 68. *BouHer, DurMot, DurRam, GreSou.*

Samson   After the premiere of *Hippolyte et Aricie* in October 1733, Voltaire* initially expressed distaste for Rameau's music, whereas six weeks later he described himself as 'infatuated' with it. During the Lulliste-Ramiste* dispute, the writer championed Rameau's cause, and the two men soon agreed to collaborate on *Samson*, a five-act *tragédie en musique**. The libretto had been drafted by December 1733, and by the following summer Rameau had composed the overture, chaconne and other dances, as well as the third and fifth acts, these being described as 'admirable' when they were rehearsed in October 1734. But meanwhile the French *parlement* had proscribed Voltaire's *Lettres philosophiques sur les anglois,* and the writer fled to his country estate at Cirey to avoid imprisonment. He nevertheless frequently returned to the *Samson* project; during the next two years, he did his best to persuade Rameau to complete it. By now, however, it was clear that the censors were unlikely to accept a libretto based on Holy Writ, given that its central theme was the struggle against tyranny and religious intolerance and that its author had already been imprisoned for his anti-clerical views. The project was thus abandoned, and Voltaire contented himself with publishing the libretto in 1745. (This was known to Saint-Saëns* and inspired the first sketch for the libretto to his *Samson et Dalila*.) Rameau is said to have recycled his *Samson* music in later operas, among them *Les Indes galantes, Castor et Pollux, Les Fêtes d'Hébé, Le Temple de la Gloire* and *Zoroastre*. Indeed, many of these works include passages whose wording is tantalizingly close to that of *Samson*, although the music, if borrowed, must have been considerably reworked before reaching its existing form. Music from *Samson* almost certainly survives as the air 'Echo, voix errante', the text of which is quoted by Voltaire himself in *La Princesse de Navarre* (II, 11), and again by

Cahusac* in the 1753 version of *Les Fêtes de Polymnie*. *BesVol, BouRam, GirVol, JacVol, RidVol, SadBor, SadHip, SadPat, SgaSam.*

Satirical engravings   One of the weapons aimed at Rameau during the Lulliste-Ramiste* dispute took the form of satirical engravings. At least five are known to have circulated, most of them issued in 1739. They excited much interest, and the significance of the 'allegory' was analysed in *nouvelles à la main** and elsewhere. Two engravings targeted the *sommeil** in *Dardanus*, likening it to the nursery rhyme 'Do do, l'enfant do'*. In another, Rameau sits beneath a Damoclean sword writing algebraic equations (an allusion to his music theory). Hanging from his desk is a quotation from *Dardanus*, while on the floor is a book of 'old harpsichord pieces for making new operas' ('Vieilles Pieces de Clavecin pour faire des opera nouveaux'). He is threatened by a devil from whose rear end falls a hail of coins; meanwhile the composer's supporters, the Ramoneurs* (chimney sweeps), are seen emerging from the fireplace. An equally salacious engraving satirizes *Les Fêtes d'Hébé*, produced earlier that year. Rameau sits playing a portative organ astride his indecently attired librettist Montdorge*, who is being pumped up from behind with bellows by the abbé Pellegrin*. This print has been shown to be an adaptation of an English engraving of c.1735 (itself based on a seventeenth-century French original) which satirizes the composer Nicola Porpora and the Opera of the Nobility; thus unlike in genuine caricatures* of Rameau, any physical resemblance to the composer is coincidental. One further engraving whose satirical intent has only recently been recognized is entitled *Triomphe de Rameau**. *See also* **Livre de caricatures**   *CerMcG, CyrHéb, DacDar, GétSat, LauDoc, MasLul, SadBor, SadPat.*

'Les Sauvages'   In September 1725 the *Mercure de France** reported an event at the Théâtre-Italien* in which two American Indians performed a sequence of three dances, evidently to their own music. Two years later, Rameau invited the librettist La Motte* to come and hear how he had 'characterized the song and dance of the savages' that he had witnessed there. This is the earliest reference to his harpsichord piece 'Les Sauvages', which was soon to appear in the *Nouvelles suites de pièces de clavecin* (1729 or 1730). In 1736, during the first run of the *opéra-ballet** *Les Indes galantes*, Rameau and Fuzelier* added a new entrée*, likewise entitled 'Les Sauvages'; this included an orchestral version of the harpsichord piece together with an elaborate *parodie**, 'Forêts paisibles', as part of the climactic Peace Pipe ceremony. In both its keyboard and orchestral forms the piece became enormously popular, as may be judged not only from the many surviving arrangements but also from the fact that the melody was perpetuated for nearly a century in works by other composers. When Rameau published a cut-down version of *Les Indes galantes* arranged as 'Quatre grands concerts'*, in which the *symphonies** are arranged for harpsichord, he included the new entrée 'Les Sauvages' at the end of the publication. His preface nevertheless makes clear that the only movements expressly arranged for harpsichord were those in the 'Quatre grands concerts'. *BloNat, BroSau, SadBor, SadInd, SavAme.*

Scarlatti, Domenico   In 1996 it was revealed that Domenico Scarlatti (1685–1757) visited Paris in May 1724 and again during the summer of 1725 while in the service of King João V of Portugal. Little is known of the Italian composer's activities in Paris, but he was evidently in contact with the financier Pierre Crozat (1660–1740) and may thus have participated in the concerts of Italian music organized by Crozat and Madame de Prie. Commentators have often remarked on certain shared elements in the keyboard music of Scarlatti and Rameau, especially in the realm of playing technique. The 'new' biographical information therefore raises the possibility of direct contact between the two composers. Scarlatti's G major sonata K547 repeatedly quotes the main theme of Rameau's 'Les Cyclopes' (*Pièces de clavessin*, 1724), while this same sonata and others employ virtuosic figuration in which the left hand rotates over the thumb, one of the *batteries** that feature prominently in 'Les Cyclopes'. There is no evidence that Scarlatti had yet developed the kind of hand-crossing where one hand passes back and forth over the other, a technique that Rameau justifiably claimed in 1724 to have been the first to demonstrate in print. At the same time, several pieces in Rameau's *Nouvelles suites de pièces de clavecin*, published only a few years after Scarlatti's second visit, feature characteristics that seem already to have become part of Scarlatti's style by the mid-1720s, among them repeated-chord accompaniments, energetic left-hand octave passages and rapid note repetition. Moreover, 'Les Trois Mains' in the *Nouvelles suites* contains elements of the fandango* and, it has been claimed, glissando*, which may possibly have featured in Scarlatti's music by that date. *See also* **'L'Entretien des Muses'**. *GirRam, SadSca.*

Scènes d'action From the outset, French opera took over three specific conventions from spoken theatre: (1) that a 'scene' began and ended at the point where one or more characters entered or left the stage; (2) that scenes should be elided, in that at least one character would have been present in the previous scene, so that the stage was never empty within a given act; and (3) that no extraneous characters should be present on stage other than the entourage ('suite') of a deity or monarch. French writers of the period often refer to the 'scènes' of an opera in a particular sense, as a shorthand for *scènes d'action* – i.e., those in which the dramatic dialogue took place and which consisted largely of recitative. Such *scènes* are distinct in their character and purpose from the divertissements*. Whereas the latter are enacted in a 'public' space, the former generally have a more 'private' character, even when the dialogue includes interjections from the chorus as onlookers. And whereas the divertissement is normally anchored within a single tonality, the recitative of the *scènes* modulates widely in response to fluctuations in the emotional temperature. Moreover the *scènes*, unlike the divertissements, were traditionally limited in terms of musical elaboration, so that nothing distracted from the dramatic interaction of the characters. Rameau inherited a tradition where the recitative, though punctuated by *petits* airs* and occasional vocal ensembles, was never interrupted by complex or virtuosic arias. This last distinction, however, became blurred as a result of progressive waves of Italian influence from the 1740s onwards and particularly in the wake of the Querelle des Bouffons*, when orchestrally accompanied *ariettes** began to appear within the *scènes*. By definition, the *air* de monologue* remained distinct from the *scènes d'action*. *AntFre, ChaRou, DilMod, GirTra, HarTou, MasOpé, NauDra, RosScè.*

School of Composition Once he had established himself as France's leading composer of keyboard music and opera, Rameau decided to create an École de Composition de Musique for music lovers ('amateurs'). Notices in the December 1737 issue of the *Mercure de France** and elsewhere announced that classes would be held three times a week, between 3 and 5 o'clock, for up to twelve people. Pupils* would be taught as a group, for a monthly fee of 1 *louis d'or* – worth 20 *livres* at that time and thus a substantial sum, though far less than the rate for his private teaching*. The notices assured readers that 'six months at most will be enough to gain an understanding of the theory and practice of harmony, [...] even for those who can scarcely read music'. Prospective students were asked to apply in writing to the Hôtel d'Effiat on the rue des Bons-Enfants, the composer's current residence, where the classes presumably took place. Rameau indicates that it was because of the eagerness of pupils already enrolled on the course that he was opening it to the public. His new school, being concerned with 'the theory and practice of harmony' rather than with vocal or instrumental tuition, appears to have been the first of its kind in France. How long it lasted is not known, though Rameau was still teaching composition in the 1750s. *See also* **'L'Art de la basse fondamentale'**. *ChrBas, ChrTho, GirRam, LauDoc, RamCtw.*

Self-borrowings   Rameau was not one of the most prolific self-borrowers of his generation: fewer than one hundred indisputable instances have so far been identified, though many others have been suggested. Among the latter are several pieces from the music to *L'Endriague** (now lost) and borrowings in opera production* scores which may have been made during his lifetime but which cannot be precisely dated. During the Lulliste-Ramiste* dispute in the 1730s, Rameau resorted to self-borrowing as a means of increasing the popular appeal of his first operas. The reuse of pieces from his best-selling harpsichord collections proved effective; audiences were presented with familiar melodies whose impact was often enhanced when these were reworked into elaborate *parodies**, as was the case with 'Les Sauvages', 'Les Niais de Sologne' and the 1724 Musette en rondeau. The reverse process is seen in the *Pièces de clavecin en concerts* (1741), which recycles movements from two operas, *Castor et Pollux* and *Dardanus*. Even so, Rameau was criticized by his detractors for pillaging his own music, and his reuse of harpsichord pieces was lampooned in two indecent satirical* engravings. As a consequence, perhaps, most of his later self-borrowings are from works which had enjoyed limited public exposure. Rameau appropriated little thematic material from other composers, although borrowings have been identified from works by Charpentier*, Campra*, Handel*, Lalande*, Telemann* and Vivaldi*. *See also* **Cantate pour le Jour de la Saint-Louis**; **Sommeil**. *MasLul, SadBor, SadHan, SadPat, TalViv.*

'La Sensible'   *See* **Royer, Joseph-Nicolas-Pancrace**.

Servandoni, Jean-Nicolas Servan, *known as*   Born in Florence of French parents, Jean-Nicolas Servan (1695–1766) was trained as an artist in Italy, where he adopted the Italian form of his name. Arriving in Paris in 1724, he had begun work as a designer at the Académie Royale de Musique* by 1726 and was appointed *premier peintre* there two years later. His first design for a Rameau opera was a magnificent Persian garden for the entrée 'Les Fleurs' in *Les Indes galantes* (1735), described extensively in two issues of the *Mercure de France**. In 1737 Servandoni temporarily abandoned work at the Académie to launch a *spectacle d'optique*, where spectators watched various optical effects in a darkened auditorium in the Salle des Machines in the Tuileries; he resumed his post, however, from 1741 until 1744. Although few of Servandoni's designs survive, abundant descriptions in the press and elsewhere give a good idea of his work. He diversified the staging by adopting the technique of painting backdrops in oblique perspective, with an off-set vanishing point. To create a further illusion of space, he would place the flats at angles and allow only the lower parts of trees or columns to be visible from the auditorium. Some of Servandoni's lighting effects were said to be so powerful that the eye could not bear to look at them directly. *CamFoi, ChaRou, GorSce, GorSer, HeySer, HorGem, MasOpé, NauDra, WooSad.*

Les Sibarites The last of Rameau's four collaborations with the librettist Marmontel*, this work began life as an independent *acte de ballet**, initially entitled *Sibaris*. It was performed at Fontainebleau before Louis XV's court on 13 November 1753, in a double bill with *La Coquette trompée*, a comedy by Charles-Simon Favart (1710–92) with music by Rameau's pupil* Antoine Dauvergne. Rameau later included it as an entrée* in *Les Surprises de l'Amour* at the 1757 revival of that work. *BouHer, BouSu2, ButCho, EmmPyg, GirRam, MasOpé, RicFon.*

Simile air One symptom of Italian influence on French opera in the mid-eighteenth century was the gradual introduction of the simile air, in which the singer's situation is likened to some natural phenomenon or activity. Interestingly, this type of aria was adopted by the French just as it was beginning to die out in Italy. In Rameau's operas, simile airs are found mainly in settings of librettos by or attributed to Cahusac*, where they often occur during the *scènes d'action** rather than in the divertissements*. A characteristic example is Anacréon's air 'Comme une fleur, quand l'hiver cesse' (*Anacréon*, scene 2), where the image in the opening line is compared to the singer's renewed feelings of pleasure. *Les Boréades* includes as many as three simile airs, two of them sung by the protagonists. Alphise's 'Un horison serein' (I, 4) compares a deceptively calm day interrupted by storms to the deceitful ties of marriage, thus anticipating her own abduction by the winds in Act III for refusing to submit to an arranged marriage. A similar allusion to this central theme occurs in Abaris's 'Que l'Amour embellit la vie' (V, 5), where love is initially likened to a stream calmly snaking its way through the meadow but later to the ravages that follow the damming of the torrent. *BouBor, SadAba, WilAna.*

'Si tu ne prends garde à toi' *See* **Modulating canon.**

Six Concerts de Mr Rameau The Decroix* collection includes five part-books, variously entitled *Six* [or *VI*] *Concerts* [or *Concertos*], that constitute the sole source of these arrangements of Rameau harpsichord pieces. From the fact that the part-books are annotated 'Decroix 1768' it has been assumed that Decroix himself was the arranger, though this is unproven. In the *Œuvres complètes** the arrangements were published as 'Six concerts transcrits en sextuor'. It is nevertheless clear from the bass part-book, which is labelled 'basses et bassons', that the arrangements were intended for orchestra rather than chamber ensemble. Moreover, the scoring for three violins, viola and bass matches the layout of the orchestra of the Concert de Lille for which Decroix supplied much material. The first five *concerts** are based on the five suites of the *Pièces de clavecin en concerts*. The arranger's technique is disarmingly simple: notes on the harpsichord's upper staff are given to violin 1, while those on the lower one are distributed between viola and bass. Meanwhile Rameau's violin line and his alternative for second violin are allotted respectively to violins 2 and 3. In the sixth *concert*, which comprises five pieces from the *Nouvelles suites de pièces de clavecin*, the arranger sticks closely to the notes and textures of the keyboard originals. We can thus rule out Rameau as the arranger: whenever he adapted his harpsichord music for orchestral use he transformed the keyboard figuration into something more idiomatic to the new scoring. *DeeRam, GirRam, HerMor, MalCon.*

Slurred tremolo   One aspect of Rameau's notation which, to judge from recent productions and recordings, is still imperfectly understood by performers, may be seen in the example overleaf. At first sight, the slurring of pairs of quavers at the same pitch indicates a string *portato*, where successive notes are gently re-articulated in the same bow-stroke. According to theorists of the time, however, the intended effect in performance was that of an organ tremulant. This phenomenon is in fact a pressure vibrato, quite distinct from the more familiar left-hand vibrato, since the fluctuations are not of pitch but of volume. The technique, nowadays known as slurred tremolo but often referred to in Rameau's day as *balancement*, originated in Italy and gradually spread to other countries including Germany and England. In France it was first used to express the shaking of the Cold People (*trembleurs*) in Lully's* *Isis* (1677). Rameau, like his contemporaries and predecessors, employs it in the context of violent natural or supernatural phenomena – tempests, earthquakes and the like: in the example below, for instance, Phèdre feels the earth tremble and Hell open beneath her feet, while in Alphise's air 'Un orison serein' (*Les Boréades*, I, 3) the notation evokes a sudden tempest. French organs of the period often had two tremulant stops – the stronger, more rapid *tremblant fort* and the gentler *tremblant doux* – and it was presumably the effect of the former that was intended in these instances. But Rameau also notates slurred tremolo in situations which, while emotionally intense, are not at all violent, as in Theseus's two prayers to Neptune in *Hippolyte et Aricie* ('Puisque Pluton est inflexible', I, 4, and 'Puissant maître des flots', III, 7); here the effect of the *tremblant doux* seems appropriate. While Rameau normally notates slurred tremolo with slurs as shown below, he sometimes replaces the slurs with horizontal wavy lines. Both notations appear in the motet *Deus noster refugium** in the passage '*mota est terra*' ('the earth *shook*') – the wavy line above the vocal lines, the slurs in the continuo bass line. In *Les Paladins* (II, 6), Rameau adopts a different notation for the same effect; on the first and last syllables of the phrase '*Et* je fré-*mis*' ('I shudder') he writes eight repeated semiquavers grouped under a slur. This powerfully expressive device remained in use in France well into the nineteenth century and may already be found, for example, in Handel* (*Dixit Dominus*, HWV 232, evoking the flowing stream at the words 'De torrente in via bibet') and Bach (*Magnificat*, BWV 243, painting the word 'fear' at 'timentibus eum'). *See also* **Rebel, Jean-Féry; Superscript dot.** *CarTre, CyrSty, GreSou, McGSpa, MilOrc, NeuOrn, NeuPer.*

Rameau, *Hippolyte et Aricie*, IV, 4

Société Jean-Philippe Rameau Founded in 1991 by Sylvie Bouissou*, this society currently acts as publisher of the Rameau *Opera Omnia* (OOR*), the complete critical edition of the composer's musical works. The society took over this task in 2003 from the publishing firm of Gérard Billaudot Éditeur, which had issued the first five volumes, beginning in 1996. Worldwide distribution of the edition is currently undertaken by Bärenreiter.

Soleinne, Alexandre Martineau de An enthusiast for all aspects of the theatre, Soleinne (1784–1842) amassed a huge collection of manuscript plays and librettos, most of which survive in the Bibliothèque Nationale de France (Département de la Musique and Bibliothèque de l'Arsenal), Paris. The Soleinne exemplar of La Bruère's* libretto to *Linus**, set by Rameau in the early 1750s, was evidently copied from one in the Decroix* collection, since it bears a note thanking the owner for having lent it: 'Mr. D[e] Soleinne est venu pour faire ses adieux à M.ʳ Decroix et lui rapporter le manuscript de *Linus* qu'il avait eu la complaisance de lui prêter'. *BouHer, BruSol, GreSou, JacBib, SadLet.*

Soliloquy *See **Air de monologue**.*

Sommeil As a staple ingredient of opera, the sleep scene emerged in Venice in the 1640s and was eventually taken up by Lully* and his librettist Quinault*. The archetypal 'sommeil', as it was known in France, occurs in the third act of Lully's opera *Atys* (1676). Among its much-imitated features was a texture dominated by pairs of slurred crotchets in mainly stepwise movement. Over half a century later, Rameau was to adopt these features in his first opera, *Hippolyte et Aricie*, in a scene where the heroine lies asleep (V, 3). It also appears during the 'Entrée des songes' [Dreams] in *Dardanus* (IV, 2), which the composer's detractors mockingly likened to the cradle song 'Do do, l'enfant do'*, and in *Les Fêtes de Polymnie* (III, 3). In later sleep scenes Rameau abandoned the Lullian model. The entrée* 'Anacréon', added to *Les Surprises de l'Amour* in 1757, includes a *sommeil* that alludes unmistakably to the slow movement of Vivaldi's* *L'autunno*, RV 293, published in *Il cimento dell'armonia e dell'inventione* in 1725. In the example opposite, Rameau's *sommeil* is transposed down a fourth to make comparison easier. Over and above their melodic and harmonic resemblances (the latter more obvious in performance than on paper), these two movements share a similar context: Rameau's occurs at the point where the poet Anacreon falls into a drunken stupor; Vivaldi's is labelled *Ubriachi dormienti* – 'sleeping inebriates'. *AntFre, MasOpé, TalHab, VlaViv, WooOrc.*

(a) Vivaldi, *L'autunno* (RV293), second movement

(b) Rameau, 'Anacréon' scene 4, *sommeil*

Son coupé   *See* **Vertical stroke**.

Sonata form   Throughout his life Rameau kept abreast of developments not only in French music but increasingly in the latest European styles and techniques. One symptom of the latter is his occasional use of sonata form, which he adopted as early as 1741: 'La Pantomime' from the *Pièces de clavecin en concerts* has a miniature exposition with contrasted first and second subject-groups, a modulatory development section and a clearly defined recapitulation of both subject-groups. Thereafter, Rameau's essays in sonata form or its variants occur mainly in the fast sections of overtures. Those to *Les Fêtes de l'Hymen*, *Zaïs*, *Naïs*, *Les Paladins* and especially *Zoroastre* come close to text-book sonata form, though they lack the structural repeats of the exposition and development-plus-recapitulation. The *Vite* section of the *Zoroastre* overture, for example, is a through-composed movement of eighty-nine bars, with a first subject-group in D major (bb. 53–68 of the overture as a whole), a transition to the dominant (bb. 68–77), a distinctive second subject-group in A major (bb. 77–89), a modulatory section that develops material from both groups (bb. 89–115), and a truncated recapitulation in the tonic in which elements from the second subject-group are sandwiched between material from the first. (The overture to *La Princesse de Navarre*, whose final movement adopts an embryo sonata form, has been shown by Julien Dubruque to be the one Rousseau composed for *Les Fêtes de Ramire**.)   *ChaRou, GreSou, MasOpé, RicFon.*

Sound effects   The predilection of French opera composers for graphic representations of storms (*tempêtes*) and other violent natural or supernatural phenomena took root at the end of the seventeenth century. From the outset, realism was enhanced by sound effects. The score of the earliest *tempête*, in Collasse's *Thétis et Pélée* of 1689 (II, 7–9), specifies rolls on a side-drum (*tambour**) placed in the wings of the theatre: in order to imitate the noise of the wind and waves, the player is instructed to make the dynamic level higher or lower in response to the rise and fall of the violin line. According to Titon du Tillet, the *tempête* in Marais's *Alcyone* (1706, IV, 4) was accompanied by continuous rolls on slackened drums ('tambours peu tendus'), which produced a muffled and gloomy noise. Jean-Jacques Rousseau*, writing in 1761, states that the sound of thunder was produced by trundling a heavy cart ('une lourde charrette') around in the wings (*La Nouvelle Héloïse*, II, letter 23). Archival documents from Rameau's time reveal that explosive charges (*boîtes*) were sometimes used to represent lightning flashes. Similar devices were doubtless employed for the cannon* shots notated in the overture to *Acante et Céphise* (1751). This piece also includes a part for 'Tocsin', or warning bell, which is sounded in repeated quavers in the rhythm of the bass line. Further sound effects were produced by the use of unusual instruments such as the flageolet* or playing techniques such as pizzicato* and portamento*. If wind machines were ever used at the Académie Royale de Musique*, their use is not documented. *BouCri, MasOpé, SadOrc, SouFêt, WooOrc.*

'Les Soupirs' Cited with evident pride in Rameau's letter of 1727 to La Motte*, 'Les Soupirs' (*Pièces de clavessin*, 1724) is one of the composer's most Couperinesque pieces, in its tender, reflective mood and its obsessive reworking of a single right-hand figure in the *style luthé**. Several unexpectedly wide leaps in the second half of this binary movement illustrate Rameau's exploitation of an innovatory technique of finger-changing on the same note. The composer's son Claude-François Rameau* used this title for the second piece in his 'Premiere suitte'. *BouHer, GirRam, GusFul.*

***Spectacle coupé**   See **Fragments**.*

***Style luthé** The arpeggiated textures characteristic of Baroque music for plucked instruments are often described nowadays as being in the *style brisé* ('broken style'), a term coined only in the early twentieth century. In *L'Art de toucher le clavecin* (1717) François Couperin* refers to 'les choses luthées' (literally 'the luted things'), and while he never explained the meaning of this expression, many French and other writers have substituted *style luthé* for *style brisé*. The former term does at least have the virtue of more aptly characterizing the adoption by harpsichord composers of an idiom and technique originally developed by lutenists. Neither term implies any particular rhythmic freedom. *AntFre, BucSty.*

Subdominant   *See **Nouveau système de musique théorique**.*

Suite   Over a period of thirty-five years, Rameau's approach to the keyboard suite evolved considerably. His *Premier livre de pièces de clavecin* (1706) comprises a single suite of ten movements, much in the tradition of Louis Marchand*. Beginning with a partly unmeasured* prelude (one of the last of its kind printed in Rameau's day), it consists mainly of the standard dances and contains only one character* piece. In the *Pièces de clavessin* (1724) and *Nouvelles suites de pièces de clavecin* (1729 or 1730), this type of suite co-exists with a newer one: each book contains a pair of suites contrasted both in tonality and in character. The first of each pair is dominated by dances (not all of them the traditional ones) and includes only two or three character pieces; the second consists almost exclusively of pieces with character titles. In their make-up, if not in their style, these latter suites are closer to the *ordres* of François Couperin*, whose first three books of *pièces de clavecin* had now been published. Given that this newer type was to dominate French harpsichord publications, Rameau can be seen to be somewhat conservative in devoting half of each collection to the older type. The traditional dance movements of the third book, and particularly the monumental allemande and courante, are indeed among the finest and most highly developed in the French repertory. Rameau's final collection, the *Pièces de clavecin en concerts* (1741), is quite different in its internal organization: whereas the suites of the first three books each contain between seven and ten movements, the *concerts** of the fourth contain only three or five. Moreover, dance movements are almost entirely supplanted by character pieces; of the nineteen movements, all but the two menuets and tambourins have character titles. Not surprisingly, all four books consist almost exclusively of binary and rondeau forms (there are no chaconnes). But whereas the first and third books are composed mainly of binary movements, more than half the pieces in the second are rondeaux. In the *Pièces* [...] *en concerts*, binary movements outnumber rondeaux by two to one. *AntFre, BouHer, GirRam, GusFul.*

Superbissimum auris judicium   Central to Rameau's theoretical writings in his later years was the belief that the ultimate arbiter was not reason but experience. He believed that not only did the sense of hearing take priority over all the other senses, but that the authority of reason could be overturned if it was contradicted by the empirical evidence of the ear. It was in this context that, beginning with the *Nouvelles réflexions sur le principe sonore** (1752), Rameau made frequent use of the Latin tag *superbissimum auris judicium* ('the judgement of the ear is best'), an adaptation of the phrase *aures, quarum est iudicium superbissimum* ('the ears, whose judgement is best') from Cicero's *Orator*. *ChrTho, RamCtw.*

Supernatural   *See* **Le merveilleux**.

Superscript dot   One potentially misleading aspect of notation in the Lully-Rameau period is that the same symbol can mean different things in different contexts. A case in point is the superscript dot. That Rameau sometimes used this to denote a staccato is explicit in the example overleaf (effectively in compound time despite the signatures **2**, **3** and **C**). An accompanying autograph note explains that these dots indicate that the notes in question should be cut short ('Les points au dessus des notes font couper le son') – presumably to enhance the comic effect of Orcan's panic attack ('Je meurs de peur ...'). Dots of this kind never normally occur in Rameau's vocal music, hence the need in this instance to clarify their purpose. In the engraved score of *Zoroastre*, superscript dots do not all have the same meaning. Those above certain crotchets in the 'Entrée des Bergers et des Pastres' (V, 7) must clearly be interpreted in the same way as the quaver-plus-quaver-rest notation used for the same figure elsewhere in this movement. In the 'Entrée des Indiens' (II, 4), however, the dots are found only on the off-beat quavers of the two anacrusis figures that form the thematic material of this movement. While it is possible that this notation distinguishes between detached and sustained quavers, a more plausible explanation is that the dots warn the players not to apply the conventions of *notes inégales** – one long-established use of the superscript dot in France. (See the third example in the article **Cadence**.) A further interpretation of the superscript dot occurs in *Les Paladins*. In the 'Entrée des Paladins' (I, 5) the autograph score includes dots over several tied dotted crotchets in the bassoon part; as

Rameau explains, each dot indicates an exhalation of air without taking a breath ('le point au-dessus d'une note [...] marque un coup de vent sans reprendre haleine'), a similar effect to that of the slurred* tremolo. At a later stage he replaced the dots with vertical* strokes, probably to make them more visible in the manuscript. *GreSou, MasOpé, SaiInt, WolInt, WolPal.*

Les Paladins, I, 6

Supposition   In his *Traité de l'harmonie*, Rameau adopted this term to refer to the addition of an extraneous bass note a third or a fifth below different varieties of seventh chord, thereby creating chords of the ninth and eleventh. In so doing, he was able to explain the resolution of suspensions, since these could be related to the resolution of the parent seventh chord above the 'sub-posed' note. In subsequent treatises, Rameau's concept of *supposition* underwent considerable refinement as he reacted to, or even appropriated, the arguments of his critics. *ChrTho, JacCtw, LesRam, LesThe, MarVie, MonDis.*

Les Surprises de l'Amour   Although Louis XV's mistress Madame de Pompadour seems to have had an ambivalent attitude towards Rameau's music, she commissioned this *opéra-ballet** for performance in her Théâtre des Petits Cabinets* in November 1748, when she created the roles of Uranie and Venus. This was Rameau's second collaboration with Bernard*. In its original form the opera comprised two entrées*, 'La Lyre enchantée' and 'Adonis'; these were preceded by a prologue ('Le Retour d'Astrée') which, like that of *Naïs*, celebrated the Treaty of Aix-la-Chapelle. The work was eventually restaged at the Académie Royale de Musique* in 1757; the prologue, no longer topical, was omitted and a new overture substituted; moreover, the original two entrées were drastically revised (the second now renamed 'L'Enlèvement d'Adonis'), and Rameau and Bernard added a new entrée, 'Anacréon'*. A few weeks later 'La Lyre enchantée' was replaced by a revised version of *Les Sibarites*, an *acte de ballet** by Marmontel* and Rameau first given at Fontainebleau in 1753. 'Anacréon' proved the most successful, remaining in the Académie's repertory until 1771. Each entrée involves a central conflict – between aggression and peace ('Le Retour d'Astrée' and 'Les Sibarites'), love and indifference ('La Lyre enchantée'), love and chastity ('Adonis'), love and wine ('Anacréon'); and in each it is Amour (Cupid) or his attendants who bring reconciliation, often in a surprising way – hence the work's title. *BouHer, BouSu1, BouSu2, EmmPyg, GirRam, GorSet, KaePom, MasOpé.*

Suspension   The table of *agréments** in Rameau's *Pièces de clavesin* of 1724 includes a compound symbol for the *suspension* (see illustration on p. 20) which indicates that the given note is to be slightly delayed. François Couperin*, who considered this to be the ornament that gave the harpsichord its soul, used an identical symbol with a similar meaning. Nowadays this expressive resource is widely applied by harpsichordists, whether or not so marked. It is worth recalling, however, that Rameau indicates the *suspension* in remarkably few places, from which we might justifiably conclude that he wished this powerful effect to be used elsewhere only selectively and with discretion. *HerMor, NeuOrn, RpeKey, Sailnt.*

Symphonie Before the mid-eighteenth century, when the symphony in its modern sense began to establish itself in France, the term *symphonie* was used in a variety of related contexts. It could denote an autonomous instrumental piece or sequence of pieces, as in *suites de symphonies, concerts de symphonies, symphonies en trio*; or the players (also known as *symphonistes*) who performed such pieces; or a discrete instrumental section – not necessarily the opening one – within an extended vocal work; or an obbligato instrumental accompaniment in a vocal work. In a cantata or motet subtitled *à voix seule avec symphonie*, individual obbligato lines are sometimes labelled 'symphonie' to indicate that they may be played by any suitable instrument or combination of instruments. *AntFre, MasOpé, SadOrc.*

Taille The French of Rameau's time distinguished two kinds of tenor: the *haute-contre** and the *taille*. The latter had a compass somewhat narrower than the modern choral tenor. At the Paris Opéra in Rameau's day, the *taille* was considered a less prestigious voice-type, suitable only for minor roles and for the 'tenor' line in the choruses. The term was also applied generically to the tenor of a family of instruments, as in *taille de violon** and *taille de flûte*. *MasOpé, SpiZas.*

Taille de violon Most of the orchestras for which Rameau composed included two viola lines, the *haute-contre de violon** and *taille de violon*, of which the *taille* was the lower. Its parts were normally written in the mezzo-soprano clef (C²), though the alto (C³) is often found in sources prepared after his death. When the two viola parts played in unison, Rameau usually labelled their line *parties**. *MasOpé, GorOrc, SadOrc, SpiZas.*

Les talents lyriques In press reports and elsewhere, Rameau's *opéra-ballet** *Les Fêtes d'Hébé* was often referred to only by its subtitle, *Les talents lyriques*; this gave a better indication of the subject-matter, each *entrée** being devoted in turn to a different 'lyric talent' – poetry, music and dance. In 1991 Christophe Rousset* adopted the eighteenth-century spelling, Les Talens Lyriques, for the name of the vocal and instrumental ensemble which he founded to explore the music of Rameau and his contemporaries. *GirRam, MalHéb, MasOpé.*

Tambour At the Paris Opéra the *tambour*, or side drum, was generally used only for sound effects*. Its most remarkable use by Rameau is at the start of the overture to *Zaïs*, a represention of the separation of the four Elements from primordial Chaos. As originally conceived, this movement began with an unaccompanied muffled drum (*tambour voilé*). At an early stage in the first run Rameau revised this opening, doubling the *tambour* with bassoons, cellos and *contrebasse**; whatever the reasons for the revision, it surely blunted the impact of this extraordinary conception. The exact nature of the 'muting' of the drum is not known. From the dramatic context we may assume that the skin was slackened and the snares released. Berlioz*, discussing a long tradition, says that, as an alternative to covering the parchment with a piece of cloth, players often contented themselves with passing a leather strap between the snares. *BlaPer, GorOrc, MasOpé, SadZaï.*

Tambour de Basque Among the attributes with which Terpsichore, Muse of Dancing, is often depicted is the *tambour de basque,* or tambourine. At the Paris Opéra this instrument was sometimes played by on-stage female dancers, a tradition dating back to the early eighteenth century. Stage directions occasionally indicate that the dancers carry 'tambours'*, as in the entrée* 'La Danse' in *Les Fêtes d'Hébé,* but in such instances it is the tambourine rather than the side-drum that is intended. *BlaPer, MasOpé.*

Tambourin Originating in Provence, where it was traditionally accompanied by *galoubet* (a three-holed pipe) and *tambourin* (a long cylindrical snare-drum struck with a single stick), this lively dance was introduced into French opera by Marin Marais in *Alcyone* (1706). It is normally notated in 2/4 metre or its equivalent, with repeated pedal notes in the bass to imitate the drum beats. One of Rameau's best-known examples, the 'Tembourin' [*sic*] in his *Pièces de clavessin* (1724), is the earliest dance of this kind to appear in a published harpsichord collection. A year earlier he had included a tambourin (possibly an early version of this same movement) in the music for *L'Endriague*, his first *opéra comique*. The keyboard piece was later incorporated, along with the Musette en rondeau from this same collection, into the *opéra-ballet* *Les Fêtes d'Hébé* (1739). Many of Rameau's other operas include tambourins, usually in pairs with one in the major and the other in the minor mode. They were usually performed with an improvised *tambourin* part. An inventory of 1748 shows that the Académie Royale de Musique* owned four of these instruments. Sometimes other dances could be performed with *tambourin* accompaniment; *Hippolyte et Aricie* includes a 'Rigaudon en tambourin' (III, 8), whose title is clarified by an annotation in the production* score: 'il faut ici le flageolet et le tambourin' ('the flageolet* and tambourin are required here'). In *Anacréon* (1754) successive passages in the Air pour les Bacchantes (scene 6) are marked 'avec tambourins / sans tambourins', these instruments being carried by the on-stage dancers along with *tambours de Basque*. *BouHi1, CyrHeb, GétTam, GorOrc, GusFul, MasOpe, SadBor, SadPir, WilAna.*

Teaching For much of his life, teaching occupied an important place in Rameau's professional activities. His earliest known experience came when he was appointed organist at Clermont* Cathedral in 1702 and again in 1715, where he was required to give 'learned instruction' to one choirboy or another person designated by the cathedral chapter. During his second period in Clermont, he developed a course in harmony and *accompagnement*, set out in the so-called 'Clermont notes'*. When he settled in Paris in 1722, he did not immediately secure an organist post, hence his principal occupation during the early years was as a teacher of continuo playing, keyboard instruments and possibly singing. With the publication of the *Traité de l'harmonie* (1722) and *Pièces de clavessin* (1724), Rameau found himself in increasing demand as a teacher. In 1728, according to Castel*, the composer had a number of pupils*, some of them well known, who after three months had learnt the whole theory of music and, after six, the entire practice of the art(!) In 1743 Rameau was said to charge a monthly fee of four *louis d'or* (worth 96 *livres* by that date – a huge sum) for twelve private lessons. By contrast, the rate for group classes at his School of Composition* was little more than a fifth of that amount. He was still giving private lessons well into the 1750s. Some idea of Rameau's approach to teaching may be gleaned from his voluminous theoretical writings, especially those with a pedagogical emphasis – the essay 'De la méchanique des doigts sur le clavessin' in his *Pièces de clavessin* (1724), the *Dissertation sur les différentes métodes d'accompagnement* (1732), the manuscript 'L'Art de la basse fondamentale' (between 1737 and 1744), 'Réflexions sur la manière de former la voix' (1752), and the *Code de musique pratique* (1760). *See also* **Giannoti, Pietro; Pupils.** *BreJeu, ChrTho, LauDoc, MorPed, QuiAnn, RamCwt, SuaCle, SuaInt, WelCle, ZasApp.*

Te Deum   *See* '**Paroles qui ont précédé le Te Deum**'.

Teding van Berkhout, Jan   Between 1739 and 1741 the Dutch patrician Teding van Berkhout (1713–66) kept a travel diary of his Grand Tour through France and Italy. This includes an account of a visit to the Lyon Opéra in April 1740 and numerous comments on the musicians whom he encountered there and in Paris the following winter. Of special relevance are his comments on Rameau and his wife. On 24 December 1740, at a dinner hosted in Paris by a 'Mr Couderc' (elsewhere spelt 'Couder' or 'Coudere') 'there were eight of us at table and we were well served. Mr Ramau [*sic*], the great opera composer, was one of us. He treated us by playing a piece on the harpsichord after dinner'. (Rameau, then aged fifty-seven, had evidently not yet developed into the unsociable figure portrayed in later descriptions.) A month later, the diarist dined at the residence of 'Mr Artraud' (presumably Jacques Autreau*), along with Rameau's wife (Marie-Louise Mangot*), Marie Fel* and Pierre Jéliote*, 'three opera persons, who sang a lot at the table'. *VlaTed.*

Telemann, Georg Philip   A committed Francophile throughout his life, Telemann (1681–1767) spent eight months in Paris between October 1737 and May 1738. Although there is no evidence that he met Rameau, Telemann must surely have attended performances of *Castor et Pollux*, whose much-heralded premiere took place only a few weeks after his arrival. He was later to defend this opera against the criticism by Carl Heinrich Graun (1704–59) that French recitative – Rameau's in particular – was 'unnatural'. During an amicable exchange of letters in 1751, Telemann asked his German colleague for examples of unsatisfactory passages. Graun responded with an analysis of an extract from *Castor* (I, 5) and provided his own alternative. The opening bars of the two versions are shown overleaf. Graun's setting, in an Italianate *secco* recitative style, has none of the vocal ornaments, shifting time-signatures, active bass line and varied harmonic rhythm of Rameau's. Telemann was not impressed. He pointed out that the vocal ornaments, if sometimes laboured by French singers, often produced melodic beauties. He drew attention to miscalculations in Graun's setting – the rest in bar 2 that interrupts the sense of the opening line; the faulty prosody whereby 'rendre_au jour' is set as four syllables; the error of placing 'jour' (b. 7) on a weak beat so that the following unstressed syllable ('à') falls on a strong one. For Telemann, Graun's harmonies were dreary and 'brackish', while the words were all rendered in the same manner despite a superficial diversity. By contrast, Telemann praises the heroic character of

Rameau's setting and the diverse emotions it captures: the word 'infortuné' ('unfortunate') is rendered tenderly; 'ressussiter' is characterized by a rolling trill ('trille roulant'); the word 'empêcher' ('to prevent') prompts a written-out retardation; 'triomphe' is haughty; 'à ce qu'il aime' tender. In his view Rameau's more active bass line, implicitly criticized by Graun, is just what was required. Further insights into the nature of French opera are found elsewhere in his lengthy correspondence with Graun, in which Telemann reveals himself to be a perceptive and non-partisan critic of French music. *See also* **Cantate pour le Jour de la Saint-Louis; Versification.** *CyrEss, FauCas, GauJug, LauTel, RosDec.*

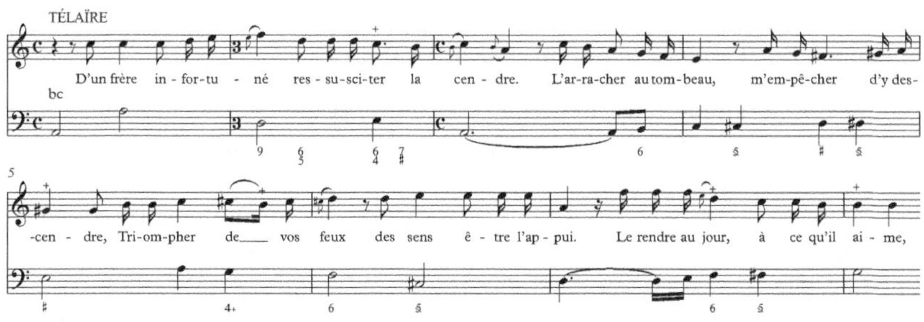

(a) Rameau, *Castor et Pollux*, I, 5

(b) The same text reset by Graun

Temperament   In his *Nouveau systême de musique théorique* (1726) Rameau advocated a modified mean-tone temperament based on B♭, in which the octaves and many of the thirds are pure but the fifths are slightly flattened. He never fully explained the details of this irregular temperament, however, so it cannot nowadays be reconstructed with any confidence. By the time he wrote *Génération harmonique* (1737), Rameau had changed his mind, arguing now in favour of equal temperament, which allowed a composer to modulate freely to any key. Whereas Rameau had earlier described with approval the different key* characteristics produced by the unequal intervals in other temperaments, he now rejected this idea. Moreover, his operas from the 1740s onwards (though not his keyboard music, written for amateur consumption) include modulations to keys as extreme as G♯ major. Given that such passages often include a figured bass, we may surmise that, for these works at least, the harpsichord was tuned to something close to equal temperament. Despite such advocacy, many French musicians proved reluctant to adopt this system; beginning with Bollioud-Mermet* and Jean-Jacques Rousseau*, a succession of theorists argued vociferously against equal temperament. *See also* **Bernouilli, Jean II**. *BarTun, ChrTho, CohEqu, MacTem, RamCtw, RouDic, ValLyo.*

Le Temple de la Gloire   Described as a 'fête' in Voltaire's* libretto, this work belongs to the genre identified in the mid-eighteenth century as *opéra-ballet**. It was commissioned for performance at court to celebrate the French victory at Fontenoy. After two performances in the Grande Écurie at Versailles, on 27 November and 4 December 1745, it was transferred to the Académie Royale de Musique* for a run of fifteen performances beginning on 7 December. After substantial revision, it was given a second run of performances, beginning in April 1746. Voltaire believed that opera should be edifying as well as entertaining and that the conventional love element, generally thought indispensable, could be minimized. Characteristically, his libretto to celebrate the victory is concerned not with love but with the nature of kingship. Three kings of contrasted character come in turn to the Temple of Glory: Belus, the power-hungry Assyrian, is refused entry because of his bloodthirsty and unjust nature; the self-indulgent Bacchus is refused because of his unbridled debauchery. Only the benevolent Roman emperor Trajan proves himself worthy, having showed magnanimity in victory. In its original form the work devoted one act to each king, together with a prologue-like Act I and epilogue-like Act V. In 1746 it was made to conform to the conventional *opéra-ballet** format: Act I became the prologue, Acts IV and V were condensed into one, and the entrée 'Belus' was almost entirely rewritten. There is reason to believe that Voltaire and Rameau incorporated some material from their abandoned *Samson**. *BesVol, BouHer, DubCon, DubRés, DubTem, GirRam, GreSou, JacVol, MalTem, MasOpé, RidVol, SadBor.*

Tempo indications   With the exception of *andante** and (very rarely) *adagio* and *allegro*, Rameau avoided Italian time words, preferring the standard French terms *lent, grave, modéré, gracieux, gai, vif* and their adverbial equivalents: *lentement, vivement* etc. These are often nuanced as *un peu lent, un peu plus gai* or *moins vite*, or adapted, as in *sans vitesse, sans lenteur, sans se presser* (without hurrying). Some indications, such as *animé, léger, majestueux, marqué, noble, fier* (proud), suggest both tempo and mood. The association of tempo and expression is also apparent in the annotation 'lent, et avec un sentiment pénétré de douleur', added by Rameau to the production* score of *Dardanus* (Iphise's air 'Les horreurs de la guerre environnent la ville', III, 4) and others in the production score of *Les Paladins*: 'très vif en peignant néanmoins le sentiment amoureux' ('very fast but nevertheless painting amorous feelings', I, 2) and 'scène débitée* vivement sans agréments' ('scene delivered rapidly without ornaments', II, 2). At the Paris Opéra in Rameau's day, great care was taken over the appropriate choice of tempo. A production score of *La Guirlande*, for example, bears a note added in red crayon by the *batteur de mesure*: 'Le mouvement de cette ritournelle doit peindre une personne qui hésite en venant' ('the tempo of this *ritournelle* must suggest a person who hesitates while approaching', scene 4). Elsewhere, a special effect might require a special tempo: for a representation of the rising dawn in the prologue to *Zaïs*, Rameau instructs the *batteur de mesure*: 'Rendez la mesure de ce morceau un peu plus lente que de coutume'. In modern times, when 'standard' tempi have become the norm, such comments are salutary. *See also* **Expressive markings**. *GreSou, MasOpé, MilOrc, SadZaï.*

'Les Tendres Plaintes'   We might instinctively interpret the mood and title of this D minor rondeau from the *Pièces de clavessin* (1724) as conveying a gentle, languid pathos. It is as well to remember, however, that when Rameau reused its refrain and first *reprise** in *Zoroastre* (1749), transposed to G minor, it was in a context where the heroine collapses, 'overwhelmed with grief' ('accablée de douleur'), while her companions dance consolingly around her. *BouHer, GirRam, GusFul, RpeCtw, SadBor, SadZo1.*

Terminology, French   Unlike most Western European countries, France tried with mixed success to resist successive waves of Italian influence during the Baroque period. Although its musical language selectively adopted elements of Italian styles and genres, its major performing institutions remained largely immune to foreign traditions. As a result, the standard Italian terminology used today is often ill-suited to the distinctive range of voice-types* and, to a lesser extent, the instruments cultivated in France. For this reason, most writers and editors nowadays retain the original French terminology.

Théâtre de la Foire   The two annual Parisian fairs, the springtime Foire Saint-Germain and autumn Foire Saint-Laurent, traditionally presented popular entertainments (plays, farces, acrobatics) in what became collectively known as the Théâtre de la Foire. In 1715 these theatres, now officially designated Théâtre de l'Opéra-Comique, leased a privilege from the Académie Royale de Musique* which allowed them to include singing and dancing in their productions but not (initially) spoken dialogue. By 1723, when Rameau first collaborated with Piron* at these Fair theatres, the ban on spoken dialogue had been lifted. The standard repertory now consisted of *opéras comiques** in which the dialogue was interspersed with lyrics set mainly to well-known tunes. *See also* **Monnet, Jean; Opéra-Comique.** *BarIns, BarVoc, CamSpe, FraOpé, GroCom, NemSéj, NoiHip, PorPre, SadPir, VenCom.*

Théâtre des Petits Cabinets   As official mistress to Louis XV since 1745, the marquise de Pompadour (1721–64) was all too aware of the need to protect the king from boredom. In 1747 she created a small private auditorium at Versailles, initially known as the Théâtre des Petits Appartements, in which to exercise her considerable skills as singer and actress. Roles in plays and operas were taken by aristocrats, while the small orchestra directed by Rebel* included a mixture of professional and amateur players. This enterprise soon established itself as the central theatrical activity at court. Much has been written about the marquise's ambivalent attitude towards Rameau and his music, yet her own tastes came second to those of the king. At first, knowing that Louis did not much enjoy Rameau's operas, she commissioned more readily accessible works by Mondonville*, Rebel* and Francœur and others. By 1748 she nevertheless felt ready to commission a Rameau *opéra-ballet**, *Les Surprises de l'Amour*, for the opening of her newly constructed theatre, now known as the Théâtre des Petits Cabinets, on the Ambassadors' staircase. Madame de Pompadour herself created the roles of Uranie and Vénus. Predictably, however, the king was bored: he would have preferred a comedy. Although the marquise's theatre company continued until 1750, it performed no further work by Rameau. *See also* **Les Beaux Jours de l'Amour.** *BouHer, BouSu1, BouThé, ChaRou, EmmPyg, GreSou, KaePom, RicFon.*

Théâtre-Italien   To replace the troupe of Italian comedians expelled by Louis XIV in 1697, a new Italian company was invited to France by the Regent, Philippe II d'Orléans, in 1716. This troupe, which became known as the Nouveau Théâtre-Italien (or the Comédie-Italienne), took up residence at the Hôtel de Bourgogne, traditional home of Italian comedy in France. Under the direction of Luigi Riccoboni (1676–1753), the company presented works in Italian or, increasingly, in French. Its repertory consisted of comedies by Marivaux and others; divertissements* including music and dance; and *parodies** of spoken plays and opera. From the 1730s its programming diversified, with the introduction of *pantomimes* choreographed by Dehesse*, *opéras comiques** and even the occasional *opera buffa*: Pergolesi's *La serva padrona* was given there in 1746, some six years before the eruption of the Querelle des Bouffons*, and again in 1754, translated as *La Servante maîtresse*. Rameau was evidently a devotee of the Théâtre-Italien: his first-known visit was in 1725, when he witnessed the dancing of the North American Indians that would inspire his harpsichord piece 'Les Sauvages'*. *AntFre, ChaRou, GroCom, LagThé, LecDeh, ThoAes.*

Theorbo   At the start of the eighteenth century the *théorbe* (the largest member of the lute family) was still popular as a continuo instrument. During the first quarter of the century, the *petit chœur** at the Académie Royale de Musique* included two theorbo players. The instrument's popularity was nevertheless declining, and when Bernard d'Alberty ('Bernardo') left the Académie in 1725 and François Campion resigned in 1730, neither was replaced. Thus by the time of Rameau's operatic debut three years later, the orchestra no longer included any hand-plucked continuo instruments, and the figured bass was realized by a single harpsichord. In performing Rameau's early motets* and *cantates françoises** the theorbo would, however, be quite appropriate. *CyrSty, GorOch, SadInv, SadKey.*

Thétis   Writing to La Motte* in 1727, Rameau stated that he had composed a cantata entitled *Thétis* 'a dozen years ago', that is to say, at the end of his time in Lyon* or during his second period in Clermont*. A cantata of this name survives in the Bibliothèque Nationale de France as a set of part-books with attributions both to Rameau and to Thomas-Louis Bourgeois (1676–1750/51). The vocal part-book was originally headed 'Thetis par bourgeois'; the composer's name was then struck out and replaced by Rameau's, though by whom or on what authority is not known. The continuo part is annotated: 'Composé par le S.ʳ Bourgeois et coppié en juillet 1718 à Paris par le S.ʳ Delaserre'. Support for the Rameau attribution comes from the composer's letter to La Motte, in which he draws attention to 'the degree of anger which I give to Neptune and to Jupiter' in accordance with certain established conventions, and the present setting certainly matches that description. Even so, the piece reveals few fingerprints of Rameau's style other than a possible anticipation of the chorus 'Tombez, tombez' in *Castor et Pollux* (III, 4), whereas it includes nothing uncharacteristic of Bourgeois. *BouHer, CyrCan, CyrChr, CyrEss, DorCan, GirRam, MonBou, TunCan.*

Thuret, Louis-Armand Eugène de   A former captain in the Picardy regiment, Thuret (d.1762) acquired the *privilège* of the Académie Royale de Musique* in May 1733, five months before Rameau made his operatic debut with *Hippolyte et Aricie*. Thuret was initially assisted by Campra* as *inspecteur général* and by

Rameau's patron the prince de Carignan* as 'protecteur'. From an artistic point of view Thuret's time as director began well: it witnessed the premieres not only of Rameau's first five operas, all regarded as among the composer's finest, but also of major works by Mouret, Rebel* and Francœur. In 1741, however, Thuret began to receive letters from the comte de Maurepas, secretary of state, complaining of falling standards; Maurepas demanded immediate reforms and called for the recruitment of better performers. Worse still, there is evidence that Rameau had by now fallen out with the management: it is surely significant that he produced no wholly new work for the Académie from the end of 1739 until after Thuret's departure five years later. Thuret was eventually to return as *directeur général* of the Académie in 1753. *See also* **Orphée aux Enfers**. *ChaPol, ChaRou, GirRam, GreSou, MalHip, SadPat, SerOpé, WooSad.*

Timbales   The first French opera to include *timbales* (kettledrums) was Lully's* *Thésée* (1675). Rameau inherited the tradition of using these instruments mainly in association with trumpets and in a martial context, where the drums are tuned to *d* and *A* or, more rarely, *c* and *G*. The *timbales* could also be used for certain sound* effects. From 1704 until about 1764, the *timbaliers* at the Académie Royale de Musique* were all members of the Caraffe family, who also played in the violin section. *BlaPer, GorOrc, MasOpé, SadInv.*

Timbre   The texts of *opéras comiques** performed at the Théâtre de la Foire* and elsewhere usually indicate the *timbre* of the popular melody to which each *vaudeville** was sung, this being the first line or refrain (e.g., 'Dans le bel âge', 'Lanturelu') or, in the case of instrumental melodies, the familiar title (e.g., 'Menuet d'Exaudiat'). Given that the original words of the melodies were well known to audiences, playwrights could exploit the relationship between these and the new words which they substituted. *See also* '**Les Niais de Sologne**'. *GroCom, LegVoi, VenCom.*

Time signatures   Apart from the fact that 3/4 and 2/2 were usually written as **3** and **2** respectively, the majority of time signatures in Rameau's day functioned much as they do in modern notation. One archaism survived, however, in the system of fluctuating metres in recitative notation of the Lully-Rameau period. These fluctuations came about because of a desire to place strong syllables on strong beats, with the caesura and rhyme word preferably falling on the first beat of a bar. Given the variety of line-lengths in French recitative, such a matching of verbal and musical stress was possible only if there was a corresponding variety of bar lengths. By Rameau's day the three signatures most commonly used in this context were **C**, **3** and **2**, in which the number of beats was respectively four, three and two. The length of the beat was in principle the same in each metre, though singers were permitted some liberty with the written rhythms in the interests of dramatic expression. The archaic element here is that while the beat in **C** and **3** is a crotchet, in **2** it is a minim, resulting in the following beat-equivalence: **C** ♩ = **3** ♩ = **2** ♪ . The **2** in this context is used as a proportional signature, the notes being read at twice the speed of those in the other two metres. This usage dates back to Lully's day, when the 'Italian' signature 2/4 was still not in general use in France. So ingrained had it become that even when 2/4 became widespread in the following century, it did not supplant the proportional use of **2** in recitative notation. The example opposite illustrates Rameau's use of the convention. In bar 3 the rhyme-word 'pou-dre' requires a shorter, two-beat bar. But because the beat in 2 is twice as fast as in the previous bars, Rameau has to halve the note values of the rapid figuration in the accompaniment, hence the semiquavers in bar 3 are performed at the same speed as the demi-semiquavers in the previous bars. *GreSou, RosDec, RosMet, WolMet.*

Rameau, *Zoroastre*, I, 2

'La Timide'   Commentators have noted similarities between the titles of several pieces by Rameau and Dandrieu* – among them this one, given by Rameau to a pair of rondeaux in the *Pièces de clavecin en concerts* (1741) and by Dandrieu to a movement in his *Second livre de pièces de clavecin* (1728). In the refrain of Rameau's first rondeau, the continuous quavers are slurred in groups of four in the violin and bass viol parts, which may indicate that they were not to be played as *notes inégales**. By contrast, in a reworking of this refrain as the 'Air gracieux [...] pour les Plaisirs' for the 1744 version of *Dardanus*, Rameau slurred the quavers in pairs, thereby implying a degree of inequality. *GusFul, FraDan, HerMor, RpeKey, SadBor.*

'Les Tourbillons'   Three years after its appearance in the *Pièces de clavessin* of 1724, Rameau explained to La Motte* that 'Les Toubillons' was intended to evoke 'the swirls of dust raised by high winds'. The increasing turbulence in this piece is achieved by rapid scales and arpeggios shared between the hands and spanning more than four octaves. Rameau's prefatory comments imply that such *roulements**, as he called them, were to be played in a seamless manner, a new development in 1724. *GirRam, HolBac, RpeKey, SadSca.*

Tous   For the most part, Rameau's orchestration follows well defined patterns, familiarity with which allows us to establish his intentions without much uncertainty. The use of the word *tous* ('all') in French opera scores of the period nevertheless requires some explanation. In many contexts there is no ambiguity – as, for instance, when it signals the end of a solo vocal or instrumental passage or the return to unison of voices or instruments divided on the same staff. An element of apparent uncertainty arises when a given staff at the start of a piece is labelled *tous* without any indication of which instruments are involved. A study of Rameau's autograph and other authoritative sources reveals, however, that *tous* in such contexts has a well-defined and restricted meaning. Applied to the bass line, it generally means unison *basses** and bassoons only – not *basses*, bassoons and continuo. Applied to a main melodic instrumental line in the French* violin clef (G¹), it normally indicates unison violins and oboes – not violins, flutes, oboes etc. Indeed, there is little evidence that the Académie Royale de Musique's* flutes and oboes ever played in unison in Rameau's day, whether because of intonation problems or disparities in dynamic* ranges. *GreSou, RosOrc.*

Tragédie en musique   The archetypal genre that Lully* established at the Académie Royale de Musique* in the early 1670s had undergone considerable evolution by the time Rameau made his operatic debut there some sixty years later. Even so, many aspects of its traditional form and character are outwardly recognizable in Rameau's *Hippolyte et Aricie* (1733) and subsequent *tragédies en musique*. Although new operatic genres had emerged in the intervening years, among them the *opéra-ballet**, the *ballet héroïque** and *comédie lyrique**, the *tragédie en musique* was still the most prestigious, and was distinguished from the other genres by its five-act structure (the others had fewer), its greater dramatic intensity and more elevated tone. By the 1720s and 1730s, the *tragédie* had nevertheless become the riskiest genre, since any new work of this kind had to measure up to those of the revered Lully, which remained the backbone of the repertoire. In other respects, however, there was less to distinguish the *tragédie* from other genres, since all of them included essentially similar musical ingredients and structures – recitative, airs, *ariettes**, *airs de monologue**, ensembles, choruses and ballet, albeit in varying proportions; each genre, moreover, distinguished between dramatic dialogue (*scènes d'action**) and divertissement*. Until 1749, the *tragédie* and other genres were normally preceded by a lengthy prologue*. In recent years the term *tragédie en musique* has generally replaced the somewhat anachronistic appellation *tragédie lyrique** by which the genre was increasingly known from the later eighteenth century onwards. *FajOpé, GirTra, GorLul, KinPoé, NauDra, VerDra, WooLul.*

Tragédie lyrique   In the nineteenth century and much of the twentieth, this was the standard term for the genre more appropriately known as *tragédie en musique**. Almost without exception, librettos printed before 1760 used the terms 'tragédie' or 'tragédie en musique', while published scores used these same terms with similar consistency, along with such variants as 'tragédie mise en musique' or, in the case of recycled librettos, '... remise en musique'. By contrast, the expression *tragédie lyrique* emerged only in the mid-eighteenth century, when it was employed in literary contexts primarily to distinguish sung ('lyric') tragedy from spoken tragedy. Not until the 1760s is the newer term found – sporadically – on title pages, while only in the following decade, after the arrival of Gluck's operas in Paris, does it appear at all frequently in this context. The use of the term *tragédie lyrique* for operas of the Lully-Rameau period is thus somewhat anachronistic; for that reason, most British, American and (increasingly) French writers nowadays prefer the term *tragédie en musique* for this repertory.

Traité de la composition des canons en musique   In his manuscript biography of Rameau, Decroix* lists an unpublished treatise with this title 'containing many examples'. Evidence has recently emerged that in 1763 Rameau sent a treatise entitled *Méthode pour faire les canons* to the Noblemen and Gentlemen's Catch Club* in London. Neither manuscript has yet been traced, however, and only a small number of Rameau canons* are known to survive, not all with undisputed attributions. *BouCan, BouRam, MonBou, RobCat, SchFam.*

Traité de l'harmonie   Evidently commissioned by the publisher Ballard*, the
Traité de l'harmonie réduite à ses principes naturels (1722) is one of the most
important and influential books of its kind ever written. This monumental
treatise immediately established Rameau as the leading music theorist of his
age, while many of the principles it established have remained fundamental
to the way we nowadays perceive harmony. The treatise comprises four
'books', two on the science of music and two on practical matters. Rameau's
achievement in the first two books was to reduce the complexities of harmonic
practice to a rational system which is governed by a single principle derived
from the mathematical and physical bases of a vibrating body. He established
the premise that, between them, the consonant perfect triad and dissonant
seventh chord constitute the source of all standard harmonies. Using the first
six divisions of a monochord, he argued that all such harmonies could be
generated from one fundamental sound (*son fondamentale*), which thus constituted the fount or principle of harmony. This in turn led to the concept of the
*basse fondamentale** – the root of a chord to which all inversions of the same
notes are related – and to the observation that the root progression within a
succession of harmonies was related to standard cadence patterns. For Rameau,
these patterns were the generating force of harmony and inculcated a sense of
tonal direction. By including the dissonant seventh as well as the consonant
triad in his concept of chord inversion, Rameau was able to explain some
hitherto puzzling aspects of dissonance treatment; if, for example, a 6/5 chord
is regarded as the first inversion of a seventh chord, the fifth above the bass
normally requires resolution as the dissonant seventh of the chord, despite the
fact that it may form a perfect consonance with the bass (as in the chord F, A,
C, D). One aspect of Rameau's theory that proved controversial was the concept
of chords by *supposition**, among them ninth and eleventh chords, suspensions
and appoggiaturas; the ninth, for example, is explained as a seventh chord with
a third 'sub-posed', as it were, beneath it. (For Rameau, this interval could not
be 'superposed' since, according to his concept of the *identité des octaves**, the
ninth was not an autonomous interval but a compound second.) Over the next
forty years Rameau was to develop and refine many of the above concepts, yet
they remained at the core of his ground-breaking system. *AndTer, BouHer, ChrBas,
ChrEig, ChrTho, CohSup, DahTra, FerEvo, GosTre, HyeBef, LegThé, LesRam, LewTra,
RamCtw.*

Travenol, Louis-Antoine   An indefatigable and pugnacious pamphleteer,
Travenol (1698/1708–1783) crossed swords with several prominent individuals,
among them Voltaire*, Jean-Jacques Rousseau* and Mondonville*. His
numerous anti-masonic writings include the poem *Brevet de la Calotte* (undated
but after 1744), in the course of which he identifies numerous individuals
as freemasons. All but one of those 'outed' were either musicians – notably
Rameau and (Roland) Marais, presumed dedicatee of 'La Marais'* – or Paris
Opéra employees. While this poem does not constitute proof that Rameau was a
mason, Travenol's 'exposures' of masonic practice were written from first-hand
experience, while the fact that he was a violinist at the Paris Opéra gives his
testimony a certain 'insider' value. *CamAca, CotMaç, LauÉco.*

Tréfontaine, Joseph Guénot de   In May 1748, following the death of Berger*,
the *privilège* to direct the Académie Royale de Musique* was acquired by

Tréfontaine with the aim, some said, of extracting as much profit from it as possible. His period as director proved disastrous: he was accused of making appointments without consulting his *inspecteurs*, Rebel* and Francœur, while the financial situation went from bad to worse: within only sixteen months he managed to spend 1,168,265 *livres* against revenues of only 915,356 *livres*. Tréfontaine was dispossessed of the *privilège* in August 1749 and evicted from his residence in the Magasin* de l'Opéra, at which point the Académie was placed under the control of the city of Paris. He died a ruined man, having been forced to petition the Académie for subsistence payments. *ChaPol, ChaRou, EmmPyg, SerOpé, WooSad.*

Tremblement, *see* **Cadence**.

Tribou, Denis-François   At the time of Rameau's debut at the Académie Royale de Musique*, Tribou (c.1695–1761) was the leading *haute-contre**. He first appeared in 1721 as Le Soleil in a revival of Lully's* *Phaëton*, where he made such a strong impression that he was promoted to the title role a few weeks later. His acting skills and declamation were much admired, and he excelled in tragic roles. It was for this well-loved singer that Rameau conceived the parts of Hippolyte (*Hippolyte et Aricie*), Tacmas (*Les Indes galantes*) and Castor (*Castor et Pollux*). In the late-1730s Tribou was increasingly overshadowed by Jéliote*, and he retired in 1741 to take up the position of theorbo player in Louis XV's Musique de Chambre. *BenVer, BouHer, CamAca, PouJél, SadInv.*

'Les Tricotets'   There is no apparent connection between this rondeau from the *Nouvelles suites de pièces de clavecin* (1729 or 1730) and surviving sixteenth-century melodies and dances with the same or similar titles; nor does Rameau's piece share the preference for three-bar phrases that are a feature of seventeenth-century *vieux tricotets* and *tricotets nouveaux*. Rather, 'Les Tricotets' consists of paired four-bar phrases, the quavers of the first phrase being grouped 3+3 and those of the second 2+2+2. Gilles Ménage's *Dictionnaire étymologique* (Paris, 1750) defines *tricotets* as 'a kind of lively dance, so called because the movement of the feet is as swift as the hand of a man or woman knitting stockings' (*tricoter*: to knit). In one sense this definition scarcely suits Rameau's piece, the tempo of which is not particularly fast. On the other hand, the continuous quaver movement and interlocking hand-patterns may be intended to suggest the clicking of needles. *BouHer, EllMar, GirRam, RpeKey.*

Trio des hautbois   A staple ingredient of French orchestral scoring dating back to the time of Lully*, the classic *trio des hautbois* comprised two oboes and bassoon, often intended to be performed with more than one instrument per part. In his first operas, Rameau adopted the tradition of including short trios of this kind as contrasting interludes in overtures, chaconnes or choruses. From the 1740s, he increasingly entrusted the accompaniments of solo vocal movements and duets to a *trio des hautbois*, though now with one instrument to a part and in contexts requiring considerable delicacy from the players. *MasOpé, SadOrc.*

Trio des Parques   The second act of *Hippolyte et Aricie* climaxes with a colossal trio in which the Fates (Parques) make the prediction that prepares the opera's tragic denouement. The trio is renowned for its use of the enharmonic* genre, introduced by Rameau 'to inspire dread and horror'. Sadly, the resulting harmonic progressions were so unfamiliar to the performers that, as the composer later complained, some of them were unable or unwilling to perform them, and the passage had to be 'abandoned for the stage'. Commentators have sometimes taken this to mean that the whole movement was cut, yet surviving sources reveal that this was not so; rather the movement was drastically shortened, from seventy-two bars to a mere twenty-nine. In the process, the offending enharmonic progression and its virtuoso accompaniment of multiply-divided strings were eliminated, as was most of the orchestral postlude with its prominent diminished sevenths and Neapolitan sixth, the latter being a chord that French opera audiences would have rarely encountered.

This movement is, in fact, one of two 'trios des Parques' in *Hippolyte et Aricie*. Comparison of the two suggests that Rameau intended a deliberate stylistic distinction between them. The first, in which the Fates explain that they cannot cut the thread of life before the appointed time, could hardly be more Lullian: it actually paraphrases a passage from the remarkably similar Trio des Parques in Lully's* *Isis* (1677), likewise concerned with the thread of life (compare the cadential bars in the example below). By contrast, the second trio represents the boldest possible statement of Rameau's modernity, in its forceful expression, its harmonic daring and orchestral virtuosity. *BarEnh, BouHi1, BouHi2, DilIma, GirRam, MalHip, MasOpé, SadHip, ThoAes.*

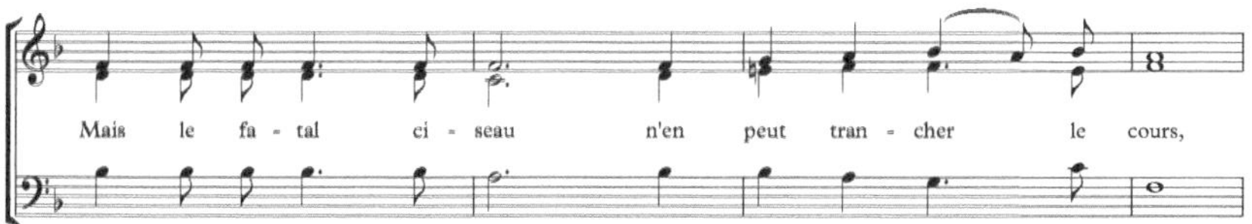

(a) Rameau, *Hippolyte et Aricie*, II, 4

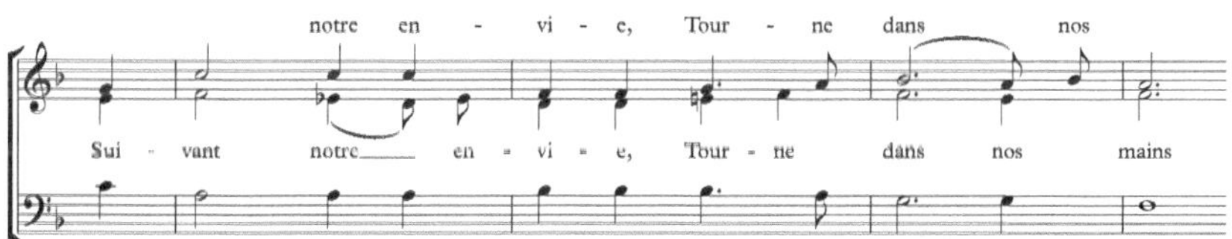

(b) Lully, Trio des Parques, *Isis*, IV, 7

'Les Triolets'   The title of this movement, from Rameau's *Nouvelles suites de pièces de clavecin* (1729 or 1730), is initially puzzling: the piece includes no triplets. In any case, the term *triolet* had not yet come into common use in that sense; rather, it normally denoted a poetic form akin to the medieval rondeau, an eight-line poem in which lines 1, 4 and 7 were identical, as were lines 2 and 8. While Rameau's piece does not follow this *forme fixe*, the reappearance of two thematic ideas at various points may be intended as an allusion to the recurrence in a triolet of the first and second lines. The composer's prefatory remarks to the *Nouvelles suites* indicate that the tempo of this movement should not be fast. *DicAut, GirRam.*

'La Triomphante'   In his preface to the *Nouvelles suites de pièces de clavecin* Rameau draws attention to the use of enharmonic* progressions in two pieces in this collection, 'La Triomphante' and 'L'Enharmonique'*. In the example below, the enharmonic change occurs in the first bar, where the B♯ in the bass is re-spelt as a C♮ in the treble, at which point the ear automatically accepts that the bass note has also become C♮, in order for it to progress to the B♮ in the next bar. *BarEnh, ChrTho, GirRam, RamCtw, RpeKey.*

Rameau, 'La Triomphante', *Nouvelles suites de pièces de clavecin*

Triomphe de Rameau   Several exemplars survive of an etching by Claude Mathieu Fessard (1740–1803) entitled *Triomphe de Rameau* and engraved after a now-lost design by Cochin* the younger. In view of its title, this engraving (illustrated below) was traditionally accepted as a tribute to the composer, yet Olivia Bloechl has observed an unmistakably satirical intention. The composer stands awkwardly on a chariot astride two monsters. Although the figure of Victory tries to place a laurel crown on his head, the chariot is being dragged backwards, away from a triumphal arch and out of the city – and by men rather than horses. Rameau meanwhile tries to conduct a group of singers and players, but they are out of sight behind the chariot and are facing in all directions. Two dogs bark at the procession, as if to comment on the implied cacophony. A fanfare is sounded by two trumpet-playing American Indians, dressed in feathered skirts and carrying bows and arrows – a clear reference to the 'savage' nature of Rameau's music. Given the date of Fessard's birth, this print presumably dates from no earlier than about 1760, yet the irreverent subject matter and the presence of Indian 'savages' suggests that Cochin's original formed part of the series of satirical* engravings issued during the Lulliste-Ramiste* dispute. *BloNat, GétPor, GétSat.*

'Triomphe de Rameau', etching by Claude Mathieu Fessard, after Charles-Nicolas Cochin II (Paris, Bibliothèque Nationale de France, Département de la Musique. Estampe Rameau J.P., 036). Reproduced by permission.

'Les Trois Mains'   Surprising though it may seem, this piece from the *Nouvelles suites de pièces de clavecin* (1729 or 1730) has been shown to include many characteristics of the Spanish fandango*. The title doubtless derives from the fact that, although the piece is written largely in two parts, the extensive use of hand-crossing* creates the illusion that three hands are required on one keyboard. Siegbert Rampe suggests that the rapid downward scales at the approach to the final cadence of each section call for the use of glissando*. *GirRam, RpeKey, SadSca.*

Underlay slurs   One notational peculiarity of the Lully-Rameau period is the *liaison de vocalises,* or what might be termed 'underlay slur', which is found exclusively in vocal music during the course of a melisma. Two of these may be seen in the example below, across the second and fourth barlines. Unlike other slurs, the *liaison de vocalise* has no bearing on articulation: its sole purpose is to clarify the textual underlay, in confirming that the melisma continues over the barline. Though strictly redundant in modern typography, such slurs are often a useful guide to the eye, hence their retention in many recent editions. *BouPri*

Rameau, 'Règne, Amour', *Zoroastre*, V, 7

Unity of Place   The classic French spoken tragedy of Pierre Corneille (1606–84) and his successors was governed by a code of rules ultimately derived from Aristotle's *Poetics.* These included the unities of time (the plot should occupy no more than a single day), action (there should be few if any subplots) and place (the action should be restricted to a single locality). In opera, by contrast, these unities were only loosely observed. Most librettos are deliberately vague about the passage of time, while the episodic nature of the genre made unity of action difficult to respect. As for unity of place, this was routinely ignored, such was the emphasis on elaborate stage spectacle; indeed, each act normally began in a new location. There is, however, the curious case of Rameau's *Hippolyte et Aricie.* The first two scenes of Act V, crucial to the resolution of the plot, were cut during the first run, leading the *Mercure de France** to explain that 'these scenes have been omitted because they cause some irregularity to the Unity of Place by the scene-change within the same act'. This explanation has given rise to some speculation. While the location does indeed change after scene 2, scene-changes during the course of an act were by no means uncommon, despite criticism in some literary quarters. Rather, the convention contravened by Pellegrin's libretto was precisely the one that permitted a new location at the start of the act. In *Hippolyte* there is, unusually, no scene change between Acts IV and V; yet it becomes clear that a period of time has elapsed since the end of the previous act – enough for Phaedra to commit suicide, having confessed her guilt to Theseus. While modern audiences have no difficulty in accepting this time-lapse, it evidently offended Rameau's contemporaries' sense of *vraisemblance* – that is, what was 'likely' or 'probable', hence the disastrous cut. *BurHip, GirTra, KinPoé, NauDra, SadHip, ThoAes, WooSad.*

Unmeasured prelude   In the *prélude non mesuré* that emerged in the mid-seventeenth century, the pitches are carefully notated but the rhythms are largely left to the player's intuition. Rameau's single contribution to this genre, in his *Premier livre de pièces de clavecin** of 1706, was one of the last to be published. It adopts a form of notation first developed by d'Anglebert in 1689, where the notes indicating chord formations are shown in semibreves, whereas melodic fragments appear in conventional notation. Only the first section is unmeasured. Thereafter, the character of the prelude changes abruptly, as the player launches into a cascade of triplet quavers that would scarcely sound out of place in the latest Italian violin sonata. It is as if Rameau, in his first publication, was announcing his intention to preserve the best features of the traditional French style while at the same time rejuvenating it with elements imported from Italy. *GusFul, MorUnm, RpeKey, TilUnm.*

Vallas, Léon   Better known for his writings on Debussy, d'Indy and Franck, Léon Vallas (1879–1956) first made his name with two monumental studies of eighteenth-century musical life in Lyon*. The first, devoted to the Académie des Beaux-Arts, was published in 1908; the second, an exhaustive study of music and theatre in the city, appeared in 1932. Both are founded on solid archival work and remain essential reading. In 1991 all Vallas's research materials were deposited in the city's Bibliothèque municipale. *HerMot, ValAca, ValLyo, ValMan, ValRam.*

Van Loo, Jean-Baptiste   An auction in Bordeaux in 1997 included a 'Portrait of Jean-Philippe Rameau' said to be by Jean-Baptiste van Loo (1684–1754). The sitter, richly attired in a blue jacket and lace sleeves, is writing unidentifiable music with a quill. His features bear little if any resemblance to those of Rameau, reliably depicted by Caffieri* and Carmontelle*, and the identification thus remains spurious. The painting is now in a private collection. *GétPor.*

'La Vanloo'   *See* **Duphly, Jacques.**

Vaudeville   The particular variety of *opéra comique** that flourished in the first half of the eighteenth century normally consisted of a spoken play interspersed with songs and instrumental music. Most of the songs were *vaudevilles*, well-known tunes to which new words were fitted. The texts of the plays include *timbres** identifying the melody. The original lyrics of these songs were so well known that playwrights could exploit the comic potential by alluding wittily to the originals, thereby introducing an element of irony, satire or double meaning. Most *opéras comiques* ended with a *vaudeville final* to which all the characters in the play contributed. Some of these were newly composed, as in several of the plays of Piron* that include music by Rameau. *BarVoc, ConPir, FraOpé, GroCom, ProPir, SadPir, VenCom.*

Vennevault, Nicolas   Among those consulted by Maret* while researching his *Éloge historique de M.ʳ Rameau* was Vennevault (1697–1775), a painter noted for his miniatures and landscapes. He was a member of the Académie Royale de Peinture and, like Maret and Rameau himself, the Académie des Sciences, Arts et Belles-Lettres de Dijon. The artist, described by Maret as one of the composer's friends, provided him with a description of Rameau's working methods, written in collaboration with Balbastre*. *BreJeu, GirRam, GreSou, MarÉlo.*

'**Vénitiénne**' [*sic*]   In choosing this title for the only character* piece in his *Premier livre de pièces de clavecin* (1706), Rameau may have been influenced by Gaspard Le Roux, whose *Pièces de clavecin* of 1705 includes a 'Courante la Venitiene'. It is possible that he already knew 'La Venitienne' by his mentor Louis Marchand*, a movement subsequently published in Ballard's *Pièces choisies pour le clavecin de différents auteurs* (1707). Neither piece resembles Rameau's, however. The young composer had probably not arrived in Paris in time to see La Barre's *comédie-ballet** *La Vénitienne*, performed at the Opéra in May and June 1705 and including an *Air des barcarolles*. Still, Rameau's choice of a lilting 3/8 metre, rare in French harpsichord music at that time, was doubtless intended to evoke the character of a gondolier's song. *BreJeu, GirRam, GusFul, RpeKey.*

'**Vérités également ignorées et interressantes tirées du sein de la nature**' Rameau's last music treatise evidently belongs to the period 1763–64, his final year. It survives in two manuscript versions, one consisting of fragments, the other (discovered by Herbert Schneider) more or less complete. Like many of Rameau's writings from the mid-1750s onwards, the fragments include direct attacks on d'Alembert*, but these had been eliminated by the time the later version was prepared. Much of the text rehearses the metaphysical arguments that feature in many of Rameau's last writings, in which the *corps sonore** is seen as the source and principle of all the arts and sciences, and as proof of the existence of the Supreme Being. Such thinking, which Thomas Christensen has shown to be influenced by the Occasionalist philosophy of Nicolas Malebranche (1638–1715), also reflects the esoteric, quasi-Rosicrucian rhetoric that is increasingly associated with freemasonry* from the 1750s onwards. *BurCor, ChrTho, JacVér, RamCtw, SchVér.*

Versification   Spoken French has a rhythmic character distinct from that of any other European language. Not only does it make little distinction between long and short syllables but it has largely eliminated word-stress in favour of group-stress: a syllable is normally accented only if it happens to be the last in a group. Hence French poetry traditionally made limited use of metre as a primary principle of organization; rather, individual poetic lines (*vers*) are classified according to the number of pronounced syllables they contain. Librettos of the Lully-Rameau period are written in *vers libres*, a fluid mixture of lines of different length. In recitative, the alexandrine (twelve syllables) alternates freely with the *décasyllabe* (ten) and *octosyllabe* (eight). Airs and choruses employ a wider variety of line-lengths. To calculate the number of syllables, a distinction is made between masculine and feminine endings: the former end with a strong syllable (e.g., 'grand'), while the latter have a 'mute *e*'* (*e muet*) after the last strong syllable ('gran-*de*'). In poetry this final *e*, though customarily pronounced, is not included in the syllable count. Other *e muets* in the line are counted unless elided with the following vowel. In the example overleaf (Rameau/Pellegrin, *Hippolyte et Aricie*, IV, 2), the + indicates the uncounted mute *e* at the feminine ending; the remaining *e muets* are either included in the syllable count or elided as shown.

1 2 3 4 5 6 | 7 8 9 10 11 12

Nous al - lons nous ju - rer   u - *ne*_im - mor - tel - *le* foi

1 2 3 4 5 6 | 7 8 9 10 11 12 +

Viens, rei - *ne* des fo - rêts,   viens for - mer no - *tre* chaî - *ne*

The last strong syllable in each line, whatever it happens to be, receives a stress. In the longer lines a secondary accent is produced by the caesura (medial pause), shown in the example above as a vertical line. This divides the alexandrine into two six-syllable *hémistiches*, each ending with a stress; a further accent occurs within each *hémistiche*, though the fact that these have no fixed position makes for greater rhythmic flexibility. In the *décasyllabe* the caesura is normally placed after the fourth syllable. French librettos of this period preserve the tradition of alternating masculine and feminine rhymes. Rhymes were usually arranged as *rimes plates* (*aabb*), *rimes croisées* (*abab*) or *rimes embrassées* (*abba*). However, the practice of constructing *parodies** on pre-existent music brought about much greater variety in this respect. *KasVer, RosDec, SchRam.*

Vertical stroke   In his table of *agréments** in the 1724 *Pièces de clavessin*, Rameau uses this symbol to indicate the *son coupé** – a detached articulation in which the note is shortened to half its notated value. The vertical stroke or narrow wedge also appears in several of Rameau's engraved scores (e.g., *Les Fêtes de l'Hymen et de l'Amour*, I, 6; *Zaïs*, II, 3; *Zoroastre*, I, 3), probably with a similar meaning. It is nevertheless worth recalling that this symbol was also used to warn against the application of *notes inégales**, and in some cases it is not easy to decide which meaning is intended. In at least one instance (*Les Paladins*, I, 6) the stroke appears as an alternative to the superscript* dot to denote an unconventional articulation. Yet another application of the vertical stroke occurs in the performing parts used by Rameau's singers, where it evidently indicates an unprepared *pincé**. *See also* **Ornaments added in rehearsal.** *GreSou, HefRhy, NeuPer, SadZaï, SawNou.*

'Le Vézinet'   Why Rameau chose this title for the second movement of his *Pièces de clavecin en concerts* is unclear. Nowadays Le Vésinet is a suburb in a loop of the river Seine to the west of Paris, but in 1741 it was still only a hamlet surrounded by forest. The composer may possibly have passed through it on visits to the palace of Saint-Germain-en-Laye, just across the river. Alternatively the area may have had some connection with one of the 'persons of taste and skill' who suggested names for pieces in this collection. At all events, there is nothing particularly rustic about the ascending scales, harpsichord *batteries** and hand-crossings that characterize this piece. *BouHer GirRam, GusFul, HerMor, RpeKey.*

'La Victoire'   *See* **Duphly, Jacques.**

Vivaldi, Antonio   If Léon Vallas* is to be believed, the earliest-known French performances of music by Vivaldi (1676–1741) took place at the Académie des Beaux-Arts in Lyon* during the period 1713–17, during concerts comprising miscellaneous operatic extracts, motets and cantatas. Vallas provides no specific programme details, but the Académie's library included *L'estro armonico* and two unidentified concertos, the latter now lost. By a happy coincidence, Rameau

was resident in the city for much of that time and may well have attended or even performed in these concerts. The Lyon initiative was not, however,
followed up immediately: Vivaldi's music remained little known in France until 1725, when *Il cimento dell'armonia e dell'inventione*, Op. 8, was published in Paris. With the appearance of this collection, Vivaldi's reputation among the French grew rapidly, reinforced by frequent performances of concertos from this publication at the Concert Spirituel* from 1728 onwards, notably *La primavera* from *Le quattro stagioni*, by the Turinese violinist Guignon* and others. Such programmatic pieces strongly appealed to the French, for whom the concept of the imitation of nature was a fundamental aesthetic goal.

Vivaldi's influence on Rameau can be sensed in much of the energetic string figuration in the latter's cantatas and operas, above all in the shuddering tremolandos that characterize his many representations of violent natural and supernatural phenomena (e.g., the 'Tonnerre' in *Hippolyte et Aricie*, I, 4). Rameau also follows Vivaldi in using pizzicato* to depict raindrops, while the *sommeil** in *Anacréon* (1754) is clearly indebted to several passages in Vivaldi's *Le quattro stagioni*. *TalHab, ValAca, ValLyo, VlaTed.*

La Vilagoise [*sic*]   The title of this gavotte-like rondeau from the *Pièces de clavessin* of 1724 may well summon up the image of a peasant girl, though the feminine article (*la*) in this context does not indicate the villager's gender. Rameau's piece, with its folksy melody and uncomplicated quaver accompaniment, may be intended to evoke a more generalized picture of village life. Even so, the elaborate semiquaver figuration of the second *reprise** seems at odds with such a homely image. Unusually, this figuration continues directly into the final return of the rondeau refrain, giving it the character of a *double**. *GirRam, RpeKey.*

'La Villeroy'   *See* **Duphly, Jacques.**

Villeroy, marquise de   In 1747 Jeanne-Louise Constance d'Aumont (1731–1816), daughter of the duc d'Aumont, married the marquis de Villeroy. One notable feature of the couple's Parisian residence, the Hôtel de Villeroy on the rue de Varennes, was a private theatre capable of seating one hundred or more spectators. The marquise was a devotee not only of spoken theatre but of opera: she is known to have co-rented a private box at the Académie Royale de Musique*. Among the events that took place in her theatre were rehearsals* of operas intended for the Académie or for Louis XV's court; these included *La Naissance d'Osiris*, the Rameau-Cahusac *Anacréon* and the ill-starred *Linus**. This last suffered a fatal blow when the marquise (or, more likely, Rameau) was taken suddenly ill, after which the score and all but one of the performing parts mysteriously disappeared. *ColJou, GirRam, GreSou, GrmCor, HenAri, WilAna.*

Viola   *See* ***Haute-contre de violon; Parties; Taille de violon.***

Violons en basse   The French originally had no term for what was elsewhere known as *bassetto* or *Bassett*, where the bass line moves temporarily to an upper register and is played by violas or violins; the expression *violons en basse* in current use derives from a comment by Jean-Jacques Rousseau* in 1750. While such a lightening of the bass occurs in French opera from its beginnings, it became widespread from the early eighteenth century not only in opera but also in the motet and *cantate françoise** repertories. Over and above its use in choruses and dance movements, this scoring came to be associated with a particular kind of soprano air accompanied by one or, more often, two obbligato flute parts. Such scoring exploited the resources of the *petit chœur** at the Académie Royale de Musique*, which in the 1710s and 1720s included not only the continuo players but also two flutes and two violins, charged with the more delicate accompaniments. Rameau made extensive use of this sonority in his first two operas: *Hippolyte et Aricie*, for example, includes nine movements accompanied wholly or partly by obbligato flutes and *violons en basse*. Thereafter, however, his use of this texture is more selective and largely confined to his minor works. *FajPré, KauVio, MasOpé, SadOrc.*

Vocalises   Extended melisma in French airs and choruses ultimately derived from seventeenth-century Italy; yet unlike other nationalities, the French restricted *vocalises* to certain 'privileged' syllables in words whose meaning somehow justified the use of melisma – 'accou-*rez*' (run), 'triom-*phez*' (triumph), '*fou*-dre' (thunder), '*chaî*-ne' (chain), '*flam*-me' (flame), 'mur-*mu*-re' (murmur) and so on. In such words, moreover, the melisma normally fell on a 'lyric' vowel – one suited to vocalisation. By contrast, the comedy *Platée* exploits the humour of melismas placed on inappropriate syllables, as in La Folie's evocation of laughter in 'refu-*sa a a a*' and 'tom-*beau eau eau*' ('Aux langueurs d'Apollon', II, 5). *CyrSin, GirRam, MasOpé.*

Voice-types, French   During the seventeenth and much of the eighteenth centuries, France maintained a performing tradition quite distinct from that of Italy and elsewhere in Europe (where Italian practice was widely adopted). In the domain of voice-types, this manifests itself both in the particular ranges cultivated in France and in the terminology found in French scores and theoretical sources. The use of standard Italian or English terms to categorize these voices can be misleading, hence most modern critical editions of French music of the period retain the original terminology – typically *dessus**, *bas-dessus*, *haute-contre**, *taille**, *basse-taille** and *basse*. Of these, the last four were sung by adult males. As in so many other ways, such emphasis on the lower voices sets France apart from Italy and indeed much of Europe, as does the French avoidance of the castrato voice in operatic roles. *CyrCho, CyrSin, MasOpé.*

Voltaire   Few writers collaborated with Rameau more than once or twice, whereas Voltaire (the pen name of François Marie Arouet, 1694–1778) provided him with three librettos and offered him a fourth. Sadly, what promised to be the one of the most high-minded collaborations in French operatic history was beset with problems and never achieved its potential. *Samson**, begun in the winter of 1733–34, was eventually abandoned; the libretto of *Pandore** was refused by Rameau in 1740, who had temporarily retired from opera composition; and *La Princesse de Navarre* and *Le Temple de la Gloire* (1745) were written in unpromising circumstances for celebrations at court. Voltaire first encountered Rameau after attending the premiere of *Hippolyte et Aricie* in 1733. He soon came to appreciate that the composer, if provided with a libretto worthy of his talent, was capable of changing the entire character of French opera. Voltaire's aim was to create a genuinely edifying type of music drama. Instead of plots centred on amorous entanglements, the action would admit romantic love only as a means to a more elevated end. Such ambitions are reflected in these librettos. The central theme of *Samson** is the Israelites' struggle against captivity and religious intolerance, in which the love between Samson and Dalila is merely an agent in precipitating the hero's destruction of the Philistine temple. *Pandore**, set against a power-struggle between the gods and Titans, points the moral that mankind's downfall is not a desire for knowledge but its credulity in trusting the gods. *Le Temple de la Gloire** provides a lesson in kingship. The Voltaire-Rameau collaboration was not a smooth one; Rameau's son Claude-François* told Decroix* that 'they squabbled quite a bit with each other, given that they were both very lively and both wanted to have the last word'. Even so, Voltaire had no doubt about the composer's towering stature, and his voluminous correspondence is peppered with affectionate references to 'Orphée-Rameau', the 'hero of the semiquavers' (*double croches*). *See also* **Collège Louis-le-Grand**; **Mercier, Louis Sébastien**. *BesVol, BouRam, DilMon, DubCon, DubRés, DubTem, GirTra, GirVol, JacVol, KafEnc, KinVol, RidVol, SawVol, SchFam.*

Voyez, François   Among rejected* portraits of Rameau is an engraving by François Voyez (1742–1806) in the Foyle Menuhin Archive at the Royal Academy of Music, London. The archive's on-line catalogue describes the image as 'A rehearsal of the ballet for Jean-Philippe Rameau's opera *Castor et Pollux*'. This modern title is derived from a pencil annotation on the mount, in what appears to be a twentieth-century hand: 'Le personnage assis à droite est le célèbre compositeur, Jean Philippe Rameau, faisant répéter à une jeune fille, le ballet de *Castor et Pollux*. / Baudouin' ('The person seated on the right is the famous composer Jean-Philippe Rameau, rehearsing a young girl in the ballet of *Castor et Pollux*'). In reality, Voyez entitled his engraving *Le Chemin de la Fortune* (The Pathway to Fortune), the print being based on a painting of that name by Pierre-Antoine Baudouin*, now lost. Baudouin had recently painted scenery for a revival of *Castor*, but why the present image, with its erotic innuendos and Hogarthian social satire, should include a score of this opera, or why the scene is presided over by a depiction of the bust of Rameau by Caffieri*, is a mystery. As for the seated male figure directing the proceedings, if this is the composer himself (as maintained in the archive's catalogue), it bears no resemblance to any known image of him, whereas Voyez's depiction of the Caffieri bust in the background is quite realistic. The original painting must date from between 1760 (the date of the bust) and Baudouin's death (1769). *GétPor.*

Walsh, John   At a time when comparatively little French music was published outside France, the London firm of Walsh issued three volumes of harpsichord music by Rameau and a translation of his *Traité de l'harmonie*. First to appear was an edition of the *Pièces de clavecin en concerts* of 1741, published in 1750 under the title *Five Concertos for the Harpsichord [...] Accompanied with a Violin or German Flute or Two Violins or Viola*. The English title, in substituting 'concertos' for 'concerts'*, is rather misleading, as is the word 'viola' as a translation of Rameau's [*basse de*] *viole*. The score itself nevertheless retains the original instrument names ('Violon', 'Viole', 'Clavecin') and prints Rameau's 'Avis aux Concertants' in French with an English translation. This edition evidently inspired Charles Avison's* three collections of accompanied* keyboard music. Walsh later published Rameau's *Pièces de clavessin* of 1724 and *Nouvelles suites de pièces de clavecin* of 1729 or 1730; both appeared under the title *A Collection* *of Lessons for the Harpsichord compos'd by Mr Rameau*, the latter in 1760 as 'opera seconda', the former in 1764 as 'opera [...]'. Walsh's edition of Rameau's *Traité* appeared in 1752 as *A Treatise of Musick, containing the Principles of Composition*. BouHer, HerMor.

Walther, Johann Gottfried   The first Rameau 'biography' in any language appeared in the monumental *Musicalisches Lexicon* (1732) by Walther (1684–1748). The information in the 29-line entry has been shown to derive almost entirely from three sources: a review of the *Traité de l'harmonie* in the Leipzig *Neue Zeitungen von gelehrten Sachen* (1723); the second edition (1708) of Rameau's *Premier livre de pièces de clavecin*; and Boivin's music catalogue for the year 1729, no longer extant. This last source is particularly useful, since the catalogue was evidently issued, as was the custom, at the end of the previous year. Given that Walther does not mention Rameau's undated *Cantates à voix seule** or the *Nouvelles suites de pièces de clavecin** (both traditionally dated 'c.1728'), we may safely conclude that neither had appeared before the beginning of 1729. BouHer, CyrChr, CyrEss, GusFul, RamCtw, WalMus, ZasApp.

Xylophone   *See* **Orgue de Barbarie.**

'La Zaïde'   *See* **Royer, Joseph-Nicolas-Pancrace.**

Zaïs   First performed at the Académie Royale de Musique* on 29 February 1748, *Zaïs* was Rameau's first opera devoted entirely to *la féerie**, the enchanted world of Middle-Eastern mythology. The work's sources are unanimous in labelling it a *ballet héroïque**, a somewhat meaningless term, given the inconsistency with which it was applied, and nowadays *Zaïs* is more logically classified as a *pastorale héroïque**. Cahusac's* libretto consists of a prologue followed by four acts with a continuous plot. As with other works of the *féerie* genre, the enchanted world provides the setting for a series of ordeals which provoke moral questions relating to social rank, fidelity and the renunciation of power; as the final chorus makes clear, the outcome was intended as an edifying lesson for contemporary society. One innovation in the libretto is the identification by Cahusac himself of intertextual links with other seminal works in the genre. The prologue, which treats the creation of the universe from primordial chaos, contains clear allusions to the tenets of freemasonry*; the ensuing trials by ordeal and use of a talisman may also be read in a masonic sense. The overture depicts the unravelling of the four Elements out of chaos, beginning with an unaccompanied muffled drum (*tambour voile**) followed by an extraordinary series of dislocated harmonic progressions. This section initially proved too revolutionary and was replaced by a blander version, though Rameau eventually insisted on reinstating the original. The opera proved popular with audiences; it was revived in 1761 and, posthumously, in 1769, notching up well over one hundred performances over a period of two decades. BouHer, BucSup, ChaRou, CotMaç, GirRam, GorSet, GreSou, KinRam, MalZaï, MasBal, MasOpé, SadZaï.

Zanotti, Francesco Maria   *See* ***Nouvelles réflexions de Mr Rameau sur sa 'Démonstration du principe de l'harmonie'.***

Zéphire   This *acte de ballet**, originally entitled *Les Nymphes de Diane*, is something of a mystery. It was apparently never performed in the eighteenth century, and nothing was known of it until Rameau's autograph score resurfaced in 1866, more than a century after his death. In identifying music on the reverse of *collettes** pasted over discarded passages, Thomas Green has narrowed down the date of composition to the period 1750–55. Other internal clues suggest that the opera may have been intended for court performance at Fontainebleau in 1753, where it would have doubtless been performed as part of composite entertainments with other works. Unusually, all the solo roles, including that of the male protagonist, are assigned to sopranos. The librettist of *Zéphire*, though unidentified in the source, was almost certainly Louis de Cahusac*. *BouHer, GreTra, GreSou, GreZép, MalPri, MasOpé, RicFon.*

Zoroastre   Premiered at the Académie Royale de Musique* on 5 December 1749, *Zoroastre* was the first new work to be produced after the Académie came under the aegis of the city of Paris. It was given an extraordinarily lavish production, with a star cast and a larger-than-usual proportion of new sets and costumes; even so, the opera was initially only a limited success, and soon after its first run Rameau and his librettist Cahusac* began an extensive revision in which the plot and music of three of the five acts were substantially new. This revised version, eventually staged on 19 January 1756, was far more successful, and the work was later chosen to inaugurate the Académie's newly rebuilt Palais-Royal* theatre in 1770. The 1749 libretto, translated into Italian by Casanova*, was staged in Dresden in 1752, with music by Johann Adam replacing most of Rameau's.

As Cahusac pointed out, *Zoroastre* represents a deliberate break with the classical legend and medieval romance that formed the conventional material of the *tragédie en musique**. Its theme, derived from Persian sources, is the struggle between Good and Evil involving the great religious reformer Zoroastre, representative of the Supreme Being, in perpetual conflict with an ambitious sorcerer Abramane, servant of the Spirit of Darkness. This dualist theme allowed Cahusac to introduce themes and rituals associated with freemasonry*, notably in the sun worshipping ceremony and in Zoroastre's initiatory voyage supported by talismans; in 1756 further masonic elements were introduced, including a more explicit initiation ceremony. With *Zoroastre* the traditional French prologue* was decisively abandoned. The overture*, designed to take its place, is the first in which Rameau prepared the audience for the drama as a whole: its three sections depict, in turn, Abramane's barbarous rule, the renewal of hope and the rejoicing of the people freed from tyranny. *BetCah, BouHer, BucSup, ChaRou, CotMaç, DilMon, GirRam, GirTra, GreGen, GreSou, LecDiv, KinPoé, KinRam, ManZor, RicZor, RusZor, SadFre, SadSaë, SadZo1, SadZo2, VerDra.*

Works

Introductory notes

1   *RCT* numbers are taken from Sylvie Bouissou and Denis Herlin, with Pascal Denécheau, *Jean-Philippe Rameau: catalogue thématique des œuvres musicales* (2003–).

2   Works are listed in the order in which they were first performed, where known; otherwise in alphabetical order.

3   The orthography of titles in the first editions of Rameau's keyboard works and theoretical writings is respected, but accents have been added where appropriate to letters originally given in upper case. The titles of his operas and other works that survive in multiple authoritative sources follow the spelling in *RCT*.

4   Where published sources are cited, only the earliest is normally given.

5   Lost works and pieces plausibly attributed to Rameau are included, but misattributions are not. Many of the latter are, however, discussed in individual entries in the dictionary.

6   Major keys are indicated by capitals, minor keys by lower case.

Abbreviations

anon.	anonymous
attrib.	attributed to
b	*basse* (bass voice, solo)
B	*basse* (bass voice, choral)
bc	*basse continue*
bdvl	*basse de viole*
bn	bassoon
bt	*basse taille* (baritone, solo)
Bt	*basse taille* (baritone, choral)
CH-Gpu	Geneva, Bibliothèque publique et universitaire
collab.	with the collaboration of
cor	horn(s)
d	*dessus* (soprano, solo)
D	*dessus* (soprano, choral)
ed./eds	editor/editors
edn	edition
fl	flute
fol./fols	folio(s)
F-Pa	Bibliothèque Nationale de France, Paris; Bibliothèque de l'Arsenal
F-Pi	Bibliothèque de l'Institut de France, Paris
F-Pn	Bibliothèque Nationale de France, Paris
F-Po	Bibliothèque Nationale de France, Paris; Bibliothèque-Musée de l'Opéra

hc	*haute-contre* (high tenor, solo)
Hc	*haute-contre* (high tenor, choral)
I-Bc	Civico Museo Bibliografico Musicale, Bologna
instr	instruments
ms., mss.	manuscript(s)
ob	oboe
rev.	revised or revised by
S-Smf	Stiftelsen Musikkulturens Främjande, Stockholm
str	strings laid out (unless otherwise stated) in the standard French manner, with one violin part which may occasionally divide, two viola parts, and a part for *basses* (cello/*contrebasse*).
vn	violin(s)

Contents

The list of works is divided into the following sections:

1   Keyboard music

2   Motets

3   Canons

4   Airs for one or more voices

5   Cantatas

6   Incidental music for plays

7   Operas

8   Theoretical writings

1 Keyboard music

RCT	Title and content	Key	Published sources and comments
1	*Premier livre de pièces de clavecin*		1st edn, Paris: author, Roussel, Foucaut, 1706 2nd edn, Paris: C. Ballard, 1708 (lost) 3rd edn, Paris: J.-B.C. Ballard, 1741, as *Pièces de clavecin [...] œuvre premier*
	Prélude	a	
	Alemande	a	
	2.ᵉ Alemande	a	
	Courante	a	
	Gigue	a	
	1.ᵉʳᵉ Sarabande	a	
	2.ᵉ Sarabande	A	
	Vénitiénne	A	
	Gavote	a	
	Menuet	a	

RCT	Title and content	Key	Published sources and comments
2–4	*Pièces de clavessin avec une méthode pour la méchanique des doigts*		1st edn, Paris: Hochereau, Boivin, author, [1724] (date of privilege) 2nd edn, Paris: Boivin, Le Clerc, author, 1731 (as *Pièces de clavecin avec une table pour les agrémens*)
	Menuet en rondeau	C	
	Allemande	e	
	Courante	e	
	Gigue en rondeau	e	
	2.ᵉ Gigue en rondeau	E	
	Le Rappel des oiseaux	e	
	1.ʳ Rigaudon	e	
	2.ᵈ Rigaudon	E	
	Double du 2.ᵈ Rigaudon	E	
	Musette en rondeau	E	
	Tembourin	e	
	La Vilageoise, rondeau	e	
	Les Tendres plaintes, rondeau	d	
	Les Niais de Sologne	D	
	1.ᵉʳ double des Niais	D	
	2.ᵈ double des Niais	D	
	Les Soupirs	D	
	La Joyeuse, rondeau	D	
	La Follette, rondeau	D	
	L'Entretien des Muses	d	
	Les Tourbillons, rondeau	D	
	Les Cyclopes, rondeau	d	
	Le Lardon, menuet	D	
	La Boiteuse	d	

RCT	Title and content	Key	Published sources and comments
5–6	*Nouvelles suites de pièces de clavecin [...] avec des remarques sur les différens genres de musique*		Paris: author, Boivin, Le Clerc, [1729 or 1730]
	Allemande	a	
	Courante	a	
	Sarabande	A	
	Les Trois Mains	a	
	Fanfarinette	A	
	La Triomphante	A	
	Gavotte	a	
	P.ʳ double de la Gavotte	a	
	2.ᵐᵉ double	a	
	3.ᵐᵉ double	a	
	4.ᵐᵉ double	a	
	5.ᵐᵉ double	a	
	6.ᵐᵉ double	a	
	Les Tricotets, rondeau	G	
	L'Indifférente	g	
	Menuet	G	
	La Poule	g	
	2.ᵉ Menuet [to be paired with the previous menuet]	g	
	Les Triolets	G	
	Les Sauvages	g	
	L'Enharmonique	g	
	L'Egiptienne	g	
7–11	*Pièces de clavecin en concerts, avec un violon ou une flûte, et une viole ou un deuxième violon*		Paris: author, Boivin, Le Clerc, 1741
	Premier Concert		
	La Coulicam	c	
	La Livri, rondeau	c	
	Le Vézinet	C	
	La Livri [...] pour le clavecin seul	c	
	Deuxiéme Concert		
	La Laborde	G	
	La Boucon, air	g	
	L'Agaçante	G	
	Premier Menuet	G	
	2.ᵉ Menuet	g	
	L'Acaçante, clavecin seul	G	

RCT	Title and content	Key	Published sources and comments
	III.ᴱ Concert		
	La Lapoplinière	A	
	La Timide, P.ᵉʳ rondeau	a	
	2.ᵉ Rondeau	A	
	P.ᵉʳ Tambourin	A	
	2.ᵉ Tambourin en rondeau	a	
	La Timide, pour le clavecin seul	a	
	2.ᵉ rondeau, pour le clavecin seul	A	
	IV.ᴱ Concert		
	La Pantomime, loure	B♭	
	L'Indiscrette	B♭	
	La Rameau	B♭	
	L'Indiscrette, rondeau pour le clavecin seul	B♭	
	Cinquiéme Concert		
	Fugue La Forqueray	d	
	La Cupis	d	
	La Marais	D	
12	La Dauphine	g	autograph ms. in *F-Pn*, Rés. Vm⁷. 550 (1)
12ᵇⁱˢ	Les Petits Marteaux	C/c	attibuted to Rameau in ms. *F-Pn*, Vm⁷. 2108; anon. in *F-Pa*, Ms. 6820 [4]
-	*Les Indes galantes, balet, reduit à quatre grands concerts*		Paris: Boivin, Le Clerc, author [c.1736]; instrumental pieces arranged for harpsichord, as are the accompaniments of some vocal items

2 Motets

RCT	Title	Genre	Key	Scoring	Comments
13	*Deus noster refugium*	motet à grand chœur	B♭	d d hc t t b D Hc T B fl ob bn str bc	psalm 45; solo vocal line of v. 10 missing
-	*Exultet caelum laudibus*	[petit motet]		3 voices and unspecified obbligato instruments and bc	lost
14	*In convertendo*	motet à grand chœur	g	d hc bt b D Hc T Bt B fl ob cor bn str bc	psalm 125, with v. 35 of psalm 68 (possibly from a lost *Salvum me fac Deus*) between vv. 5 and 6
16	*Laboravi*	quinque (quintet)	d	d d hc t b bc	psalm 68, v. 4; probably from a lost setting of *Salvum me fac Deus*; published in *Traité de l'harmonie* (Paris: J.-B.C. Ballard, 1722)
15	*Quam dilecta*	motet à grand chœur	b	d d hc t bt b D Hc T Bt B fl bn str bc	psalm 83, vv. 1–5, 8–9 and 13
-	*Salvum me fac Deus*	motet à grand chœur			psalm 68; lost

3 Canons

RCT	Title	Genre	Key	Comments
17	*Ah! loin de rire*	four-part modulating canon at the 5th		published in Rameau, *Traité de l'harmonie* (Paris: J.-B.C. Ballard, 1722)
18	*Avec du vin, endormons-nous*	four-part modulating canon at the 4th		published in *Recueil d'airs sérieux et à boire* (Paris: J.-B.C. Ballard, November 1719) and in Rameau, *Traité de l'harmonie*
18bis	*L'Épouse entre deux draps*	three-part canon at the unison or octave	d	attributed to François Couperin, but now thought to be possibly by Rameau
18[bis(1)]	*Frère Jacques*	four-part canon at the unison	G	attributed to Rameau in ms. additions to L.-J. Francœur's *Diapason général* (*F-Pn*, Ms. 1843)
18[bis(2)]	*Grégoire est mort*	canon at the unison	G	published without attribution in La Borde, *Essai sur la musique ancienne et moderne*; attributed to Rameau in ms. additions to L.-J. Francœur's *Diapason général* (*F-Pn*, Ms. 1843)
18ter	*Je suis un fou*	three-part canon at the unison or octave	C	attributed to Rameau (see BouCan)
19	*Mes chers amis*	six-part canon at the unison or octave	G	attributed to Rameau in J.-B. de La Borde, *Essai sur la musique ancienne et moderne*, 4 vols (Paris: P.-D. Pierres and E. Onfroy, 1780)
20	*Réveillez-vous dormeur sans fin*	five-part canon at the unison or octave	C	published in Rameau, *Traité de l'harmonie*
20bis	*Si tu ne prends garde à toi*	three-part modulating canon at the 5th	F	published in La Borde, *Essai sur la musique ancienne et moderne*

4 Airs for one or more voices

RCT	Title	Key	Scoring	Comments
21[1]	*L'Amante préoccupée* ('À l'objet que j'adore')	a	d, bc	a version of the air 'Au Berger que j'adore' (*Naïs*, II, 6), with minor modifications of textual underlay
21[2]	'Lucas, pour se gausser de nous'	C	d, b, bc	first published in *Recueil d'airs sérieux et à boire* (Paris: C. Ballard, February 1707), entitled 'Air à boire, [...] Deux paysans'
21[3]	'Non, non, le dieu qui sait aimer'	a	d, bc	attributed to Rameau by Silvestre in 1763; text printed as 'Madrigal' in anon., *Le Trésor du Parnasse* (London: [n.p.], 1762), vol. 3
21[4]	'Un Bourbon ouvre sa carrière'	D	hc, 2 vn, bs, bc	described by Rameau's son Claude-François as an ariette for the birth of the duc de Bourgogne; originally intended as part of *Acante et Céphise*

5 Cantatas

RCT	Title	Key	Scoring	Comments
22	*Les Amants trahis*	g	d/[hc], b, bdvl, bc	by 1721
23	*Aquilon et Orithie*	e	b, vn/fl, bc	c.1715–19, revised version published in Rameau, *Cantates françoises à voix seule avec simphonie [...] livre premier* (Paris: author, Boivin, Le Clerc, [1729 or 1730])
24	*Le Berger fidèle*	d	d, 2 [vn], bc	by 22 Nov 1728; published in Rameau, *Cantates françoises à voix seule avec simphonie [...] livre premier*
25	*Cantate pour le jour de la Saint-Louis*	B♭	d, [vn], bc	c.1737–41; autograph ms. in *F-Pn*
26	*L'Impatience*	a	d/[hc], bdvl, bc	c.1715–22
27	*Orphée*	G	d, vn, bdvl, bc	by 1 June 1721
28	*Thétis*	D	b, vn, bc	by 1718; also attributed to [Thomas-Louis] Bourgeois
-	*Médée*			lost
-	*L'Absence*			lost

6 Incidental music for plays

RCT	Title	Genre and no. of acts	Playwright	First production	Comments
36	*L'Endriague*	*opéra comique*; 3 acts	A. Piron	Foire Saint-Germain, 8 Feb 1723	text published in *Œuvres complettes d'Alexis Piron* (Paris: M. Lambert, 1776); music lost
37	*L'Enrôlement d'Arlequin*	*opéra comique*; 1 act	A. Piron	Foire Saint-Laurent, 3 Feb 1726	text published in *Œuvres complettes d'Alexis Piron*; music lost
55	*La Robe de dissension, ou Le faux prodige*	*opéra comique*; 2 acts	A. Piron	Foire Saint-Laurent, 7 Sept 1726	text published in *Œuvres complettes d'Alexis Piron*; music lost
55bis	*Le P[ucelage], ou La rose*	*opéra comique*; 1 act	A. Piron	Completed by July 1726	text published in *Œuvres complettes d'Alexis Piron*; music lost; revised as *Le Jardin de l'Hymen, ou La rose* for Foire Saint-Laurent, 5 Mar 1744
33	*Les Courses de Tempé*	*pastorale*; 1 act	A. Piron	Comédie-Française, 30 Aug 1734	text published in *Œuvres complettes d'Alexis Piron*, with vocal line of airs from Rameau's divertissement
-	*Le Procureur dupe sans le savoir*	*opéra comique mêlé de vaudevilles*; 1 act	anon.	?	text said to have been copied from a score found in Rameau's papers; music lost

7 Operas

RCT	Title	Genre and no. of acts	Librettist	First production (at Académie Royale de Musique unless otherwise stated)	First publication and other comments
43	*Hippolyte et Aricie*	*tragédie en musique;* prologue, 5 acts	S.-J. Pellegrin	1 Oct 1733	Paris: author, Boivin, Le Clerc, [1733]
56	*Samson*	*tragédie en musique;* prologue, 5 acts	Voltaire	Unperformed	libretto published in Voltaire, *Œuvres diverses* (London: Jean Nourse, 1746); most music lost
44	*Les Indes galantes*	*ballet héroïque* [*opéra-ballet*]; prologue, 2–4 entrées: 'Le Turc généreux', 'Les Incas du Pérou', 'Les Fleurs', 'Les Sauvages'	L. Fuzelier	23 Aug 1735	original title: *Les Victoires galantes*; added entrées: 'Les Fleurs' (28 Aug 1735), 'Les Sauvages' (10 March 1736); items from prologue and first three entrées arranged and published as 'Quatre grands concerts' (Paris: Boivin, Le Clerc, author, [1736])
32	*Castor et Pollux*	*tragédie en musique;* prologue, 5 acts	P.-J. Bernard (? with others)	RCT 32a: 24 Oct 1737 RCT 32b: 11 Jan 1754	*RCT 32a:* Paris: Prault fils, veuve Boivin, Le Clerc, Duval, author, [1737] *RCT 32b:* major revision (1754) in which the prologue was replaced by a new Act I; former Acts I–V reworked as Acts II–V; published Paris: author, [1754]

RCT	Title	Genre and no. of acts	Librettist	First production	First publication and other comments
41	*Les Fêtes d'Hébé, ou Les talents lyriques*	*ballet* [*opéra-ballet*]; prologue, 3 entrées: 'La Poésie', 'La Musique', 'La Danse'	A.-C.-G. de Montdorge	21 May 1739	Paris: author, veuve Boivin, Le Clerc, [1739]
35	*Dardanus*	*tragédie en musique*; prologue, 5 acts	C.-A. Le Clerc de La Bruère (? with P.-J. Pellegrin)	*RCT* 35a: 19 Nov 1739 *RCT* 35b: 23 Apr 1744	*RCT* 35a: Paris: author, veuve Boivin, Le Clerc, Monet, [1739] *RCT* 35b: major revision (1744) in which Acts III–V have a new plot and largely new music; published as 'nouvelle tragédie', Paris: author, veuve Boivin, Le Clerc, [1744]
54	*La Princesse de Navarre*	*comédie-ballet*; 3 acts	Voltaire	Versailles, 23 Feb 1745	for the wedding of the Dauphin and Maria Teresa of Spain
53	*Platée*	*ballet bouffon* [*comédie lyrique*]; prologue, 3 acts	J. Autreau	Versailles, 31 Mar 1745	for the wedding of the Dauphin and Maria Teresa of Spain; libretto adapted by A.-J. Le Valois d'Orville; revised version, perf. Académie Royale de Musique, 9 Feb. 1749; Paris: author, veuve Boivin, Le Clerc, [1749]
39	*Les Fêtes de Polymnie*	*ballet héroïque* [*opéra-ballet*]; prologue ('Le Temple de Mémoire'), 3 entrées: 'La Fable', 'L'Histoire', 'La Féerie'	L. de Cahusac	12 Oct 1745	Paris: Mme Boivin, Le Clerc, author, [1753]; commemorates the victory of Fontenoy

RCT	Title	Genre and no. of acts	Librettist	First production	First publication and other comments
59	Le Temple de la Gloire	*fête*, 5 acts	Voltaire	Versailles, 27 Nov 1745	for the victory of Fontenoy; revised as *opéra-ballet* with prologue ('La Caverne de l'Envie') and 3 entrées ('Bélus', 'Bacchus', 'Trajan'), perf. Académie Royale de Musique, 19 April 1746
40	Les Fêtes de Ramire	*acte de ballet*	Voltaire, rev. J.J. Rousseau	Versailles, 22 Dec 1745	adapted by Rousseau from *La Princesse de Navarre*
38	Les Fêtes de l'Hymen et de l'Amour, ou Les Dieux d'Égypte	*ballet héroïque* [*opéra-ballet*]; prologue, 3 entrées: 'Osiris', 'Canope', 'Aruéris, ou Les Isies'	L. de Cahusac	Versailles, 15 Mar 1747	Paris: author, veuve Boivin, Le Clerc, [1748]; written for wedding of the Dauphin with Maria-Josepha of Saxony; revised for Académie Royale de Musique, 5 Nov 1748
60	Zaïs	*ballet héroïque* [*pastorale héroïque*]; prologue, 4 acts	L. de Cahusac	29 Feb 1748	Paris: author, veuve Boivin, Le Clerc, [1748]
52	Pigmalion	*acte de ballet*	Ballot de Sovot, after H. de La Motte	27 Aug 1748	Paris: author, veuve Boivin, Le Clerc, [1748]; libretto adapted from the entrée 'La Sculpture' in La Motte, *Le Triomphe des arts*

RCT	Title	Genre and no. of acts	Librettist	First production	First publication and other comments
58	*Les Surprises de l'Amour*	*divertissement* [*opéra-ballet*]; prologue ('Le Retour d'Astrée'), 2 entrées: 'La Lyre enchantée', 'Adonis'	P.-J. Bernard	*RCT* 58a: Versailles, 27 Nov 1748 *RCT* 58b: 31 May 1757	*RCT* 58a: prologue celebrates the Treaty of Aix-la-Chapelle *RCT* 58b: revised and restructured version of 1748 original, first performed at Académie Royale de Musique 31 May 1757; prologue omitted, 4 entrées: 'L'Enlèvement d'Adonis', 'La Lyre enchantée', 'Anacréon', 'Les Sibarites'; published Paris: Le Clerc, Bayard, Mlle Castagnery, Daumont [1757]
49	*Naïs*	'Opéra pour la Paix' [*pastorale héroïque*]; Prologue ('L'Accord des Dieux'), 3 acts	L. de Cahusac	2 Apr 1749	prologue celebrates the Treaty of Aix-la-Chapelle
62	*Zoroastre*	*tragédie en musique*; 5 acts	L de Cahusac	*RCT* 62a: 5 Dec 1749 *RCT* 62b: 20 Jan 1756	*RCT* 62a: Paris: veuve Boivin, Le Clerc, Le Castaniere, author, [1749] *RCT* 62b: major revision (1756) in which Acts II, III and V have a new plot and largely new music
42	*La Guirlande, ou Les fleurs enchantées*	*acte de ballet*	J.-F. Marmontel	21 Sep 1751	Paris: author, veuve Boivin, Le Clerc, [1751]; celebrates the birth of the duc de Bourgogne

RCT	Title	Genre and no. of acts	Librettist	First production	First publication and other comments
29	*Acante et Céphise, ou La sympathie*	*pastorale héroïque*; 3 acts	J.-F. Marmontel	19 Nov 1751	Paris: author, veuve Boivin, Le Clerc, [1751]; celebrates the birth of the duc de Bourgogne
34	*Daphnis et Églé*	*pastorale héroïque* [*acte de ballet*]	C. Collé	Fontainebleau, 29/30 Oct 1753	
57	*Les Sibarites*	*acte de ballet*	J.-F. Marmontel	Fontainebleau, 13 Nov 1753	Paris: Le Clerc, Bayard, Castagnery, Daumont, [1757]; original title: *Sibaris*; revised version incorporated into *Les Surprises de l'Amour* in 1757
48	*La Naissance d'Osiris*	*ballet allégorique* [*acte de ballet*]	L. de Cahusac	Fontainebleau, 12 Oct 1754	celebrates the birth of the duc de Berry; former title: *Les Fêtes Pammilies*; originally intended as prologue to *Les Beaux Jours de l'Amour*, a projected *opéra-ballet*
30	*Anacréon*	*ballet héroïque* [*acte de ballet*]	L. de Cahusac	Fontainebleau, 23 Oct 1754	
51	*Les Paladins*	*comédie-ballet* [*comédie lyrique*]; 3 acts	anon., possibly by D. de Monticourt or P.J. Bernard	12 Feb 1760	alternative title: *Le Vénitien*
31	*Les Boréades*	*tragédie en musique*; 5 acts	attrib. L. de Cahusac	Unperformed	alternative title: *Abaris*; rehearsed in Apr 1763 for performance at court
45	*Io*	*acte de ballet*	anon.	Unperformed	incomplete; probably written before 1745

RCT	Title	Genre and no. of acts	Librettist	First production	First publication and other comments
46	*Linus*	*tragédie en musique*; 5 acts	C.-A. Le Clerc de La Bruère	Unperformed	rehearsed in or before 1751; libretto and violin part survive in *F-Pn* but other music lost
47	*Lisis et Délie*	*acte de ballet*	J.-F. Marmontel	unperformed	intended for performance at Fontainebleau, 6 Nov 1753, but considered too similar to *Daphnis and Églé* and abandoned; lost
50	*Mirthis*	*acte de ballet*	probably L. de Cahusac	unperformed	entitled *Nélée et Mirthis* in one posthumous source; intended as one entrée in *Les Beaux Jours de l'Amour*, a projected *opéra-ballet*
61	*Zéphire*	*acte de ballet*	probably L. de Cahusac	unperformed	original title: *Les Nymphes de Diane*

8 Theoretical Writings

Title	First publication and other comments
Traité de l'harmonie réduite à ses principes naturels	Paris: J.-B.C. Ballard, 1722
'De la méchanique des doigts sur le clavessin'	in *Pièces de clavessin* (Paris: Hochereau, Boivin, author, [1724])
Nouveau système de musique théorique	Paris: J.-B.C. Ballard, 1726
'Remarques ... sur les différens genres de musique'	in *Nouvelles suites de pièces de clavecin* (Paris: author, Boivin, Le Clerc, [1729 or 1730])
'Examen de la conférence sur la musique'	*Mercure de France* (Oct 1729), pp. 2369–77
'Observations sur la méthode d'accompagnement pour le clavecin qui est en usage, et qu'on appelle échelle ou règle de l'octave'	*Mercure de France* (Feb 1730), pp. 253–63
'Plan abrégé d'une méthode nouvelle d'accompagnement pour le clavecin'	*Mercure de France* (March 1730), pp. 489–501
'Réplique du premier musicien à la réponse du second'	*Mercure de France* (June 1730), vol. 2, pp. 1337–44
'Lettre de M. à M. sur la musique'	*Mercure de France* (Sept 1731), pp. 2126–45
Dissertation sur les différentes métodes d'accompagnement pour le clavecin, ou pour l'orgue	Paris: Boivin, Le Clerc, 1732
'Lettre de M.ʳ Rameau au R.P. Castel, au sujet de quelques nouvelles réflexions sur la musique'	*Journal de Trévoux* (July 1736), vol. 2, pp. 1691–1709
Génération harmonique, ou Traité de musique théorique et pratique	Paris: Prault fils, 1737
'Remarques de M.ʳ Rameau sur l'extrait qu'on a donné de son livre intitulé "Génération harmonique" dans le Journal de Trévoux, décembre 1737'	*Le Pour et contre* 14 (Paris, 1738), no. 196, pp. 74–96; no. 197, pp. 141–3
'Mémoire où l'on expose les fondemens du Système de musique théorique et pratique de M.ʳ Rameau' [collab. D. Diderot]	1749; mss. in *F-Pi*, dossier Rameau, Archives de l'Académie des Sciences, Paris; and *F-Po*, Ms. B 24 (8) fols 119–128v
Démonstration du principe de l'harmonie [collab. D. Diderot]	Paris: Durand, Pissot, 1750
Nouvelles réflexions de M.ʳ Rameau sur sa 'Démonstration du principe de l'harmonie'	Paris: Durand, Pissot, 1752
'Lettre de M.ʳ Rameau à l'auteur du Mercure'	*Mercure de France* (May 1752), pp. 75–7
'Réflexions sur la manière de former la voix'	*Mercure de France* (Oct 1752), pp. 89–100
'Extrait d'une réponse de M.ʳ Rameau à M. Euler sur l'identité des octaves'	*Mercure de France* (Dec 1752), pp. 6–31
Observations sur notre instinct pour la musique	Paris: Prault fils, Lambert, Duchesne, 1754

Title	First publication and other comments
Erreurs sur la musique dans l'Encyclopédie	Paris: Jorry, 1755
Suite des erreurs sur la musique dans l'Encyclopédie	[Paris: n.p, 1756]
Prospectus où l'on propose au public, par voye de souscription, un 'Code de musique pratique', composé de sept méthodes [collab. F. Arnaud]	[Paris: Jorry, 1757]
Réponse de M.ʳ Rameau à MM. les éditeurs de l'Encyclopédie sur leur dernier Avertissement	Paris: Jorry, 1757
'Réflexions sur le principe sonore'	ms. c.1758–9 in *I-Bc*, 'Martini, P. Giambattista. Miscellanea', I/45
Code de musique pratique, ou Méthodes pour apprendre la musique [...] avec de nouvelles réflexions sur le principe sonore [collab. F. Arnaud]	Paris: L'Imprimerie Royale, 1760
Lettre à M. d'Alembert sur ses opinions en musique	Paris: [n.p.], 1760
'Réponse de M.ʳ Rameau à la lettre de M. d'Alembert'	*Mercure de France* (April 1761), vol. 2, pp. 127–9
'Source où, vraisemblablement, on a dû puiser la première idée des proportions'	*Mercure de France* (April 1761), vol. 2, pp. 129–33
'Origine des modes et du tempérament'	*Mercure de France* (June 1761), pp. 152–70
'Suite de la Réponse'	*Mercure de France* (July 1761), vol. 1, pp. 150–8
Origine des sciences, suivie d'une controverse sur le même sujet	Paris: Jorry, [1762]), approbation dated 31 December 1761
'Lettre de M*** à M. D**** sur un ouvrage intitulé "l'Origine des sciences"'	*Mercure de France* (April 1762), vol. 1, pp. 103–19
'Seconde lettre de M*** à M*** ou Extrait d'une controverse entre le Géomètre & l'Artiste sur "l'Origine des sciences"'	*Mercure de France* (April 1762), vol. 2, pp. 125–143
'Observations de M.ʳ Rameau sur son ouvrage intitulé, "Origine des sciences"'	*Mercure de France* (June 1762), pp.139–143
'Conclusion sur l'origine des sciences'	*Journal encyclopédique* (July 1762), 5/1, pp. 91–101
'Lettre aux Philosophes'	*Journal de Trévoux* (August 1762), pp. 2035–53
'Vérités également ignorées et interressantes tirées du sein de la nature'	ms. after Sept 1763; in *S-Smf*
'L'Art de la basse fondamentale par Rameau'	ms. (between 1737 and 1744) in *F-Pi*, d'Alembert archive, Ms. 2474; revised and published by Pietro Gianotti as *Le Guide du compositeur* (Paris: Durand, Le Clerc, 1759); a second ms., in Rameau's hand, survives among J.J. Rousseau's papers in *CH-Gpu* (ms. fr. 230)
Traité de la composition des canons en musique	Lost

Bibliography

AgaLet   Frédéric d'Agay (ed.), *Lettres d'Italie de Charles de Brosses*, 2 vols (Paris: Mercure de France, 1986).

AntFre   James R. Anthony, *French Baroque Music from Beaujoyeulx to Rameau*, rev. and expanded edn (Portland, Oregon: Amadeus Press, 1997).

AntOpe   James R. Anthony, 'The French Opera-Ballet in the Early 18th Century: Problems of Definition and Classification', *JAMS* 18 (1965), 197–206.

AquSiè   Pierre-Louis d'Aquin de Château-Lyon, *Siècle littéraire de Louis XV, ou Lettres sur les hommes célèbres* (Amsterdam and Paris: Duchesne, 1754).

ArgMém   René Louis de Voyer, marquis d'Argenson, *Journal et Mémoires du marquis d'Argenson*, 9 vols, ed. E. J. B. Rathery (Paris: Veuve J. Renouard, 1859–1867).

ArgNot   René-Louis de Voyer de Paulmy, marquis d'Argenson, 'Notices sur les Œuvres de théâtre', ed. Henri Lagrave, *SVEC* 42–3 (1966).

AutCol   Philippe Autexier, *La Colonne d'harmonie: histoire, théorie et pratique* (Paris: Détrad, 1995).

BacMém   Louis Petit de Bachaumont, *Mémoires secrets pour servir à l'histoire de la république des lettres en France* (London: John Adamson, 1780–89).

BarAct   Dene Barnett, *The Art of Gesture: The Practices and Principles of 18th-Century Acting* (Heidelberg: Winter, 1987).

BarCam   Maurice Barthélemy, *André Campra (1660–1744): étude biographique et musicologique*, rev. 2nd edn (Arles: Actes du Sud, 1995).

BarEnh   Patrizio Barbieri, *Enharmonic Instruments and Music, 1470–1900* (Bari: Il Levante, 2008).

BarMus   M. Elizabeth C. Bartlet, 'A Musician's View of the French Baroque after the Advent of Gluck: Grétry's *Les trois âges de l'opéra* and its Context', in *HajLul*, 291–318.

BarPla   M. Elizabeth C. Bartlet (ed.), *Platée* (1749 version, 1745 'compléments'), in *OOR* IV.10 (2005).

BarRam   Michel Baridon, 'Le Concept de nature dans l'esthétique de Rameau', in *GorDij*, 445–59.

BarTem   J. Murray Barbour, *Tuning and Temperament*, 2nd edn (East Lansing: Michigan State College Press, 1953).

BarThé   Clifford R. Barnes, 'Instruments and Instrumental Music at the "Théâtres de la foire" (1697–1762)', *RMFC* 5 (1965), 142–68.

BarVoc   Clifford R. Barnes, 'Vocal Music at the "Théâtres de la foire" (1697–1762)', *RMFC* 8 (1968), 141–60.

BazDid   Jean-Michel Bardez, *Diderot et la musique* (Paris: H. Champion, 1975).

BeaDan   Cyril W. Beaumont, *Three French Dancers of the 18th Century: Camargo, Sallé, Guimard* (London: Beaumont Press, 1934).

BédMan   Henri Bédarida, 'Jacques-Simon Mangot à Parme', *RdM* 14 (1925), 70–5.

BeeMau   David Beeson, *Maupertuis: An Intellectual Biography* (Oxford: Voltaire Foundation, 1992).

BenMus   Marcelle Benoit, *Musiques de cour: Chapelle, Chambre, Écurie, 1661–1733* (Paris: Picard, 1971).

BenVer   Marcelle Benoit, *Versailles et les musiciens du roi, 1661–1733: étude institutionelle et sociale* (Paris: Picard, 1971).

BerPan   Gösta M. Bergman, 'La Grande Mode des pantomimes à Paris vers 1740 et les spectacles d'optiques de Servandoni', *Theatre Research / Recherches Théâtrales* 2 (1960), 71–81.

BerPri   Jonathan W. Bernard, 'The Principle and the Elements: Rameau's Controversy with D'Alembert', *JMT* 24 (1980), 37–62.

BerPyg   Christian Berger, 'Ein "Tableau" des "Principes de l'harmonie": *Pygmalion* von Jean-Philippe Rameau', in *GorDij*, 371–84.

BesVol   Theodore Besterman (ed.), *Voltaire: Correspondence and Related Documents* (Geneva: Institut et musée Voltaire, 1968–77).

BetCah   Thomas Betzwieser, 'Cahusac und die Folgen: Überlegungen zum Aufführungscharakter von *L'Huomo* in Bayreuth 1754', in Thomas Betzwieser (ed.), *Opernkonzeptionen zwischen Berlin und Bayreuth: das musikalische Theater der Markgräfin Wilhelmine* (Würzburg: Königshausen & Neumann, 2016), 195–221.

BetCho   Thomas Betzwieser, 'Musical Setting and Scenic Movement: Chorus and *chœur dansé* in Eighteenth-Century Parisian Opera', *COJ* 12 (2000), 1–28.

BézBro   Yvonne Bézard, *Lettres du Président de Brosses à Ch.-C. Loppin de Gemeaux* (Paris: Firmin-Didot, 1929).

BigSch   Michelle Biget and Rainer Schmusch (eds), *'L'Esprit français' und die Musik Europas: Entstehung, Einfluß und Grenzen einer aesthetischen Doktrin* (Hildesheim: Olms, 2007).

BlaPer   James Blades, *Percussion Instruments and their History* (London: Faber and Faber, 1970).

BloNat   Olivia A. Bloechl, *Native American Song at the Frontiers of Early Modern Music* (Cambridge: Cambridge University Press, 2008), esp. 'Rameau's *Les Sauvages* and the Aporia of Musical Nature', 177–215.

BouAix   André Bourde (ed.), *L'Opéra au XVIIIe siècle: actes du colloque organisé à Aix-en-Provence par le Centre aixois d'études et de recherches sur le XVIIIe siècle, les 29, 30 avril et 1er mai 1977* (Aix-en-Provence: Université de Provence, 1982).

BouBor   Sylvie Bouissou, *Jean-Philippe Rameau, 'Les Boréades', ou la tragédie oubliée* (Paris: Méridiens Klincksieck, 1992).

BouCan   Sylvie Bouissou, 'Rameau's *Treatise on the Composition of Musical Canons*: New Discoveries and Attributions', *EM* 44 (2016), 553–65.

BouCri   Sylvie Bouissou, *Crimes, cataclysmes et maléfices dans l'opéra baroque en France* (Paris: Minerve, 2011).

BouDen   Sylvie Bouissou and Pascal Denécheau, 'Les Copistes de musique en France à l'époque de Rameau', in *BouSad*, 215–54.

BouHer   Sylvie Bouissou and Denis Herlin, with Pascal Denécheau, *Jean-Philippe Rameau: catalogue thématique des œuvres musicales*, 5 vols (Paris: Bibliothèque Nationale de France and CNRS Éditions, 2003–).

BouHi1   Sylvie Bouissou (ed.), *Hippolyte et Aricie* (1733 version), in *OOR* IV.1 (2002).

BouHi2   Sylvie Bouissou (ed.), *Hippolyte et Aricie* (1757 version, 1742 'compléments'), in *OOR* IV.6 (2006).

BouLiv   Sylvie Bouissou, 'Le "Livret" d'opéra baroque: une source d'information pour le geste, la danse et la composition des ballets', in *WaeGes*, 96–113.

BouNot   Sylvie Bouissou, 'Entre notation et pratique musicale: le role du clavecin dans les opéras baroques en France', in Cécile Reynaud and Herbert Schneider (eds), *Noter, annoter, éditer la musique: mélanges offerts à Catherine Massip* (Geneva: Droz, 2012), 191–211.

BouPas   Sylvie Bouissou, '"Les Boréades" de J. Ph. Rameau: un passé retrouvé', *RdM* 69 (1983), 157–85.

BouPri   Sylvie Bouissou, *Jean-Philippe Rameau, Opera Omnia: Principes éditoriaux, ou Petit traité d'édition critique* (Paris: Société Jean-Philippe Rameau, 1997).

BouRam   Sylvie Bouissou, *Jean-Philippe Rameau, musicien des Lumières* (Paris: Fayard, 2014).

BouSad   Sylvie Bouissou, Graham Sadler and Solveig Serre (eds), *Rameau, entre art et science* (Paris: École des Chartes, 2016).

BouSu1   Sylvie Bouissou (ed.), *Les Surprises de l'Amour* (1757–1758 version), vol. 1, in *OOR* IV.27/1 (1996).

BouSu2   Sylvie Bouissou (ed.), *Les Surprises de l'Amour* (1757–1758 version), vol. 2, in *OOR* IV.27/2 (2000).

BouThé   Thierry-G. Boucher, 'Rameau et les théâtres de la cour (1745–1764)', in *GorDij*, 565–77.

BoyFam   Marie-Thérèse Bouquet-Boyer, 'Rameau et l'esprit de famille', in *GorDij*, 51–9.

BoyTur   Marie-Thérèse Bouquet, *Musique et musiciens à Turin de 1648 à 1775* (Paris: Picard, 1969).

BreCla   Michel Brenet, 'Rameau, Gossec et les clarinettes', *Le Guide musical* 49 (1903), 183–5, 203–5, 227–8.

BreCon   Michel Brenet, *Les Concerts en France sous l'Ancien Régime* (Paris: Fischbacher, 1900).

BreJeu   Michel Brenet, *La Jeunesse de Rameau* (Turin: Bocca, 1902); reprinted in *Rivista musicale italiana* 9 (1902), 658–93, 860–87; 10 (1903), 62–85, 185–206.

BreLib   Michel Brenet, 'La Librairie musicale en France de 1653 à 1790', *Sammelbände der internationalen Musikgesellschaft* 8 (1906–07), 401–66.

BreNot   Michel Brenet, 'Notes et croquis sur Jean-Philippe Rameau', *Le Guide musical* 44 (1898), 383–6, 407–10, 578–82.

BriDem   Roger Lee Briscoe, *Rameau's 'Démonstration du principe de l'harmonie' and 'Nouvelles réflexions de M.ʳ Rameau sur sa démonstration du principe de l'harmonie': An Annotated Translation of Two Treatises by Jean-Philippe Rameau* (doctoral dissertation, Indiana University, 1975).

BroBou   Aymar de Brosses, 'Rameau jugé par deux Bourguignons: le Président de Brosses et Loppin de Gemeaux', in *GorDij*, 127–30.

BroCla   Jean-Patrice Brosse, *Le Clavecin des Lumières* (Paris: Bleu Nuit, 2004).

BroDic   Sébastien de Brossard, *Dictionnaire de musique* (Paris: Christophe Ballard, 1703) (and later editions).

BroSau   Howard Brofsky, 'Rameau and the Indians: The Popularity of Les Sauvages', in Allan Atlas (ed.), *Music of the Classic Period: Essays in Honor of Barry S. Brook* (New York: Pendragon Press, 1985), 43–60.

BruSol   Charles Brunet, *Table des pièces de théâtre décrites dans le catalogue de la bibliothèque de M. de Soleinne* (Paris: Damascène Morgand, 1914).

BucSty   David J. Buch, '*Style brisé, style luthé,* and the *choses luthées*', *MQ* 71 (1985), 52–67.

BucSup   David J. Buch, *Magic Flutes and Enchanted Forests: The Supernatural in Eighteenth-Century Music Theater* (Chicago: University of Chicago Press, 2008).

BurCor   Geoffrey Burgess, 'Enlightening Harmonies: Rameau's *corps sonore* and the Representation of the Divine in the *tragédie en musique*', *JAMS* 65 (2012), 383–462.

BurHip   Geoffrey Burgess, '"Le théâtre ne change qu'à la troisième scène": The Hand of the Author and Unity of Place, Act V of *Hippolyte et Aricie*', *COJ* 10 (1998), 275–87; repr. in *DilOpe*, 63–75.

BurHis   Charles Burney, *A General History of Music from the Earliest Ages to the Present Period*, 4 vols (London: Becket and others, 1776–89) (and later editions).

ButCho   Rohan Butler, *Choiseul* (Oxford: Clarendon Press, 1980), vol. 1, 'Father and Son, 1719–1754'.

CahDan   Louis de Cahusac, *La Danse ancienne et moderne, ou Traité historique de la danse* (Paris: Jean Neaulme, 1754); annotated edn by Nathalie Lecomte, Laura Naudeix and Jean-Noël Laurenti (Paris: Desjonquères: Centre national de la danse, 2004).

CamAca   Émile Campardon, *L'Académie royale de musique au XVIIIᵉ siècle:*

Documents inédits découverts aux Archives nationales, 2 vols (Paris: Berger-Levrault, 1884).

CamSpe   Émile Campardon, *Les Spectacles de la Foire* (Paris: Berger-Levrault, 1877).

CanLet   Rosy Candiani, 'Una lettera inedita di J.-Ph. Rameau a F.M. Zanotti (1752)', *Note d'archivio per la storia musicale* 5 (1987), 235–38.

CanPhi   Belinda Cannone, *Philosophies de la musique, 1752–1789* (Paris: Aux Amateurs de Livres, 1990).

CarTre   Stewart Carter, 'The String Tremolo in the 17th Century', *EM* 19 (1991), 43–59.

CazHip   Chantal Cazaux (ed.), 'Rameau: *Hippolyte et Aricie*', *L'Avant-Scène Opéra* 264 (2011).

CerMcG   Xavier Cervantes and Thomas McGeary, 'Handel, Porpora and the "Windy Bumm"', *EM* 29 (2001), 607–16.

CesCha   Catherine Cessac, *Marc-Antoine Charpentier*, rev. and enlarged edition (Paris: Fayard, 2004).

CesReb   Catherine Cessac, *Jean-Féry Rebel (1666–1747): musicien des 'Éléments'* (Paris: CNRS Éditions, 2007).

ChaÉlo   Michel Paul Guy de Chabanon, *Éloge de M.ʳ Rameau* (Paris: Michel Lambert, 1764).

ChaHib   David Charlton and Sarah Hibberd, '"My Father was a Poor Parisian Musician": A Memoir (1756) concerning Rameau, Handel's Library, and Sallé', *JRMA* 128 (2003), 161–99.

ChaMaî   David Charlton, '"A *maître d'orchestre* ... conducts": New and Old Evidence on French Practice', *EM* 21 (1993), 340–53.

ChaPol   David Charlton, 'Politics and Payments at the Paris Opéra, 1749–1757', in Marie-Alexis Colin (ed.), *Mélanges en l'honneur de Frank Dobbins* (Turnhout: Brepols, forthcoming).

ChaRou   David Charlton, *Opera in the Age of Rousseau: Music, Confrontation, Realism* (Cambridge: Cambridge University Press, 2013).

ChdNou   B. Glenn Chandler, *Rameau's 'Nouveau système de musique théorique': An Annotated Translation with Commentary* (doctoral dissertation, Indiana University, 1975).

ChiGén   Jacques Chailley, 'Pour une lecture critique du premier chapitre de la *Génération harmonique*', in *GorDij*, 279–85.

ChlCar   Laurence Chatel de Brancion, *Carmontelle au jardin des illusions* (Château de Saint-Rémy-en-l'Eau: Monelle Hayot, 2003).

ChoPré   Anne-Marie Chouillet, 'Présupposés, contours et prolongements de la polémique autour des écrits théoriques de Jean-Philippe Rameau', in *GorDij*, 425–43.

ChrBas   Thomas Christensen, 'Rameau's "L'Art de la basse fondamentale"', *Music Theory Spectrum* 9 (1987), 18–41.

ChrCor   Thomas Christensen, 'Eighteenth-Century Science and the *corps sonore*: The Scientific Background to Rameau's Principle of Harmony', *JMT* 31 (1987), 23–50.

ChrDid   Thomas Christensen, 'Diderot, Rameau and Resonating Strings: New Evidence of an Early Collaboration', *SVEC* 323 (1994), 131–52.

ChrEig   Thomas Christensen, 'Eighteenth-Century Science and the *corps sonore*: the Scientific Background to Rameau's Principle of Harmony', *Journal of Music Theory*, 31 (1987), 23–50.

ChrPub   Thomas Christensen, 'Public Music in Private Spaces: Piano-Vocal Scores and the Domestication of Opera', in Kate van Orden (ed.), *Music and the Cultures of Print* (New York: Garland, 2000), 67–94.

ChrRèg   Thomas Christensen, 'The *Règle de l'octave* in Thorough-Bass Theory and Practice', *Acta musicologica* 64 (1992), 91–117.

ChrThe   Thomas Christensen, 'A Theorist for Our Times', in *BouSad*, 329–44.

ChrTho   Thomas Christensen, *Rameau and Musical Thought in the Enlightenment* (Cambridge: Cambridge University Press, 1993).

ChsInt   Marie-Françoise Christout, 'Quelques interprètes de la danse dans l'opéra de Rameau', in *GorDij*, 533–49.

ClaCon   Jane Clark and Derek Connon, *The Mirror of Human Life: Reflections on François Couperin's 'Pièces de clavecin'*, rev. 2nd edn (London: Keyword Press, 2011).

CleAct   Paulette Cleyet-Faure, 'L'Activité musicale lyonnais au XVIIIe siècle', in *PaqAsp*, 37–52.

CNRS   Centre National de la Recherche Scientifique, a research organization overseen by the French Ministry of Higher Education and Research.

CoeThe   Barbara Coeyman, 'Theatres for Opera and Ballet during the Reigns of Louis XIV and Louis XV', *EM* 18 (1990), 22–37.

CohAca   Albert Cohen, *Music in the French Royal Academy of Sciences: a Study in the Evolution of Musical Thought* (Princeton: Princeton University Press, 1982).

CohCor   Albert Cohen, 'Rameau on Corelli: A Lesson in Harmony', in *Convention in Eighteenth- and Nineteenth-Century Music: Essays in Honor of Leonard G. Ratner*, ed. Wye Jamison Allanbrook and Janet M. Levy (Stuyvesant, NY: Pendragon Press, 1992), 431–45.

CohDis   Albert Cohen, '"La Supposition" and the Changing Concept of Dissonance in Baroque Theory', *JAMS* 24 (1971), 63–84.

CohEqu   Albert Cohen, 'Rameau, Equal Temperament, and the Academy of Lyon: A Controversy Revisited', in *CowTho*, 121–7.

CohGif   David Cohen, 'The "Gift of Nature": Musical Instinct and Musical Cognition in Rameau', in *Music Theory and Natural Order from the Renaissance to the Early Twentieth Century*, ed. Suzannah Clark and Alexander Rehding (Cambridge: Cambridge University Press, 2001), 68–92.

COJ   *Cambridge Opera Journal.*

ColJou   Charles Collé, *Journal historique, ou Mémoires critiques et littéraires sur les ouvrages dramatiques et sur les événements les plus mémorables depuis 1748 jusqu'en 1772*, 3 vols, ed. Antoine-Alexandre Barbier (Paris: Imprimerie bibliographique, 1807).

ConPir   Derek Connon, *Identity and Transformation in the Plays of Alexis Piron* (Leeds: Legenda, 2007).

CooQue   Elisabeth Cook, 'Challenging the *ancien régime*: The Hidden Politics of the "Querelle des Bouffons"', in Andrea Fabiano (ed.), *La 'Querelle des Bouffons' dans la vie culturelle française du XVIIIᵉ siècle* (Paris: CNRS Éditions, 2005), 141–60.

CotMaç   Roger Cotte, *La Musique maçonnique et ses musiciens*, rev. 2nd edn (Paris: Éditions du Borrégo, 1987).

CowOri   Georgia Cowart, *The Origins of Modern Musical Criticism: French and Italian Music, 1600–1750* (Ann Arbor: UMI Research Press, 1981).

CowTho   Georgia Cowart (ed.), *French Musical Thought, 1600–1800* (Ann Arbor: UMI Research Press, 1989).

CowWom   Georgia Cowart, 'Of Women, Sex and Folly: Opera under the Old Regime', *COJ* 6 (1994), 205–20; repr. in *DilOpe*, 165–80.

CucPou   Georges Cucuel, *La Pouplinière et la musique de chambre au XVIIIᵉ siècle* (Paris: Fischbacher, 1913).

CudFit   Charles Cudworth, 'Fitzwilliam and French Music of the Baroque', in *French Music and the Fitzwilliam* (Cambridge: Fitzwilliam Museum, 1975), 7–11.

CyrBas   Mary Cyr, '*Basses* and *Basse continue* in the Orchestra of the Paris Opéra, 1700–1764', *EM* 10 (1982), 155–70; repr. in *CyrEss*.

CyrCan   Mary Cyr, 'Towards a Chronology of Rameau's Cantatas', *MT* 124 (1983), 539–41; repr. in *CyrEss*.

CyrCho   Mary Cyr, 'The Paris Opéra Chorus during the Time of Rameau', *M&L* 76 (1995), 32–51; repr. in *DilOpe*, 341–60.

CyrChr   Mary Cyr, 'Pour une nouvelle chronologie des cantates de Jean-Philippe Rameau', in *GorDij*, 227–33.

CyrEss   Mary Cyr, *Essays on the Performance of Baroque Music: Opera and Chamber Music in France and England* (Aldershot: Ashgate, 2008).

CyrGes   Mary Cyr, 'The Dramatic Role of the Chorus in French Opera: Evidence for the Use of Gesture, 1670–1770', in Thomas Bauman and Maria Petzoldt McClymonds (eds), *Opera and the Enlightenment* (Cambridge: Cambridge University Press, 1995), 105–18; repr. in *CyrEss*.

CyrHau   Mary Cyr, 'On Performing 18th-Century Haute-Contre Roles', *MT* 118 (1977), 291–95; repr. in *CyrEss*.

CyrHéb   Mary Cyr, *Rameau's 'Les fêtes d'Hébé'* (doctoral dissertation, University of California, Berkeley, 1975).

CyrInc   Mary Cyr, '"Inclina Domine": A Marian Motet Wrongly Attributed to Rameau', *M&L* 58 (1977), 318–25; repr. in *CyrEss*.

CyrNew   Mary Cyr, 'A New Rameau Cantata', *MT* 120 (1979), 907–9; repr. in *CyrEss*.

CyrPer   Mary Cyr, 'Performing Rameau's Cantatas', *EM* 11 (1983), 480–9.

CyrSin   Mary Cyr, 'Eighteenth-Century French and Italian Singing: Rameau's Writing for the Voice', *M&L* 61 (1980), 318–37.

CyrSty   Mary Cyr, *Style and Performance for Bowed String Instruments in French Baroque Music* (Farnham: Ashgate, 2012).

CyrTra   Mary Cyr, 'Rameau e Traetta', *Nuova Rivista Musicale Italiana* 12 (1978), 166–82.

CyrVio   Mary Cyr, 'Rameau and the Viol: The Enigma of the *musette en rondeau*', *MT* 154 (2013), 43–58.

DacDar   Émile Dacier, 'L'Opéra au XVIIIe siècle: les premières représentations du *Dardanus* de Rameau (novembre–décembre 1739)', *La Revue musicale* 3 (1903), 163–73.

DaiCor   J. Alan Dainard *et al.* (eds), *Correspondance de Madame de Graffigny*, 16 vols (Oxford: Voltaire Foundation, 1985–).

DalElé   Jean Le Rond d'Alembert: *Elémens de musique théorique et pratique, suivant les principes de Mr Rameau* (Paris: David l'aîné, 1752; enlarged edn, Lyon: Jean-Marie Bruyset, 1762).

DavHer   Cécile Davy-Rigaux and Denis Herlin, with Sylvie Bouissou (eds), *Dardanus* (1739 version), in *OOR* IV.5.

DawBus   Aileen Dawson, 'A Little-known Bust of Jean-Philippe Rameau in London', *EM* 44 (2016), 515–21.

DecAmi   Jacques Joseph Marie Decroix, *L'Ami des arts, ou Justification de plusieurs grands hommes* (Amsterdam: Les Marchands de Nouveautés, 1776).

DecRam   Jacques Joseph Marie Decroix, 'Rameau', in *Biographie universelle, ancienne et moderne*, ed. Louis-Gabriel Michaud, vol. 37 (Paris: Michaud, 1824), 28–33.

DecRam   Laurence Decobert, 'Decroix et sa collection des œuvres de Rameau', in *BouSad*, 291–325.

DemCam   Marie Demeilliez, 'Campra maître de musique au collège Louis-le-Grand de la Compagnie de Jésus', in Catherine Cessac (ed.), *Itinéraires d'André Campra (1660–1744): d'Aix à Versailles, de l'Église à l'Opéra* (Wavre: Mardaga, 2012), 61–75.

DenNaï   Pascal Denécheau (ed.), *Naïs*, in *OOR* IV.18 (in preparation).

DenSer   Pascal Denécheau and Solveig Serre, 'Sauts, gambades et monnaie de singe: les représentations pour la capitation du personnel de l'Opéra sous l'Ancien Régime', *RdM* 97 (2011), 35–60.

DevLes   Anik Devriès and François Lesure, *Dictionnaire des éditeurs de musique français des origines à 1820* (Geneva: Minkoff, 1979).

DevPre   Anik Devriès-Lesure, *L'Édition musicale dans la presse parisienne au XVIIIe siècle: catalogue des annonces* (Paris: CNRS Éditions, 2005).

DicAut   *The ARTFL Project: Dictionnaires d'autrefois.* University of Chicago, Division of the Humanities: http//artfl-project.uchicago.edu/content/dictionnaires-dautrefois

DidDév   Béatrice Didier, 'Le Développement de la critique musicale au XVIIIe siècle: autour du monologue d'*Armide*', in *BouSad*, 431–46.

DidLiv   Béatrice Didier, *Le Livret d'opéra en France au XVIIIe siècle* (Oxford: SVEC, 2013).

DidLum   Béatrice Didier, *La Musique des Lumières: Diderot, l'Encyclopédie, Rousseau* (Paris: Presses Universitaires de France, 1985).

DigDém   Nancy Diguerher-Menelin, 'La *Démonstration du principe de l'harmonie* face à ses *Mémoires* (1749–1750): enjeux nouveaux d'une démonstration, entre mise en pièces et mise en scène', in *BouSad*, 381–94.

DilCre   Charles Dill, 'Creative Process in Rameau's *Castor et Pollux*', in *The Creative Process*, Studies in the History of Music, 3 (New York: Broude Brothers, 1993), 93–106.

DilIma   Charles Dill, 'Rameau's Imaginary Monsters: Knowledge, Theory, and Chromaticism in *Hippolyte et Aricie*', *JAMS* 55 (2002), 433–76.

DilInf   Charles Dill, 'The Influence of Linguistics on Rameau's Theory of Modulation', in *BouSad*, 397–408.

DilLul   Charles Dill, 'Rameau reading Lully: Meaning and System in Rameau's Recitative Tradition', *COJ* 6 (1994), 1–17.

DilMod   Charles Dill, 'Eighteenth-century Models of French Recitative', *JRMA* 120 (1995) 232–50.

DilMon   Charles Dill, *Monstrous Opera: Rameau and the Tragic Tradition* (Princeton: Princeton University Press, 1998).

DilOpe   Charles Dill (ed.), *Opera Remade, 1700–1750* (Farnham: Ashgate, 2010).

DilPel   Charles Dill, 'Pellegrin, Opera and Tragedy', *COJ* 10 (1998), 247–57.

DorCan   Jérôme Dorival, *La Cantate française au XVIIIe siècle* (Paris: Presses Universitaires de France, 1999).

DouMus   Joëlle-Elmyre Doussot, *Musique et société à Dijon au siècle des Lumières* (Paris: Honoré Champion, 1999).

DouRam   Jean-Paul Dous, *Rameau: un musicien philosophe au siècle des Lumières* (Paris: L'Harmattan, 2011).

DraBla   Benoît Dratwicki, *François Colin de Blamont (1690–1760): une carrière officielle dans les institutions musicales françaises du Grand Siècle au Siècle des Lumières* (doctoral thesis, Université Paris-Sorbonne, 2014).

DraCha   Benoît Dratwicki, 'Chanter Rameau à l'époque de Gluck (1764–1785), in *BouSad*, 157–79.

DuaInd   Alain Duault, 'Rameau: *Les Indes galantes*', *L'Avant-Scène Opéra* 46 (1982).

DubCon   Julien Dubruque, 'Contenter Trajan? Les enjeux esthétiques du remaniement du *Temple de la Gloire*', *RdM* 95 (2009), 299–318.

DubRés   Julien Dubruque, 'La Résistance de Rameau à la réforme dramatique de Voltaire dans *Le Temple de la Gloire*', in *BouSad*, 39–49.

DubTem   Julien Dubruque (ed.), *Le Temple de la Gloire*, in *OOR* IV.12.

DubVan   Julien Dubruque and Jean-Claire Vançon, 'Pour une réévaluation critique du ramisme de Debussy', in Myriam Chimènes and Alexandra Laederich (eds), *Regards sur Debussy* (Paris: Fayard, 2013), 337–56.

DucRéf   Jean-Jacques Ducharger, *Réflexions sur divers ouvrages de Mr Rameau* (Rennes: J.-C. Vatar, 1761).

DucVal   Marie-Elisabeth Duchez, 'Valeur épistémologique de la théorie de la basse fondamentale de Jean-Philippe Rameau: connaissance scientifique et représentation de la musique', *SVEC* 245 (1986), 91–130.

DufNou   Norbert Dufourcq, 'Nouvelles de la cour et de la ville (1734–1738)', *RMFC* 10 (1970), 101–6.

DurAca   Jacques-Bernard Durey de Noinville, *Histoire du théâtre de l'Opéra en France depuis l'établissement de l'Académie de musique jusqu'à présent* (Paris: J. Barbou, 1753).

DurMot   Jean Duron, 'Le Grand motet: Rameau face à ses contemporains', in *GorDij*, 331–70.

DurRel   Jean Duron (ed.), *Jean-Philippe Rameau, La musique religieuse: Laboravi clamans, Quam dilecta tabernacula, Deus noster refugium, In convertendo Dominus* (Versailles: Éditions du CMBV, 2005).

EckRam   Théophile Eck, 'Un portrait de Rameau par Maurice-Quentin De La Tour', in *OC* 16 (1911), vii–xii.

EllDij   Katharine Ellis, 'Rameau in Late Nineteenth-Century Dijon: Memorial, Festival, Fiasco', in *French Music, Culture, and National Identity, 1870–1939*, ed. Barbara L. Kelly (Rochester: University of Rochester Press, 2008), 197–214.

EllEar   Katharine Ellis, *Interpreting the Musical Past: Early Music in Nineteenth-Century France* (Oxford: Oxford University Press, 2005).

EllKey   Katharine Ellis, 'Saint-Saëns and Rameau's Keyboard Music', in Jann Pasler (ed.), *Saint-Saëns and His World* (Princeton: Princeton University Press, 2012), 266–70.

EllMar   Meredith Ellis and Carol Marsh, *La Danse noble: An Inventory of Dances and Sources* (Williamstown, MA: Broude Brothers, 1992).

EM   *Early Music.*

EmmNaï   Maurice Emmanuel and Martial Ténéo, 'Commentaire bibliographique: *Naïs*', in *OC* 18, vii–cxix.

EmmPyg   Maurice Emmanuel and Martial Ténéo, 'Commentaire bibliographique: *Pygmalion, Les Surprises de l'Amour, Anacréon, Les Sybarites*', in *OC* 17, part 1, ix–clix.

FabBou   Andrea Fabiano and Sylvie Bouissou (eds), *La Querelle des Bouffons dans la vie culturelle française du XVIIIe siècle* (Paris: CNRS, 2005).

FadInv   Don Fader, 'The Invention of the *Cantate françoise*: Patronage, Social History, and the "Goûts-réunis" in "Préramiste" France' (in preparation).

FaiSty   Edmund Fairfax, *The Styles of Eighteenth-Century Ballet* (Lanham, MD: Scarecrow Press, 2003).

FajAch   Robert Fajon (ed.), with Sylvie Bouissou, *Achante et Céphise, ou La sympathie*, in *OOR* IV.21 (1998).

FajOpé   Robert Fajon, *L'Opéra à Paris du Roi Soleil à Louis le Bien-Aimé* (Geneva: Slatkine, 1984).

FajPré   Robert Fajon, 'Le Préramisme dans le répertoire de l'Opéra', in *GorDij*, 307–29.

FauCas   Joël-Marie Fauquet (ed.), 'Rameau: *Castor et Pollux*', *L'Avant-Scène Opéra* 209 (2002).

FauPal   Joël-Marie Fauquet, 'Rameau: *Les Paladins*', *L'Avant-Scène Opéra* 219 (2004).

FavMot   Thierry Favier, *Le Motet à grand chœur: Gloria in Gallia Deo* (Paris: Fayard, 2009).

FerEvo   Joan Ferris, 'The Evolution of Rameau's Harmonic Theories', *JMT* 3 (1959), 231–56.

FosRam   Donald Foster, *Jean-Philippe Rameau: A Guide to Research* (New York: Garland, 1989).

FraDan   Brigitte François-Sappey, *Jean François Dandrieu, 1682–1738, organiste du roy: contribution à la connaissance de la musique française de clavier* (Paris: Picard, 1982).

FraOpé   Lorenzo Frassà (ed.), *The Opéra-Comique in the Eighteenth and Nineteenth Centuries* (Turnhout: Brepols, 2011).

FulAcc   David Fuller, 'Accompanied Keyboard Music', *MQ* 60 (1974), 222–45.

FulMar   David Fuller, 'Les Petits Marteaux de M.ʳ Rameau', *EM* 11 (1983), 516–17.

FulPor   David Fuller, 'Of Portraits, "Sapho" and Couperin: Titles and Characters in French Instrumental Music of the High Baroque', *M&L* 78 (1997), 149–74.

GarDia   *The Diary of David Garrick, being a Record of his Memorable Trip to Paris in 1751*, ed. Ryllis Clair Alexander (New York: Oxford University Press, 1928).

GarOrg   Jacques Gardien, *L'Orgue et les organistes en Bourgogne et en Franche-Comté au dix-huitième siècle* (Paris: Droz, 1943).

GasPau   Amadée Gastoué, 'Les Notes inédites du marquis de Paulmy sur les œuvres lyriques françaises, 1655–1775', *RdM* special series 1 (1943), 1–7.

GauJug   Jean Gaudefroy-Demombynes, *Les Jugements allemands sur la musique française au XVIIIᵉ siècle* (Paris: Librairie Orientale et Américaine, 1941).

GérEgl   Bernadette Gérard, 'La Musique dans les églises de la cité aux XVIIe et XVIIIᵉ siècles, d'après les registres paroissiaux (1611–1773)', *RMFC* 16 (1976), 153–86.

GesHom   Martin Gester, liner note to *Denoyé – Corrette d'après Vivaldi: Hommages* (Ambronay AMY014, 2007).

GétHer   Florence Gétreau and Denis Herlin, 'Portraits de clavecins et de clavecinistes au XVIIIᵉ siècle', *Musique, Images, Instruments: Revue française d'organologie et d'iconographie musicale* 3 (1998), 64–88.

GétPor   Florence Gétreau, 'The Portraits of Rameau: A Methodological Approach', *Music in Art* 36 (2011), 275–300.

GétSat   Florence Gétreau, 'Satirical Portraits and Visual Lampoons of Rameau and his Works', *EM* 44 (2016), 523–37.

GétTam   Florence Gétreau, 'Tambours-bourdons en France au XVIIIᵉ siècle', *Musique, Images, Instruments: Revue française d'organologie et d'iconographie musicale* 7 (2005), 67–85.

GiaGui   Pietro Gianotti, *Le Guide du compositeur* (Paris: Durand, 1759).

GiaHot   Tula Giannini, 'Jacques Hotteterre le Romain and his Father, Martin: A Re-examination based on Recently Found Documents', *EM* 21 (1993), 377–95.

GilRam   Kenneth Gilbert, Preface to *Jean-Philippe Rameau: Pièces de clavecin* (Paris: Heugel, 1979).

GirAut   Henri Giroux, 'Autour de Jean-Philippe Rameau', *Mémoires de l'Académie des sciences, arts et belles-lettres de Dijon* 117 (1963–65), 87–116.

GirRam   Cuthbert M. Girdlestone, *Jean-Philippe Rameau: His Life and Work*, rev. 2nd edn (New York: Dover, 1969).

GirTra   Cuthbert M. Girdlestone, *La Tragédie en musique (1673–1750) considérée comme genre littéraire* (Geneva: Droz, 1972).

GirVol   Cuthbert M. Girdlestone, 'Voltaire, Rameau et *Samson*', *RMFC* 6 (1966), 133–43.

GiuEnr   Élizabeth Giuliani, 'Jean-Philippe Rameau enregistré (1904–2014), in *BouSad*, 199–211.

GlaNob   Viscount Herbert John Gladstone *et al.*, *Noblemen and Gentlemen's Catch Club: Three Essays towards its History* (London: Cypher Press, 1996).

GorDec   Jérôme de La Gorce, 'Décors et machines à l'Opéra au temps de Rameau: inventaire (1748)', *RMFC* 21 (1983), 145–57.

GorDij   Jérôme de La Gorce (ed.), *Jean-Philippe Rameau: colloque* international organisé par la Société Rameau, Dijon 21–24 septembre 1983: actes (Paris-Geneva: Éditions Champion-Slatkine, 1987).

GorLul   Jérôme de La Gorce, *Jean-Baptiste Lully* (Paris: Fayard, 2002).

GorOpé   Jérôme de La Gorce, *L'Opéra à Paris au temps de Louis XIV: histoire d'un théâtre* (Paris: Desjonquères, 1992).

GorOrc   Jérôme de La Gorce, 'L'Orchestre de l'Opéra et son évolution de Campra à Rameau', *RdM* 70 (1990), 23–44.

GorSce   Jérôme de La Gorce, 'Scénographie des opéras de Rameau représentés à Paris du vivant du compositeur', *Rameau: le coloris instrumental* (Paris: Société des amis du Musée Instrumental du Conservatoire national supérieur de musique, 1983), 53–60. Exhibition catalogue.

GorSer   Jérôme de La Gorce, 'Un Grand Décorateur à l'Opéra au temps de Rameau: Jean-Nicolas Servandoni', in *GorDij*, 579–94.

GorSet   Jérôme de La Gorce, 'Twenty Set Models for the Paris Opéra in the Time of Rameau', *EM* 11 (1983), 429–40.

GosTre   Philip Gossett (trans.), *Treatise on Harmony: Jean-Philippe Rameau* (New York: Dover, 1971).

GouRec   Jean-Philippe Goujon, 'Les *Recueils d'airs sérieux et à boire* des Ballard (1695–1724)', *RdM* 96 (2010), 35–72.

GreAri   Robert A. Green, 'Aristophanes, Rameau and *Platée*', *COJ* 23 (2011) 1–26.

GreDou   Michael D. Greenberg, 'Perfecting the Storm: The Rise of the Double Bass in France, 1701–1815', *The Online Journal of Bass Research*, 1 (July 2003), http://www.ojbr.com/docs/OJBR-Volume-1-Number-1.pdf. Accessed July 2013.

GreGen   Thomas R. Green, 'La Genèse d'une ariette de Rameau', *Les Sources en musicologie: actes des Journées d'études de la Société française de musicologie à l'Institut de recherche et d'histoire des textes d'Orléans-La Source, 9–11 septembre 1979* (Paris: CNRS Éditions, 1981), 151–7.

GreSou   Thomas R. Green, *Early Rameau Sources: Studies in the Origins and Dating of the Operas and Other Musical Works* (doctoral dissertation, Brandeis University, 1992).

GreTra   Thomas R. Green, '"Chants d'allégresse": le travail contrapuntique de Rameau', in Marc Honegger and Christian Meyer (eds), *La Musique et la rite sacré et profane: actes du XIII congrès de la Société internationale de musicologie, Strasbourg, 29 août–3 septembre 1982* (Strasbourg: Association des publications près les Universités de Strasbourg, 1986), vol. 2, 555–78.

GreZép   Thomas R. Green, 'Les Fragments d'opéras dans la partition autographe de *Zéphyre*', in *GorDij*, 265–76.

GriMus   Jean Gribenski, Marie-Claire Mussat and Herbert Schneider (eds), *D'un opéra l'autre: Hommage à Jean Mongrédien* (Paris: Presses de l'Université de Paris-Sorbonne, 1996).

GrmCor   Friedrich Melchior Grimm, *Correspondance littéraire, 1753–1773*,

	critical edition under the direction of Ulla Kölving (Ferney-Voltaire: Centre international d'étude du XVIIIe siècle, 2006–).

GroCom   Donald J. Grout, 'The Opéra-Comique and the Théâtre-Italien from 1715 to 1762', *Miscelánea en homenaje a Monseñor Higinio Anglés* (Barcelona: Consejo Superior Investigaciones Cientificas, 1958–61), vol. 1, 369–77.

GusFul   Bruce Gustafson and David Fuller, *A Catalogue of French Harpsichord Music, 1669–1780* (Oxford: Oxford University Press, 1990).

GutPié   Stephen Gutman, '"Ces Piéces éxécutées sur le Claveçin seul ne laissent rien à désirer": Reflections on Playing Rameau's *Pièces de clavecin en concerts* on Solo Keyboard', *EM* 44 (2016), 567–78.

HajGil   John Hajdu (ed.), *Jean Gilles, Requiem (Messe des morts)* (Madison: AR Editions, 1984).

HajLul   John Hajdu Heyer (ed.), *Jean-Baptiste Lully and the Music of the French Baroque: Essays in Honor of James R. Anthony* (Cambridge: Cambridge University Press, 1989).

HamMem   John Hammond, *The Music for Rameau's Memorial Services: A Study and Critical Edition of the 'Messe de Morts' by Jean Gilles as Performed in 1764* (doctoral dissertation, University of Hull, 2010).

HarBal   Rebecca Harris-Warrick, 'Ballet, Pantomime, and the Sung Word in the Operas of Rameau', in Cliff Eisen (ed.), *Coll' astuzia, col giudizio: Essays in Honor of Neal Zaslaw* (Ann Arbor: Steglein Publishing, 2009), 31–61.

HarCom   Rebecca Harris-Warrick, 'Comment terminer un opéra?', in *BouSad*, 87–101.

HarPro   Rebecca Harris-Warrick, 'Le Prologue de Lully à Rameau', in *NoiSer*, 199–212.

HarTou   Rebecca Harris-Warrick, '"Toute danse doit exprimer, peindre...": Finding the Drama in the Operatic Divertissement', *Basler Jahrbuch für Musikpraxis* 23 (1999), 297–316.

HayGen   Deborah Hayes, *Rameau's Theory of Harmonic Generation: An Annotated Translation and Commentary of 'Génération harmonique' by Jean-Philippe Rameau* (doctoral dissertation, Stanford University, 1968).

HayNou   Deborah Hayes, 'Rameau's "Nouvelle Méthode"', *JAMS* 27 (1974), 61–91.

HayPit   Bruce Haynes, *A History of Performing Pitch: The Story of 'A'* (Lanham, MD: The Scarecrow Press, 2002).

HeaCon   Daniel Heartz, 'The Concert Spirituel in the Tuileries Palace', *EM* 21 (1993), 240–8.

HeaEur   Daniel Heartz, *Music in European Capitals: The Galant Style* (New York: W.W. Norton, 1981).

HefRhy   Stephen E. Hefling, *Rhythmic Alteration in Seventeenth- and*

Eighteenth-Century Music: 'Notes Inégales' and Overdotting (New York: Schirmer, 1993).

HenAri   David Hennebelle, *De Lully à Mozart: aristocratie, musique et musiciens à Paris (XVIIe–XVIIIe siècles)* (Paris: Champ Vallon, 2009).

HénIdé   Charles Hénin, 'De "L'Idée des concerts de province", d'après le manuscrit de Ducharger, jusqu'à l'invitation de Léopold Mozart à Dijon en 1766 par Louis-Joseph de Condé, gouverneur de Bourgogne', in Francis Claudon (ed.), *Itinéraires mozartiens en Bourgogne* (Paris: Klincksieck, 1992), 85–100.

HerCas   Denis Herlin, 'Une Source méconnue de *Castor et Pollux*', in *BouSad*, 255–70.

HerMor   Denis Herlin and Davitt Moroney (eds), *Pièces de clavecin en concerts*, in *OOR* I.2 (1996).

HerMot   Bénédicte Hertz, *Le Grand Motet dans les pratiques musicales lyonnaises (1713–1773): étude des partitions et du matériel conservés à la bibliothèque municipale de Lyon* (doctoral dissertation, Université Lumière-Lyon 2, 2010).

HeySer   Christel Heybrock, *Jean Nicolas Servandoni (1695–1766). Eine Untersuchung seiner Pariser Bühnenwerke* (Cologne: Author, 1970).

HilDan   Wendy Hilton, *Dance of Court & Theatre: The French Noble Style, 1690–1725* (Princeton: Princeton Book Company, 1981).

HolBac   Douglas Hollick, 'J. S. Bach and Left-hand–Right-hand Distribution', *EM* 23 (1995), 365–6.

HorGem   Clare Hornsby, 'Geminiani's Artistic Collaborator in Paris, Giovanni Niccolò Servandoni', in Christopher Hogwood (ed.), *Geminiani Studies* (Bologna: Ut Orpheus Edizioni, 2013), 89–111.

HowNeo   William Driver Howarth, *French Theatre in the Neo-Classical Era* (Cambridge: Cambridge University Press, 1997).

HyeBef   Brian Hyer, 'Before Rameau and After', *Music Analysis* 15 (1996), 75–100.

HyeSig   Brian Hyer, '"Sighing Branches": Prosopopoeia in Rameau's *Pigmalion*', *Music Analysis* 13 (1994), 7–50.

IshDal   Robert M. Isherwood, 'The Conciliatory Partisan of Musical Liberty: Jean Le Rond d'Alembert, 1717–1783', in *CowTho*, 95–119.

IshQue   Robert M. Isherwood, 'Nationalism and the *Querelle des Bouffons*', in *GriMus*, 323–30.

JacBib   Paul L. Jacob (ed.), *Bibliothèque dramatique de Monsieur de Soleinne*, 6 vols (Paris: Alliance des Arts, 1843–45).

JacEnl   Margaret Jacob, *Living the Enlightenment: Freemasonry and Politics in Eighteenth-Century Europe* (Oxford: Oxford University Press, 2001).

JacMar   Erwin R. Jacobi, 'Rameau and padre Martini: New Letters and Documents', *MQ* 1 (1964), 452–75.

JacNou   Erwin R. Jacobi, 'Nouvelles lettres inédites de Jean-Philippe Rameau', *RMFC* 3 (1963), 145–58.

JacPiè   Erwin R. Jacobi (ed.), *Jean-Philippe Rameau: Pièces de clavecin* (revised 3rd edition, Kassel: Bärenreiter, 1966).

JacVér   Erwin R. Jacobi, '"Vérités intéressantes": le dernier manuscrit de Jean-Philippe Rameau', *RdM* l (1964), 76–109.

JacVol   François Jacob (ed.), *Voltaire à l'Opéra* (Paris: Classiques Garnier, 2011).

JAMS   *Journal of the American Musicological Society.*

JMT   *Journal of Music Theory.*

JonLiv   Colin Jones, Juliet Carey and Emily Richardson (eds), *The Saint-Aubin 'Livre de caricatures': Drawing Satire in Eighteenth-Century Paris* (Oxford: Voltaire Foundation, 2012).

JouBér   Sophie Jouve-Ganbert, 'Bérard et l'art du chant en France au XVIIIe siècle', *RMFC* 29 (1996–98), 103–62.

JRMA   *Journal of the Royal Musical Association.*

KaePom   Winston Haverland Kaehler, *The Operatic Repertoire of Madame de Pompadour's Théâtre des Petits Cabinets (1747–1753)* (doctoral dissertation, University of Michigan, 1971).

KafEnc   Frank A. Kafker in collaboration with Serena L. Kafker, *The Encyclopedists as Individuals: A Biographical Dictionary of the Encyclopédie*, *SVEC* 257 (1988).

KasVer   Leon Kastner, *A History of French Versification* (Oxford: Clarendon Press, 1903).

KauVio   Deborah Kauffman, '*Violons en basse* as Musical Allegory', *The Journal of Musicology* 23 (2006), 153–85.

KidSon   Ronald R. Kidd, 'The Emergence of Chamber Music with Obligato Keyboard in England', *Acta musicologica* 44 (1972), 122–44.

KinPoé   Catherine Kintzler, *Poétique de l'opéra français de Corneille à Rousseau* (Paris: Minerve, 1991).

KinRam   Catherine Kintzler, *Jean-Philippe Rameau: splendeur et naufrage de l'esthétique du plaisir à l'âge classique* (Paris: Le Sycomore, 1983; rev. and enlarged edition, Minerve, 1988).

KinVol   Catherine Kintzler, 'Rameau et Voltaire: les enjeux théoriques d'une collaboration orageuse', *RdM* 67 (1981), 139–68.

KneRou   Claude Knepper and Isabelle Rouard, 'Les "Leçons de musique" du Fonds Rousseau de la Bibliothèque de Genève, manuscrit autographe du traité de composition inédit de J.-Ph. Rameau: "L'Art de la basse fondamentale"', *Annales de la Société Jean-Jacques Rousseau* 51 (2013), 117–71.

KocDap   Érik Kocevar (ed.), *Daphnis et Églé*, in *OOR IV.22*.

KocOrg   Érik Kocevar, 'L'Orgue du Collège Louis-le-Grand au XVIIe siècle à la lumière d'un marché d'orgues inédit', *RMFC* 31 (2004–07), 165–80.

KocRel   Érik Kocevar, 'Les Relations sociales des Rameau à la lumière des archives judiciaires de la ville de Dijon', in *BouSad*, 105–116.

KocSer   Érik Kocevar, 'Les Servitudes des organistes de l'église de Notre-Dame de Dijon au XVIIIe siècle', *L'Orgue* 252 (1999), 3–84.

KocWil   Érik Kocevar, 'New Light on Jean-Philippe Rameau's Biography revealed by Revisions to his Father's Will', *EM* 44 (2016), 539–51.

LabEss   Jean-Benjamin de La Borde, *Essai sur la musique ancienne et moderne*, 4 vols (Paris: Philippe-Denis Pierres and Eugène Onfroy, 1780).

LagThé   Henri Lagrave, *Le Théâtre et le public à Paris de 1672 à 1750* (Paris: Klincksieck, 1972).

LajBib   Théodore de Lajarte, *Bibliothèque musicale du théâtre de l'Opéra: catalogue historique, chronologique, anecdoctique*, 2 vols (Paris: Librairie des bibliophiles, 1878).

LalDar   Nicole Lallement, 'Iconography of Rameau's Operas: The *Dardanus* Example', *Music in Art: International Journal for Music Iconography* 34 (2009), 165–75.

LanBel   Francine Lancelot, *La Belle Danse: catalogue raisonné* (Paris: Van Dieren, 1996).

LauCla   Lionel de La Laurencie, 'Rameau et les clarinettes', *Mercure musical S.I.M.* 9 (1913), 27–8.

LauDoc   Lionel de La Laurencie, *Quelques documents sur Jean-Philippe Rameau et sa famille* (Paris: L.-M. Fortin, 1907); repr. in *Le Mercure musical et Bulletin français de la SIM* 3 (1907), 541–614.

LauÉco   Lionel de La Laurencie, *L'École française du violon de Lulli à Viotti* (Paris: Delagrave, 1922–24).

LauGen   Lionel de La Laurencie, 'Rameau, son gendre et ses descendants', *SIM Revue musicale mensuelle* 7 (1911), 12–23.

LauLet   Lionel de La Laurencie, 'Lettres d'Eurydice à Orphée', *RdM* 11 (1930), 38–41.

LauRam   Lionel de La Laurencie, *Rameau: biographie critique* (Paris: Laurens, 1908).

LauSai   Lionel de La Laurencie, 'La Grande Saison italienne de 1752: les Bouffons', *Revue musicale SIM* 8 (1912), no. 6, 18–33; no. 7, 13–22.

LauTel   Lionel de La Laurencie, 'G.-Ph. Telemann à Paris', *RdM* 13 (1932), 75–85.

LauVal   Jean-Noël Laurenti, *Valeurs morales et religieuses sur la scène de l'Académie Royale de Musique (1669–1737)* (Geneva: Droz, 2002).

LawGes   Hedy Law, '"Tout, dans ses charmes, est dangereux": Music, Gesture, and the Dangers of French Pantomime (1748–1775)', *COJ* 20 (2008) 241–68.

LayQue   Denise Launay (ed.), *La Querelle des Bouffons* (Geneva: Minkoff, 1983), facsimile of 61 pamphlets published 1752–54.

LebDec   Élisabeth Lebeau, 'J.J.M. Decroix et sa collection Rameau', in *MélMas* 2, 81–91.

LebFon   Élisabeth Lebeau, 'Un Fonds provenant du Concert Spirituel à la Bibliothèque nationale', *RdM* 37 (1955), 187–91, and 38 (1956), 54–61.

LecDeh   Nathalie Lecomte, 'Jean-Baptiste François Dehesse, chorégraphe à la Comédie-Italienne et au Théâtre des Petits Appartements de Madame de Pompadour', *RMFC* 24 (1986), 142–91.

LecDiv   Nathalie Lecomte, 'Les Divertissements exotiques dans les opéras de Rameau', in *GorDij*, 551–63.

LegPar   Raphaëlle Legrand, 'Rameau parodié dans les opéras comiques: la notion d'auteur au risque du vaudeville', in Lorenzo Frassà (ed.), *The Opéra-Comique in the Eighteenth and Nineteenth Centuries* (Turnhout: Brepols, 2011), 205–19.

LegPla   Raphaëlle Legrand *et al.*, 'Platée', *L'Avant-Scène Opéra* 189 (1999).

LegPou   Raphaëlle Legrand, *Rameau et le pouvoir de l'harmonie* (Paris: Cité de la musique, 2007).

LegThé   Raphaëlle Legrand, 'La Théorie de Rameau: un outil d'analyse?', in *BouSad*, 447–64.

LegVau   Raphaëlle Legrand, 'Rameau des villes et Rameau des champs: itinéraires de quelques mélodies ramistes de la bergerie au vaudeville', *Musurgia* 9 (2002), 7–18.

LegVoi   Raphaëlle Legrand, 'Les Voies de l'intertextualité dans *Dardanus*, parodie de Favart, Panard et Parmentier', in Herbert Schneider (ed.), *Timbre und Vaudeville: Zur Geschichte und Problematik einer populären Gattung im 17. und 18. Jahrhundert. Bericht über den Kongreß in Bad Homburg 1996* (Hildesheim: Olms, 1999), 205–25.

LeiRou   Jean-Jacques Rousseau, *Correspondance complète de Jean-Jacques Rousseau*, vol. 2, 1744–1754, ed. Ralph A. Leigh (Geneva: Institut et musée Voltaire, 1965), 'Rousseau et Rameau', 338–42.

LemHip   Edmond Lemaître, '*Hippolyte et Aricie*: la "haute-contre de violon" dans les parties séparées du fonds La Salle', *GorDij*, 235–43.

LemMen   Pauline Lemaigre-Gaffier, 'Les Menus-Plaisirs, gestionnaires de la vie théâtrale des Lumières entre cour et ville au XVIIIe siècle', in Sabine Chaouche and Roxane Martin (eds), *European Drama and Performance Studies. Le Développement du 'grand spectacle' en France: politiques, gestion, innovations (1715–1864)* (Paris: Classiques Garnier, 2013), 49–75.

LesCon   Philippe Lescat, 'Conclusion sur l'origine des sciences', in *GorDij*, 409–24.

LesOpé   François Lesure, *L'Opéra classique français, XVIIe et XVIIIe siècles* (Geneva: Minkoff, 1972).

LesRam   Joel Lester, 'Rameau and Eightenth-Century Harmonic Theory', in Thomas Christenson (ed.), *The Cambridge History of Western Music Theory* (Cambridge: Cambridge University Press, 2002), 753–77.

LesThe   Joel Lester, *Compositional Theory in the Eighteenth Century* (Cambridge: Harvard University Press, 1992).

LetCam   Gabriel Letainturier-Fradin, *La Camargo, 1710–1770* (Paris, Flammarion, 1908).

LevCav   Brigitte Level, *À travers deux siècles, 1726–1939: le Caveau, société bachique et chantante* (Paris: Presses de l'Université de Paris-Sorbonne, 1988).

LewTra   David Lewin, 'Two Interesting Passages in Rameau's "Traité de l'harmonie"', *In Theory Only*, 4 (1978), 3–11.

LibPor   Laurence Libin, 'A Rediscovered Portrayal of Rameau and *Castor et Pollux*', *EM* 11 (1983), 510–13.

LinAri   Lowell Lindgren, 'Ariosti's London Years, 1716–29', *M&L* 62 (1981) 331–51.

LinPat   Lowell Lindgren, 'Parisian Patronage of Performers from the Royal Academy of Music (1719–28)', *M&L* 58 (1977) 4–28.

LocVar   Nicholas Lockey, 'Formal structure in Vivaldi's Variation Sets', in Michael Talbot (ed.), *Vivaldi* (Farnham: Ashgate, 2010), 364–86.

M&L   *Music & Letters*.

MacÉga   Armand Machabey, 'Jean-Philippe Rameau et le tempérament égal ("Nouveau système de musique théorique", 1726)', *RM* 260 (1965), 113–32.

MacMon   Roberte Machard, *Jean-Joseph Cassanéa de Mondonville: virtuose, compositeur et chef d'orchestre* (Beziers: Centre International de Documentation Occitane, 1980).

MacMus   Roberte Machard, 'Les Musiciens en France au temps de Jean-Philippe Rameau d'après les actes du secrétariat de la Maison du Roi', *RMFC* 11 (1971), 5–177.

MagNev   André Magnan, *Rameau le Neveu: textes et documents* (Paris: CNRS Éditions, 1993).

MalCan   Charles Malherbe, 'Commentaire bibliographique: *Cantates*', in *OC* 3, ix–xxxi.

MalCas   Charles Malherbe, 'Commentaire bibliographique: *Castor et Pollux*', in *OC* 8, xv–cxix.

MalCon   Charles Malherbe, 'Commentaire bibliographique: *Pièces de clavecin en concerts, Six concerts en sextuor*', in *OC* 2, xvii–xxxv.

MalDar   Charles Malherbe, 'Commentaire bibliographique: *Dardanus*', in *OC* 10, xv–cxl.

MalHéb   Charles Malherbe, 'Commentaire bibliographique: *Les Fêtes d'Hébé*', in *OC* 9, ix–lxxx.

MalHip   Charles Malherbe, 'Commentaire bibliographique: *Hippolyte et Aricie*', in *OC* 6, iii–lxxxix.

MalHym   Charles Malherbe, 'Commentaire bibliographique: *Les Fêtes de l'Hymen et de l'Amour*', in *OC* 15, vii–cx.

MalInd   Charles Malherbe, 'Commentaire bibliographique: *Les Indes galantes*', in *OC* 7, ix–cviii.

MalMot   Charles Malherbe, 'Commentaire bibliographique: *Motets*', in *OC* 4, iii–xxxvii, and 5, ix–xix.

MalPiè   Charles Malherbe, 'Commentaire bibliographique: *Pièces de clavecin*, in *OC* 1, xxix–xxxix.

MalPla   Charles Malherbe, 'Commentaire bibliographique: *Platée*', in *OC* 12, vii–lix.

MalPol   Charles Malherbe, 'Commentaire bibliographique: *Les Fêtes de Polymnie*', in *OC* 13, vii–lxxii.

MalPri   Charles Malherbe, 'Commentaire bibliographique: *La Princesse de Navarre, Les Fêtes de Ramire, Nélée et Myrthis, Zéphyre*', in *OC* 11, vii–lxxiv.

MalTem   Charles Malherbe, 'Commentaire bibliographique: *Le Temple de la Gloire*', in *OC* 14, xiii–xciv.

MalZaï   Charles Malherbe, 'Commentaire bibliographique: *Zaïs*', in *OC* 16, xiii–cxlii.

ManZor   Jean Malignon, 'Zoroastre et Sarastro', *RMFC* 6 (1966), 145–58.

MapEar   Catherine Massip, 'Berlioz and Early Music', in Peter Bloom (ed.), *Berlioz: Past, Present, Future* (Rochester, NY: University of Rochester Press, 2003), 19–33.

MapRam   Catherine Massip, 'Rameau et l'édition de ses œuvres: bref aperçu historique et méthodologique', in *GorDij*, 145–57.

MarAuv   Christiane Marandet, 'Notes pour servir à l'histoire des orgues et des organistes en Auvergne', *Bulletin historique de l'Auvergne* 85 (1971), 81–108.

MarÉlo   Hugues Maret, *Éloge historique de M.ʳ Rameau* (Dijon: Causse, Delalain, 1766).

MarHis   Friedrich Wilhelm Marpurg, *Historisch-kritische Beyträge zur Aufnahme der Musik*, 5 vols (Berlin: J. J. Schützens sel. Wittwe, and G. A. Lang, 1754–78).

MarRam   Friedrich Wilhelm Marpurg, 'Hr. Johann Baptist Rameau', *Historisch-kritische Beyträge zur Aufnahme der Musik* (Berlin: J. J. Schützens sel. Wittwe, 1754), 1, 454–8.

MarVer   Friedrich Wilhelm Marpurg, *Versuch über die musikalische Temperatur, nebst einem Anhang über den Rameau- und Kirnbergerschen Grundbass und vier Tabellen* (Breslau: Johann Friedrich Korn, 1776).

MarVie   Nathan John Martin, 'Rameau's Changing Views on Supposition', *JMT* 56 (2012), 121–67.

MasBac   Paul-Marie Masson, 'Deux chansons bachiques de Rameau', *SIM Revue musicale mensuelle* 6 (1910), 298–308.

MasBal   Paul-Marie Masson, 'Le Ballet héroïque', *RM* 9 (1928), 1–33.

MasLet   Paul-Marie Masson, 'Une Lettre inédite de Rameau', in *Mélanges de musicologie offerts à M. Lionel de La Laurencie* (Paris: Droz, 1933), 201–7.

MasLul   Paul-Marie Masson, 'Lullistes et Ramistes, 1733–1752', *Année musicale* I (1911), 187–211.

MasOpé   Paul-Marie Masson, *L'Opéra de Rameau* (Paris: Laurens, 1930).

MasPol   Paul-Marie Masson, 'Une Polémique musicale de Claude Rameau en faveur de son frère (1752)', *RdM* 18 (1937), 39–47.

McCDan   Sarah McCleave (ed.), *Dance & Music in French Baroque Theatre: Sources & Interpretations* (London: Institute of Advanced Musical Studies, 1998).

McCEng   Sarah McCleave, 'English and French Theatrical Sources: The Repertoire of Marie Sallé', in *McCDan*, 13–32.

McCSal   Sarah McCleave, 'Marie Sallé and the Development of the Ballet in Action', in *WaeGes*, 175–195.

McGSpa   Nicholas McGegan and Gina Spagnoli, 'Singing Style at the Opéra in the Rameau Period', in *GorDij*, 209–26.

MélMas   *Mélanges d'histoire et d'esthétique musicales offerts à Paul-Marie Masson*, 2 vols (Paris: Richard-Masse, 1955).

MelPar   Flora Mele, 'Les Parodies de Favart: entre la Foire et L'Académie royale de musique', in *BouSad*, 69–85.

MerÉlo   'Essai d'Eloge historique de feu M.ʳ Rameau', *Mercure de France* I (October 1764), 182–99.

MerTab   Louis-Sébastien Mercier, *Le Tableau de Paris*, 2 vols, ed. Jean-Claude Bonnet (Paris: Mercure de France, 1994).

MilGor   Sylvette Milliot and Jérôme de La Gorce, *Marin Marais* (Paris: Fayard, 1991).

MilOrc   Sylvette Milliot, 'Rameau et l'orchestre de l'Académie royale de musique d'après le exemplaires des répétitions de ses opéras', in *GorDij*, 201–8.

MilRoy   Leta E. Miller, 'Rameau and the Royal Society of London: "New" Letters and Documents', *M&L* 66 (1985), 19–33.

MonBou   Jean-Paul C. Montagnier and Sylvie Bouissou (eds), *Cantates, Canons, Airs*, in *OOR* III.1 (2008).

MonDis   Jean-Paul Montagnier, 'Heavenly Dissonances: The Cadential Six-Four Chord in French *grands motets* and Rameau's Theory of the "accord par supposition"', *JMT* 47 (2003), 305–23.

MooAug   Charles Jay Moomaw, *Augmented Mediant Chords in French Baroque Music* (doctoral dissertation, University of Cincinnati, 1985).

MorHip   Jacques Morel, '"Hippolyte et Aricie" de Rameau et Pellegrin dans l'histoire du mythe de Phèdre', in *GorDij*, 89–99.

MorPed   Marie-Germaine Moreau, 'Jean-Philippe Rameau et la pédagogie', *RM* 260 (1965), 47–64.

MorUnm   Davitt Moroney, 'The Performance of Unmeasured Harpsichord Preludes', *EM* 4 (1976), 143–58.

MouPoè   François Moureau, 'Les Poètes de Rameau', in *GorDij*, 61–73.

MouRép   François Moureau (ed.), *Répertoire des nouvelles à la main: dictionnaire de la presse manuscrite clandestine, XVIe–XVIIIe siècle* (Oxford: Voltaire Foundation, 1999).

MQ   *The Musical Quarterly.*

MT   *The Musical Times.*

NauDra   Laura Naudeix, *Dramaturgie de la tragédie en musique (1673–1764)* (Paris: H. Champion, 2004).

NemSej   Joachim Christophe Nemeitz, *Séjour de Paris* (Leiden: Jean van Abcoude, 1727).

NeuOrn   Frederick Neumann, *Ornamentation in Baroque and Post-Baroque Music, with Special Emphasis on J.S. Bach* (Princeton: Princeton University Press, 1978).

NeuPer   Frederick Neumann, *Performance Practices of the Seventeenth and Eighteenth Centuries* (New York: Schirmer Books, 1993).

NoiHip   Michel Noiray, 'Hippolyte et Castor travestis: Rameau à l'Opéra-Comique', in *GorDij*, 109–25.

NoiSer   Michel Noiray and Solveig Serre (eds) *Le Répertoire de l'Opéra de Paris (1671–2009): analyse et interprétation* (Paris: École des Chartes, 2010).

NorPhe   Buford Norman, 'Remaking a Cultural Icon: *Phèdre* and the Operatic Stage', *COJ* 10 (1998), 225–45.

NovLet   Jean Georges Noverre, *Lettres sur la danse, et sur les ballets* (Lyon: Aimé de La Roche, 1760); translated by Cyril W. Beaumont as *Letters on Dancing and Ballets, by Jean Georges Noverre* (London: C.W. Beaumont, 1930).

OC   Jean-Philippe Rameau, *Œuvres complètes* (Paris: Durand, 1895–1924), 18 vols: vol. 1, *Pièces de clavecin* (ed. Camille Saint-Saëns, 1895); vol. 2, *Musique instrumentale; pièces de clavecin en concerts; six concerts en sextuor* (ed. Camille Saint-Saëns, 1896); vol. 3, *Cantates* (ed. Camille Saint-Saëns, 1897); vol. 4, *Motets*, part 1 (ed. Camille Saint-Saëns, 1898); vol. 5, *Motets*, part 2 (ed. Camille Saint-Saëns, 1899); vol. 6, *Hippolyte et Aricie* (ed. Vincent d'Indy, 1900); vol. 7, *Les Indes galantes* (ed. Paul Dukas, 1902); vol. 8, *Castor et Pollux* (ed. Auguste Chapuis, 1903); vol. 9, *Les Fêtes d'Hébé* (ed. Alexandre Guilmant, 1904); vol 10, *Dardanus* (ed. Vincent d'Indy, 1905); vol. 11, *La Princesse de Navarre, Les Fêtes de Ramire, Nélée et Myrthis, Zéphyre* (ed. Paul Dukas, 1906); vol. 12, *Platée* (ed. Georges Marty, 1907); vol. 13, *Les Fêtes de Polymnie* (ed. Claude Debussy, 1908); vol. 14, *Le Temple de la Gloire* (ed. Alexandre Guilmant, 1909); vol. 15, *Les Fêtes de l'Hymen et de l'Amour* (ed. Reynaldo Hahn, 1910); vol. 16, *Zaïs* (ed. Vincent d'Indy, 1911); vol. 17, part 1, *Pygmalion, Les Surprises de l'Amour;* part 2, *Anacréon, Les Sybarites* (ed. Henri Büsser, 1913); vol. 18, *Naïs* (ed. Reynaldo Hahn, 1924).

OliEnc   Alfred Oliver, *The Encyclopedists as Critics of Music* (New York: Columbia University Press, 1947).

OOR *Jean-Philippe Rameau: Opera Omnia* (Paris: Billaudot, 1993–2002; Kassel: Bärenreiter/Société Jean-Philippe Rameau, 2003–).

OpdPig Olivier Opdebeeck, 'Pigmalion de Rameau: étude des sources et propositions pour une édition', *GorDij*, 245–64.

PalBar Claude V. Palisca, '"Baroque" as a Music-Critical Term', in *CowTho*, 7–21.

PalRam Charles Palissot de Montenoy, 'Rameau', *Le Nécrologe des hommes célèbres de France*, 1 (Paris: Imprimerie de Moreau, 1767).

PapDid John N. Pappas, 'Dans les "registres" de l'ancien régime: des réponses officielles à Rameau, Diderot et Voltaire', *XVIIIe siècle* 7 (1975), 21–5.

PaqAsp Daniel Paquette (ed.), *Aspects de la musique baroque et classique à Lyon et en France* (Lyon: Université de Lyon, 1989).

PaqRam Daniel Paquette, *Jean-Philippe Rameau: musicien bourguignon* (Saint-Seine-l'Abbaye: Éditions de Saint-Seine-l'Abbaye, 1984).

ParFal Andrew Parrott, 'Falsetto and the French: "une toute autre marche"', *Basler Jahrbuch für historisches Musikpraxis* 26 (2002), 129–48.

PaulInd Charles B. Paul, 'Rameau, d'Indy and French Nationalism', *MQ* 58 (1972), 46–56.

PazBor Michel Pazdro (ed.), 'Rameau: *Les Boréades*', *L'Avant-Scène Opéra* 203 (2001).

PetFau Françoise Petit, 'Jean-Philippe Rameau et l'art de la fauconnerie', *RMFC* 16 (1976), 7–8.

PieCon Constant Pierre, *Histoire du Concert Spirituel 1725–1790* (Paris: Société française de musicologie, Heugel et Cie, 1975).

PirŒu Alexis Piron, *Œuvres complètes*, ed. Rigoley de Juvigny (Paris: Michel Lambert, 1776), 9 vols.

PitDar Spire Pitou, 'Rameau's "Dardanus" at Fontainebleau in 1763', *SVEC* 116 (1973) 281–305.

PorFoi Bertrand Porot, 'Rameau et les théâtres de la Foire: nouvelles perspectives', in *BouSad*, 51–67.

PorNov Bertrand Porot, 'Noverre à l'Opéra-Comique: nouvelles perspectives et nouvelles découvertes (1743–1755)', *Colloque international Jean-Georges Noverre (1727–1810)*, *Musicorum* 10 (2011), 39–64.

PorPre Bertrand Porot, *Le Premier Opéra-comique (1697–1757): histoire institutionnelle et artistique* (Éditions Vrin, in preparation).

PouJél Arthur Pougin, *Un Ténor de l'Opéra au XVIIIe siècle: Pierre Jélyotte et les chanteurs de son temps* (Paris: Fischbacher, 1905).

PowPas David M. Powers, 'The *Pastorale héroique*: Problems of Definition and Classification', *RMFC* 29 (1996–98), 53–66.

PraGil Michel Prada, *Un Maître de musique en Provence & en Languedoc, Jean Gilles (1668–1705): l'homme et l'œuvre* (Béziers: Société de musicologie de Languedoc, 1986).

PRMA   *Proceedings of the Royal Musical Association.*

ProFel   Jacques-Gabriel Prod'homme, 'Marie Fel (1713–1794)',
              Sammelbände des internationalen Musikgesellschaft 4 (1902–03),
              485–518.

ProMus   Jacques-Gabriel Prod'homme, 'La Musique à Paris, de 1753
              à 1757, d'après un manuscrit de la bibliothèque de Munich',
              Sammelbände der internationalen Musikgesellschaft 6 (1904–05),
              568–87.

ProNev   Jacques-Gabriel Prod'homme, 'Une *prise de possession* à l'Opéra
              en 1753: le neveu de Rameau', *Bulletin de la Sociéte française de
              musicologie* 8 (1921), 102–5.

ProPir   Gunnar von Proschwitz (ed.), *Alexis Piron, epistolier: choix de ses
              lettres* (Göteborg: Université de Göteborg, 1982).

QuiJeu   Henri Quittard, *Les Années de jeunesse de J.-P. Rameau* (Paris: H.
              Welter, 1902); repr. in *Revue d'histoire et de critique musicales* 2
              (1902), 61–3, 100–14, 152–70, 208–18.

RamAva   'Mort de M.ʳ Rameau'; 'Paralle [*sic*] de Lully & de Rameau', *L'Avant-
              coureur* 41 (1764), 648–54.

RamCtw   Jean-Philippe Rameau, *Complete Theoretical Writings*, 6 vols,
              ed. Erwin R. Jacobi (Rome: American Institute of Musicology,
              1967–1972).

RaySav   Marcie Ray, 'Savage Love: the Indifferent Woman, Violent
              Seduction, and 18th-century French Cantatas', *EM* 44 (2016),
              579–91.

RdM   *Revue de musicologie.*

RecGen   *Recueil général des opéra*, 3 vols (Paris: Ballard, 1703–45).

ReiCha   Edward R. Reilly, 'Chabanon's Éloge de M.ʳ Rameau', *Studies in
              Music from the University of Western Ontario* 8 (1983), 1–24.

ResGal   Jean Bernard Restout, *Galerie françoise, ou Portraits des hommes et
              des femmes célèbres qui ont paru en France* (Paris: Herissant le Fils,
              1770).

RicFon   Paul F. Rice, *Fontainebleau Operas for the Court of Louis XV of France
              by Jean-Philippe Rameau (1683–1764)* (Lewiston, NY: Edwin Mellen
              Press, 2004).

RicZor   Paul Rice, 'Mid-Eighteenth-Century Changes in French Opera:
              The Two Versions of Rameau's *Zoroastre*', *RMFC* 21 (1983),
              128–44.

RidVol   Ronald S. Ridgway, 'Voltaire's Operas', *SVEC* 189 (1980), 119–51.

RivFil   Gina Rivera, 'Les Filles de l'Opéra in the Early Eighteenth Century'
              (doctoral dissertation, Harvard University, 2013).

RM   *La Revue musicale*, musicological journal founded in 1920 by Henry
              Prunières (and distinct from earlier periodicals with the same or
              similar titles).

RMFC   *Recherches sur la musique française classique.*

RobCat   Brian Robins, *Catch and Glee Culture in Eighteenth-Century England* (Woodbridge, The Boydell Press, 2006).

RodAvi   Jacques Rodriguez, 'La Musique et les musiciens à la cathédrale d'Avignon au XVIIIe siècle', *RMFC* 13 (1973), 64–101.

RolCos   Marianne Roland-Michel, 'Costumes de ballet au temps de Rameau', in *GorDij*, 595–600.

RolVau   Romain Rolland, 'Un Vaudeville de Rameau', *Le Mercure musical* 1 (1905), 19–24.

RosArm   Lois Rosow, *Lully's 'Armide' at the Paris Opéra: A Performance History 1686–1766* (doctoral dissertation, Brandeis University, 1981).

RosDec   Lois Rosow, 'French Baroque Recitative as an Expression of Tragic Declamation', *EM* 11 (1983), 468–79.

RosDes   Lois Rosow, 'From Destouches to Berton: Editorial Responsibility at the Paris Opéra', *JAMS* 40 (1987), 285–309.

RosEnt   Lois Rosow, 'Making Connections: Some Thoughts on Lully's Entr'actes', *EM* 21 (1993), 231–38.

RosLal   Lois Rosow, 'Lallemand and Durand: Two Eighteenth-Century Music Copyists at the Paris Opéra', *JAMS* 33 (1980), 142–63.

RosMet   Lois Rosow, 'The Metrical Notation of Lully's Recitative', in Jérôme de La Gorce and Herbert Schneider (eds), *Jean-Baptiste Lully: Actes du colloque Saint-Germain-en-Laye, Heidelberg 1987* (Laaber: Laaber-Verlag, 1990), 405–22.

RosOrc   Lois Rosow, 'Paris Opéra Orchestration, 1686–1713: Deciphering the Code in the Orchestral Parts', in *McCDan*, 33–53.

RosPer   Lois Rosow, 'Performing a Choral Dialogue by Lully', *EM* 15 (1987), 325–35.

RosScè   Lois Rosow, 'Structure and Expression in the *scènes* of Rameau's *Hippolyte et Aricie*', *COJ* 10 (1998), 259–73.

RouArt   Isabelle Rouard, '*L'Art de la basse fondamentale* de Rameau, pratique et pédagogie raisonnées de la composition harmonique', in *BouSad*, 367–80.

RouCon   Jean-Jacques Rousseau, *Confessions*, trans. J.M. Cohen (Harmondsworth: Penguin, 1953).

RouDic   Jean-Jacques Rousseau, *Dictionnaire de musique* (Paris: Veuve Duchesne 1768) (and later editions).

RpeKey   Siegbert Rampe (ed.), *Rameau: Complete Keyboard Works*, 3 vols (Kassel: Bärenreiter, 2004).

RusZor   Paolo Russo, 'Les Incertitudes de la tragédie lyrique: *Zoroastre* de Louis de Cahusac', *RdM* 75 (1989), 47–64.

SadBor   Graham Sadler, 'A Re-examination of Rameau's Self-Borrowings' in *HajLul*, 264–76.

SadCan   Graham Sadler, 'The Orchestral French Cantata (1706–30): Performance, Edition and Classification of a Neglected Repertory',

	in Michael Talbot (ed.), *Aspects of the Secular Cantata in Late Baroque Italy* (Farnham: Ashgate, 2009), 227–54.
SadCou	Graham Sadler, 'A Philosophy Lesson with François Couperin? Notes on a Newly Discovered Canon', *EM* 32 (2004), 541–8.
SadDan	Graham Sadler, 'The Paris Opéra Dancers in Rameau's Day: A Little-Known Inventory of 1738', in *GorDij*, 519–31.
SadFre	Graham Sadler, 'Rameau, Cahusac and the Rituals of French Freemasonry: Curious Parallels between *Zoroastre* and a Contemporary Masonic "Exposure"', in *BouSad*, 117–32.
SadHan	Graham Sadler, 'From Themes to Variations: Rameau's Debt to Handel', in *BigSch*, 592–607.
SadHip	Graham Sadler, 'Rameau, Pellegrin and the Opéra: The Revisions of "Hippolyte et Aricie" during its First Season', *MT* 124 (1983), 533–7.
SadInd	Graham Sadler, 'Rameau's Harpsichord Transcriptions from *Les Indes galantes*', *EM* 7 (1979), 18–24.
SadInv	Graham Sadler, 'Rameau's Singers and Players at the Paris Opéra: A Little-Known Inventory of 1738', *EM* 11 (1983), 453–67.
SadKey	Graham Sadler, 'The Role of the Keyboard Continuo in French Opera, 1673–1776', *EM* 7 (1980), 148–57.
SadLet	Graham Sadler, 'A Letter from Claude-François Rameau to J.J.M. Decroix', *M&L* 59 (1978), 139–47.
SadOrc	Graham Sadler, 'Rameau and the Orchestra', *PRMA* 108 (1981–82), 47–68.
SadPat	Graham Sadler, 'Patrons and Pasquinades: Rameau in the 1730s', *JRMA* 113 (1988), 314–37.
SadPir	Graham Sadler, 'Rameau, Piron and the Parisian Fair Theatres', *Soundings* 4 (1974), 13–29.
SadSaë	Graham Sadler, 'Saint-Saëns, d'Indy and the Rameau *Œuvres complètes*: New Light on the *Zoroastre* Editorial Project (1914)', in Deborah Mawer (ed.), *Historical Interplay in French Music and Culture* (Abingdon: Routledge, at press).
SadSca	Graham Sadler, 'When Scarlatti met Rameau? Reflections on a Probable Encounter in the 1720s', in Bruce Gustafson (ed.), *The Worlds of Harpsichord and Organ: Liber Amicorum David Fuller* (Hillsdale, NY: Pendragon Press), at press.
SadVin	Graham Sadler, 'Vincent d'Indy and the Rameau *Œuvres complètes*: A Case of Forgery?', *EM* 21 (1993), 415–21.
SadZaï	Graham Sadler (ed.), *Zaïs*, in *OOR* IV.15 (2011).
SadZas	Graham Sadler and Neal Zaslaw, 'Notes on Leclair's Theatre Music', *M&L* 41 (1980), 147–57.
SadZo1	Graham Sadler (ed.), *Zoroastre* (1749 version), in *OOR* IV.19 (1999).
SadZo2	Graham Sadler (ed.), *Zoroastre* (1756 version), in *OOR* IV.26 (at press).

SaiInt   Jean Saint-Arroman, *L'Interprétation de la musique française 1661–1789* (Paris: H. Champion, 1988).

SavAme   Roger Savage, 'Rameau's American Dancers', *EM* 11 (1983), 441–52.

SawBor   Lionel Sawkins, 'Rameau's Last Years: Some Implications of Re-discovered Material at Bordeaux', *PRMA* 111 (1984–85), 66–91.

SawDou   Lionel Sawkins, '*Doucement & Légèrement*: Tempo in French Baroque music', *EM* 21 (1993), 365–74.

SawNou   Lionel Sawkins, 'Nouvelles sources inédites de trois œuvres de Rameau: leur signification pour l'instrumentation et l'interprétation du chant', in *GorDij*, 171–200.

SawPig   Lionel Sawkins: 'New Sources for Rameau's *Pigmalion* and Other Works', *EM* 11 (1983), 490–6.

SawVol   Lionel Sawkins, 'Voltaire, Rameau, Rousseau: A Fresh Look at *La Princesse de Navarre* and its Revival at Bordeaux in 1763', *SVEC* 265 (1989), 1335–9.

SchBar   André Schaeffner, 'L'Orgue de barbarie de Rameau', in *MélMas* 2, 135–50.

SchCan   Herbert Schneider, 'Canevas als Terminus der lyrischen Dichtung', *Archiv für Musikwissenschaft* 42 (1985), 87–101.

SchFam   Herbert Schneider, 'Rameau et sa famille: nouveaux documents', *RMFC* 23 (1985), 94–130.

SchRam   Herbert Schneider, 'Rameau et la tradition lulliste', in *GorDij*, 287–306.

SchVér   Herbert Schneider, *Jean-Philippe Rameaus letzter Musiktraktat, 'Vérités également ignorées et interressantes tirées du sein de la nature' (1764): Kritische Ausgabe mit Kommentar* (Stuttgart: Franz Steiner, 1986).

SclOtt   Jochen Schlobach and Véronique Otto (eds), *Correspondance privée de Frédéric-Melchior Grimm* (Geneva: Slatkine, 2009).

SemBal   Richard Semmens, *The 'Bals publics' at the Paris Opéra in the Eighteenth Century* (Hillsdale, NY: Pendragon, 2004).

SerOpé   Solveig Serre, *L'Opéra de Paris (1749–1790): politique culturelle au temps des Lumières* (Paris: CNRS Éditions, 2011).

SgaDic   Jean Sgard (ed.), *Dictionnaire des journaux: 1600–1789* (Paris: Universitas, 1991).

SgaSam   Jean Sgard, 'Le Premier *Samson* de Voltaire', in *BouAix*, 513–25.

SIM   Société internationale de musique (section de Paris).

SouCah   Thomas Soury, 'Louis de Cahusac, librettiste et théoricien: un collaborateur majeur à l'œuvre de Rameau', *RdM* 99 (2013), 33–60.

SouFêt   Thomas Soury, *'Les Fêtes de l'Hymen et de l'Amour' de Jean-Philippe Rameau: étude historique, générique et critique* (doctoral dissertation, Université François-Rabelais de Tours, 2013).

SouHym   Thomas Soury (ed.), *Les Fêtes de l'Hymen et de l'Amour*, in *OOR* IV.14.

SouRéc   Thomas Soury, 'La Réception de Rameau à Lille à travers les matériels Raparlier du fonds Decroix', in *BouSad*, 271–90.

SouSlo   Françoise Souchal, *Les Slodtz, sculpteurs et décorateurs du Roi (1685–1764)* (Paris: É. de Boccard, 1967).

SpiZas   John Spitzer and Neal Zaslaw, *The Birth of the Orchestra: History of an Institution, 1650–1815* (New York: Oxford University Press, 2004).

StaSer   Bert O. States, 'Servandoni's Successors at the French Opera: Boucher, Boquet, Algieri, Girault', *Theatre Survey* 3 (1962), 41–58.

SteKey   Rita Steblin, *A History of Key Characteristics in the Eighteenth and Early Nineteenth Centuries* (Ann Arbor: UMI Research Press, 1983).

SuaCle   René Suaudeau, *Le Premier système harmonique, dit clermontois, de Jean-Philippe Rameau* (Clermont-Ferrand: École Nationale de Musique, 1958).

SuaInt   René Suaudeau, *Introduction à l'harmonie de Rameau* (Clermont-Ferrand: École Nationale de Musique, 1960).

SusDeb   Anya Suschitzky, 'Debussy's Rameau: French Music and its Others', *MQ* 86 (2002), 398–448.

SVEC   *Studies on Voltaire and the Eighteenth Century*, a literary series published by the Voltaire Foundation, University of Oxford.

TalHab   Michael Talbot, '"Le plus habile compositeur qui soit à Venise": Vivaldi's Reputation in Eighteenth-Century France', in Marie-Alexis Colin (ed.), *Mélanges en l'honneur de Frank Dobbins* (Turnhout: Brepols, forthcoming).

TérAba   Mary Térey-Smith, *Jean Philippe Rameau: 'Abaris, ou Les Boréades': A Critical Edition* (doctoral dissertation, Eastman School of Music, 1971).

TesBoq   André Tessier, 'Les Habits d'opéra au XVIIIᵉ siècle: Louis Boquet, dessinateur et inspecteur général des Menus-Plaisirs', *Revue de l'art* 49 (1926), 15–26, 89–100, 173–84.

TesCor   André Tessier, 'Correspondance d'André Cardinal des Touches et du prince Antoine Iᵉʳ de Monaco (1709–1731)', *RM* 8/2 (1926–27), 97–114; 8/4 (1926–27), 104–17; 8/5 (1926–27), 209–24; 8/6 (1926–27), 149–62.

ThmDid   Jean Thomas, 'Diderot, les Encyclopédistes et le grand Rameau', *Revue de synthèse* 28 (1951), 46–67.

ThoAes   Downing Thomas, *Aesthetics of Opera in the Ancien Régime, 1647–1785* (Cambridge: Cambridge University Press, 2002).

ThoPla   Downing Thomas, 'Rameau's *Platée* Returns: A Case of Double Identity in the Querelle des Bouffons', *COJ* 18 (2006), 1–19.

ThpCro   Shirley Thompson, 'Once More into the Void': Marc-Antoine Charpentier's *croches blanches* Reconsidered', *EM* 30 (2002), 82–92.

TieRam   Julien Tiersot, 'Lettres inédites de Rameau', *RM* 16 (1935), 15–21.

TilUnm   Colin Tilney, *The Art of the Unmeasured Prelude: France 1660–1720*
(London: Schott, 1991).

TroArn   Rodolphe Trouilleux, *N'oubliez pas Iphigénie: biographie de la
cantatrice et épistolière Sophie Arnould (1740–1802)* (Grenoble: Alzieu,
2002).

TroÉvo   Rémy-Michel Trotier, 'Évolutions du langage et mutations
formelles: l'architecture harmonique des tragédies en musique de
Rameau représentées par l'Académie royale de musique de 1733 à
1757', in *BouSad*, 409–30.

TunCan   David Tunley, *The Eighteenth-Century French Cantata*, rev. 2nd edn
(Oxford: Clarendon Press, 1997).

ValAca   Léon Vallas, *La Musique à l'Académie de Lyon au XVIIIᵉ siècle* (Lyon:
Éditions de la Revue musicale de Lyon, 1908).

ValLyo   Léon Vallas, *Un Siècle de musique à Lyon, 1688–1789* (Lyon: P.
Masson, 1932).

ValMan   Léon Vallas, 'Jacques-Simon Mangot: un beau-frère de Rameau,
symphoniste, compositeur et directeur d'Opéra', *RdM* 5 (1924),
123–6.

ValRam   Léon Vallas, 'Rameau à Lyon', *Revue musicale de Lyon* 6 (1908–09),
73–84.

ValVoy   Simon de Valhebert, *L'Agenda du voyageur, ou Le calendrier des fêtes*
(Paris: chez DesHayes, 1727; veuve de Laulne, 1732, 1736).

VenCom   Philippe Vendrix (ed.), *L'Opéra-Comique en France au XVIIIᵉ siècle*
(Liège: Mardaga, 1992).

VerDev   Cynthia Verba, 'The Development of Rameau's Thoughts on
Modulation and Chromatics', *JAMS* 26 (1973), 69–91.

VerDra   Cynthia Verba, *Dramatic Expression in Rameau's Tragédie en
Musique: Between Tradition and Enlightenment* (Cambridge:
Cambridge University Press, 2013).

VerNic   Thomas Vernet, 'Nicolas-Louis Dran (1687–1774), "amateur de
l'harmonie" et lecteur de Rameau', in *BouSad*, 143–53.

VerMod   Cynthia Verba, 'Rameau's Views on Modulation and their
Background in French Theory', *JAMS* 31 (1978), 467–79.

VerMus   Cynthia Verba, *Music and the French Enlightenment: Reconstruction
of a Dialogue 1750–1764* (Oxford: Clarendon Press, 1993).

VerRec   Cynthia Verba, 'What Recitatives Owe to the Airs: A Look at the
Dialogue Scene, Act 1, Scene 2 of Rameau's *Hippolyte et Aricie* –
Version with Airs', *COJ* 11 (1999), 103–34; repr. in *DilOpe*, 361–92.

VlaTed   Kees Vlaardingerbroek, '"The Promised Land of Music": Jan Teding
van Berkhout in Italy, 1739–1741', *Recercare* 24 (2012), 107–36.

VlaViv   Kees Vlaardingerbroek, 'Vivaldi alla francese: Guido and Rameau
"à la manière vivaldienne"', *Informazioni e studi vivaldiani* 18 (1997),
60–80.

WaeGes   Jacqueline Waeber (ed.), *Musique et geste en France de Lully à la*

Révolution: études sur la musique, le théâtre et la danse (Berne: Peter Lang, 2009).

WalMus   Johann Gottfried Walther, 'Rameau', in *Musicalisches Lexicon, oder musicalische Bibliothec* (Leipzig: Wolfgang Deer, 1732), 512.

WebWan   William Weber, '*La Musique ancienne* and the Waning of the *ancien régime*', *The Journal of Modern History* 56 (1984), 58–88.

WelCle   Louise Welter, 'Quelques précisions sur le second séjour de Rameau à Clermont, en qualité d'organiste', *Bulletin historique et scientifique de l'Auvergne* 71 (1951), 62–4.

WilAna   Jonathan Huw Williams (ed.), with Sylvie Bouissou and Cécile Davy-Rigaux, *Anacréon*, in *OOR* IV.25 (2004)

WilAnx   Peter Williams, 'Is there an Anxiety of Influence discernible in J.S. Bach's *Clavierübung I*?', in Christopher Hogwood (ed.), *The Keyboard in Baroque Europe* (Cambridge: Cambridge University Press, 2003), 140–56.

WisVer   Valérie de Wispelaere and Thomas Vernet, '"J'ai trop confiance, Monseigneur, en vos lumières et en votre justice": une lettre inédite de Rameau retrouvée à la Bibliothèque de l'Arsenal', *RdM*, 99 (2013), 325–41.

WokEss   Robert Wokler: 'Rameau, Rousseau, and the "Essai sur l'origine des langues"', *SVEC* 117 (1974), 179–238.

WolAut   R. Peter Wolf, 'Rameau's *Les Paladins*: from Autograph to Production', *EM* (1983) 11, 497–504.

WolInt   R. Peter Wolf, Introduction to *Jean-Philippe Rameau: Les Paladins, comédie lyrique* (New York: Pendragon, 1986).

WolMet   R. Peter Wolf, 'Metrical Relationships in French Recitative of the Seventeenth and Eighteenth Centuries', *RMFC* 18 (1978), 29–49.

WolŒu   R. Peter Wolf, 'An Eighteenth-Century *Œuvres complètes* of Rameau', in *GorDij*, 159–67.

WolPal   R. Peter Wolf, *Jean-Philippe Rameau's comédie lyrique 'Les Paladins' (1760): A Critical Edition and Study* (doctoral dissertation, Yale University, 1977).

WolRam   Hellmuth Christian Wolff, 'Rameaus "Les Indes galantes" als musik-ethnologische Quelle', *Jahrbuch für musikalische Volks- und Völkerkunds* 3 (1967), 105–8.

WooLul   Caroline Wood, *Music and Drama in the 'tragédie en musique', 1673–1715: Jean-Baptiste Lully and His Successors* (New York: Garland, 1996).

WooOrc   Caroline Wood, 'Orchestra and Spectacle in the *tragédie en musique* 1673–1715: oracle, *sommeil* and *tempête*', *PRMA* 108 (1981–82), 25–46.

WooSad   Caroline Wood and Graham Sadler, *French Baroque Opera: A Reader* (Aldershot: Ashgate, 2000).

YeaAwk   David Yearsley, 'The Awkward Idiom: Hand-Crossing and the European Keyboard Scene around 1730', *EM* 30 (2002), 225–35.

ZasApp	Neal Zaslaw, 'Rameau's Operatic Apprenticeship: The First Fifty Years', in *GorDij*, 23–50.
ZasEni	Neal Zaslaw, 'The Enigma of the Haute-Contre', *MT* 115 (1974), 939–41.
ZasNew	Neal Zaslaw, 'The New Rameau Edition', *MT* 124 (1983), 28–30.
ZasOpe	Neal Zaslaw, 'At the Paris Opéra in 1747', *EM* 11 (1983), 515–16.
ZasScy	Neal Zaslaw, '*Scylla et Glaucus*: A Case Study', *COJ* 4 (1992), 199–228.

Printed and bound by CPI Group (UK) Ltd, Croydon, CR0 4YY

07/07/2026

14916224-0005